W9-APX-890

The Social History
of the Reformation

EDITED BY

LAWRENCE P. BUCK

AND JONATHAN W. ZOPHY

OHIO STATE UNIVERSITY PRESS — COLUMBUS

Library of Congress Cataloging in Publication Data

Main entry under title:

The Social history of the Reformation.

"In honor of Harold J. Grimm."

CONTENTS: The control of morals in Calvin's Geneva, by R. M. Kingdon.—The Reformation in Nürnberg, by G. Seebass.—Hard work, good work, and school work: an analysis of Wenzeslaus Linck's conception of civic responsibility, by C. E. Daniel. [etc.]

1. Reformation—Addresses, essays, lectures.
2. Grimm, Harold John, 1901-   I. Grimm, Harold John, 1901-   II. Buck, Lawrence P., 1944-   ed. III. Zophy, Jonathan W., 1945- ed.

BR307.S6   270.6   72-5952

ISBN 0-8142-0174-1

IN HONOR OF HAROLD J. GRIMM

Contents

Foreword   xi

Preface   xvii

Acknowledgments   xxi

PART ONE: The Municipal Setting of the Reformation

The Control of Morals in Calvin's Geneva
Robert M. Kingdon   3

The Reformation in Nürnberg
Gottfried Seebass   17

Hard Work, Good Work, and School Work: An
Analysis of Wenzeslaus Linck's Conception of Civic
Responsibility
Charles E. Daniel, Jr.   41

The Lawyers, Dr. Christoph Scheurl, and the
Reformation in Nürnberg
Phillip Norton Bebb   52

Patricians in Dissension: A Case Study from
Sixteenth-Century Nürnberg
Jackson Spielvogel   73

PART TWO: The Impact of the Reformation on Society

The Dynamics of Printing in the Sixteenth Century
Richard G. Cole   93

The Reformation and the German Peasants' War
Hans J. Hillerbrand 106

Christian Humanism and the Freedom of a
Christian: Johann Eberlin von Günzburg to the
Peasants
Kyle C. Sessions 137

The Two Social Strands in Italian Anabaptism
ca.1526–ca.1565
George H. Williams 156

John Foxe and the Ladies
Roland H. Bainton 208

Wittenberg Botanists during the Sixteenth Century
Karl H. Dannenfeldt 223

Luther's Social Concern for Students
Lewis W. Spitz 249

Albrecht Dürer's "Four Apostles": A Memorial
Picture from the Reformation Era
Gerhard Pfeiffer 271

The Significance of the Epitaph Monument for
Early Lutheran Ecclesiastical Art
Carl C. Christensen 297

PART THREE: The Organization of the Reformation

The Lutheran Church of the Reformation: Problems
of Its Formation and Organization in the Middle
and North German Territories
Irmgard Höss 317

Protestant Endowment Law in the Franconian
Church Ordinances
Hans Liermann 340

The Second Nürnberg Church Visitation, 1560-1561
Gerhard Hirschmann 355

Notes on the Contributors   381

Index   385

LIST OF ILLUSTRATIONS
(Following page 280)

1. Philip Melanchthon. Copper engraving by Albrecht Dürer. Germanisches Nationalmuseum, Nürnberg.

2. Joachim Camerarius the elder. 1559.

3. Heronymous Paumgartner. Medal by Joachim Deschler in 1553. Reproduced in Paul Grotemeyer, *Da ich het die Gestalt* (Munich, 1957), plate 59.

4. Michael Roting. Copper engraving in the Stadtbibliothek, Nürnberg. Reproduced in G. W. Panzer, *Verzeichnis von Nürnbergischen Portraiten* (Nürnberg, 1970).

5. "The Four Apostles," by Albrecht Dürer. Bayer. Staatsgemäldesammlungen, Munich.

Foreword

"Historians are the most useful people and the best teachers," wrote Luther in the *Preface to Galeatius Capella's History*, "so that one can never honor, praise, and thank them enough." As one of America's leading historians of the Reformation era, Harold J. Grimm merits the honor, praise, and thanks not only of the entire historical profession but of the thousands of students who have learned from him and the tens of thousands who have read his books. He has enjoyed a most distinguished academic career and has played an important role in the maturation of American historical scholarship.

Professor Grimm is truly a "son of the Middle Border." He was born in Saginaw, Michigan, August 16, 1901, and received his basic education in the Midwest. His preparatory school was Woodville Academy, and he took his A.B. degree at Capital University in 1924. His life then took a serious theological turn, for he entered the Evangelical Lutheran Theological Seminary in Columbus and received his diploma, the equivalent of a bachelor of divinity degree, in 1927. A line of interior identification with the great Reformer was clearly in evidence, and two years later he published his first book, *Martin Luther as a Preacher* (Columbus, 1929). From theology he now turned to history, enrolling at the school with which his name has ever since been prominently associated, Ohio State University. He took his M.A. degree there in 1928, then studied for a year at the Universities of Leipzig and Hamburg, and returned to take his Ph.D. at Ohio State in 1932. To rehearse all the academic honors garnered under way would indeed be gilding the golden rose.

Professor Grimm's career of teaching and administration has been one of perpetual motion. From 1925 to 1937 he taught at his alma mater, Capital University. From 1937 to the present he has taught at Ohio State, serving as chairman from 1958 to 1967. His three decades of service at Ohio State were interrupted by a four-year interlude, 1954 to 1958, while he served as chairman of the history department at Indiana University. He taught as a Fulbright professor at the University of Freiburg in 1954 and taught summer sessions at West Virginia, Texas, and San Diego State College. Great teaching and research are a natural combination, but it takes a man of unusual ability to have served as chairman of two major history departments and still win fame as one of the nation's great teachers. Two of Professor Grimm's most cherished honors are his selection as Honored Professor of the Year at Ohio State in 1950 and the Alumni Award for Distinguished Teaching in 1963. Harold and his charming wife, Thelma, have opened their home to countless students at a university where by virtue of its size alone things are inclined to be impersonal. Beyond his impact upon countless undergraduates, Professor Grimm served as *Doktorvater* for over two dozen graduate students who took their Ph.D.'s in Renaissance and Reformation history and now hold important teaching and research positions literally from coast to coast. Judicious and diligent, he served as chairman and member of many major university committees through the years, such as the Executive Committee of the College of Arts, the Religious Affairs committee, and the University Archives committee. He was rewarded for outstanding teaching and university service with a Regents Professorship in 1968.

Professor Grimm has been a leader in the major professional organizations for many years. He joined the American Historical Association in 1935, served on numerous committees, especially of the modern European history section, and has been most faithful in attending the meetings even under the most trying circumstances. He contributed several papers and served frequently as chairman or critic. On one occasion he rose from a sickbed to present his paper, so weakened by Asian flu that he literally had to cling to the lectern for support. He was elected president of the American Society of Church History and president of the American Society for Reformation Research. He has served as a member of the board of trustees of the Ohio Historical Society, as a council member of the Renaissance Society of America, and as a board member of the Foundation for Reformation Research in St. Louis. He is a member of the *Hansischer Geschichtsverein*, the Ohio Academy of History, the Ohio Historical Society, the Royal Historical Society, and the Royal Society of Arts (British). His service has extended to the community as well, for he was for many years on the board of trustees of both the Bexley Public Library and the Bexley Public Schools, and headed up the Campus United Appeal, 1959–60. In the early days of the American Society for Reformation Research, Professor Grimm served as an American editor of the *Archive for Reformation History*. With virtually no operating budget, he personally received, wrapped, and mailed all the United States copies of that distinguished journal, a real labor of love. Modest and unassuming, Professor Grimm is anything but a busy, aggressive organization man. The honors and burdens of office seemed to seek him out, so that he became almost involuntarily a strongman in the professional societies.

Luther once responded, when asked why he stayed in his "ivory tower" as a university professor, "I send forth my books into all the world." Professor Grimm, too, has been the kind of historian who writes history and sends forth his books into all the world. He has found the proper balance between the active life and the studious life, like Luther, who resolved the apparent tension between the two by pronouncing in the *Table Talks*: "Every great book is an action, and every great action is a book." It is characteristic of Professor Grimm's pedagogical drive that his most comprehensive work should have been written as a text for students, *The Reformation Era 1500–1650* (New York, 1954, 1965). "The widespread interest of the present generation in religion in general," he wrote in the preface, "and in the various contemporary forms of Christianity in particular is sufficient justification for the publication of a comprehensive study of the Reformation. This interest has prompted me to tell the story of the rise of Protestantism and the Catholic reforms in their complete setting." This excellent survey combines a broad scope with precise detail, for the author possesses to an eminent degree that "genius for accuracy" which Gibbon once attributed to Tillemont. He gives Wittenberg and the Holy Roman Empire a very prominent place in the volume, but as an American he transcends the national parochialism that afflicts so many European Reformation scholars. Professor Grimm's deep concern with education is evident also from the subjects of his "Martin Luther Lectures" presented at Luther College in Decorah, Iowa, and published in 1960, *Luther and Culture*. Choosing "Luther and Education" as his theme, he spoke on "Luther's Impact on the Schools," "Luther as a Teacher in the Pulpit" and "Luther's Catechisms as Textbooks." He is co-author with F. J. Tschan and J. D. Squires of the two-volume history *Western Civilization: Decline of Rome to the Present* (Philadelphia, 1942). He proved evidence of his philological ability and editorial skill as translator and editor of the *Career of the Reformer I*, volume 31 of the American edition of *Luther's Works* (Philadelphia, 1957). His control of the bibliography and understanding of the scholarly literature in the field can best be seen in the survey he prepared for the American Historical Association's Service Center for Teachers, volume 54, *The Reformation in Recent Historical Thought* (New York, 1964). His own place in recent historical thought can be seen best by another.

The true biography of an intellectual is the life of his mind. A survey of Professor Grimm's contributions to the scholarly journals and of the dissertations he has directed reveals a fascinating interior development. From a more traditional interest in Luther and religious subjects, he has moved to a concern with the social nexus within which the Reformation as a historical movement evolved. A few of his articles may be cited by way of example: "Lorenzo Valla's Christianity," *Church History* 18 (June, 1949): 75–88; "The Human Element in Luther's Sermons," *Archive for Reformation History* 49 (1958): 50–59; "Luther Research Since 1920," *Journal of Modern History* 32 (June, 1960): 105–18. The focus of Professor Grimm's later scholarship has been on the social forces operative in the Reformation, the role of townsmen and of city councils in introducing and promoting the evangelical cause. Again, a few representative titles will tell the story: "The Relations of Luther and Melanchthon with the Townsmen," *Luther and Melanchthon*, ed. Vilmas Vajta (Philadelphia, 1961), pp. 32–48; "Social Forces in the German Reformation," *Church History* 31 (1962): 3–13; "Lazarus Spengler, the Nürnberg City Council, and the Reformation," *Luther for an Ecumenical Age*, ed. Carl S. Meyer (St. Louis, 1967), pp. 108–19; "Luther's Contributions to Sixteenth-Century Organization of Poor Relief," *Archive for Reformation History* 61 (1970): 222–33. From the earlier days when he wrote on the "genealogist as historian," he has been cutting a wider and wider swath, reaching unexplored corners of a very big field. He has twice been honored by the mayor of Nürnberg for his distinguished contributions to the history of that *Schatzkästchen* of the empire. Professor Grimm's graduate students have written theses in the field of social history and are already contributing to learned journals such as the *Archive for Reformation History*. The members of this *Nachwuchs* who have already attracted scholarly attention include Carl Christensen, Richard Cole, John Constable, Charles Daniel, Allan Dirrim, James Estes, George Robbert, Kyle Sessions, Jackson Spielvogel, and others. "The young, too," said Luther, "must soon stand up and speak out after us."

This festschrift is a fitting tribute to a man who has meant so much to the development of Reformation studies in America. He has been a tower of strength, not to say "a mighty fortress," as a teacher, administrator, active professional, and historian. We may well say also of this *viator* that he was a good man a long season, and we thank him for it.

LEWIS W. SPITZ

Preface

The main purpose of this volume is to honor Professor Harold J. Grimm on the occasion of his retirement from regular teaching duties at the Ohio State University. It is dedicated to him as an expression of the gratitude of all of his students, past and present, for his kindness, his concern, and his interest in each of them as individuals. A devoted teacher and scholar, he has provided an inspirational example to thousands of students both undergraduate and graduate.

Hoping to reflect, as far as possible, Professor Grimm's own research interests, we have chosen social history as our general topic. The contributors include former students of Professor Grimm and other scholars who have been associated with him as friends and colleagues. The articles thus reflect a wide range of approaches to the social history of the Reformation.

This being the case, the volume can also serve the purpose of indicating current trends and emphases in the writing of social history of the Reformation. In 1967 Professor Grimm wrote that today's "great desideratum" is an analysis of the various "social forces" operating at the time of the Reformation. In recent years interest in social history has produced a sizeable literature dealing with the impact of the Reformation upon social problems and societal institutions, and upon the various classes or "estates" of men found in the cities and princely territories, university towns, and peasant villages of sixteenth-century Europe.

The essays in the first section concern the reception of the Reformation in cities and towns and the restructuring of municipal institutions that this religious movement caused. The contributors have directed their attention to two important centers of the Reformation, Geneva and Nürnberg. Professor Kingdon's article attempts to discover the genesis of modern moral puritanism in the enforcement of morality in Calvin's Geneva. Since Professor Grimm has, in recent years, devoted special attention to the history of Nürnberg, it is fitting that this "outpost of Wittenberg in southern Germany" be well represented in the volume. Dr. Seebass's essay surveys the origins, development, and effects of the Reformation in Nürnberg. The contributions by Charles E. Daniel, Phillip N. Bebb, and Jackson Spielvogel examine, in greater detail, the roles played by representative members of Nürnberg society during the Reformation, namely the preacher Wenzeslaus Linck, the lawyer Christoph Scheurl, and the humanist Willibald Pirckheimer.

The second section deals with the impact of the Reformation on various groupings of men in society. The first three essays concern the interrelationship of the Reformation and the Peasants' Revolt, with special attention devoted to the place of pamphlet literature. Richard G. Cole's contribution investigates the role of the sixteenth-century pamphlet in changing the "consciousness of society" and thus raises the question of the interconnection of printing and social change. Professor Hans J. Hillerbrand looks specifically at the interrelationship of the Reformation and the Peasants' Revolt as reflected in contemporary pamphlet literature. Kyle C. Sessions discusses a pamphlet written by the humanist and evangelical preacher Johann Eberlin von Günzburg to the peasantry of the Margravate of Burgau urging them not to participate in rebellion and concludes his contribution with a translation into English of a large excerpt from the original pamphlet.

The next three articles treat some of the newest fields of historiographic investigation. Professor George H. Williams looks at Italian Anabaptism, especially at the appeal of this sectarian movement to various social and ethnic groups in sixteenth-century Italy. Professor Roland H. Bainton's delightful essay deals with the timely topic of women in the Reformation, in particular, female martyrs portrayed by John Foxe. In line with recent interest in the history of science, Karl H. Dannenfeldt has investigated the role of the University of Wittenberg in producing a group of sixteenth-century botanists. Professor Lewis Spitz's contribution deals likewise with the University of Wittenberg, specifically with Luther's concern for the social well-being of Wittenberg students.

Professor Gerhard Pfeiffer and Carl C. Christensen, in the last two essays of the second section, have directed their attention to the impact of the Reformation on artists of the sixteenth century. Professor Pfieffer has analyzed the various social and religious forces that might have influenced Albrecht Dürer when he painted his "Four Apostles." He concludes that the founding of the *Gelehrtenschule* in Nürnberg provided the actual occasion for Dürer to make a gift of the "Four Apostles" to the city council. Carl C. Christensen, instead of concentrating on one artist, has turned his attention to the question of the impact of the Lutheran Reformation on the fine arts and, in particular, Lutheran patronage of the art form of the epitaph monument.

The final section of the festschrift treats the organization and spread of the Reformation, the bureaucratic and legal changes that it brought about, and the consequent problems of enforcement. Professor Irmgard Höss's article analyzes the establishment of a Lutheran territorial church in Saxony, Brunswick-Wolfenbüttel, and Prussia. Professor Hans Liermann has a careful look at the far-reaching changes in endowment law that the Reformation wrought. Finally, Dr. Gerhard Hirschmann presents a comprehensive study of the second Nürnberg church visitation of 1560–61, undertaken to evaluate popular knowledge of Reformation teachings, to enforce religious changes adopted in 1525, and to establish a new regulation of the religious life in the Nürnberg territory.

In preparing their essays the contributors have taken different approaches and have utilized the findings of diverse fields of historical inquiry. This is proper, for the social historian must draw his materials from a wide variety of sources. Nevertheless, each author has dealt with the impact of the Reformation on some aspect of society in sixteenth-century Europe. It is this central concern that gives the volume unity and coherence.

The authors and editors dedicate these articles to Professor Harold J. Grimm with the hope that they will both honor him and contribute to our knowledge of the social history of the Reformation.

Acknowledgments

By its very nature a collection of essays when brought together in book form requires the assistance of a large number of individuals. In this limited space we can mention only a few of the many who helped make this volume possible. The editors would like to pay special tribute to Professor Robert Bremner, who has served as the guiding force behind this book almost from its inception. Professor Harry Coles helped to secure financial support for the preparation of the manuscript. Indeed, the entire Department of History of the Ohio State University has given support, aid, and encouragement to this undertaking.

A team of students, colleagues, and friends of Professor Grimm assisted greatly in the various scholarly tasks connected with this volume. Jann Whitehead Gates, Kurt Hendel, and Frank P. Lane did much of the difficult work of preparing translations. Our deepest thanks to Sidney Fisher, June Fullmer, Judith Harvey, Charles Morley, and Angela Zophy for their gracious aid and encouragement. Ohio State University Press editor Robert Demorest rendered admirable service.

We would like to thank the editors and publishers of the following for permission to reprint materials already published: Augsburg Publishing House, Evangelische Verlagsanstalt, Melanchthon-Gymnasium, Mitteilungen des Vereins für Geschichte der Stadt Nürnberg, and Zeitschrift für bayerische Kirchengeschichte. Finally, the editors wish to express their appreciation and gratitude to our contributors who have shown their respect and affection for Harold J. Grimm by honoring him with these fine examples of their scholarship. Any inadequacies that remain are solely the responsibility of the editors.

LAWRENCE P. BUCK
JONATHAN W. ZOPHY

LIST OF ABBREVIATIONS

ADB   *Allgemeine deutsche Biographie*

AEG   Archives d'Etat Genève

ARG   *Archiv für Reformationsgeschichte*

BB   Briefbücher (letters) of the Nürnberg City Council located in the Staatsarchiv, Nürnberg.

CO   Calvin, John. *Ioannis Calvini Opera quae supersunt omnia.* ed. G. Baum, E. Cunitz, and E. Reuss. 59 vols. Brunswick, 1863–1900.

CR   *Corpus Reformatorum.* A. Brettschneider et. al. eds. 28 vols. Halle, 1834–60.

KO   Sehling, Emil, ed. *Die evangelischen Kirchenordnungen des XVI. Jahrhunderts.* Tübingen, 1902–69.

LW   Lehmann, Helmut T., and Pelikan, Jaroslav, eds. *Luther's Works.* 55 vols. St. Louis and Philadelphia, 1955–71.

MQR   *Mennonite Quarterly Review*

MVGN   *Mitteilungen des Vereins für Geschichte der Stadt Nürnberg.*

RB   Ratsbücher, minutes from the meetings of the Nürnberg City Council, located in the Staatsarchiv, Nürnberg.

RC   *Registres du Conseil de Genève, publiés par la Société d'Histoire et d'Archéologie de Genève.*

RCP   Bergier, Jean-Francois, and Kingdon, Robert M., eds. *Registres de la Compagnie des Pasteurs de Genève au temps de Calvin.* 2 vols. Geneva, 1962, 1964.

RV   Ratsverlässe, protocol from the Nürnberg City Council meetings.

SD   Rivoire, Emile, and van Berchem, Victor, eds. *Les sources du droit du Canton de Genève.* 4 vols. Aarau, 1927–35.

StAN   Staatsarchiv, Nürnberg.

WA   *D. Martin Luthers Werke.* Weimar, 1883–.

WA Br   *D. Martin Luthers Werke. Briefwechsel.* Weimar, 1930–48.

THE MUNICIPAL SETTING OF THE REFORMATION

THE CONTROL OF MORALS IN CALVIN'S GENEVA

Robert M. Kingdon

Calvinism is often thought to be an important source of that drive for moral austerity or asceticism that is commonly labeled "puritanism." Some think this is bad, and blame Calvinism for introducing into modern society a repressiveness that has killed joy and led to many serious problems. Others think this is good, and praise Calvinism for introducing into modern society a measure of discipline that has made it both more cohesive and more productive. But most people who have thought about the matter, seem to think that men formed by the Calvinist tradition have usually set for themselves higher standards of private morality, including sexual morality and morality in business dealings, than the ordinary run of men, and that these Calvinists have had greater success in living up to these high standards. They have thus often set a moral tone that became pervasive throughout our society. This belief, no doubt, has something of the character of a folk myth, and folk myths are often imprecise and have a way of becoming anachronistic. It is obviously a very gross generalization, and could not apply with equal force to every Calvinist in every place at every time. But, like most folk myths, it almost certainly contains a very important kernel of truth. It thus poses an interesting problem in historical explanation. Where did this moral austerity come from? Why have Calvinists been more concerned with morals than other men?

If one tries to explain this phenomenon in exclusively theological terms, it seems to me that one must fail. I do not think that Calvinist theology values the moral life more than other types of Christian theology. Indeed, since it accepts the basic doctrine of all sixteenth-century magisterial Protestantism, of "justification by faith alone," one might well conclude that it values the moral life less than either Catholic theology or certain types of radical Protestant theology. If one could demonstrate that a moral life is a sure sign of election to salvation in Calvinist theology, one could establish an important place for morality as allied to the strong doctrine of predestination so characteristic of Calvinism. Such a link can apparently be discovered in certain varieties of late Calvinist or Puritan theology. But if it is present in the thought of Calvin himself, it is in a highly attenuated form.

Similarly, I do not think that it can be argued that Calvinist theologians taught a different kind of morality than other Christians, except, of course, for the clergy, who are absolved from such special requirements imposed upon them by Roman Catholicism as celibacy. For the generality of mankind, Calvinism taught the same code of morals, derived from such biblical texts as the Ten Commandments and the moral teachings of Jesus, as almost all systems of Christian thought.

The real explanation of the moral austerity that characterized Calvinism from the beginning, lies, it seems to me, in the fact that early Calvinist communities *enforced* morality. And they enforced it by the creation and effective use of a new institution, the Calvinist consistory. The model for this body was the consistory established in Geneva by Calvin himself. It is in the history of this body that one must search, I am convinced, for the essential source of modern moral puritanism. This search, thus, demands the talents not of a historian of thought but rather of a historian of municipal institutions.

The Genevan Consistory was not, of course, created out of a vacuum. It was created in response to a need felt by the Genevan community.[2] For centuries, morals controls in Geneva had been quite lax. Although the city was an ecclesiastical principality, ruled by a bishop, aided by a chapter of cathedral canons, these clergymen had never tried to impose a strict code of morals on the population. What controls were adopted simply tried to regulate moral lapses regarded as inevitable. Prostitution, for example, was accepted and permitted. Repeated attempts were made to limit prostitutes to certain parts of the city, to require them to wear distinctive dress, to organize themselves under an elected or appointed "queen," to limit the times they could enter the public baths where they apparently did much of their soliciting. But no attempt was made to outlaw prostitution. Similarly, illegitimacy was accepted as inevitable. If a father would acknowledge and provide financial support for his illegitimate children, the authorities were content. Even adultery was punished only occasionally and lightly.

Furthermore, there was no institution in medieval Geneva charged with primary responsibility for maintaining morality. The actions that were taken against those who had flouted Christian morality in notorious ways were taken by the city council, an elected group of lay businessmen and professionals, charged by the bishops with the responsibility for maintaining order in the city. But this council had so many other responsibilities more important and pressing to its members that they rarely considered morals cases. They could be assisted in locating and punishing morals offenders by the "official," an officer of the bishop. And their decisions could be reviewed by the bishop's court. But these agents of the church did not seem to be very concerned about morality either.

This rather loose situation began to change early in the sixteenth century. Growing criticism from the general population began to force the authorities to consider ways of controlling morals. This criticism tended to focus increasingly on clergymen found guilty of such moral lapses as frequenting prostitutes, maintaining concubines, and the like. It thus combined with the general tide of rising discontent that led to the ejection of Roman Catholicism and the introduction of Protestantism. The first concrete result of this popular puritanism was the enactment of a number of laws regulating morals on the very eve of the Reformation. These laws were enacted by the lay members of the city council entirely on their own authority. Some of them may have been persuaded to this action by William Farel, the flamboyant Protestant preacher who was actively agitating for the outlawry of Catholicism in the city. But they acted before Farel had been named to any position of authority, and before John Calvin had even arrived in Geneva. On February 28, 1534, the council ordered all fornicators and adulterers to "abandon their wicked life" or be whipped and banished.[3] On April 30, 1534, it ordered the caretakers of the baths to keep all prostitutes out of those establishments.[4] On March 7, 1536, the prostitutes were ordered either to abandon their trade or leave the city.[5] The ordinance establishing the Reformation was not adopted until May 21, 1536.[6] Calvin did not arrive in Geneva until several months after that.

Systematic enforcement of these laws, however, had to wait for several years. The first years of the Reformation regime in Geneva witnessed considerable turmoil. Farel and Calvin became the principal ministers of the Reformed church, but they were forced out of the city in 1538. It was only on Calvin's return, in 1541, that the building of a Reformed society could really begin. One of the first of Calvin's accomplishments was to persuade the city council to establish the consistory. In his very first interview with the council on returning to Geneva, he asked that a consistory be established and that ordinances be drafted describing the nature and functions of this and other Genevan ecclesiastical institutions.[7] A committee made up of all the pastors of the city and selected lay members of the governing councils immediately went to work on this project. After a draft had been prepared and modified in meetings of the councils, the new ecclesiastical ordinances were adopted, about two months after Calvin's return.[8] A few weeks later, the Genevan Consistory met for the first time.[9]

This new institution was at once an agency of both the state and the church. Its members included both elected lay elders and the ordained pastors of the city. The elders were elected annually, in the February elections in which all municipal officials were chosen. In those elections, the entire voting population of Geneva gathered together to select four governing magistrates, called syndics; members of three governing councils, the most important of which, the small council, met almost every day to handle government business for the city and possessed the real sovereign power in Geneva; members of a number of standing committees that handled such problems as the maintenance of city fortifications, the maintenance of city grain supplies, the control of city funds, the judgment of both criminal and civil legal cases. In most of these elections, however, the voters simply ratified slates of candidates prepared by the outgoing small council. In only a few of the elections, in those for syndics, for example, were the voters given a choice between two candidates for each office. The crucial decisions, consequently, were made by the small council, in drawing up its lists of nominees.[10]

The consistory fitted into this constitutional structure as a new standing committee of the government. Its lay members were chosen in much the same way as members of the committees controlling fortifications and grain supplies. Two of them had to be members of the small council itself, and one of these customarily came to be a ruling syndic; four of them had to come from the less important and less active council of sixty; six had to come from the council of two hundred. They were so selected that each geographic section of the city would be represented.[11] The elder who was also a syndic for the year, acted as the presiding officer of the consistory.[12]

Only in one way did the selection of these elders differ from the selection of the members of the city's other standing committees. But that difference was crucial. The ecclesiastical ordinances provided that the small council consult the city's pastors on the nominations it made annually both of the elders and of the deacons, who were responsible for maintaining the city's programs of social welfare. They further provided that the council would decide, at the end of every year, which elders should be reelected and which should be replaced, presumably again in consultation with the pastors. It was expected that an elder who was doing a satisfactory job would normally be reelected for a period of several years.[13] The pastors, headed by Calvin, thus gained an important legal right to share in the selection of elders and deacons.

This right does not seem to have been exercised for some time in the selection of deacons. Not until 1562, only two years before Calvin's death, is there sure evidence that the pastors were, in fact, consulted by the small council when it drew up its annual slate of nominees for the office of deacon.[14] This right may not have been exercised right away in the selections of elders, either.

Election records are not clear on this point. But it clearly was exercised sooner and more forcefully. In 1546 and 1547, "the ministers" were consulted on the selection of elders; in 1552, "the ministers . . . through their spokesman, M. Calvin," were consulted; Calvin, again representing the entire corps of pastors, was consulted in 1556, 1557, and 1558; two other pastors were consulted in 1559; from 1560 on, the entire body of pastors was invited to the small council session at which the slate of elders for the coming year was drawn up.[15]

Until 1560, the elders, like most other elected officials of the Genevan state, were always native-born citizens. In that year, Calvin and his fellow pastor Pierre Viret persuaded the council to permit the election also of members of the council of two hundred who were immigrant "bourgeois," who had obtained that position of legal and political privilege by special action of the council without having been born in the city.[16] In the election which followed this breakthrough, the Marquis Galeazzo Carraciolo, a prominent Italian convert to Calvinism, was made an elder. This change tended to increase the authority of Calvin among the lay members of the consistory, since many of his most fervent supporters came from the large group of religious refugees in Geneva.

The remaining members of the consistory, the ordained pastors, were also technically agents of the Genevan state. They were salaried employees, hired by the small council, on the nomination of the company of pastors, of which Calvin was moderator, but they were considerably more independent of state control. It was clear that it was the company, not the council, that had the decisive role in their initial selection. They normally held office for life. If they were deposed, for bad behavior or incorrect belief, it was normally, although not invariably, at the initiative of the company. If they were released to take positions elsewhere, it was normally the permission of the company that was decisive.[17] Furthermore, none of the pastors were native-born citizens of Geneva, for no Genevans could be found who possessed the requisite education. Most of them became "bourgeois" sooner or later. Calvin, surprisingly, was one of the last to become a "bourgeois," not being elevated to that position until 1559.[18] The number of pastors grew significantly during Calvin's lifetime, from nine in 1542, the first full year of his service after his return, to nineteen in 1564, the year of his death.[19] A few of these men were deputed to serve in small churches in the outlying villages dependent on Geneva, and thus would not have been always present for the weekly meetings of the consistory. But most of them lived and served in the city, and were regularly available for consistory duty. This was the only civic duty to which the pastors were all assigned, and they took it very seriously. The elders often had many other civic duties to which they had to devote attention. Those who sat on the small council had to spend most of their time working for the city government. And many of them held positions on other standing committees of the city. However, the elders also, in spite of these distractions, took their consistory duty seriously. Attendance at the weekly meetings was almost always nearly full, with generally only members who were ill or who had to leave the city on government or personal business being absent.

This seriousness may be explained in part by the fact that both pastors and elders were not only agents of the state but also ministers of the church. Both Calvinist theology and Genevan law are explicit on this point. The Calvinist ministry was made up of four orders: preaching pastors, teaching doctors, disciplining elders, and charity-directing deacons. All were parts of the organization dictated by God and described, if fleetingly, in the New Testament. All were equal in dignity and value, if different in function and length of tenure.[20]

The functions of the Genevan Consistory were various.[21] In the beginning, particularly, it devoted much of its energy to wiping out vestiges of Roman Catholicism. It stopped such practices as the saying of traditional prayers in Latin. It punished those who left Geneva to receive Catholic sacraments. It complained of acts labeled "superstitious" to which Catholic authorities had not objected. For example, a number of Genevans were disciplined for going to a country spring to collect samples of a water believed to have the miraculous ability to cure certain diseases. The consistory also worked hard to uphold the honor of God, of the Reformation of His worship, and of its leaders. Many

Genevans were punished for blasphemies of various sorts; for public insults to the consistory, to the Reformed pastors, above all to Calvin himself; for failure to attend church services or catechism. Occasionally the consistory considered charges of doctrinal error, although the most celebrated of those cases, the trials of Bolsec and Servetus, were handled primarily by other institutions. For our purposes, however, its really important function was to expose and punish immorality of many kinds, particularly sexual immorality. These cases occupied a good deal of its time and energy. In handling them, the consistory came to act like a morals court.

The procedures of the consistory were simple. Its members, both elders and pastors, were supposed to be constantly on the alert for signs of unchristian belief or behavior. If they spotted cases that were not serious, that were perhaps even private or secret, they were to reprimand the sinner involved. If these reprimands did not induce repentance, or if the sins involved were open and serious, the sinner would be referred to the entire consistory. Cases could thus be referred to the consistory by any of its members. They could also be referred by the city council or by the standing governmental committees devoted to judicial matters. They could apparently also be referred by any individual citizen who thought his neighbor's belief required correction or behavior merited discipline. These cases thus reflected a fair amount of spying by the residents of Geneva on each other.

Those summoned before the consistory were sharply questioned. If found guilty, they were subjected to vehement tongue-lashings, at which Calvin was particularly adept. Often this scolding would reduce a sinner to tears and repentance, and be deemed punishment enough. If the sinner proved stubborn, however, or if his sins were deemed sufficiently serious, he could be turned over to the small council for further discipline. The small council could then apply to him its usual summary justice, ending often in secular punishment—ranging from a spectacular public humiliation, to a short prison term, a small fine, or even death, executed in several brutal ways (by burning, drowning, strangling, hanging, or decapitation). The small council could also find the consistory in error, and release the sinner without punishment. It could also find the consistory overly severe, and administer a relatively mild punishment.[22]

The only further punishment that the consistory itself could administer was ecclesiastical. It could excommunicate, bar a sinner from receipt of Communion, a terrible penalty in a day when regular receipt of Communion was regarded as an essential sign of the operation of God's saving grace. This power of excommunication made the Calvinist consistory unusual, setting it apart from many of the institutions to control morals that preceded it in a number of other Protestant cities in both Switzerland and southern Germany.[23] It was also the feature of the consistory's operation that aroused the most vehement opposition among Protestants otherwise disposed to accept Calvin's leadership. It was the root cause of the Erastian quarrel, which first boiled up in the Palatinate, between Erastus and Calvin's student Olevianus,[24] and which later became a serious issue in such other Protestant countries as England. Opponents of consistorial excommunication felt that it usurped powers really belonging to the secular courts, that it put into human hands decisions that should be made by God alone, and that it permitted an intolerable intrusion into human privacy.

Some of this resistance to consistorial excommunication can be found within Geneva itself. It became so bitter, in fact, that it threatened Calvin's position in the city. It suggests that the systematic enforcement of morality was new to Calvin's Geneva, or at least relatively new. The small council was not at all certain that the ecclesiastical ordinances had in fact granted a sole right of excommunication to the consistory. It tried to intervene in the consistory's punishments by lifting sentences of excommunication when it judged those upon whom they were levied to be penitent. There were some particularly important cases of this sort involving Genevans of great prominence between 1553 and 1555. Calvin reacted against this intervention with fury, absolutely refusing to administer Communion to these sinners and persuading the other pastors to join him in this stand, even threatening to leave the city over this issue. In the resulting showdown, Calvin won a complete victory. His enemies were forced to give in completely, or were driven from the city or even put to death.[25]

An immediate result of this dramatic victory was a kind of moral reign of terror in Geneva. After 1555, no one could oppose the consistory effectively. There was a sharp increase in the number of morals cases referred by the consistory to the council and then acted upon, perhaps reaching a peak in 1557 and 1558.[26] Complaints were made to the council, but they had no effect. At one point, for example, a delegation appeared before the council to argue that the standards of sexual morality demanded by the consistory were humanly impossible, and to suggest that if the consistory continued to insist on such pure behavior, they feared their wives might all be tied in weighted sacks and thrown into the river (the punishment for flagrant adultery). The delegation was scolded for being frivolous and its leader was imprisoned.[27] Only after 1560, when Calvin and his colleagues began to be distracted by the demands of a tremendous missionary campaign in France, was there any slackening in the consistory's campaign to purify Geneva.

This campaign for morality produced results that were most impressive to visitors. John Knox, for example, who came to Geneva for the first time during these years, reported that in other cities he had found true doctrine preached, but in no other city had he seen such good behavior.[28] It seems to me that one finds in this stern enforcement of morality the essential explanation for the moral austerity of the entire Calvinist movement. Enforcement of morality was not, of course, unique to Calvin's Geneva. One can find analogous enforcement and sometimes even analogous institutions of enforcement in such other places as Savonarola's Florence, several decades earlier, and in the German and Swiss cities influenced by Zwingli, in the years immediately preceding the establishment of Calvin's regime in Geneva. A program of enforcement as strong as Geneva's, moreover, could not be imposed upon every community in which Calvinists were active. But it was imposed on many. And the very fact of its frequent existence in Calvinist communities gave a special sanction to the stern Calvinist education in morality that internalized this austerity and passed it on to succeeding generations. At least, this seems to me to be the most important element in any explanation of Calvinist moral austerity.

The main outlines of the history of the Genevan Consistory during Calvin's lifetime are already known. There are even some rather detailed studies of its operations, perhaps the best of which is Walther Köhler's *Zürcher Ehegericht und Genfer Konsistorium*, a monograph that traces with great skill the development of the Reformed methods for treating sexual and marital problems from Zwingli's establishment of a marriage court for Zurich in 1525 through similar developments in a number of south German and Swiss cities, to the full flowering of the Calvinist consistory in Geneva.[29] Those of us who have worked in the Genevan State Archives, however, know that these studies are far from definitive. They are based, at best, on a random sampling of the records of the consistory's operations. For those records are not only voluminous but also peculiarly difficult to use. There are some twenty manuscript registers in those Archives containing minutes of the weekly meetings of the consistory during the period when Calvin was its most prominent member, and dozens of registers for the succeeding periods. In these same Archives, one can also find hundreds of dossiers of manuscript trial records, which include records of cross-examinations, judgments, even on occasion private papers impounded as evidence, all in the cases of sinners referred by the consistory to the small council and the criminal courts of Geneva. No one, to my knowledge at least, has ever gone through this entire mass of manuscript material. It is not only dismayingly bulky, but its use also poses severe technical problems. These manuscripts were all written by hand, sometimes at top speed, as hearings before the consistory or council were in progress. They are in a French that is not only four hundred years old and includes many abbreviations, but that also contains many peculiar local usages. To read these manuscripts at all requires some training or experience in paleography. Even with experience, the reading of these materials is a slow and laborious process, as I can testify from personal experience. Most scholars who have tried to use these materials have given up in despair. Both Walther Köhler and Emile Doumergue, for example, based their studies of the consistory on a selection of transcribed excerpts from the consistory's Registers, prepared in the nineteenth century by A.

Cramer,[30] a local antiquarian who seems to have been the only man in history to have read much of these materials.

Yet a really intensive study of them might well yield some extremely interesting results. It should make possible studies of a much greater precision than can normally be attempted of how morality can be controlled in a community determined to do so. One could develop statistics on the various kinds of moral aberrations brought to the consistory's attention, and with them establish which aberrations were most prevalent in Calvin's Geneva. One could find out how each variety of aberration was treated by the consistory and the council, and thus estimate which aberrations were regarded as serious and which were accepted as petty. One could discover how many cases were handled by the consistory alone and how many were referred to the council, thus fixing the relative role of church and state in punishing moral offenders in Geneva. One could establish how many of the sinners referred to the council were punished as the consistory wished, how many were let off with lighter punishments, and how many were released without punishment, thus measuring in another way the relative weight of the church's moral influence in the community. Finally, one could measure how all these statistics changed over the years, with the annual changes in the personnel of both consistory and council and the shifts in the primary interests of these men, both affecting institutional reactions to moral lapses, and in turn revealing how the climate of opinion in Geneva developed.

At the moment, however, all of these possibilities remain nothing but possibilities. They can only be realized by intensive archival research, which may be beyond the capacity of any one historian, requiring the work of an entire team of scholars. The definitive history of the Genevan Consistory remains to be written. And the full history of the centuries-long devotion to moral austerity that issued from Calvin's Geneva lies still farther in the future.

1. François Wendel, *Calvin: sources et évolution de sa pensée religieuse* (Paris, 1950), pp. 209–10 (hereafter cited as *Calvin*).

2. On the pre-Reformation history of morals controls in Geneva, see Henri Naef, *Les origines de la Réforme à Genève*, 2 vols. (Geneva, 1936), 1:chap. 5

(hereafter cited as *Origines*). See also chap. 2, section 1, on the various government agencies to which police powers were attributed.

3. *SD*, 2:300. Noted by Naef, *Origines*, p. 234.

4. *RC*, 12 (Geneva, 1936): 533. Noted by Naef, *Origines*, pp. 229-30.

5. *RC*, 13 (Geneva, 1940):480. Noted by Naef, *Origines*, p. 230.

6. *SD*, 2:312-13; *RC*, 13:576-77.

7. *CO*, 21:282.

8. For copies of the full text, see *CO*, 10a:15-30; *SD*, 2:377-90; *RCP*, 1:1-13.

9. E. Doumergue, *Jean Calvin, les hommes et les choses de son temps*, 7 vols. (Lausanne, 1899-1927) 5:169 (hereafter cited as *Jean Calvin*).

10. This information comes from my own examination of the annual election records in the Archives d'Etat de Genève (hereafter cited as AEG), manuscript Registres du Conseil (hereafter cited as RC), for the period of Calvin's ministry.

11. *RCP*, 1:7.

12. A rule established by custom, not ordinance. See AEG, manuscript Registres du Consistoire de l'Eglise de Genève.

13. *RCP*, 1:7.

14. Robert M. Kingdon, "Social Welfare in Calvin's Geneva," *American Historical Review* 76 (1971):63.

15. Ibid., p. 62, based on AEG, RC, vol. 41, fol. 9, Feb. 8, 1546; vol. 42, fol. 17v, Feb. 11, 1547; vol. 46, fol. 151v, Feb. 11, 1552; vol. 51, fol. 7-7v, Feb. 12, 1556; vol. 53, fol. 7v, Feb. 11, 1557; vol. 54, fol. 77, Feb. 8, 1558; vol. 55, fol. 4v, Feb. 9, 1559; vol. 56, fol. 4v, Feb. 8, 1560; vol. 56, fol. 147, Feb. 13, 1561; vol. 57, fol. 5, Feb. 12, 1562; vol. 58, fol. 5, Feb. 11, 1563; vol. 59, fol. 3v, Feb. 10, 1564.

16. *CO*, 21:726-28.

17. Robert M. Kingdon, *Geneva and the Consolidation of the French Protestant Movement, 1564–1572* (Geneva and Madison, Wis., 1967), pp. 38-39.

18. Robert M. Kingdon, *Geneva and the Coming of the Wars of Religion in France, 1555-1563* (Geneva, 1956), p. 7. On Calvin, see also *CO*, 21:725.

19. Amédée Roget, *Histoire du peuple de Genève depuis la réforme jusqu'à l'Escalade*, 7 vols. (Geneva, 1870-83), supplies lists of the pastors active in every year from 1542 to 1567. For the 1542 list, see 2,2:335; for the 1564 list, see 7, 2:265.

20. Wendel, *Calvin*, pp. 230-31.

21. The analysis that follows is based on my own survey of Genevan records. Cf. the analogous analysis of Doumergue, *Jean Calvin*, 5:189-97; Walther Köhler, *Zürcher Ehegericht und Genfer Konsistorium*, 2 vols. (Leipzig, 1932, 1942), 2:580-88 (hereafter cited as *Konsistorium*).

22. For two examples, dating from shortly after Calvin's death, see *RCP*, 2:109.

23. See Köhler, *Konsistorium*, passim; above all, in his conclusion, 2:661-62.

24. On which see, inter alia, Ruth Wesel-Roth, *Thomas Erastus: Ein Beitrag zur Geschichte der reformierten Kirche und zur Lehre von der Staatssouveränität* (Lahr/Baden, 1954), pp. 43–81.

25. Köhler, *Konsistorium*, 2:604-14.

26. Revealed by the inventories of *procès criminels*, or criminal trials, still preserved in the AEG. Cf. the tabulation of sentences of excommunication, also increasing sharply in these years, in Köhler, *Konsistorium*, 2:614 n. 544.

27. See register entries excerpted in *CO*, 21:656 and 657; noted by Köhler, *Konsistorium*, 2:592.

28. John Knox to Mrs. Locke, December 9, 1556, in David Laing, ed., *The Works of John Knox*, 4 (Edinburgh, 1855):240.

29. Walter Köhler, *Zürcher Ehegericht und Genfer Konsistorium*, 2 vols. (Leipzig, 1932, 1942). There are extended reviews of vol. 1, by Jean Adam and François Wendel, in *Revue d'histoire et de philosophie religieuse* 13 (1933): 448-57.

30. AEG, A. Cramer, *Notes extraites des registres du Consistoire de l'Eglise de Genève, 1541–1814* (Geneva, 1853). Cited by Doumergue, *Jean Calvin,* 5:189; Köhler, *Konsistorium*, 2:vii, 568.

THE REFORMATION IN NÜRNBERG

Gottfried Seebass

Theology and evangelism of the Christian church have gone beyond the borders of confessions and denominations (often crossing them and making them relative), rediscovering the dimension of the "political." Certainly a shift will take place in the work of ecclesiastical historians. "Church history as a history of scriptural exegesis" will give greater attention to the extent to which the social milieu influenced biblical interpretation and whether or not exegesis might break down or change the social structure. Thus social history in the broadest sense of the word has become a relevant field of investigation for the church historian. A central question, then, for Reformation history is what effect did Luther's rediscovery of the gospel have for his time; what relevance did that passage from the third chapter in Romans "that a man is justified by faith without the deeds of the law" possess; and in what way could this passage be transferred into sociopolitical action.[1]

One does well to turn with this question to the free imperial cities of the time, where, in distinction to many other territories, one finds particularly copious sources, which allow one to make a broad survey of the gradual process or the sudden reversal of the Reformation. Furthermore, Reformation preaching very early evoked an enthusiastic echo in the cities. This was the case especially in municipalities in southern Germany, where the economic, social, cultural, and intellectual life was far more illustrious than in the imperial cities of other areas. Zurich and Strassburg, Memmingen and Constance must be named as the first Protestant communities. Nürnberg also belongs to this group, distinguished, however, by the fact that, being from the outset closely connected with Wittenberg, it adhered to the Lutheran form of the Reformation. In this regard it exercised a strong influence on many other smaller Franconian imperial cities that followed the lead of powerful Nürnberg on many questions. It may therefore without exaggeration be called an outpost of Wittenberg in southern Germany.

The above mentioned question will be studied below in terms of the history of the Reformation in Nürnberg. To be sure, there is a wealth of problems contained in our question. However, in order to present a short, general survey of the new epoch of the Reformation in Nürnberg, only three principal questions will be treated: first, how did the Reformation begin, and what strata of the urban society supported it; second, how did it proceed in Nürnberg; and finally, what changes did it bring with it. With this three-part subdivision one may at the same time approximately indicate the main chapters and most important stages of the history of the Reformation in Nürnberg: After a period of penetration of Lutheran doctrine, until about 1523, there follows, in 1523 and 1524 the first changes in the liturgical life, until the slow, steady organization of a city with Protestant character is completed in the period from 1525 to 1533. With the promulgation of the Nürnberg-Brandenburg Church Ordinance of 1533, the Reformation in Nürnberg is essentially finished. Thus, for the purposes of this study, developments after 1533 need be mentioned only now and then.

One must not forget that the following treatment of the Reformation in Nürnberg holds true only for the small area of this city. By no means can the history of its Reformation be considered exemplary for that of other cities. On the contrary! Bernd Moeller has recently shown in his valuable work "Reichsstadt und Reformation"[2] that Nürnberg even represents in many respects an exception.[3] Indeed, among the German imperial cities of the sixteenth century there were such differences in social and economic situation, in constitution and law, that general conclusions may be drawn and attempts at typology made only with extreme caution. In spite of the various relations of the cities with each other, and their slowly awakening interest in a unified policy at the imperial diets, where they formed their own group after 1498, each of them must first of all be considered as a "micro-*corpus christianum*,"[4] as a world in itself. One must take this limitation into consideration in the following discussion.

I

How did the Reformation begin and what strata of society supported it? It has often been considered necessary to answer this question in terms of mutually exclusive alternatives. It has been concluded on the one hand that the Reformation involved a religious movement that seized hold of the majority of the citizens and that had to establish itself slowly against the opposition of the hesitant or even hostile city councils. Thus, for example, Franz Lau asserted, with reference to the demands of guilds or newly formed assemblies of the citizenry in the north German cities, "there are no Reformations from councils, much less Reformations which proceed from the territorial ruler acting in the capacity of a city ruler";[5] and Moeller maintained the validity of this observation for all of Germany.[6] On the other hand, as Luther noted in his *Address to the Christian Nobility,* the Reformation, as a "levelling of the first wall of the Romanists," that is, the levelling of the distinction between clerics and laymen, played into the hands of the late-medieval ecclesiastical policy of the city councils that were striving for control of the church. Prior to the Reformation the councilmen supervised church property in parishes and monasteries and administered all care for the poor. They had procured for themselves the right to make church appointments, to supervise the schools, and they also regulated the entire social life of the city, from the clothing and jewelry of the citizens to the drinking of toasts in taverns. It is thus understandable that they also, where necessary, watched over the morals of the clergy and undertook needed reforms in the monasteries. Such extensions of competence, which were to be achieved only after lengthy negotiation or even legal struggle with the church, had a dual background. For one thing, the council attempted to exclude any interference in city affairs from the outside, be it from pope, bishop or superiors of religious orders; for another, and this factor must not be underestimated, within the *civitas christiana*, which the city represented, it felt itself responsible for not only the bodily but also the eternal well-being of the citizens. With an eye to these ambitions Josef Kraus said, "Wittenberg offered what Rome could never offer, fulfillment of the last wish of Nürnberg's ecclesiastical policy, ecclesiastical sovereignty in its perfection. . . . All due respect to nobler motivations! But these tempting prospects doubtlessly weighed heavy when it came to making a decision."[7] Such a conception will always be inclined to look for the driving force of the Reformation in the city council. How does this alternative apply in Nürnberg?

The first beginnings of the Reformation in Nürnberg are found not in the broad mass of citizens but with a small circle of men who were representatives of that typically south German humanism that was biblically molded by Erasmus and that recently has been rightly designated as an important point of departure for the Reformation in the cities.[8] In Nürnberg humanism had found its patrons early in the Pirckheimer family, whose house on the marketplace the arch-humanist Celtis praised as a "hostel of poets and scholars."[9] But other patrician families also proved their love for learning when they let their sons study at Upper Italian or German universities. Thus it was chiefly members of the patriciate who joined together in the humanist circle that included the two *Losunger* Anton Tucher and Hieronymus Ebner, the brothers Martin and Endres Tucher and Christoph and Sigmund Fürer, also Caspar Nützel, Hieronymus Holzschuher, Albrecht Dürer, Lazarus Spengler, and finally the jurist Christoph Scheurl, to whom we owe the notes about the group.

The sermons of Johann von Staupitz, vicar general of the Augustinian observants and Luther's confessor, served as the focal point of their gatherings. He preached in the Nürnberg Augustinian monastery on the occasion of his frequent visits in the years 1512, 1515, and 1517. Even if he himself considered it to be rare, this man possessed the talent of interpreting Holy Scripture so "that it applies consolation and help to men and is used more for enjoyment than for despair."[10] In his sermons he explained that it should be the "characteristic of a pious righteous Christian that he look at almighty God not as an evildoer imagining the hangman whom he must fear, but rather as a dear son thinking of his father whom he loves."[11] The effect was that he attracted attention and drew the people into the monastery church. These sermons had a more permanent effect on the humanist circle, which met with the Augustinians thereafter, and which, in humanistic fashion, bore the name "sodalitas Staupitziana" in honor of its founder. What Staupitz had begun was continued by Wolfgang Volprecht, the prior of the Augustinians, and Wenzeslaus Linck, who had been transferred from Wittenberg to Nürnberg by Staupitz. Linck was a good friend of Luther, and, like him, a doctor of theology, who formerly had been dean of the theological faculty in Wittenberg. Through him and Scheurl contact was made with the Wittenberg Augustinian monk, whose "Disputatio contra scholasticam theologiam" of September and whose "Ninety-five Theses Concerning Indulgences," of October 31, 1517, were greeted joyfully and discussed zealously. In the following year there was an opportunity to greet Luther in Nürnberg on his journey to Augsburg. The group again changed its name, this time from "Augustiniana" to "Martiniana"; "omnis ferme super coenam sermo de uno Martino," as Scheurl wrote at that time to his friends.[12] The circle grew noticeably and gradually was able to draw the majority of the council to its side.

The difficulties that Nürnberg was having with its clerics surely contributed to this shift. It was not enough that the council had to intervene against immoral behavior of regular and secular clergy; there were also clashes regarding the right of asylum of the monasteries. Finally it came to the point that two citizens of the city of high standing, Spengler and Willibald Pirckheimer, who had taken part in writing in the feud between Luther and Eck following the Leipzig disputation, were placed by Eck onto the same bull that threatened Luther with excommunication. Only after long, humiliating negotiations were the two able to receive absolution. However, it would be wrong to trace the decision of the councilors in favor of the Reformation only to the need for reform of the church. Naturally the council was cognizant of the financial drain connected with the system of indulgences and hoped to defend against it, just as against the propagation of new saints. Surely the criticism made by humanism and popular literature against the clerics fell on fertile soil in Nürnberg also. But that had not been able to lessen the importance of the church as mediator of all graces. Just as always, processions were held, persons acquired membership in confraternities, children were sent into the respected monasteries of the city, and at Saint Sebald's alone, twenty-five clerics read masses.

But Scheurl could nevertheless write as early as 1520 that "the patriciate, the multitude of the other citizens and all scholars stand on Luther's side."[13] At that time, however, Luther's teaching, proclaimed by a great number of circulating pamphlets and tracts, already had found its adherents among the citizenry. The path for the gospel to the broad masses did not open until the council made reappointments to the most important church offices in the years 1520-22: Hector Pömer and Georg Bessler were appointed as provosts, Andreas Osiander and Dominikus Schleupner as preachers at the parish churches of the city. They were joined not much later by the humanist Thomas Jäger. They were all young men—hardly any had passed thirty—who in part had been Luther's pupils at Wittenberg or had been instructed in his writings.

Doubtlessly Osiander was the most important one among them. As a cleric from Gunzenhausen, he had been educated at Ingolstadt in the writings of Reuchlin and Erasmus to the point of being a humanist and a *homo trilinguis*. In 1520 after his ordination to the priesthood, he had become instructor of the Hebrew language among the Nürnberg Augustinians. It was probably there in the monastery that he was won over to the Reformation by the reading of Luther's writings from the years 1519–20. After his installation as preacher he represented the cause of the new doctrine in the pulpit of the Church of Saint Lorenz with the relentless determination that was peculiar to him. His sermons, of which none is completely preserved for us, developed in very lively fashion the basic concepts of the doctrine of justification from constantly new points of church dogma, and exerted an attraction not only upon the citizens of Nürnberg. A large number of the princes and envoys who were staying in the city between 1522 and 1524 for the meetings of the imperial governing council and the imperial diets went to them. Osiander's zeal could not even be tempered by the presence of the papal nuncio in Nürnberg; from the pulpit he referred to the pope as the Antichrist.

These sermons found their echo among the people, who expressed their partisanship for Luther in pamphlets like those of the weaver Niklas Cadolzburger or the painter Hans Greiffenberger, and above all, in the famous "Wächterlied" (Song of the Watchman) of Hans Sachs, in which Luther is celebrated as the "Wittenberg nightingale" that announces to the people the dawning of a new day after a long darkness.

Naturally the council had to intercede against attacks of the aroused mob who cursed monks, disturbed divine services in the monasteries by shouting, or even broke window panes. To preserve external appearances, it also on occasion forbade the sale of Lutheran booklets, which were to be had everywhere and by no means just from bookdealers. Of course, at the same time the councilmen received copies of them from Saxony. To be sure, the preachers were exhorted again and again not to hold controversial sermons; but such exhortations were aimed almost exclusively at the Catholic monastic preachers. It is characteristic that the council, following advice that Osiander had drafted for his colleagues, banned a Franciscan preacher from the city as early as 1522. The fact that there was no serious intention of hindering the propagation of the Reformation was obvious when, at the beginning of 1523, a papal legate demanded the imprisonment of the Lutheran preachers, particularly of Osiander. At that point the city government, with the justification that it "might be conducive to despondency and more outrage among the community to fail to observe that such a thing, as a human fear, would move God without doubt to disfavor,"[14] protected its preachers and showed itself ready to defend them with weapons if need be. A more unambiguous position could not have been taken. Thus, at the end of 1524 there was still earnest opposition to the Reformation only in the monasteries, especially among the Dominicans and Franciscans and in the two convents. They were joined by the small group of citizens and patricians who either wanted to hold onto tradition or who—one thinks of Willibald Pirckheimer and

Christoph Scheurl—reapproached the old church, having been repulsed and disappointed by the Reformation and the disorders connected with it. The Lutheran message, however, had won over the great majority of the populace and the council. It was soon apparent that this camp was not at all in agreement on questions of how the Reformation was to be undertaken. But this lies outside the sphere of the question of how the Reformation began in Nürnberg.

In searching for an answer to this question, one sees that the alternative of "popular movement" or "conciliar Reformation" cannot be established for Nürnberg. There was neither an evangelical movement outside of, or opposed to, the council, nor a "new dogma" imposed upon the citizenry by the council. The statement arrived at by Moeller for the cities is thus valid also for Nürnberg: "Nowhere else was the success of the Reformation so little influenced by suppression or promotion by force."[15] Indeed, there would have been no chance of success for an evangelical popular movement in the face of a hostile council. The oligarchic patrician city government sat so firmly in control that without its agreement any movement for reform would have been condemned to failure. In fact, it was on the basis of the religious decision of the council members and through the strong influence of the secretary of the council, Lazarus Spengler, that a reforming evangelic movement that encompassed all classes was made possible, and led within two years to the first changes.

II

How did the Reformation proceed?

It has already been noted that one can scarcely overemphasize the significance of the fact that from 1520 on, men sympathetic to the Lutheran cause administered the most important church offices in the city. Their installation was in no way illegal. The bishop of Bamberg confirmed the appointment of the provosts after their presentation by the council, and they in turn—as was their right—installed the preachers with the consent of the council. The jurisdictional power of the bishop thus remained intact.

The same was the case with the promulgation of the new alms ordinance in the year 1522, which in its preface clearly betrayed the influence of Lutheran preaching. The charitable works of the community were no longer understood as a good work of men, well-pleasing to God, but as thanks for the grace of absolution: "Faith and love, as Christ says in the gospel, Matthew 22, are the two chief points of a just Christian existence, in which all other laws of God are included, on which also hang all the laws and the prophets. For to love Christ, to trust him alone and to do to my neighbor as I believe Christ has done to me, that is the only proper way to become pious and attain salvation, and there is no other. Through faith man becomes just, is born to life and attains salvation."[16] Likewise, in reorganizing the welfare system the council did not exceed its rightful powers.

In the following years it appeared that the council and the provosts, were disposed, as far as was possible, to carry out the Reformation legally. Thus during Lent in 1523 and 1524 the city government undertook all sorts of changes in the elaborate ceremonies, but it was always a case of things that were abolished because of "improper carryings-on which were prevalent" or because they "have been more conducive to vexation and frivolity than to piety."[17] Even the bishop of Bamberg did not care to protest against this. It was a different case with the extensive demands of the provosts and preachers who appeared as early as 1523 before the council at the request of the members of the community for permission to celebrate the Eucharist under both kinds. As was demanded by the ordinance, the council, despite its desire to approve their request, referred them to the bishop of Bamberg, who, as was to be expected, did not give his approval. If then in spite of this such celebrations of the Eucharist were held at Easter time in 1523 and in 1524 in the Augustinian monastery, and Osiander dared even to offer the chalice to the sister of the emperor at the castle, this action marked the path of open resistance against the jurisdiction of the bishop. The same holds true for the unauthorized use of the German language. After Osiander translated the Bamberg ordinance, German was used from early in 1524 on at baptisms in the parish churches; in the Augustinian monastery, which had long been the seat of those in the forefront of the movement, it was even used in a newly created order of the mass.

One would like to know how far the right of codetermination of the communities went in such questions; that is to say, to what extent it was really a matter of their desires aroused by the sermons and not just a matter of the desires of the preachers. Osiander's statements in letters from that time clearly show that he was the driving force. In any case, the active participation of the communities, in the form of citizens' meetings or petitions to the council, is nowhere to be seen. Repeatedly, the provosts and preachers were the ones who passed on the wishes of the communities to the council.

In addition, soon after the imperial diet and imperial governing council left the city, at the beginning of June, 1524, they carried out some basic changes without first informing their superiors; the significance of these was later clothed in the words: the pope has been sent on vacation. Certainly Osiander's name was the one signed when the provosts agreed in nineteen articles to a new regulation of pastoral care and ecclesiastical ministration; likewise, he led in the working-out of a cautious change in the liturgy of the mass. Thus the first form of an evangelical church ordinance was created for Nürnberg. To be sure, this contested once again the authoritative competence of the bishop in matters of ceremony.

These changes, at least at this point, went too far for the council. It demanded at first the restoration of the old ordinances, but relented, however, when Osiander drafted a voluminous defense for the provosts in which he depicted in detail the faithfulness to the letter of all measures. Indeed, he defended himself to the imperial representative and the bishop of Bamberg with the statement that he had not known anything about the reforms, but would, even so, intervene against them only if their unchristian character were proved. Therefore, the excommunication, which after a short trial at Bamberg was issued against the provosts of the parish churches and the Augustinian prior, and against which those concerned appealed to a general council, remained completely without effect in the city. In refusing to carry out the bishop's judgment, the council, for all practical purposes, suspended the bishop's jurisdiction. Basically, by virtue of this act, it assumed responsibility for the entire ecclesiastical life of the city.

In its negotiations with the imperial representative and the bishop, the council could point with justification to the fact that a reversal of the changes would lead to disturbance and alarm in the city. This, as the secular authority, it had to prevent. In actual fact, there was in the city a third group inclined to revolt. The lower class, composed of the poor and beggars, workers and apprentices, made up an unruly element. Not the sermons of the Lutheran clerics but other ideas, those of Carlstadt and Müntzer, had spread among them. Thus the liturgical reform, now completed, by no means accommodated all the wishes voiced in the community. Much earlier, in and around the city lay preachers had appeared who attempted to make the council unpopular among the people; some peasants were already plotting to protect such preachers from measures taken on the part of the authorities. Right at the time of those changes introduced by the provosts and preachers, there were dangerous omens in the villages around the city and among the urban proletariat. The Forchheim peasant revolt, prelude to the great Peasants' War in Franconia, also affected Nürnberg subjects. Invoking "Christian freedom," they refused to pay the tithes and at night burned the grain in the fields which was to be delivered. Placards directed against the council appeared on church doors and house walls. Partisans of Müntzer from outside the city, who were, to be sure, soon banned, fanned the flames. Journeymen printers and journeymen of the smith and dye trades proved to be particularly susceptible to such influences. These are the same circles that tended toward the Carlstadt-Zwinglian doctrine of the Eucharist; therefore, Osiander wrote especially for the council a short "Report on the Causes Which Might Move the Common Uneducated Man to Consider the Holy Sacrament of the Altar to be Merely Wine and Bread and not the Flesh and Blood of Christ."[18]

The council had two of the trouble-makers executed publicly. Otherwise, however, it attempted to prevent a revolt by calling attention to the favorable situation of the peasants in the Nürnberg area and by careful easing of the peasants' burdens. In

actual fact, the Peasants' War later did not extend to the area of
the city, and Nürnberg was able to protest against the barbaric
reprisals of the army of the Swabian League. Twenty years later,
the council still remembered thankfully the help that Osiander
had been to it at this time. Along with Spengler, Hans Sachs,
and others, it was he above all who, in his sermons, inculcated
the difference between Christian and worldly freedom in the
face of the careless conjoining of the two on the part of the peasants. Thus the council succeeded with the help of Lutheran
preachers in preventing a "radical Reformation."

In the fall of 1524, if the council, in spite of demands from
various sides, still hesitated in seeking a solution to the religious
question for the city, then it was only a question of time as to
when it would have to do so. Two factors, already briefly mentioned earlier, pushed in this direction. First, the council was concerned about peace and quiet among the citizenry; hence, the
stereotyped admonitions to the preachers not to bring controversial doctrines into the pulpits. For this reason action was taken
against the partisans of Carlstadt and Zwingli and later against
the Anabaptists. There was a strong conviction that division in
faith must lead to disturbance and tumult in the citizenry, since
dissimilar preaching brings with it "division among our citizenry
. . . destruction of civil peace, and general repugnance." In its
measures the council had merely sought "the prevention of imminent intolerable damage that every authority is duty bound
to prevent for the preservation of honorable city government and
civil order."[19]

In addition there was a feeling of responsibility for the eternal
well-being of the citizens. If the council would not make God's
Word the guiding principle of life in the city, it would have to
fear the punishment of God. This responsibility had been impressed upon the ruling men by Osiander at the end of his defense of the provosts with the words "As we are the servants of
Your Honors and of a common city and Your Honors as the
temporal authority have power over our possessions, body and
life, we ask that you diligently wish to reflect upon the fact that
not less, but rather much more depends upon you as the government, and should the Word of God be wrenched from the peo-

ple, their faith weakened and their soul neglected, God would very earnestly demand them from your hands, even if it would remain unpunished in the eyes of the world. For we see how earnestly God commanded the authorities in the Old Testament about heeding his word."[20]

The Nürnberg religious colloquy held by the council at the beginning of March, 1525, in the assembly room of the city hall must be understood in this context. Holding such a debate for the purpose of removing religious controversies, at least on the level of the city, was an obvious alternative after a planned national council, for which Nürnberg had prepared with detailed expert briefs, had been forbidden by the emperor in the fall of the previous year. For the council the final reason (for the colloquy) was the controversy that had arisen between the Protestant provost and the other monks in the Carthusian monastery. The council was not interested in a fundamental settlement: out of a citizenry that had disintegrated into the most varied factions, there was to arise anew a united Christian community. In this respect use was made of Luther's comment "that a Christian assembly or community has the right and power to judge all doctrine." To be sure, in contrast especially to the cities of Upper Germany, the multitude of the people, also on this occasion, took part only as an audience in front of open windows. They gave expression to their opinion so violently, however, that the council had to have the monks accompanied under military guard into the monasteries. The real desire of the patrician government for a decision of the whole citizenry is seen in the fact that the council of the two hundred "Genannte," which met on extremely rare occasions and in which the craftsmen were represented, was convened so that it could follow the disputation on the twelve articles that had been worked out as a basis for the debate. In order to abbreviate the process, a spokesman was chosen immediately for the Catholic and Protestant factions. Certainly, the preacher of the Franciscan monastery, who represented the monks, was inferior to the eloquent Osiander. Thus the colloquy ended with a complete victory for the Protestant side. This result was admittedly to be foreseen, insofar as the agenda for the day contained chiefly points of Protestant dogma. Scheurl's opening speech read: "But after the ram has nested so deeply in the garden that the children on the street, not to mention the women cry, "Scripture! Scripture!" it is considered to be most necessary, profitable, and good that in your colloquy you leave out popes, councils, fathers, tradition, holiness, statute, decree, usage, old custom and everything that is not founded on the Word of God, and use only the pure gospel and Scripture, for at this market no other coin will be current."[21] In the last meeting of the debate, at which the monks, who previously had repeatedly declined a colloquy, did not appear, Osiander, in a two-hour speech, summarized Protestant doctrine and then called upon the council to wait no longer for a (church) council, but rather to draw all the resultant consequences from the Reformation for the city.

Thus the council was officially charged by its most capable theologian with a reordering of all church affairs. It was a task that it discharged with great conscientiousness and care in the years between 1525 and 1533. With the promulgation of the Nürnberg-Brandenburg Church Ordinance in this year, the Reformation of the city was considered to be essentially complete, and the council was not at all happy when the theologians kept on demanding changes, whether the abolition of general absolution or the introduction of a special act of ordination for clerics. This, however, anticipates the last question.

As for the question of how the Reformation proceeded in Nürnberg, one can now answer: The Reformation was undertaken by the city council. It, however, did not thus act arbitrarily, but mostly followed slowly and with pensive hesitation the wishes of the community conveyed to it by the theologians. All fanatic stirrings or attempts to draw sociorevolutionary consequences from the gospel were rejected by the council with the support of the preachers. Nevertheless, the carrying-out of the Reformation was certainly in the minds of the great majority of the citizens after 1525, even if they were not directly involved in it.

III

What did the Reformation change? In posing this question one must first make clear the limits of this investigation. It is, of course, not at all intended to trace far and wide, in the comprehensive fashion of Max Weber, Ernst Troeltsch, and Werner Elert, the effects of the Reformation in the areas of the family and society, the state and justice, scholarship and art, in order to show to what extent the Reformation was a phenomenon that either ushered in or inhibited modernity. Rather, this investigation is interested concretely in what actual changes took place in Nürnberg after the religious colloquy of 1525 until the promulgation of the church ordinance of 1533.

The most far-reaching change, doubtlessly, concerned the completely altered relationship between secular authority and the church. It has already been possible to show how the council in pre-Reformation times, proceeding from the concept of the *corpus christianum*, attempted to get broad powers in the ecclesiastical area. In spite of all this, however, the powerful spectacle and organization of the church remained a rival to be respected, whose power one had to reckon with and not seldom had occasion to feel. This rival now disappeared, since even the city's theologians themselves, in distinction to Luther's conception, accepted the complete administration of the church by the council as the legitimate power. Thus the continual disputes with the pope, bishop, and monasteries ceased, even if the defense of the Reformation against these powers at first required much effort. That did not mean, however, that the council now could have ruled, or would have wanted to rule, at will in ecclesiastical affairs. For the period right after 1525 one may in no way speak of "governmental rule of the church"; for later periods one may do so only with great qualification. Osiander, the leading theologian, was of the opinion that all necessary changes in the ecclesiastical life of the city would have to come at the direction of the council and be carried out by it, although he immediately added:

> We want to and should commend all such things . . . to Your Honors as Christian . . . authorities, and yet in each instance advise in these matters, and as it happens remind and admonish Your Honors of the same, for that is proper to us out of duty and by virtue of our office in which we teach everyone, but primarily authorities, to lead a Christian government in right belief. . . . [We] therefore ask that

Your Honors take our direction and admonition to heart and put it into
practice so that it will not be necessary for us to speak about it from
the pulpit; that will be . . . pleasing to the Almighty, to the esteem
of Your Honors and will be conducive to general peace and civil
obedience.[22]

Accordingly, between 1525 and 1533 the staff of the city
preachers together with the provosts formed an advisory body for
the ruling patricians, comparable to the assembly of lawyers.
Briefs from the provosts and preachers were collected together
with those of the lawyers as part of the council's records (*Ratschlagbücher*). Nevertheless, this was neither a case of a special representation of the Christian community nor a matter of a truly
independent ecclesiastical authority, since the composition and
convening of the body as well as the topics to be treated in its
sessions were determined solely and entirely by the council. In
this body, which had to meet particularly often after the religious
colloquy of 1525, Osiander no doubt held a scarcely contested
preeminence. This is proved by the many opinions that originate
from his pen, but that were handed to the council in the name of
the preachers. However, if his view did not dominate, he not infrequently handed in his own suggestions along with those of his
colleagues to the council. Accordingly, his influence on the reforming changes in Nürnberg cannot be overestimated.

In dealing with the problems presented to the theologians for
advice, one touches an important limitation on their influence;
namely, their right of consultation was limited, and once more by
their own agreement, to the area of doctrine and preaching, liturgical life and welfare, marital laws, and school questions. Regarding social, economic, or political questions, their opinion was
usually not heard at all. Thus it is not surprising that the Reformation scarcely penetrated as a reforming factor into the area
of public life.

In spite of opposition to it among the people in the countryside and among the citizenry, there was no change in the old
oligarchic constitution of the city. Indeed, after the Schmalkaldic
War, when the patrician councils were restored in the cities of
Upper Germany, Nürnberg's constitution was even taken as a
model since the relation between city constitution and conserva-

tive ecclesiastical reform was very well recognized.[23] A contribution to the solution of social problems is just as little in evidence. The justified questions and demands that had been expressed in the unruliness of the urban proletariat and the peasant revolts died away without being heard, if one discounts some steps to ease the burden of deliverance of the tithe and the new alms ordinance. And if the council right at that time repeatedly called upon the theologians to explain quite clearly "Christian freedom," it was exactly their intent to impress upon the common man that the Reformation and secular freedom had nothing to do with one another. Nevertheless, the attitude of the Nürnberg Council in the Peasants' War was a pleasant relief from that of many other Protestant governments.

In the area of economics the most important occurrence was the abolition of the special status of the clerics—and above all, of the monasteries—in the matter of tax exemption and other special rights that had long been a thorn in the flesh of the citizens. On the other hand, no limitation was imposed upon usury, as Luther had demanded in his writing on business transactions and usury, and as Hans Sachs had also at times desired in his pamphlets. However, the drastic reduction of the number of church holidays, a measure that was undertaken immediately after the religious colloquy, must have had an advantageous effect on commerce and trade.

By no means can one assert that the Reformation entailed a noticeable elevation of the moral attitude of the citizenry. This is proved not only by the various mandates of the council having to do with morals, which were continually repeated, but also by the charge that Hans Sachs raises: "It is true for one thing if you Lutherans would behave modestly and inoffensively, your doctrine would have better respect in the eyes of all men; those who now call you heretics would speak well of you, those who now despise you would learn from you. But with the eating of meat, uproar, defamation of priests, quarreling, derision, scorn, and all immodest behavior, you Lutherans have yourselves caused a great scorn for the Protestant doctrine. It is regrettably evident."[24] In view of the many matrimonial cases (*Ehehändel*), a swift reforming of the marriage law would have been especially indispensable. However, precisely this action was delayed, since in this area the views of the lawyers and theologians were widely divergent. Thus there was for a long time a definite uncertainty that could not have an advantageous effect.

The Reformation, however, meant a real step forward for the school system. To be sure, school attendance at first declined; however, it soon improved again. In addition the council provided for adequate pay for teachers and at intervals installed commissions that concerned themselves with everything from the school building to the course of instruction. Above all, however, the fruitful connection of the Reformation and humanism may be seen here among the councilmen and theologians of the city. Since it was believed that the rebirth of the three ancient languages was the precondition for theological reorientation—not infrequently did Osiander in one breath name Reuchlin, Erasmus, and Luther as reformers—the step was taken toward the creation of a *Gymnasium* to which prominent scholars were summoned as teachers. Even if this did not benefit the youth of all classes, concern was nevertheless shown them in that childrens' sermons and catechism classes were at least established alongside the existing Latin schools.

If one surveys the "secular sphere" in this fashion, one sees that the Reformation produced only few changes here. In general, it strengthened tendencies already evident before the Reformation. However, one must not forget that in a collection of such individual points it is exactly the earth-shaking discovery of the Protestant message that could not come up for discussion: namely, the fact that with the abolition of the distinction between clerics and laymen, even the slightest trace of inferiority was taken away from secular life as opposed to the perfect life of the monk. Now a councilman and a craftsman could view work in his social rank as a call of God to "good works." Justifiably this has been called a "Copernican turning-point."[25]

Before turning to the effect of the Reformation in the "ecclesiastical sphere" it must be stressed once again that, for reasons already mentioned, there was no distinction made between the civil and the ecclesiastical community. The council watched cautiously so that no form of independent ecclesiastical administration could be established anywhere. It turned down Osiander's suggestion for the establishment of a court staffed with theologians for marital cases; in the absolution controversy after 1533 it resisted all attempts at exercise of an independent ecclesiastical discipline; and it refused to permit the ordination of Lutheran preachers as a special ecclesiastical act along with their installation by the council.

This unity of civil and religious community, however, also prevented the possibility of tolerance for different creeds in the city. It has been noted that the religious colloquy was supposed to serve exactly the purpose of establishing the unity of the message to be preached. Hence, after this debate, action was taken against all tendencies deviating from the Lutheran dogma: the establishment of one denomination in the city began. On the one hand, this affected the monks and nuns, who opposed all innovations. They were forbidden to hold mass and forced to hear Protestant preachers. Charitas Pirckheimer, the well-educated abbess of the Convent of Saint Clara, reported from her experience that the preachers called upon the citizens "that they exterminate us godless people, tear down the monasteries, and drag us forcefully out of the cloisters, for we were supposed to be in a damnable state . . . and would have to be the devil's eternally."[26] The city council put the monasteries and convents, as it were, into a state of extinction by not allowing them additional new admissions. That they proceeded on the whole quite cautiously, however, was no doubt partly due to the fact that several daughters of the most respected families of the city lived in the convents. The council acted more vigorously from the outset against all socalled fanatics, which term indiscriminately designated the followers of Carlstadt and Müntzer as well as the representatives of the Zwinglian Sacramentarian doctrine and the Anabaptists. All of them, who found their followers mainly in the lower levels of the population, were banned from the city, providing that long imprisonment and attempts at conversion made by the preachers proved fruitless. But in Nürnberg, in distinction to many other areas, the death penalty was not used against them. In general, the theologians also followed Luther's statement that heresy must be overcome not with the sword but rather with the Word. Nev-

ertheless, one gets an impression of what was possible when one
hears that Osiander answered the question of whether children
of the Anabaptists might be baptized forcefully with a clear
"no," but at the same time showed a way out: one could punish
the parents with exile, retain the children, however, with the
other belongings, establish a guardian, and in this fashion have
them baptized and reared Lutheran.

Of course there was a censorship board in the city, which
closely watched over what books and writings were permitted to
be printed and sold. Here one clearly sees that freedom of conscience, in the sense that every citizen be permitted to live his
belief, in no way belonged among the results of the Reformation. It is characteristic that an Augsburg citizen could write about
the citizens of Nürnberg, "What Osiander holds and believes,
they must also believe."[27]

The actual sphere of Reformation changes was in the ecclesiastical life of the city.

Here the refashioning of liturgical forms must first be noted.
It was completed in slow succession and in very careful fashion.
Thus there was no iconoclasm in Nürnberg, in spite of many
derogatory statements about images. There was, rather, an attempt to take over from tradition whatever did not stand in obvious contradiction to the doctrine of justification as the mid-
point of scripture. The baptismal rite translated by Osiander into
German preserved all of the traditional ceremonies. Another of
Osiander's accomplishments, the liturgical regulation of the parish churches, which later became generally binding, featured as
its essential reform simply a German reading of the epistle and
gospel and the dropping of the *canon missae*. The entire external
course of the liturgy, however, was retained. The liturgy was sung
in Latin, and the traditional vestments of the mass were used in
the celebration of the Eucharist, which was interpreted, however,
in a German "exhortation" as the chalice was distributed. The
various strictly German orders of the mass that at first were also
to be found in Nürnberg again disappeared. Bernhard Klaus
rightly concluded that the external appearance of these church
services hardly differed from that of pre-Reformation times.[28]

Attempts at adapting tradition by means of interpretation become particularly apparent in the question of whether one might still swear an oath "by all saints." Osiander answered yes, since the word "saints" in this oath does not refer to the saints of the Roman Church but, rather, calls upon the now-living members of the Christian community as witnesses, just as *hoi hagioi* in the New Testament simply designated the Christians.

Of course, the theologians would gladly have made more radical changes on some points. However, they were hindered in this at the beginning of the Reformation by consideration for those "weak in faith" and by the general political situation in the empire, and later by the council. It was only at the express wish of the council that, for example, some feast days of Mary and the feasts of the twelve apostles continued to be celebrated; only its command later prevented the exclusive use of German in the liturgy. After the promulgation of the Ecclesiastical Ordinance of 1533, it became more and more difficult to push through any changes in the council.

Of course, one should not underestimate the innovations. The numerous private masses that had been celebrated in churches and monasteries on the basis of the most diverse bequests were done away with. The ostentatious processions and a great number of other ceremonies were no longer performed. These reforms penetrated more deeply into the liturgical life than one is able today to estimate. After all—and this is particularly important—there was thus a shift of the emphasis from visual perception of sacred actions in the liturgy to auditory perception of the Word of Holy Scripture as revealed by the sermon.

In addition, the formation of an entirely new class of Protestant pastors must be emphasized. Since the differentiation between clerics and laymen had been abolished, all clerics were also obliged to swear the oath of citizenship and to assume the burdens and duties of a citizen. Their earlier exempt status was thus removed. On the other hand, the council also assumed complete care for its clerics. To begin with, this meant that they were given a sufficient salary. The means for this came from the wealth of the churches and monasteries, which was administered by the council by means of special boards, from which the costs of the schools and of welfare were also defrayed. In an extensive brief

Osiander had advised in favor of such a use of church property and,endowments. Thus the church property was administered conscientiously by the council. It also took responsibility for the legal protection and safety of the Protestant theologians, and not a few of them needed this protection. Since after the religious colloquy the council no longer wanted to tolerate the old keeping of concubines, most of the clerics had married and thus had been outlawed and excommunicated. With these measures, and above all by virtue of the facts that there was also an interest taken in the continuing education of the clerics and that preachers were appointed only after an examination, the council contributed much to the change and moral elevation of the old class of clerics. To be sure, the Protestant clerics thus all too quickly fell into a completely dependent situation that could easily have allowed them to become mere servants of the council. Only a few of them possessed the courage, like Osiander, to resist the authorities where it seemed necessary for the sake of faith. The interim period can serve in a certain fashion as proof of this. When at that time the council ordered for the first time basic changes in the liturgy, against the will of the theologians, only a few of the clerics gave up their office along with Osiander.

Once again, with this enumeration of various points, the actual change has not been touched upon: it consisted of the fact that the message of the Reformation placed man in a new relationship to God that was no longer characterized by the law of one's own work, but rather by trust and love. This entailed, however, a freeing of consciences from church laws, which was greeted with thanks by all strata of the people and the scope of which can in no way be judged in our day.

To be sure, it must be noted here—and thus is formulated the answer to the third question—that the "Christian freedom" discovered by the Reformation operated in Nürnberg exclusively as a possibility for reorganization of those areas that, with the claim of absolute validity, had been previously regulated by canon law. In this matter the reformers proceeded very carefully at first, in the face of tradition, but they contemplated for the future more basic changes, which for various reasons did not come about. Thus only very conservative reforms were made. Since all changes were approved and carried out by the council, the Reformation favored de facto the tendencies of urban ecclesiastical policy of the late Middle Ages, and was not able to resist a slowly emerging regulation of the churches on the part of the authorities, in spite of several attempts. Of course, the changes mentioned above operated also in the sociopolitical area, insofar as the Christian and the civil communities still formed an undivided unit. But there were no basic transformations in the secular sphere, which was freed by Reformation theology from ecclesiastical control. By proclaiming the basic freedom of this sphere without developing individual suggestions for a reform, which was necessary in view of the peasant disturbances, the status quo was simply de facto strengthened.

1.   This essay was first published in the *Mitteilungen des Vereins für Geschichte der Stadt Nürnberg*, 65 (1967/68): pp. 252–63. It has been revised for its inclusion in this volume (translation by David Armborst, revised by the editors). Gerhard Ebeling, *Kirchengeschichte als Geschichte der Auslegung der Heiligen Schrift* ("Sammlung gemeinverständlicher Vorträge," Vol. 189 [Tübingen, 1947]); reprinted in Gerhard Ebeling, *Wort Gottes und Tradition: Kirche und Konfession* ("Veröffentlichungen des Konfessionskundlichen Instituts des Konfessionskundlichen Instituts des Evangelischen Bundes," Vol. 7 [Göttigen, 1964]), pp. 9-27, especially pp. 24 f.

2.   Bernd Moeller, *Reichsstadt und Reformation* ("Schriften des Vereins für Reformationsgeschichte," Vol. 69 [Gütersloh, 1962]).

3.   Ibid., pp. 25-27.

4.   Ibid., p. 15.

5.   Franz Lau, "Der Bauernkrieg und das angebliche Ende der lutherischen Reformation als spontaner Volksbewegung," *Luther-Jahrbuch*, 26 (1959); 109-34, especially p. 119.

6.   Moeller, *Reichsstadt und Reformation*, p. 33.

7.   Quoted in Gerhard Pfeffer, "Das Verhältnis von politischer und kirchlicher Gemeinde in den deutschen Reichsstädten," in W. P. Fuchs, ed., *Staat und Kirche im Wandel der Jahrhunderte* (Stuttgart, 1966), p. 83.

8.   Moeller, *Reichsstadt und Reformation*, p. 19; E. W. Kohls, "Evangelische Bewegung und Kirchenordnung in oberdeutschen Reichsstädten," *Theologische Literaturzeitung* 92(1967): 322.

9.   Quoted in Hans von Schubert, *Lazarus Spengler und die Reformation in Nürnberg* ("Quellen und Forschungen zur Reformationgeschichte," Vol. 17, ed. Hajo Holborn [Leipzig, 1934]), p. 112.

10.   Quoted in Friedrich Roth, *Die Einführung der Reformation in Nürnberg 1517-1528* (Würzburg, 1885), p. 53.

11.   Quoted in von Schubert, *Lazarus Spengler*, p. 114.

12.   Quoted in ibid., p. 163.

13. Quoted in ibid., p. 205.

14. Hans von Schubert, *Die Reformation in Nürnberg* (Nürnberg, 1925), p. 17.

15. Moeller, *Reichsstadt und Reformation*, p. 33.

16. Emil Sehling, *Die evangelischen Kirchenordnungen des XVI. Jahrhunderts*, Vol. 11: Bayern, Pt. 1, Franken (Tübingen, 1961), p. 23.

17. Adolf Engelhardt, "Die Reformation in Nürnberg," *MVGN* 33 (1936): 119.

18. Wilhelm Möller, *Andreas Osiander: Leben und ausgewählte Schriften* (Elberfeld, 1870), p. 67.

19. Quoted in Pfeiffer, "Das Verhältnis von politischer und kirchlicher Gemeinde," p. 89.

20. W. F. Schmidt and Karl Schornbaum, *Die fränkischen Bekenntnisse* (Munich, 1930), p. 177.

21. Quoted in Roth, *Die Reformation*, p. 196.

22. Quoted in Gottfried Seebass, *Das reformatorische Werk des Andreas Osiander*, ("Einzelarbeiten aus der Kirchengeschichte Bayerns," Vol. 44 [Nürnberg, 1967]), p. 180.

23. Moeller, *Reichsstadt und Reformation*, p. 66.

24. Quoted in Roth, *Die Reformation*, p. 125.

25. Quoted in Moeller, *Reichsstadt und Reformation*, p. 36.

26. Joseph Pfanner, *Die Denkwürdigkeiten der Caritas Pirckheimer* ("Caritas Pirckheimer Quellensammlung," Vol. 2 [Landschut, 1967]), p. 52.

27. Quoted in Seebass, *Andreas Osiander*, p. 117.

28. Bernhard Klaus, "Die Nürnberger Deutsche Messe 1524," *Jahrbuch für Liturgik und Hymnologie*, 1 (1955): 24.

HARD WORK, GOOD WORK, AND SCHOOL WORK: AN ANALYSIS OF WENZESLAUS LINCK'S CONCEPTION OF CIVIC RESPONSIBILITY

Charles E. Daniel, Jr.

Martin Luther once said of Wenzeslaus Linck that he "preaches so that the common man learns something. . . . I must write a book sometime about smart preachers."[1] Luther never wrote that book, but he was correct in his assessment of Linck, whose popularity testifies to the sensitivity he had for the ideals of his parishioners. His sermons can serve as a mirror of the aspirations and ethics of sixteenth-century townsmen in Germany.

Wenzeslaus Linck, born January 8, 1483, of a burgomaster of Colditz in Saxony, attended the University of Leipzig and found his vocation in the Augustinian-observants' cloister at Waldheim, not far from his birthplace. Some scholars have tried to construct parallels between the lives of Linck and Luther. At least two major points should be noted: they received a similar influence from Johann von Staupitz, and they were close friends from the time they were both on the faculty of the University of Wittenberg until Luther's death.[2]

Staupitz introduced Linck to the humanist circle at Nürnberg and arranged for him to be the preacher in the Augustinian cloister there. In 1520 Linck left Nürnberg to become vicar-general of the Augustinians. During his short term he released the monks at Wittenberg from their vows.[3] In 1523 Frederick the Wise selected him to become preacher at Saint Bartholomew's in Altenburg. During his stay there the church left the control of the papacy and Linck married. He helped to establish economic and social reforms that partially mitigated the ravages of the Peasants' Revolt in the area.[4]

The Nürnberg City Council had reformed the town's churches

and offered Linck a post at the New Hospital Church. For the last twenty-two years of his life, he faithfully served the needs of the poor, cooperated with the city council, published several works, and served on church ordinance commissions. He died in 1547, one of the last of those who had initiated the original reforms.[5]

When Wenzeslaus Linck left the world of the monastery and entered the life of the town as a preacher, he left the relatively secluded world of the clergy and entered the secular world. There he applied his theological principles in an attempt to reconstruct society. His whole life was a testimony to his belief in the preeminence of religion as a remedy for all that troubled man. Thus he based his reforms for the secular world on his conception of the sufficiency of Christ.

Linck reconciled the world to his religious ideas. He had abandoned the idea of earning merit for salvation by good works and had given expression to his new theology in early attacks on the idle life of the monks. Such polemics he felt were necessary so that man could understand clearly the message of justification by faith and see that no special merit could be earned by any external practice.

Wenzeslaus Linck's polemics against the Catholic theology of good works meant that he had to redefine work.

> Work is medicine given man after the fall, through which he should atone and return to God, avoid and stay away from evil, get closer to good, kill the old Adam, and attain the new Christ, and through which he should become a new creature, and carry the cross of Christ, follow the law of God obediently, and flee from the devil, death, and sin, etc.[6]

Work was the first law God imposed upon Adam. For Linck this signified that man in the active life returned to God by atonement and beatification. For man there was work for atonement, for woman there was the pain of childbirth. Linck clearly transferred his earlier mystical emphasis on humility and suffering to work and pain.

He changed from the traditional views of the age that work was the curse of mankind because of original sin. Linck incorporated work into God's plan of atonement. Work received new dignity because it was no longer degrading; it was part of the divine plan. By emphasizing the transcendent quality of labor, it was no longer an end in itself, but a means to an end. He had early come to the conclusion that the consequence of looking upon human toil as an end in itself was vanity and lust. The end of work, he preached, was not only earthly satisfaction but primarily a Christian life lived in accord with God's divine calling. Toil did have therapeutic value for the individual, however, because it gave him no time for earthly lust. In this way Linck changed his individualized mysticism of humility into a generalized temporal virtue that all could attain.

Work is good because it "furthers the general welfare."[7] Linck maintained that God sanctified what was useful to society. He spoke, not only in theological terms, but in terms understandable to tax-paying, economically oriented townsmen. He had a new argument against the clergy: a doctrine of the usefulness of work. They were no longer useful theologically or economically to society.

Linck also maintained that there were two types of work. Physical labor is all "which one does to be serviceable and useful to others, like the work which that person does who farms the land." Teaching or preaching in the pulpit is acceptable spiritual toil. If a person can do neither of these two, he should find other occupation. If he can do no work whatsoever, he will suffer. By such reasoning Wenzeslaus Linck anticipated the Puritans, who put such a high value upon work.[8]

His attitude toward labor is similar to Luther's conception of *Beruf*, or vocation. Both took certain aspects of their monastic experience, modified them, and widened the spiritual aspects of work to apply to all men. Man must, both believed, labor in the temporal world to live according to the will of God.

By emphasizing the spiritual value of work, it would at first appear that Linck was close to Calvin's view that man served God through his vocation. However, he always emphasized that toil was the way one kept his soul humble and his spirit meek. He believed that work, by producing humility and meekness, aids man in finding faith for salvation.

His ideas of civic responsibility, social welfare, care of the sick, and aid for the poor all stemmed from his conception of work. Linck looked at society and saw its needs and problems. He tried to solve them within the framework of his religious ideas. As an evangelical preacher, his message had to make sense to the world and answer the questions that the world asked of religion. From his religious ideas he saw that man had a responsibility as a citizen of the world. He tried to base his social views on the commandment, Love thy neighbor. This was related to his belief that the gospel could be exemplified only in the midst of the secular world.[9]

The Golden Rule, Linck believed, should have an ameliorating effect upon society; man should correct past wrongs in society, should repay all whom he has "cheated, insulted or damaged."[10] He also taught that love of neighbor is charity and expanded this as the basis for social welfare. His view had evolved beyond the traditional conceptions of giving alms, which for him was a passive activity because the individual who gives is not involved in any further responsibility. One should have an active sense of responsibility for what society does for the welfare of all.

Linck felt that if the city council expelled all those who did not want to work, the community could more easily take care of its own. He believed that all clergymen still employed in saying masses were unnecessary and served no useful purpose. He appealed to the townsmen's sense of *Gemeinde*. Since the clergy did not choose to be part of the city because of their exemptions from civic responsibilities, the money spent on them was misspent. He thought that the money that did not go to the clergy could go to the poor and thus alleviate the local distress that was causing increasing unrest.

Many of Wenzeslaus Linck's ideas reflect his experience in Nürnberg and his friendships there, particularly his close relationship with Lazarus Spengler.[11] His proposals indicate a reading of the Nürnberg ordinances of 1522, written by Spengler. Whether he first influenced Spengler or whether he was influenced by the ordinances is impossible to determine. What is of importance is that Linck, from an evangelical pulpit, was preaching social concern.

In 1523 he preached to the congregation at Zwickau on the need for social welfare. He debated with Mayor Hermann Mühlpfordt of Altenburg over the problem of Christian death and burial. Afterward he preached on the composition of the last wills and testaments and the execution of legacies. Linck maintained that gifts to the church, as endowments for the recitation of death masses or any other spiritual legacies, was an exploitation of man by the church; that the clergy seemed to suggest that a dying man would receive eternal benefits from an endowment to the church. He claimed that even if the testator stated that he agreed to the testament of his own free will, he had sworn under the fear of eternal damnation. More important, economically and socially he argued for the absolute necessity of leaving goods to one's natural heirs so that they would not be future burdens on society. Linck used his pulpit, in this case, to plead for what he considered social justice and civic responsibility in a totally secularized situation. Such an attack upon the recitation of masses for the dead and bequests had such a popular appeal to the townsmen that this sermon was reprinted in Nürnberg, Zwickau, and Magdeburg.[12]

Wenzeslaus Linck was concerned not only with social welfare but also with education. His very first sermons show that he believed that the preacher had a special responsibility to educate.[13] The idea of the universal priesthood of all believers changed the basic concept of education. No longer was it limited to the clergy; it was expanded to the whole congregation. At the time of the Reformation, the whole purpose of education was broadened. Wenzeslaus Linck, the evangelical preacher, cooperated with the city councils at Altenburg and Nürnberg in setting up and maintaining schools.

He also developed a new theoretical framework for the need for education. In so doing he deviated from usual Lutheran doctrine by drawing upon a principle primarily known to us for its use by John Locke, *tabula rasa*.[14]

Man from his physical birth is, with respect to his will like *ein blosse Tafel* (an empty tablet), upon which nothing has been written or that does not have any form; it is formed by education, teaching, or upbringing, and at the same time is born again spiritually.[15]

Thus he denigrated the significance of the fall of Adam. He continued to speak about how man became sinful and full of lust from the world, but this is because improper education shaped the physical individual and his will followed suit.

He emphasized that one needed to keep a child healthy, to shelter him properly, and to teach him the manners of society. This process he called necessary upbringing. Though necessary, it was not enough. More important were family relationships and education. Education was more than reading and writing, for through education man was the very creator of the child's psyche, his personality, his moral training, and also his capacity for the reception of the Word of God or immortality.

This *tabula rasa* of man's will has no form, but unless there is a total network of instruction, man learns to be disobedient, proud, and to embrace all the other vices that make him see a distorted reality and reject God's divine grace. Through education the total man is formed; that is, man is born again spiritually. This means that man will not be blinded by his inadequacies, but will see the total reality of God living in the world. A partial education perverts the will as well as the physical man. Therefore, there is no such thing as only religious education or only secular education. They are intertwined. Apart, they are the basis of man's corruption. "Man by nature is greedy for the good."[16] His instincts are for the good, but he must learn true reality. That is why Linck, as a Reformation preacher, saw education as important.

Through education, man receives the grace of God and is reborn within the world, where, Linck argued, one must live his religion. Empirically, he said, "faith and trust must be tried out."[17] Once reborn, man has a responsibility to do physical and spiritual work to serve the general welfare. Linck therefore saw education as the way to apply his Christian principles to reconstruct society. He took special efforts to apply his ideas in a practical way. Education led people to the good. He attempted to elucidate and implement the Word of God through his own words.

The purpose of all sermons, for Linck, was to instruct. This is best illustrated in his first major series of sermons, which he called *A Wholesome Teaching*. They represent an attempt to establish criteria for the new education. These sermons on the seven beatitudes were preached about the same time that Luther preached his first sermons on the Ten Commandments, but Linck's were designed to prepare people for a confession for Christ and to illustrate the method preachers used in their instruction.[18]

Wenzeslaus Linck also became active in cooperating with local governments in setting up new evangelical schools. While he was at Altenberg, the council built two new schools. The Bartholomew school became a Latin school for higher education and the other was a coeducational elementary school.[19] He wholeheartedly supported the calling of Melanchthon to Nürnberg to establish a gymnasium in that city. Melanchthon visited with Linck while he was there. Though Melanchthon himself did not stay as its head, as the city council wanted him to do, the school became a landmark in the development of the German school system. At the same time the Augustinian monastery was reopened and used as a school for boys and girls.[20]

One of Linck's most famous books was *Preparation of Children for Communion*, published in 1528.[21] It is called the first catechetical evangelical work. Wenzeslaus Linck, like Martin Luther, worked hard to develop the materials necessary to improve Christian education. Normally in midweek he preached a children's sermon. In his lifetime he worked on several types of catechetical materials. He published a simplified commentary on the Lord's Prayer to aid in understanding this important part of the church service.[22] Furthermore, he tried to put the essentials of Christian belief into the hands of the people. His sermons, in general, were examples of the Christian message. His polemic sermons were presented to rid the people of nonevangelical ceremonies. He attempted to build materials for a Christian education in his paraphrase of the Psalms and the Old Testament,[23] simplifying them so they would be easier to read and understand. Because of his interest in children, he reinstituted children's sermons in Nürnberg and specialized in children's preaching.

Linck promoted not merely secular education in Nürnberg but also spiritual education because he believed they were interrelated. He saw the church service itself as a form of education.

In connection with this he wrote music because he knew that
songs were one of the most inspirational means of spiritual
teaching. The Reformation in Nürnberg was carried out by the
city council, many of whose members had been greatly influenced by Linck during his first period as a preacher there. Therefore, when the post of preacher at the New Hospital Church
became open, they wrote to Linck offering him the position.[24]

At Nürnberg Linck served on almost every evangelical committee established by the city council. He attended most of the
important meetings of the Lutherans held during his lifetime.
His opinion was constantly sought by fellow preachers and fellow citizens.[25] In 1533 the city council of Nürnberg, realizing
the need for a consolidated policy for its churches, joined with
Margrave George of Ansbach to draw up a church ordinance to
unify the churches under their jurisdictions and provide a common administration. The council appointed a committee of the
town's ministers, including Linck. Andreas Osiander, minister of
Saint Lorenz Church, and Johann Brenz from Schwäbisch Hall,
did the actual work of drawing up the ordinance.[26]

The main disagreement among the ministers concerned the
Offene Schuld, a combination of general confession and absolution used in the churches in Nürnberg. The *Offene Schuld* had
been used in Bavaria since the eleventh century and later spread
elsewhere. Although Luther knew this practice, he did not use
it because he considered the gospel as a form of absolution. He
also supported private confession as important to the individual
sinner.[27]

When the church ordinance was drawn up, the *Offene Schuld*
was omitted. It was printed before the council noted this omis-
sion, but a new introduction was simply added including the
Offene Schuld as composed by Wenzeslaus Linck:

> Since we all have sinned and are in need of the grace of God, humble
> your hearts before God the Lord and confess your sins and needs with
> sincere hearts and desire His divine grace and help with firm belief
> and trust in your hearts each one his neighbors in order that Our Heav-
> enly Father also will forgive your sins and misdeeds. If you do so,
> I absolve you again in the name of the holy Christian church and Jesus
> Christ, for He said, 'Those whom you forgive their sins are forgiven

all their sins,' in the name of the Father and the Son and the Holy Ghost. Amen.[28]

To Osiander and the city council the general confession and absolution were closely tied to the power of excommunication. Osiander wanted the church ordinance to give this power to the clergy. Not only the city council but the other members of the committee opposed this. To men like Linck and Spengler freedom from the jurisdiction of the bishop had been won with great effort, and they did not intend to relinquish it now to another authority.[29]

The grounds given by the members of the council for the retention of the general confession were a blend of economics, history, and knowledge of their citizens. The city council and Linck had always been in close touch with the citizens and perhaps in no other situation is this so clearly shown. Osiander, Luther, Melanchthon—indeed, the whole of the evangelical movement might oppose them, but Wenzeslaus Linck and Lazarus Spengler stood firm in what they knew was the wish of the people. Linck's *Offene Schuld* was retained as part of the church service until 1790.[30]

The wide circulation of Linck's sermons, his close friendship with Nürnberg humanists and reformers, and his obstinate insistence upon the *Offene Schuld* indicate his popularity with the townsmen of Nürnberg.[31] His social views undoubtedly met the same wide acceptance as the rest of his preaching. Whether or not his ideas preceded the formulation of social reform concepts in the minds of his congregation, his sermons furnished a religious basis for the reforms instituted in Nürnberg. His continuing efforts for the poor and his support and aid to education represent a man attuned to the aims and wishes of Nürnbergers. To paraphrase Luther, Dr. Linck taught and lived so that the common man learned. That is a smart preacher.

1.　D. *Martin Luthers Werke, Tischreden* (Weimar, 1883—), 4: No. 5047.

2.　Compare Hermann Wilhelm Caselmann, "Wenzeslaus Linck's Leben für christliche Leser insgemein aus den Quellen erzählt," *Leben der Altväter der lutherischen Kirche*, ed. Moritz Meurer (Leipzig and Dresden, 1863), pp. 335-38, with Wilhelm Reindell, *Doktor Wenzeslaus Linck aus Colditz 1483-1547: Nach ungedruckten und gedruckten)Quellen; Erster Teil; Bis zur reformatorischen Thätigkeit in Altenburg; Mit Bildnis und einem Anhang enthaltend die zugehörigen Documenta Linckiana 1485-1522* (Marburg, 1892), pp. 16, 27–28; see also Th. Kolde, *Die deutsche Augustiner-Congregation und Johann von Staupitz; Ein Beitrag zur Orderns-und-Reformations-geschichte nach meistens ungedruckten Quellen* (Gotha, 1879), p. 356; Wenzeslaus Linck, *Sacra Superioris aevi analecta, in quibus variorum ad Venceslaum Lincum epistolae plures quam septuaginta . . . ex tabulis Manuscriptis in lucem protulit,* ed. Albert Meno Verpoortennius (Colburg, 1708), pp. 11, 87.

3.   Franz von Soden and J. K. F. Knaake, eds., *Christoph Scheurls Briefbuch: Ein Beitrag zur Geschichte der Reformation und ihrer Zeit,* 2 vols. (Potsdam, 1867–72), 1:36; 2:1,6, 42; R. Bendixen, "Wenzeslaus Link," *Zeitschrift für kirchliche Wissenschaft und kirchliche Leben* 8 (1887) : 45; Kolde, *Augustiner-Congregation,* pp. 226, 230. 235, 242, 257. For an overall summary see Gerhard Pfeiffer, "Nürnberger Patriziat und fränkische Reichsritterschaft," *Beiträge zur Nürnberger Geschichte* (Nürnberg, 1961), 35–55. The actual material on what Scheurl calls at times the *Sodalitas Linckiana* is too broad to include here.

4.   Caselmann, "Linck," pp. 387–88, 93; George Löhlein, "Die Gründungsurkunde des Nürnberger Heilig-Geistspitals von 1399," *MVGN* 52 (1963/64), 65–79; W. P. Fuchs, ed., *Akten zur Geschichte des Bauernskrieges in Mitteldeutschland* (Leipzig and Jena, 1924–42), 2: 549–50.

5.   Joh. Paul Priem, *Geschichte der Stadt Nürnberg: von dem ersten urkundlichen Nachweis ihres Bestehens bis auf die neueste Zeit,* ed. Emil Reicke (Nürnberg, n. d.), p. 687.

6.   Wenzeslaus Linck, "Von Arbeit und Betteln," *Wenzel Lincks Werke,* ed. Wilhelm Reindell (Marburg, 1894), p. 152 (hereafter cited as *Werke*).

7.   Ibid., p. 156.

8.   Ibid., p. 160. For comparison with traditional views, see: Max Weber, *The Protestant Ethic and the Spirit of Capitalism,* trans. Talcott Parsons (New York, 1958), pp. 79–82. For a discussion of overall views and further bibliography, see Robert W. Green, *Protestantism and Capitalism: The Weber Thesis and Its Critics* (Boston, 1959), and Sidney A. Burrell, "Calvinism, Capitalism and the Middle Class: Some Afterthoughts on an Old Problem," *Journal of Modern History* 32 (1960): 129–1.

9.   Wenzeslaus Linck, *Ein Hailsame lere wie das hertz oder gewissen durch die siben selighkeyt: als siben sewlen des geystlichenn bawes: auff das wort gottes gebauet wirdt* (Nürnberg, 1519), Sermon 16.

10.   Ibid., Sermon 24.

11.   Willi Rüger, *Mettalalterliches Almonsenwesen: Die Almosenordnungen der Reichsstadt Nürnberg* (Nürnberg, 1932), p. 37.

12.   Linck, "Ein Bedenken über Abfassung und Vollstreckung von Testamenten," *Werke,* p. 261.

13.   Linck, "Eselspredigt," *Werke,* p. 6.

14.   The idea was transmitted to the Renaissance through Plutarch and Boethius. The origin of the idea can be found in Plato's dialogue *Theaetetus,* 191C. See *The Collected Dialogues of Plato,* ed. Edith Hamilton and Huntington Carins (New York, 1963), p. 189.

15.   Linck, "Der christliche Adel," *Werke,* p. 279.

16.   Linck, *Ein Hailsame lere,* Sermon 21.

17.   Linck, "Homiletische Betrachtung des Lätareevangeliums von der Speisung der Fünftausend Joh. VI, 1–14," *Werke,* p. 214.

18.   Linck, *Ein Hailsame lere*, Sermon 21.

19.   Caselmann, "Linck," p. 390.

20.   Adolf Engelhardt, "Die Reformation in Nürnberg," *MVGN* 33 (1936): 233–35. For a recent summary see Gerald Strauss, *Nuremberg in the Sixteenth Century* (New York, 1966), pp. 154–86.

21.   Wenzeslaus Linck, *Unterrichtung der Kinder so zu Gottes Tische gehen wollen* (Nürnberg, 1528).

22.   Linck, "vater Unser," *Werke*, pp. 287–92.

23.   Linck's Old Testament with an introduction by Martin Luther was published in three parts in Strassburg between 1543 and 1545.

24.   StAN, RB, No. 13, fol. 5 and 49.

25.   Caselmann, "Linck," pp. 405–6.

26.   Ibid., pp. 403–5; Wilhelm Möller, *Andreas Osiander* (Elberfeld, 1870), pp. 179–80; Bernard Klaus, *Veit Dietrich: Leben und Werke* (Nürnberg, 1958), p. 151.

27.   *WA, Briefe*, 6, 446 ff., 454 ff.

28.   Klaus, *Viet Dietrich*, p. 150.

29.   Caselmann, "Linck," pp. 410–19.

30.   Priem, *Geschichte der Stadt Nürnberg*, p. 781.

31.   Engelhardt, "Die Reformation in Nürnberg," *MVGN* 34 (1937): 29–51.

THE LAWYERS, DR. CHRISTOPH SCHEURL, AND THE REFORMATION IN NÜRNBERG

Phillip Norton Bebb

Recent studies of the Protestant Reformation have concentrated on the means by which this fundamentally religious movement spread from one area to another. As a result, there is a growing awareness of the roles played by various social groups in adhering to and disseminating Reformation principles.

The free imperial cities in the Holy Roman Empire offer a favorable point of departure for investigating the social groups. Each of these cities was sovereign, except for owing allegiance to the emperor, and each possessed a government, a code of law, and a body of officials that carried out the policies and functions of the government. As a commercial entity that housed its populace in a relatively compact area, the city clearly exhibited the distinctions and tensions among the social groups that comprised the community. Moreover, most of the imperial cities accepted the Protestant Reformation.[1]

The imperial city of Nürnberg, one of the first municipalities officially to adopt Lutheranism, presents a prime example for the study of the spread of the Reformation. As the most prominent ctiy of Franconia, and one of the two or three most influential in southern Germany, Nürnberg also occupied an important place in the political, economic, and cultural affairs of the empire during the late fifteenth and early sixteenth centuries. Following upon Nürnberg's success in maintaining its independence vis-à-vis neighboring territorial princes, other municipalities often turned to it for advice.[2]

The political sovereign of Nürnberg was the city council, a small, self-perpetuating group of patricians who held the executive, legislative, and judicial powers of government in its hands.[3]

Forty-two councilors comprised the council; eight of these were "commoners," however, and virtually devoid of real power. The remaining councilors were patricians, and it was to them that the major employees of the city owed their positions.

Because of the power of the city council and the role this body played in Nürnberg's Reformation—the council convoked the religious colloquy early in 1525, the result of which was the city's official adoption of Lutheranism—historians have tended to explain the city's acceptance of the Reformation by concentrating upon the council and its policies.[4] Less attention has been paid, therefore, to groups that influenced the decisions of the council. Consequently, this essay will treat one of these groups, the lawyers, and the way in which the lawyers, and Dr. Christoph Scheurl in particular, aided the council in the years before 1525.

Subsidiary to the council, but reinforcing Nürnberg's growing prominence as a free imperial city, were the lawyers trained in Roman and canon law employed by the government. As a result of the increasing involvement of the city in imperial affairs from the middle of the thirteenth century onward, official representatives of Nürnberg were commissioned by the council to handle public concerns that transcended local boundaries. While it is likely that the notary found employment in the city from the time of its origin,[5] no list of council employees before the fourteenth century appears extant. Significantly, however, the first two documented secretaries of the council, dated in the first half of the fourteenth century, possessed notarial designations. Thus, M. Friedrich von Eybach and Georg Herdegen were noted respectively as *protonotarius* and *notarius civium*.[6]

The connection between legal knowledge and the office of the secretariat in Nürnberg is important because it indicates, in part, the reasons why council secretaries often were nominated to accompany legations. Because the scribe handled the city's correspondence, he was educated in Latin grammar and rhetoric, both of which were necessary for the study of law; because of his education, he functioned both as an adviser and a secretary. Hence Master Erhard, the first man called a "jurist" in the council records, performed the duties of a secretary and a legal consultant.[7]

Church officials in Nürnberg also advised the council on legal problems, originally, it seems, because of their knowledge of canon law principles and procedures. At the same time, many of these administrators knew the Roman legal code. The council often appointed a cleric with a doctorate in canon law (*decretorum doctor*) or one in canon and Roman law (*doctor juris utriusque*) to an administrative position in one of the city's churches,[8] especially after its acquisition of the right of presentation.

When the council received the privilege from Pope Sixtus IV in 1477 to nominate its own candidates for the position of provost in the city's two parish churches, Saint Sebald and Saint Lorenz, the bishop of Bamberg as the city's ordinary consequently lost some of his authority to control religious affairs in Nürnberg.[9] Although the right of presentation applied, at first, only to six months of the year, it was extended early in the sixteenth century to cover the entire year. By applying this privilege, the council insured itself of loyal employees in the most important clerical posts in Nürnberg. Moreover, from the time the government received this right until 1525, every new provost had acquired his doctorate in law prior to his appointment.[10]

Thus, through its secretaries and church administrators, the city council employed scholars who were skilled Latinists and trained jurists. In addition, by the end of the fifteenth century, other types of lawyers began to emerge whose primary concerns were advising and advocating. These lawyers, in general, formed the three colleges of the procurators, the advocates, and the legal advisers or jurisconsults.

The procurators were council employees whose functions were to represent individual citizens in their actions at court. Although the procurators had direct contact with the citizenry as a result of their position, they did not seem to be able to influence the council's policies. Furthermore, since the procurators were also the least educated among the class of lawyers in the city—one year's study was customary[11]—the council consulted them rarely.

The college of the advocates, on the other hand, seems to have been more influential. Though the term *advocate* was used in the fifteenth century, the college did not come into existence until 1514.[12] Members of this group served the citizenry by rendering their legal opinions outside of the courts. They were also distinguished from the procurators by virtue of their advanced study of jurisprudence: only doctors or licentiates became advocates. Because they possessed degrees, the advocates might acquire more prestigious positions from the council. Of the five members of the college listed in the council records for 1516, for example, four were doctors and one was a licentiate. These were Dr. Michael Marstaller, Dr. Georg Pessler, Lic. Heinrich Voyt, Dr. Johann Zeitelmayer, and Dr. Johann Engelender. The first three of these came from prominent local families. In the space of a few years, Marstaller and Voyt became members of the class of jurisconsults, and Pessler became the last provost of Saint Sebald Church.[13] Zeitelmayer and Engelender appear to have come from outside the city, and each occupied his position for a short period of time only.[14]

While the secretaries and provosts offered legal advice to the council upon request, they had other duties to perform. Hence, the council created a special college of lawyers, known as legal advisers or jurisconsults (*Ratskonsulenten*), which it employed on a fulltime basis. This college, composed of five or six specially contracted men, was the most influential and prestigious body of legal scholars in the city. Each member was a professionally trained jurist who seems to have acquired varied legal experience prior to signing his contract with the government.[15]

Since the jurisconsults were contract employees, the content of the contracts indicated their duties. Because the contract was the same for each adviser, there was little formal distinction among members of the college; differences between individual lawyers were the result of special competency in particular types of cases, such as feudal and testamentary actions, and may be detected only by delineating the commissions given to each lawyer by the council.

One of these legal advisers was Dr. Christoph Scheurl, a native Nürnberger who had patrician relatives, through marriage, on the council. Scheurl received his doctorate in Roman and canon law at the University of Bologna in 1506, and then became a professor of law at the University of Wittenberg from 1507 to 1512.[16] In 1512 Scheurl returned to Nürnberg to enter the college of legal advisers.[17] The document to which he affixed his seal on April 5, 1512, obliged him to the city council for five years.[18] In return for the performance of his duties, he received an annual salary of two hundred gulden, a rather considerable sum.

According to the contract, one of the main duties of the legal adviser was to render his professional legal opinion upon any subject when asked by the councilors. This opinion, which was often submitted in writing and preserved by the council, was then consulted by the government to aid in making laws and settling disputes.[19]

The contract listed other functions of the jurisconsult, most of which concern the stipulation that he was to defend the interests of the city both at home and abroad. He was to warn the government of any subversion or possible injury to the city that he might uncover; to disclose no secret of the council as long as he lived, even if he severed his relationship with Nürnberg; and to translate Latin into German and German into Latin, orally and in writing, upon the council's command. To avoid conflict of interest, the agreement specifically stipulated that no jurisconsult would represent private citizens without the council's prior consent. If the council found the lawyer guilty of malfeasance, he would be released from his obligations; otherwise, he was committed for the term of his contract.

The concern of the councilors and the advisers with the whole community is evinced in the effort to create a comprehensive body of civil law. The codification of Nürnberg's laws, published by Anton Koberger in 1484 and known as the *Reformation*,[20] is significant not only because it was the first city statute book printed in Germany, but also for its influence on other German municipalities and territories.[21]

Since Nürnberg's legal advisers aided the committee established to formulate the *Reformation*, it is not surprising that the final code exhibited Roman law principles and Roman and canon legal procedures. The result was a series of prescribed formulas by which complaints were to be submitted, witnesses heard, and appeals made.[22] For the most part, these procedures were innovations in Nürnberg's courts, and their effect was to insure the continued importance of the lawyers in the juridical affairs of the city.

The code was reissued in 1488, 1498, and 1503. By September, 1514, the council decided to review the entire *Reformation* in order to evaluate every law. The commission appointed for the task consisted of three councilors, three jurors of the city court, and the college of legal advisers.[23]

The revision of the city statutes, which took more than seven years to complete, was finally published in 1522.[24] It seems apparent that the work involved in reviewing and revising the laws was in the hands of the lawyers while the other commissioners acted as advisers and intermediaries between the committee and the council. Ultimately, of course, changes in the code rested upon the decision of the city council, but this should not obscure the influence of the jurisconsults on the formation of the new *Reformation*. Dr. Scheurl and Dr. Prenninger, for example, were involved in writing a new fugitive law,[25] and Dr. Scheurl was explicitly mentioned in a council protocol in 1518 with respect to a new law for witnesses testifying in civil cases.[26]

To enforce this code and to administer justice to the people over whom the council acquired jurisdiction, Nürnberg possessed an elaborate court structure that treated criminal as well as civil cases. Much of our knowledge of the city's judicial machinery is found in the letter that Dr. Scheurl wrote to his friend Johann von Staupitz, the vicar general of the Augustinian-observants, upon the latter's request.[27] This significant document gives a firsthand account of Nürnberg's government and delineates, in part, the important aspects of Nürnberg's court structure.

Because the council was sovereign, all the courts in Nürnberg were responsible to it. Quite often, therefore, the council was a court of final instance in cases arising among the burghers. It also acted as the sole court trying serious transgressions of the criminal code.[28] The entire council, represented by thirteen of its members called jurors (*Schöffen*), handled such cases as murder, theft, treason, and slander. Some of the jurors presided at the torture of a suspected criminal and copied his confession. All thirteen were present when judgment was pronounced, although the decision had been agreed upon beforehand by a majority vote of the city council.[29]

A small court of five councilors (*Fünfergericht*) treated less serious criminal offenses. Roman legal procedures were not applied by this court, and judgment was, as Scheurl stated, "quick and speedy."[30] Although no appeal could be made from the judgment of this court, the more important cases were discussed and decided upon in the council prior to the final decree.

The courts composed of the councilors employed the jurisconsults on an ad hoc basis. They were permanently attached, however, to the municipal court for civil affairs *(Stadtgericht)*. This court consisted of eight men selected by the city council from the more important citizenry. It was divided into two benches that convened at established times each week. One councilor and one or two legal advisers also sat on each bench as assessors. The lawyers interpreted the written law and recommended action.[31]

Cases treated by the city court generally were divided into two categories, those involving claims of less than thirty-two gulden and those involving more. In the former, judgment was promptly rendered; in the latter, however, the final decision was considered more thoroughly, probably because an injured party might appeal the judgment to the council. In cases involving more than 600 gulden, appeals might be made directly to the imperial supreme court.[32] Since the city council apparently did not care to countenance any kind of appeal, either to itself or to an imperial court, the city court possessed extensive competency. It also preserved its proceedings in writing.

Although these were the primary courts that employed the jurisconsults—depending, of course, upon the desire of the council—the lawyers might also be called to advise on a case pending in any of the city's other courts, such as the territorial court, the forest court, and the widows and orphans court. Especially important, in this connection, was the peasants' court *(Bauerngericht)*, authorized to settle disputes arising among people in the territories over which Nürnberg claimed jurisdiction.[33] In the 1520s Dr. Scheurl and four councilors began to sit with it.[34]

The employees already described—the secretaries, provosts, procurators, advocates, and jurisconsults—held their positions from the council. Hence, their employment in the future rested upon the extent to which they fulfilled their obligations. In Dr. Scheurl's case, the council renewed his contract every five years until his death in 1542, even though he remained Catholic after the city became Lutheran.

When Scheurl entered the service of Nürnberg in 1512, he was already thirty years old and had achieved some renown as a result of his humanistic and legalistic activities.[35] His study at Bologna, and his positions on the faculty of law at Wittenberg and as assessor to the supreme court of Saxony,[36] brought him into contact with a number of people. Through these contacts, Scheurl was able to influence in some measure the spread of Luther's ideas.

By carefully reading the council minutes and collating the specific commissions given to Scheurl with the other official documents of the city, one can develop a fairly accurate picture of the adviser's formal activity. Yet his first connection with the Reformation movement in Nürnberg was not the result of his legal position, but rather a consequence of his connection to the Nürnberg humanist circle. This group, originally called the *sodalitas Celtica* in honor of the humanist Conrad Celtis who resided in the city during the latter years of the fifteenth century and around whom it formed,[37] later referred to itself as the *sodalitas Staupitziana* out of respect for Johann von Staupitz, the influential vicar general of the Augustinians and Luther's spiritual adviser.[38] Composed of the city's leading intellectuals, this group espoused many of the same principles identified with German mysticism, but did so under the name of Christian humanism.[39]

Scheurl played a leading role in this group, and through his correspondence we are informed of its activities. When Staupitz was in Nürnberg late in 1516, he spoke so highly of Luther that Scheurl wrote to the monk in January, 1517, asking him to become a member of the Nürnberg circle.[40] A few weeks later, Scheurl wrote to another friend, Dr. Johann Eck, professor of theology at the University of Ingolstadt and a man who eventually became one of Luther's bitterest opponents, relating news about Staupitz and the latter's regard for Luther.[41] Through this correspondence, Scheurl introduced Luther to Eck.

Because Scheurl continued to correspond with his friends at Wittenberg, he was continually informed of Luther's work. When the reformer posted his ninety-five theses later in 1517,

Ulrich Dinstedt, a canon at Wittenberg and one of Scheurl's closest friends, immediately sent a copy of the propositions to the Nürnberg lawyer. In turn, Scheurl sent copies of the theses to his friends Kilian Leib, the humanist-prior at Rebdorf; Conrad Peutinger, the city secretary at Augsburg; and Johann Eck at Ingolstadt.[42] At the same time, the Nürnberg councilor and humanist Caspar Nützel translated the theses into German for publication.

Luther's propositions impressed the members of the city's humanist circle. In January, 1518, for example, Scheurl wrote to Caspar Güttel, an Augustinian monk at Eisleben, that the city's intellectual elite "admire and treasure Luther's views."[43] Eck, Scheurl continued, would travel miles just to debate Luther. Because the Nürnberg humanists respected the reformer, they changed the name of the circle to the *Martiniana,* later in 1518.[44]

Scheurl also corresponded with people close to Elector Frederick the Wise of Saxony. One of these was Georg Spalatin, a humanist and priest whom Scheurl had probably met while he was still at Wittenberg, and who was the elector's secretary and tutor for his sons.[45] In his letter to Spalatin in December, 1518, Scheurl kept the secretary abreast of the machinations of Carl von Miltitz, the papal nuncio sent to deal with Luther.[46]

Nürnberg's legal adviser seems also to have influenced the development of the Reformation in the city in a less conspicuous manner. He advised young Nürnbergers to study at Wittenberg. In one case, at least, his advice had a considerable effect. Scheurl wrote to Spalatin in November, 1517, that he was sending three students, among whom was Hector Pömer, to Wittenberg.[47] Pömer later returned to Nürnberg imbued with Lutheran ideas, and succeeded Georg Beheim as provost at Saint Lorenz.[48] Moreover, it was on Pömer's recommendation in 1522 that Andreas Osiander, one of the most influential Lutheran theologians of the sixteenth century, became the preacher at Saint Lorenz.[49]

The council supported Luther before and after he had been spiritually excommunicated and temporally outlawed. It exemplified this support by appointing his adherents to the important administrative posts and preaching positions in the city's parish churches between 1520 and 1522. As a result, the cause of Lutheranism in the city was considerably advanced.

The Reformation, nevertheless, did not become a legal phenomenon in Nürnberg until March, 1525. That is, until the government officially adopted Lutheranism, the city remained, at least theoretically, obedient to the papacy. Prior to 1525, therefore, the council dealt circumspectly with papal nuncios sent to the city, presumably biding time to consider its formal position with respect to the religious problem. The government also adhered to the decisions of the imperial estates. In this light, Dr. Scheurl's discussions in 1524 with Cardinal Campeggio, Archduke Ferdinand, and the bishop of Bamberg present an important facet of the council's bearing before avowing Lutheranism.

Cardinal Lorenzo Campeggio traveled to Nürnberg in March, 1524, as papal legate to the third diet of the empire convened in the city from 1522 to 1524.[50] For some time before 1510, the year when he was ordained, Campeggio lived in Bologna where his father, Giovanni Campeggio, taught civil law at the university. Dr. Scheurl, as a student, attended the lectures of Giovanni, and Lorenzo tutored the Nürnberger in law during the evenings.[51] Therefore, because of the relationship between its adviser and the cardinal, the city council commissioned Scheurl officially to receive Campeggio in 1524.[52]

The reception did not occur, however, as the council had planned. Coming to Nürnberg from Augsburg, where he had been mocked, caricatured, and slandered,[53] Campeggio entered the city incognito and refused to go into the church of Saint Sebald.[54]

Because of the pro-Lutheran feeling he perceived in Nürnberg, negotiation with the legate appeared difficult. Again, probably drawing upon Scheurl's former relationship with the cardinal, the council commissioned him to visit Campeggio to try to obtain permission for the bestowal of a number of endowed benefices in the city's two parishes.[55] Since the council did not press its request for this permission after Scheurl had met with him,[56] the adviser's major task, presumably, was to discover Campeggio's intentions regarding Nürnberg. This assumption accords with Scheurl's written statement about his discussion with the cardinal.[57]

The chief causes of Campeggio's visit, Scheurl stated, were the innovations undertaken and the preaching offered in the city's church services.[58] The cardinal expressed his surprise that the "wise government of Nürnberg" permitted the expression of Lutheran heresies such as the publication and sale of Lutheran books, the eating of meat on fast days, and public preaching against the pope within the city. Furthermore, the government allowed these things to take place in the opinion that man would find salvation through faith alone. Campeggio went on to say that there were probably forty different religious conceptions *(mäynung, und opinion)* existing in the city; that the council had been indulgent for so long that it no longer had any authority over the burghers; and that it could expect evil results from its laxity.

When Campeggio concluded by implying the possible invoking of ecclesiastical power against the city, Dr. Scheurl responded to his charges. First, Scheurl said, Campeggio undoubtedly knew from the visits of Cajetan and d'Este—two cardinal-legates who had previously come to Nürnberg and with whom Scheurl had spoken[59]—that Nürnberg adhered to the papacy. The city had never attempted to alienate itself from the pope, and it had given no occasion for one to think that it had. Second, Scheurl believed that it was the intention of the common man "to hold only to Christ and His pure gospel."[60] Thus, the citizens were not in league with Luther. Third, the government did not countenance heresy but, in fact, prohibited it. He supported this statement by referring to the fact that the council published the Edict of Worms, forbade the sale of pro-Lutheran books, and inhibited certain preachers only because of the public disorder they caused by their sermons.

After denying Campeggio's complaint that the government permitted unorthodoxy, Scheurl turned the argument toward the church, referring to Saint Paul, who said that man should enjoy what is placed before him; thus, eating meat was no sin. Furthermore, Scheurl maintained, neither pope nor council were superior to the gospel, but both were subject to it.[61] Councils could, and, in fact, had erred, and this was readily apparent in the decisions made by one council which were later changed by another.

Scheurl's argument, thus, revolved around two major points. In the first place, he appealed to the traditions of the city and the power of the city's government. Both, he declared, were loyal to the pope and to the notion of church unity. Second, however, if certain unorthodox innovations and questionable preachers were present in the city, their existence was not due to the council's permissiveness but to the obscurity of some church laws and confusion about others. In this event, the fault lay with the organization and traditions of the Roman church, not with the government of Nürnberg. Certainly the common man, who desired only Christ, could not be held responsible. Since the government of the city was pious and Christian, Scheurl implied in his conclusion that papal power should not be brought against Nürnberg.

When he finished, Campeggio responded only to two statements made by the lawyer: the prohibition of "orthodox" sermons, and the council's acceptance of what its citizens were writing as merely an expression of the desire for knowledge. Thus, according to Scheurl, the cardinal's complaints were partially ameliorated, for the moment at least. On the other hand, because of the unfavorable religious situation he perceived in Nürnberg, Campeggio desired to depart as soon as possible. He, therefore, may have cut short the conversation.

Because Archduke Ferdinand, the brother of Emperor Charles V and Hapsburg regent in Germany, and Cardinal Campeggio desired further discussions regarding the problems of political and religious unrest in the empire, the city council, on June 17, 1524, nominated Clement Volckamer and Christoph Kress, and Dr. Scheurl to attend a meeting at Regensburg.[62] The instructions given to the commission reflected the familiar themes of Nürnberg's imperial status and the city's obedience to the desires of the emperor and his representatives.[63] The council, the instructions stated, had obeyed the recent imperial decision directing the estates to carry out the provisions of the Edict of Worms insofar as they were able.[64] In particular, the council had prohibited the publication of Lutheran books and lampoons against the church. Certain other provisions could not be enforced, however, and for this reason the present embassy had been formed.

Of major importance was that section of the instructions informing the ambassadors of the answers they should give to questions raised by the imperial advisers. If they were asked about the changes that had occurred in the ceremonies and services held in Nürnberg's parish churches, the ambassadors were to answer that the changes were introduced without the government's knowledge or desire. The council "had neither commanded, advised, nor agreed to these changes."[65] The provosts, however, when summoned by the council to account for the innovations, had responded that they were valid.

The ambassadors also were instructed to remind the imperial advisers of the decision of the second Diet of Nürnberg, 1522–23, namely with respect to the provision permitting preachers to teach the holy gospel as interpreted by the church fathers until a general church council had decided otherwise.[66] Although some authorities had already decided the provosts erred in their changes and, accordingly, had instructed the council to punish those preachers who did not abstain from erroneous teachings, the council maintained that the populace was so enthused by the word of God that to rescind such changes before the meeting of a church council was to risk bloodshed and rebellion. The council knew that the emperor and his advisers did not desire rebellion; yet, at the same time, it wished to remain obedient.

On June 25, Ferdinand and his advisers received the Nürnberg legation. From Scheurl's report of the meeting, the council learned the content of the conversation.[67] The archduke, Scheurl stated, recognized the city's continued obedience and service to the emperor and to Austria.[68] Ferdinand was pleased that the city also had carried out part of the provisions of the Edict of Worms; but for the council's failure to fulfill the remaining provisions, the embassy had to answer to the imperial viceroy, who possessed the power and authority to proceed against the city. Then following a discussion between Ferdinand's advisers and the ambassadors—one that resulted in the reiteration that Ferdinand, since he was not meeting with the imperial governing council, was able to do nothing legally to delay a process against Nürnberg for the city's failure to carry out all the demands of the Edict of Worms—the advisers stated that Ferdinand would attempt to aid the council if it desired.[69]

When the embassy prepared to depart Regensburg, Campeggio

called Scheurl to discuss, "in a brotherly fashion," problems disturbing the cardinal. In many ways, the content of this meeting was similar to their conversation a few months previously. From Scheurl's report of the discussion, composed on June 29, it was clear that Campeggio desired information about a number of specific occurrences in Nürnberg, all of which reflected the council's behavior during the time the legate had been away from the city.[70] Particularly vexatious to the cardinal was the treatment accorded to the city's priests by the populace. One priest, Campeggio said, had been recently expelled from the city, and others were slandered, caricatured, and maligned in their person and property. Furthermore, changes had been made in the office of the mass, the service was presented in German, and Communion in both kinds was permitted.[71] All of these actions, he maintained, were countenanced by the council.

Campeggio concluded his statements in a manner akin to the conclusion of his previous conversation with Scheurl when he had implied the possible use of papal power against Nürnberg. Now the cardinal clearly said that the government of Nürnberg did not realize the extent of papal authority.[72] The city had received many privileges and favors from the papacy in the past, but these could be withdrawn if the city were disobedient. Campeggio wanted Scheurl to transmit to the council these threats as well as his complaints.

Similar to the embassy's response to Archduke Ferdinand and his advisers, Dr. Scheurl informed Campeggio that the council remained steadfast in its allegiance to God, the pope, and the emperor, giving what was due to each. He did not deny that a priest had been expelled from Nürnberg, but maintained, instead, that this punishment was the result of disobedience and was justified. The council had never proceeded against the priests; on the contrary, it continued to protect them as always. Finally, Scheurl claimed he knew nothing of the lampoons and slander of the clergy because these were forbidden by the government.

During his discussion, Scheurl referred to the fact that the council refused to permit any religious action in the city that had been prohibited by an imperial mandate. If some travesty had occurred in Nürnberg, however, it was done out of ignorance. And if this was the case, Scheurl was convinced, the council desired to be better informed, not by threats and bulls but by Scripture. At the same time, he mentioned that the provost of the city's churches had presented to the council an extensive report justifying the changes they had introduced in the church service. Because the provosts believed these changes were theologically warranted, the alterations would probably be retained.[73] In these statements, Scheurl implied that the responsibility for any changes lay with the clergy, that is those who were trained in theology, not with the council.

Scheurl's implication formed the basis of the instructions given to an embassy sent to Bamberg in July, 1524.[74] The purpose of this commission, composed of the councilors Christoph Kress and Martin Tucher, and Dr. Scheurl, was to report to the bishop the innovations undertaken in the city's parish churches. The council protocol of July 19, the day that the embassy was created, clearly indicated that the government was operating in conjunction with its officials in the churches because the provosts and preachers were to be "informed of the council's intention." Like the instructions written for the embassy to Regensburg a month before, they stated that the ambassadors were to inform the bishop that "recently, the provosts of Nürnberg's two parish churches introduced certain changes in the holy service and ceremonies by themselves, and these had not been agreed to, commanded, or advised by the council."[75] Because complaints had been submitted to the council, the instructions continued, it had ordered the provosts to answer for the changes. This the provosts did, both orally and in writing.

When Scheurl presented the council's instructions to the bishop and his advisers on July 22, he reiterated the council's plea of innocence.[76] He then stated that if the bishop desired more information, he should hear the provosts and preachers at a special trial since such proceedings were authorized as part of his clerical office. If the bishop called this trial, the council would dutifully obey.

The suggestion that the bishop summon Nürnberg's provosts and preachers to Bamberg for a trial was realized. In his answer to the ambassadors, the bishop said he did not know whether the council was pleased or displeased regarding the changes in the church service, but he accepted and would remember the apologies transmitted to him by the legates. As proof of sincerity, however, he expected the council's aid if the city's parish officers and preachers proved recalcitrant in responding to his forthcoming summons.[77] The hearing, which took place in September, resulted in the pronouncement of a major excommunication against the two provosts and the Augustinian prior, and the demand that they be removed from office.[78]

Because appeals were made, the proceedings did not conclude with the bishop's sentence. Yet the council appeared to effect its purpose. Through Scheurl, it suggested to the bishop that those responsible for the changes in the church service be summoned before the ordinary of the diocese, the bishop himself. Because the bishop certainly knew the extent of his authority, the suggestion must probably be interpreted as signifying the council's willingness to send its officials to a meeting. When the trial took place, however, Nürnberg's officials refused to recognize the competency of the bishop to judge the proceedings because he was one of the contending parties.

Throughout Scheurl's negotiations with Archduke Ferdinand, Cardinal Campeggio, and the bishop of Bamberg, a rather consistent defense was argued. The line of continuity was twofold. With regard to imperial affairs, the council referred to the estates' position that until a general church council decided the religious problem, the gospel was to be preached in accordance with the views of the church fathers. In spiritual affairs, the council maintained that the innovations were undertaken by the clergy, not by the government. Because this was so, it was not the council's prerogative to interfere in the internal affairs of the church.

Although no final changes in the city's religious practices took place without discussion in the council, the Reformation in Nürnberg was a fact before it was officially proclaimed in March, 1525. The process of instituting church reform had been gradual, but at every stage the government coordinated its activities with those of the lawyers and the city's clergy: innovations in the services were investigated and, if approved, were supported on the juridical level by the legal advisers.

When the council finally decided to hold a religious colloquy in order to unify the practices of the city's churches, it appointed Dr. Scheurl as chairman.[79] Scheurl's commencement address on March 3 was of some importance due to the nature of the discussion. The previous autumn, Emperor Charles had forbidden the convocation of any religious disputation in the empire by the Edict of Burgos.[80] Scheurl clearly stated in his opening remarks that no one should evoke Charles's Edict in an attempt to abolish or discredit the meeting in Nürnberg because the colloquy was not a disputation. It was, rather, a Christian and brotherly discussion directed toward reestablishing unity among the preachers in an effort to avoid "discontent and rebellion."[81] Therefore, since it was a friendly discussion, Scheurl admonished the participants to be kind to one another and to refrain from slander.

As a result of the colloquy of 1525, the Reformation in Nürnberg became official. Yet the council's declaration was meaningful only because the government was able to enforce it. That is, the council had the backing of the most important and powerful groups in the city. By a process that had been taking place for quite some time prior to 1525, it had acquired authority and administrative rights from these groups. In the acquisition of this power, the lawyers played a fundamental role.

Although there was a plethora of legal problems to be decided after March, 1525, such as the transfer of property and goods from the religious houses to the city, the legal pattern established to handle these problems had already been worked out. Dr. Scheurl and the other lawyers had been specifically employed by the government to help in the creation of this legal pattern. Hence, what occurred after March, 1525, had been fixed on a juridical level during the preceding years.

1. See, for example, Bernd Moeller, *Reichsstadt und Reformation* ("Schriften des Vereins für Reformationsgeschichte," Vol. 69 [Gütersloh, 1962]).

2. The literature on Nürnberg is extensive. Among the better accounts, see Emil Reicke, *Geschichte der Reichsstadt Nürnberg* (Nürnberg, 1896); Georg Ludewig, *Die Politik Nürnbergs im Zeitalter der Reformation* (Göttingen, 1893); Gerald Strauss, *Nuremberg in the Sixteenth Century* (New York, 1966). For the city's relationship with other powers, see Eugen Franz, *Nürnberg, Kaiser und*

Reich (Munich, 1930), and Fritz Schnelbögl, "Die fränkischen Reichstädte," *Zeitschrift für bayerische Landesgeschichte* 31 (1968): 421–74.

3. Julie Meyer, "Die Entstehung des Patriziats in Nürnberg," *MVGN* 27 (1928): 1–96; Strauss, *Nuremberg in the Sixteenth Century*, pp. 57–115.

4. Friedrich Roth, *Die Einführung der Reformation in Nürnberg, 1517-1518* (Würzburg, 1885); Adolf Engelhardt, "Die Reformation in Nürnberg," *MVGN* 33 (1936): 3–258; cf. Gerald Strauss, "Protestant Dogma and City Government: The Case of Nuremberg," *Past and Present*, No. 36 (1967): 38-58.

5. The notary played an important role in commercial activity. Ottmar Böhm, *Die Nürnbergische Anwaltschaft um 1500 bis 1806, ihr Verhältnis zum örtlichen Gerichtswesen sowie ihrer Stellung im reichsstädtischen Organismus* (Erlangen, 1949).

6. Friedrich Ellinger, "Die Juristen der Reichsstadt Nürnberg vom 15. bis 17. Jahrhundert," *Genealogica, Heraldica, Juridica. Reichsstadt Nürnberg, Altdorf und Hersbruck* (Nürnberg, 1954), pp. 157–58.

7. Johann Christien Siebenkees, *Materialien zur Nürnbergischen Geschichte*, 4 vols. (Nürnberg, 1792–95), 3, 96. Although the exact dates during which Master Erhard served the council are not known, Ellinger concludes that he was employed between 1369 and 1392 ("Die Juristen," pp. 132-33).

8. Cf. StAN. Handschriftensammlung No. 203.

9. Adolf Engelhardt, "Der Kirchenpatronat zu Nürnberg," *Zeitschrift für bayerische Kirchengeschichte* 7 (1932): 1–16, 65–80.

10. Ibid.; cf. Reicke, *Geschichte der Reichsstadt Nürnberg*, pp. 689–90.

11. Böhm, *Die Nürnbergische Anwaltschaft*, p. 20.

12. Ibid., pp. 12–16; cf. StAN. Ämterbüchlein No. 34.

13. StAN. Ämterbüchlein Nos. 36–42.

14. Böhm, *Die Nürnbergische Anwaltschaft*, p. 16.

15. Cf. Otto Stobbe, *Geschichte der deutschen Rechtsquellen*, 2 vols. (Leipzig, 1860–64), 2: 59-61.

16. On Scheurl, see Franz von Soden, *Beiträge zur Geschichte der Reformation und der Sitten jener Zeit mit besonderem Hinblick auf Christoph Scheurl II* (Nürnberg, 1855), hereafter cited as Soden, *Beiträge*; Felix Streit, *Christoph Scheurl, der Ratskonsulent von Nürnberg und seine Stellung zur Reformation* (Plauen i. V., 1908); Wilhelm Graf, *Doktor Christoph Scheurl von Nürnberg*, ("Beiträge zur Kulturgeschichte des Mittelalters und der Renaissance," vol. 43 [Leipzig and Berlin, 1930]). Many of Scheurl's letters have been published; see Franz von Soden and J. K. F. Knaake (eds.), *Christoph Scheurls Brieflbuch. Ein Beitrag zur Geschichte der Reformation und ihrer Zeit*. 2 vols. (Potsdam, 1867–72) (hereafter cited as Scheurls Br.).

17. Cf. the correspondence from the head of Nürnberg's government, Anton Tucher, to Scheurl; BB 67, fol. 186ʳ–187ʳ, 239ʳ⁻ᵛ. See RV 539, fos. 4ʳ, 8ᵛ; 540, fol. 18ʳ; 542, fol. 10ᵛ.

18. StAN. 35 neue Laden der unteren Losungsstube, V 43/i No. 1604; the following summary is taken from this document. Scheurl's first *Bestallungsbrief* was printed by Franz von Soden, *Christoph Scheurl der Zweite und sein Wohnhaus in Nürnberg* (Nürnberg, 1837), pp. 129–32.

19. Many of these opinions were collected and bound, forming the Ratschlagbücher in the Staatsarchiv, Nürnberg.

20. *Gesetze der neuen Reformacion der Stat Nuremberg Nach crist gepurt Tausend vierhundert Und in dem neun u. sibentzigsten Jare fürgenommen.* The publication of this code followed immediately upon Koberger's edition of

the *Corpus juris civilis*, the first printed edition of the civil law in Germany; see Stobbe, *Geschichte der deutschen Rechtsquellen*, 2: 299.

21. Ibid., p. 298; Roderich Stintzing, *Geschichte des Deutschen Rechtswissenschaft* (Munich and Leipzig, 1880), p. 541; Hans Liermann, "Nürnberg als Mittelpunkt deutschen Rechtslebens," *Jahrbuch für fränkische Landesforschung* 2 (1936): 1–17; Werner Schultheiss, "Die Einwirkung Nürnberger Stadtrechts auf Deutschland, besonders Franken, Böhmen und die Oberpfalz (Der nürnberger Stadtrechtskreis)," *Jahrbuch für fränkische Landesforschung* 2 (1936): 18-54.

22. Cf. Daniel Wa'dmann, "Die Entstehung der Nürnberger Reformation von 1479 (1484) und die Quellen ihrer prozessrechtlichen Vorschriften," *MVGN* 18 (1908): 1–98.

23. RV 575, fol. 9ᵛ; *cf.* fol. 8ʳ. Although the protocol stated simply "alle gelerten," a term consistently employed by the council for the jurisconsults, this referred to Drs. Ulrich Nadler, Johann Protzer, Peter Dotz'er, Marsilius Prenninger, and Christoph Scheurl.

24. RV 664, fol. 24ʳ; 672, fol. 16ʳ.

25. RV 626, fol. 21ᵛ; cf. Ratschlagb. 2, fol. 40ᵛ–46ᵛ.

26. RV 628, fol. 4ʳ.

27. "Christoph Scheur's Epistel über die Verfassung der Reichsstadt Nürnberg. 1516," *Die Chroniken der deutschen Städte* 11 (Leipzig, 1874): 781–804 (hereafter cited as Scheurls Epistel). The following description is taken basically from this letter.

28. Siebenkees, *Materialien zur Nürnbergischen Geschichte*, 2: 532-50; "Nürnbergische Halsgerichts-Ordnung vom Jahr 1481."

29. "Scheurls Epistel," p. 796.

30. Ibid., p. 797.

31. Ibid., p. 801.

32. This was the result of a privilege granted to Nürnberg by Emperor Maximilian in 1508; see Reicke, *Geschichte der Reichsstadt Nürnberg*, p. 640. Cf. Ratschlagb. 2, fos. 215ʳ–ᵛ.

33. "Scheur's Epistel," p. 802. See also Horst Espig, *Das Bauerngericht von Nürnberg* (Würzburg, 1937).

34. RB 12, fol. 39ʳ–ᵛ; RV 676, fol. 7ʳ. Cf. RB 13, fos. 275ᵛ–276ʳ.

35. For Scheurl's published works, see Maria Grossmann, "Bibliographie der Werke Christoph Scheurls," *Archiv für Geschichte des Buchwesens* 70 (1968): 658–70.

36. Gustav Bauch, "Christoph Scheurl in Wittenberg," *Neue Mitteilungen aus dem Gebiet historisch-antiquarischer Forschungen* 21 (1903): 33-42.

37. Ludwig Keller, *Johann von Staupitz und die Anfänge der Reformation* (Leipzig, 1888), p. 28.

38. Scheurls Br. 150; cf. Harold J. Grimm, "Lazarus Speng'er, the Nürnberg City Council, and the Reformation," in *Luther for an Ecumenical Age*, ed. Carl S. Meyer (St. Louis, 1967), p. 111.

39. Roth, *Die Einführung der Reformation in Nürnberg, 1517–1528*, pp. 26–48; Bernd Moeller, "Die deutschen Humanisten und die Anfänge der Reformation," *Zeitschrift für Kirchengeschichte* 70 (1959): 46–61.

40. Scheurls Br. 114.

41. Scheurls Br. 115.

42. Scheurls Br. 154-56.

43. Scheurls Br. 160.

44. Hans von Schubert, *Lazarus Spengler und die Reformation in Nürnberg* ("Quellen und Forschungen zur Reformationsgeschichte," Vol. 17, ed. Hajo Holborn [Leipzig, 1934]), p. 163; cf. Roth, *Die Einführung der Reformation in Nürnberg, 1517–1528*, p. 64.

45. Irmgard Höss, *Georg Spalatin, 1484–1545* (Weimar, 1956).

46. See, for example, Scheurls Br. 184.

47. Scheurls Br. 149.

48. Siebenkees, *Materialien zur Nürnbergischen Geschichte*, 2: 559–66; "Von Hector Pömer, dem letzten Probst zu St. Lorenzen."

49. See Gottfried Seebass, *Das reformatorische Werk des Andreas Osiander* ("Einzelarbeiten aus der Kirchengeschichte Bayerns," vol. 44 [Nürnberg, 1967]).

50. Edward Victor Cardinal, *Cardinal Lorenzo Campeggio* (Boston, 1935).

51. Scheurls Br. 25, 138. Cf. Graf, *Doktor Christoph Scheurl von Nürnberg*, p. 29.

52. RV 700, fol. 21r; RB 12, fol. 227v.

53. Cardinal, *Cardinal Lorenzo Campeggio*, p. 85.

54. RV 701, fol. 4v.

55. RV. 701, fol. 9r.

56. Cf. RV 702, fol. 24r.

57. StAN. S. I L. 78, No. 12 fasc 1. The following summary is taken from this document. Cf. Soden, *Beiträge*, pp. 169 ff.

58. For the religious background, see Engelhardt, "Die Reformation in Nürnberg," *MVGN* 33 (1936): chaps. 5–6.

59. Cardinal Hippolyte d'Este visited Nürnberg in January, 1513, and Cardinal Cajetan, late in February, 1519. On both occasions, the city council commissioned Scheurl to be the official receptionist for the city. Copies of Scheurl's speeches are found in the private Scheurl family archive, Fischbach über Nürnberg; see Codex K, fol. 80v–81v (d'Este), and Codex C, fol. 254r–256v, 260r (Cajetan). I wish to thank Herr Siegfried Freiherr von Scheurl for his kind permission to view these documents.

60. StAN. S. I L. 78, No. 12 fasc. 1.

61. Ibid.

62. RV 704, fol. 19r. Pfeiffer, *Quellen*, p. 7.

63. StAN. S. I L. 30, No. 5. Pfeiffer, *Quellen*, pp. 261–63. Cf. Soden, *Beiträge*, pp. 182 ff.

64. Adolf Wrede, ed., *Deutsche Reichstagsakten, Jüngere Reihe*, Vol. 4: *Deutsche Reichstagsakten unter Kaiser Karl V* (Göttingen, 1905), pp. 615–20. Decision of April 18, 1524.

65. Pfeiffer, *Quellen*, p. 262.

66. Cf. Adolf Wrede, ed., *Deutsche Reichstagsakten, Jüngere Reihe*, Vol. 3: *Deutsche Reichstagsakten unter Kaiser Karl V* (Göttingen, 1901), pp. 745-48. The Recess was dated Febryary 9, 1523. See also Grimm, "Lazarus Spengler, the Nürnberg Council, and the Reformation," p. 114.

67. StAN. S. I L. 30, No. 5. Pfeiffer, *Quellen*, pp. 264–65.

68. Pfeiffer, *Quellen*, p. 264.

69. Ibid., p. 265.

70. StAN. S. I L. 78, No. 12 fasc 2. Pfeiffer, *Quellen*, pp. 265–67. Cf. Soden, *Beiträge*, pp. 188–91.

71. Pfeiffer, *Quellen*, p. 266.

\ 72. "Wir wusten nit, wi weit sich des babsts gwalt [*sic*] erstrecket . . . " (ibid.).

73. Ibid., p. 267.

74. RV 705, fol. 21r. Pfeiffer, *Quellen*, pp. 13–14.

75. Pfeiffer, *Quellen*, pp. 271–73.

76. Ibid., pp. 273–75. Cf. Soden, *Beiträge*, pp. 193–97.

77. Ibid., pp. 275–76.

78. For the substance of the trial and the Bishop's sentence, see ibid., pp. 286–88.

79. RV 713, fol. 20v–21r. Pfeiffer, *Quellen*, p. 51.

80. See Lazarus Spengler's lengthy opinion concerning the Edict of Burgos and other problems, in Pfeiffer, *Quellen*, pp. 168–77.

81. The speech is printed by Soden, *Beiträge*, pp. 225–26.

PATRICIANS IN DISSENSION: A CASE STUDY FROM SIXTEENTH-CENTURY NÜRNBERG

Jackson Spielvogel

Reformation historians have usually looked upon sixteenth-century Nürnberg as a model of effective government by a city council composed of patricians. These patricians formed a closed group, tied together formally by marriage and informally by their economic, social, and political activities. Only they could sit in the powerful small council, and in ruling this free imperial city, they displayed a common purpose and unanimity of viewpoint befitting a city of Nürnberg's stature. Such is the traditional picture, and although largely accurate, it nevertheless overlooks much of the discord and petty caviling that occurred among the members of Nürnberg's ruling elite.

The government of Nürnberg in the sixteenth century was administered by two councils, a large council of *Genannte* and a small council (the *Erber Rat* in the city documents). It was the latter council that stood at the head of the administrative system. Of the forty-two members of the small council, eight were representatives of the craft guilds with virtually no power in the affairs of the council; eight were known as the *Alte Genannte*, who participated, but not necessarily actively; and twenty-six were burgomasters, who formed the active core of the small council. The twenty-six burgomasters were, in turn, divided into thirteen senior and thirteen junior burgomasters. From the group of thirteen senior burgomasters were chosen seven men who comprised a select committee known as the *ältere Herren*. From these seven were selected three captains general (*Oberste Hauptmänner*) and from these three, two treasurers known as *Losunger*. Finally, the senior *Losunger*, distinguished by senior-

ity in office, was considered the formal chief of the council and
first man in the city. These gradations were not merely titular,
but were actually gradations of powers, with power heavily concentrated toward the top. Although it was the twenty-six burgomasters who openly conducted the city's business, the real power
of the government rested in the hands of the seven *ältere Herren*.
Together with the captains general and *Losunger*, who were
chosen from their own ranks, they effectively ruled the city.
These seven handled all secret affairs of state and also discussed
all serious matters before they came to the attention of the other
councilmen.

Membership in this small council, with the exception of the
eight representatives of the craft guilds, was limited by tradition
to a select circle of patrician families, forty-three in number in
1521.[1] Although the members of the small council (except the
Alte Genannte) were formally elected, the election process itself was carefully calculated to maintain the oligarchical structure. Thus, the electoral commission established for this process
regularly reelected those members already seated on the council.[2]

Nürnberg's system of government, then, was carefully arranged in such a way that power resided in the hands of a select
number of patrician families who formed a "closed corporation"
for the sake of dominating the city. It was, consequently, imperative that these families remain united in order to continue
their exalted position. Although they generally did so, there was
considerable dissension among the patricians, often expressed in
bickering that might appear petty on the surface, but that had
serious implications in a communal government of the sixteenth
century. A firsthand account of this discord has been provided
for us by Willibald Pirckheimer. Although more famous outside Nürnberg and to subsequent generations as a literary man,
patron of the arts, and close friend of Albrecht Dürer, Pirckheimer was, nevertheless, an active participant in the governing
of Nürnberg. Born into a patrician family that had first entered
the small council in 1386, Willibald served as a junior burgomaster from 1496 to 1502, and as an *Alte Genannte* from 1505
to 1523. He left behind in his letters and especially in his auto-

biography some intimate glimpses of his struggles with his fellow councilors. An examination of these will indicate some aspects of the dissension among the ruling Nürnberg patricians in the first half of the sixteenth century.[3]

In his autobiography Willibald Pirckheimer presented himself as a man beset and oppressed by numerous enemies in his native city. In fact, over half of this short work was devoted to a discussion of the numerous local intrigues plotted against him. Pirckheimer perhaps exaggerated the nature and extent of these intrigues, but their story still basically reveals much about the dissension in Nürnberg's city council. His opponents included not only members of the city government but others who were apparently being used by city councilors to achieve their ends.[4]

The first of a long series of altercations with his antagonists came to fruition in 1502 when Pirckheimer withdrew from the council. His ostensible reason, given to those who were not intimate companions, was that the labors of the state were a burden that drew him away from the study of the humanities, which singularly pleased him. For that reason he had freed himself of the affairs of state.[5] However, Pirckheimer's most revealing statement of his motivations came in a letter written in the summer of 1502, probably to Kilian Leib, a relatively close friend:

> Speaking frankly with you, our governors are by no|means pleasing to me, for into how many disturbances have they led and daily lead the republic, the deed itself demonstrates; oh, that I am said to have performed foolishly and not more wisely![6] I acknowledge that we are indebted to the state and republic, and that we should not reject any labor for these, if we can turn something to account by doing so. But as soon as you arouse only hate in your work, then it is the most extreme foolishness to remain in the same.[7]

In his autobiography, Pirckheimer's resentment toward the city council, as expressed in this letter, was converted into charges of persecution by an enemy bent on eliminating him.

This enemy, although not specifically named by Pirckheimer, was Paul Volckamer, who held the prominent conciliar position of first *Losunger* in 1502.[8] He and Pirckheimer had become embittered in 1497–98 over a conflict in which Volckamer, who was the ecclesiastical administrator for the church of Saint Sebald, quarreled with Pirckheimer and his brother-in-law Hans Rieter over possession of the eternal lamps of the Rieter-Volckamer foundation.[9] According to Pirckheimer, when Volckamer was unable to make him conform with his malicious plans, he began to disturb him by force. Gradually, Pirckheimer grew so tired of these attacks that he wished to withdraw from the council. The death of his father (May 3, 1501) provided him with a legitimate excuse for leaving the council, since he now needed time to pursue domestic business. However, when his adversary died suddenly,[10] he decided to reenter the council and was elected again with a large majority.[11]

After his reentry in 1505, Pirckheimer remained in the council until 1523, but not without further altercations. In 1511, probably at the beginning of August, he was suddenly invited before the seven *ältere Herren* and presented with four charges in which he had violated his duty as a city councilor. These were that he did not forfeit his tokens (*Zeichen*) when he was absent from council sessions;[12] that he disturbed his fellow councilors by his interruptions during the voting and debating; that he did not wait for the council sessions to end, but took walks outside and inside the town hall during the sessions; and that he served as legal advocate for private individuals, a service which did not befit a city councilor.[13]

In the middle of August, Pirckheimer defended himself against these charges before the entire assembled city council. In view of his own great personal wealth, he easily rejected the first charge as patently false and absurd.

> If I had wanted to be unfaithful to the state, I had many better opportunities, as, for example, in the Swiss War, where several thousand gulden were entrusted to me. . . . I could easily have kept half the money, and no one could have found out, . . . but such a thought never came into my mind. What need do I have that, for the sake of such a despicably small sum of money, not even two or three gulden a year, I should forget my honor, my oath, and my conscience?[14]

Pirckheimer did not deny the second charge that he had interrupted in the debating and voting. He argued, however, that in so doing he was only fulfilling his duty.[15] He objected strongly to the third accusation and stated that, since the last election, he had missed only two sessions; but that it made little difference whether he attended the sessions or not since he was not used for anything when he was there, nor was he asked any more to execute decisions of the council.[16] That, he stated, was how the city council showed its appreciation for his previous service.

> Have I not faithfully served you and the state for many years, unsparing of my body and property? First, in the Swiss War, where I not only offered my life, but also my possessions and spent over 150 gulden. In all the following affairs, in which you used me, I have faithfully served you according to my abilities, in the negotiations with Cunz Schott, the Margrave, and the Elector of the Palatinate. In all of these I was regarded not slovenly, as I am now accused, but useful to you to such an extent that . . . I received honor from it. But I ask all of you, what thanks or reward have I received up to this hour from such service? This is the reward: that my honor is greatly slandered. Whether this is right or just, I leave to you to judge.[17]

Finally, Pirckheimer did not deny the fourth accusation that he had served as a legal advocate. He explained, however, that he didn't do it for the sake of money, which he didn't need, but for his friends, poor people, widows, and orphans. For this reason it was certainly no detriment to the city.[18]

Having defended himself against the four charges, Pirckheimer then went over to the offensive. He declared that even if he had attended every council session, said nothing during the sessions, and had not devoted himself to private legal practice, these accusations against him still would have been made, for behind all these reproaches there stood only the hate and envy of his enemies in the city council. For that reason, he wanted to withdraw from the council and requested it to release him.[19]

Pirckheimer's defense was quite successful. In its decision of August 18, the city council declared that it had erred on the first three charges and apologized for them. On the fourth point, however, it enjoined him to quit his service as a legal counsel. It was not absolutely forbidden to him, however, since he might serve as advocate for his friends, relatives, and "poor, miserable persons."[20] The council also informed him that it could not grant his request for dismissal from the council since it was not usual to do so in the middle of the year. He should remain until the new election and then take his leave if he wanted.[21]

Pirckheimer apparently considered himself vindicated by the decision for he did not withdraw from the council in the election of 1512. But the absolution of 1511 did not bring an end to the problems he had with the enemies he had referred to in his written defense. His chief antagonist was Anton Tetzel, whose position in the council hierarchy enabled him to create many difficulties for Pirckheimer.

Pirckheimer had at one time been a close friend of Tetzel. In 1505, when he and Tetzel had undertaken a diplomatic mission to Cologne together, Pirckheimer had considered him "a colleague very dear to himself."[22] At that time, Tetzel had been the third captain general, but was raised to the position of second *Losunger* in 1507. Pirckheimer's hostility toward him developed soon after Tetzel had obtained this position. Pirckheimer later came to consider him an arrogant, deceitful, and greedy man who, along with the faction that supported him, "preferred their private interests to the state's." Consequently, Tetzel and his faction became violent opponents. As Pirckheimer related it, they tried to force him out of the city council, keep him from the important affairs of the city, and prevent him from advancing to higher offices. In fact, Pirckheimer claimed that he had to guard against ambushes and that "his rivals were so insane that, when he went on diplomatic missions, he had to conceal the day of his going and coming."[23]

Pirckheimer probably exaggerated the situation, but an affair involving Pirckheimer and Tetzel in violent disagreement from 1509 to 1513 indicates that many members of the city council partially accepted Pirckheimer's opinion of his opponent. Anton Tetzel's son had married Anna Haller, the widow of Karl Haller, in 1509. In 1508, Karl Haller had been granted controlling authority over Sigmund Oertel's possessions, which were valued at 1,250 gulden and bore a rent of fifty gulden for a foundation established by a member of the Rieter family. The possessions had been placed in trust due to Haller's spending habits, and

Anna Haller, after the death of her husband and marriage to Tetzel's son, now attempted to claim possession of the estate. The Rieter family, thinking the Rieter foundation was being threatened, opposed her actions and complained to the city council. In this effort, they received the help of Pirckheimer as legal counsel, who was related to the Rieters through his wife.[24]

By 1511, the affair had advanced to the point that Pirckheimer and Tetzel, who was supporting the claims of his daughter-in-law, were exchanging angry words in the council sessions. Tetzel disputed the right of the Rieters and their lawyer, Pirckheimer, to meddle in the case.[25] Anna Tetzel went so far as to introduce a pamphlet containing complaints about Pirckheimer. The city council, now incensed over the entire business, decided on October 14, 1511, that Pirckheimer was guiltless and had been "attacked unfairly." It also demanded that Anton Tetzel see to an orderly arrangement of the entire business.[26]

The affair was not finally resolved then, for in 1513, Jorg Rieter, who had been pressing the case for his family, lost his patience and threatened to take the case to the Swabian League. When he informed the city council of his decision, it pushed again for a settlement of the affair. This led to another violent debate between Pirckheimer and Tetzel. This time the council asked the two opponents to leave the council room while the remaining members debated the situation and then informed them of its decision. Tetzel was given a formal reproach for behavior unbecoming a councilor of his rank. Pirckheimer was not formally rebuked, but both men were enjoined to see that the affair did not reach the Swabian League.[27] The council's action ended the controversy at this point.

In 1514, Pirckheimer was subjected to a libelous attack that resulted in a vexatious affair lasting for four years. This was outwardly the work of Hans Schütz, but as the affair unfolded, it was evident that Anton Tetzel was the instigator behind Schütz's efforts. It is possible that other city councilors were also implicated.

Hans Schütz was a Nürnberg merchant who had for many years created problems for the council. He was finally forced to leave Nürnberg on account of his debts, even though his father had been one of the richest men in the city.[28] On March 19, 1514, the city council received from Schütz a libelous tract against Pirckheimer. He also sent copies of the same work to twenty-five persons in Nürnberg. In it, Pirckheimer was pictured not only as the chief source of Schütz's financial troubles but as a purveyor of many "malicious actions." Schütz requested the city council to punish Pirckheimer for these actions and to help him gain 5,000 gulden compensation for all the damages Pirckheimer had caused him. If the council would not cooperate with him, Schütz threatened to take his complaints to the emperor and all the estates of the empire.[29]

At the time of Schütz's attack, Pirckheimer was on a diplomatic mission to Linz and Innsbruck. Instead of notifying Pirckheimer directly, the council asked Caspar Nützel, his traveling companion, to inform him at an "opportune" time of Schütz's attack. It is clear from the council's letter to Nützel that it did not consider this affair to be Schütz's work alone. It characterized Schütz as a "disobedient citizen" and stated that this had not happened "from his own head, but out of the envious hate and direction of certain evil people," who must have had much knowledge of the council's affairs. Nützel was to assure Pirckheimer that the council would spare no effort or cost in proceeding against Schütz and all his backers.[30] This last point is rather ironic in view of the eventual action of the council.

When Pirckheimer had returned to Nürnberg from his diplomatic mission, he composed a lengthy defense which he presented orally to the council on April 24.[31] In the introduction, he stated that this indictment against him really originated, not from Schütz, but from his enemies in the city council. Only through these, Pirckheimer charged, could Schütz have revealed things he would not otherwise have known.[32] Pirckheimer then proceeded to a point-by-point refutation of the charges levied against him. Schütz had dredged up the old charge of 1511 that Pirckheimer served as a legal advocate contrary to the council's regulations.[33] This Pirckheimer easily refuted, going into detail about the eight specific cases his opponent had mentioned.[34] To the accusation that he had said malicious things about the *Losunger* and *ältere Herren*, Pirckheimer indicated his regret that some of these officials conducted themselves in such a way that one could say nothing good about them, although they themselves believed that one should speak well of them regardless of what they did.[35]

One charge Schütz had made against Pirckheimer was undoubtedly a great source of amusement to his fellow councilors; namely, that Pirckheimer, "as had happened in Bologna, Florence, and many other powerful communes," planned to make himself lord of Nürnberg. Pirckheimer did not even bother to refute it, but used it as an opportunity to attack his enemies. If it were possible, he said, that anyone could have made himself lord of Nürnberg, it would have happened in the past several years when some councilors had ruled by pure wantonness. Indeed, no one, regardless of how pious, honest, or capable he was, could have been promoted by them. Pirckheimer was plainly thinking of himself here, for he went on to say that he had been in the way of these people, which had led them to attempt to force him out of the city council several years earlier (1511).[36] Pirckheimer next catalogued a long list of malicious deeds perpetrated by his enemies and reproached the council for having permitted these to continue so long. Without its indulgence the present situation would never have happened. In conclusion, he presented three requests: that the council accept his answer; that it allow no injury to him in this vicious affair; and that the council let him know if it would allow him to go to court against several of the perpetrators.[37]

The council gave its reply to Pirckheimer on the same day. Concerning the first two requests it stated that it had already, through Caspar Nützel,[38] expressed itself with respect to his innocence and had condemned the business undertaken by Schütz. However, in regard to his third request, it could give no answer because it was worded too generally. If Pirckheimer could give some specific names, the council would deliberate further.[39]

This reply brought about a violent exchange of words between Pirckheimer and Tetzel in the council session on April 25. Two days later Pirckheimer was reprimanded for his behavior. The council indicated its displeasure with these speeches against Tetzel, "since nothing good will follow from them." For the future, Pirckheimer was advised to refrain from invectives against Tetzel, since he had no cause for them. As it had already demonstrated, the council concluded that it was inclined in the Schütz affair to help Pirckheimer as much as possible.[40]

The city council began to implement this offer of help on April 25 when it wrote to Schütz and stated its refusal to undertake anything whatsoever against Pirckheimer.[41] Nevertheless, the problem of Hans Schütz was not eliminated that easily since he had threatened to take his complaints to higher authorities. The council, realizing this, now made attempts at mediation, in which Caspar Nützel for the council and Hans Scharpff, a Bamberg magistrate, for Schütz, played the chief roles. This attempt revolved primarily around the effort to get Schütz to make an apology to the council and Pirckheimer for his attacks as well as a solemn agreement to forgo any further accusations. It is evident in the rough draft of the apology that the council was being quite generous to Schütz and even gave him the possibility of shifting guilt from himself to those who had undertaken this and supported him.[42] But Schütz refused all of these first attempts at compromise.

Pirckheimer was now able to gain some satisfaction even though these mediation attempts had foundered. In November, 1514, Anton Tetzel, his chief enemy and the instigator of Schütz's action, was relieved of all his high offices and put into prison. This was done, however, not because of the Hans Schütz affair but because of other instances in which Tetzel had received bribes and given state secrets to his relatives.[43] But Pirckheimer could not enjoy for long the pleasure of seeing his opponent fall, since the Schütz business continued unabated. Attempts were made in 1515, by Schutz's brother Gregory and cousins Dr. Hieronymus Schütz and Hans Pauer, to effect a settlement with Pirckheimer. But their conception of a settlement was the granting of compensation to Hans Schütz for the damages he had suffered, which the council categorically refused.[44] These efforts were therefore also in vain, and Schütz reacted in November, 1515, by issuing new threats and libelous statements against Pirckheimer and the city council. The council responded with a new pledge of support for Pirckheimer.[45]

By the end of 1515 and the beginning of 1516, the city council, obviously tired of this burdensome affair, was beginning to incline toward an amicable settlement with Schütz. For that reason, following a suggestion of Schütz himself,[46] the council now separated Pirckheimer's case with Schütz from its own and made arrangements for a "friendly hearing" before the bishop of Bamberg on March 3, 1516.[47] Pirckheimer, however, did not believe that an honorable conclusion could be reached in this way. His own solution to the affair had been proposed as early as July, 1514, and he adhered to it throughout the four-year affair. Pirckheimer wanted the matter brought as a legal case before a proper judge, namely, a Nürnberg city court, since both he and Schütz were Nürnberg citizens. If Schütz, however, was not willing to have this, then the case should be tried before anyone Schütz wanted, but with the stipulation that neither contender be given safe-conduct, so that each party would have to subject himself unreservedly to the punishment meted out by the judging party.[48] Neither the council nor Schütz had yet agreed to this proposal by the beginning of 1516. Consequently, Pirckheimer was quite dissatisfied with the entire situation. This is demonstrated in a letter to Hieronymus Emser in which Pirckheimer discussed the forthcoming session between Schütz and the council before the bishop of Bamberg:

> My case has been entirely excluded because I, in no way, on account of the grave injuries, aim to act and reply otherwise than in criminal proceedings and those without a safe conduct, which my adversary is continually unwilling to accept. . . . Therefore I shall wait.

Pirckheimer also indicated that Schütz, after negotiations with the city council, had finally demanded a reward of 1,000 gulden, for which he would reveal the names of all the people in Nürnberg who were involved in the affair against Pirckheimer. This the council was not prepared to pay.[49]

The effort before the bishop of Bamberg was also a failure, and Schütz now, in 1516 and 1517, turned to various secular lords, including the landgrave of Leuchtenberg in the Upper Palatinate and Duke George of Saxony. The city council had to explain in lengthy letters the real situation to these different lords.[50] It is obvious from these extensive efforts by the council that it greatly feared, as had happened before in Nürnberg's history, that Schütz would win over to his cause some of the Franconian landed nobility who would be only too willing to begin a feud with the city. Pirckheimer realized this, as well as the possible personal danger to himself, when he asked the city council if he could hire a bodyguard.[51]

With these considerations in mind it was understandable that the council now reacted favorably to the attempt of Gregory Schütz, in November, 1517, to bring about a reconciliation between the council and his brother.[52] The council decided on November 24 that, if Schütz were to make sufficient promises to desist from any further actions against it, it would "free him from worry for his past actions." Nevertheless, Pirckheimer would still be allowed to bring his case against Schütz before a regular court of law.[53] After some altercations over the exact wording of his written promise, the council and Schütz reached a settlement at the beginning of February, 1518.[54]

Since Pirckheimer's argument with his opponent had been excluded from this agreement, he now requested and received permission from the council to bring his case against Schütz before the court of the *Fünf Herren*.[55] Pirckheimer appeared before the court on April 13 and presented his charges.[56] On the following day a written citation was sent to Schütz requesting him to appear before the court to answer to Pirckheimer's charges.[57] The council's efforts to get Schütz to appear before the court dragged on for months. To Pirckheimer, the city council appeared to be delaying deliberately, due to its leniency toward Schütz, over which he bitterly complained.[58] Finally, on November 19, Schütz was judged *in contumaciam* to four months imprisonment, although he could commute two months to a money payment. He was also supposed to pay all of the court costs.[59] Since Schütz did not return to the city to accept the punishment, he lost his Nürnberg citizenship forever.

The final decision could not have given Pirckheimer much satisfaction, for it had been at the cost of four years of effort and vexation. It was, as is evident from his correspondence, especially disconcerting that the city council, which had been helpful in the beginning, showed itself eventually to be only too willing to consider its interests at the expense those of Pirckheimer.

During the Hans Schütz affair, Pirckheimer came into open conflict with another city councilor, Conrad Imhoff, who had been at odds with him for years. Although the issues involved appear rather insignificant, the council's reaction provides a good commentary on its attitude toward dissension among the ruling patricians. Pirckheimer and Imhoff had been in constant opposition to one another in the council sessions for years.[60] Even the marriage of Pirckheimer's daughter Felicitas to Conrad Imhoff's nephew Hans, in 1515, failed to lessen the hostility between the two men, for in May, 1517, they abused each other so violently in a council session that the council formally censured them both.

This scene occurred during an innocuous debate over the procedure of wine inspection in Nürnberg. After the exchange of some mild unpleasantries, each became disturbed enough to request a hearing to prove that the other had no right to be a member of the city council. Three days after this event, the senior burgomasters and *Alte Genannte* met to discuss this affair and after "diligent examination" arrived at a decision that was then communicated to Pirckheimer and Imhoff. In a statement that reflects the council's position on patrician dissension, the two men were first reminded of the necessity to maintain a peaceful and faithful concert among the city councilors.

> For whoever is unfaithful to the maintenance and promotion of the common good and such good faithfulness for the sake of his own interest, presents also an evil example to subjects and the common man, and a diminution of the rulers and their own persons.[61]

Neither Pirckheimer nor Imhoff, the council continued, had the prerogative to challenge the other's right to sit in the council. They justly deserved a punishment for their accusations, but instead the council commanded them hereafter to refrain from such arguments and to keep peace with one another "in word and deed." To buttress this, Pirckheimer and Imhoff had to promise formally to adhere to this command, as well as to swear an oath to this effect in the presence of the other city councilors.

The council's policy was effective, for there is no further mention of disagreements between them before Imhoff's death in 1519.

After his struggles with Schütz and Imhoff, Pirckheimer would probably have been quite willing to enjoy a respite from factional strife. But he was not that fortunate, for, according to his autobiography, he was confronted now with another faction in the council whose leader was a man who had been a close friend of Pirckheimer. By his favor, he said, the man had greatly increased his power, and "by the pretense of uprightness" had secured a considerable reputation.[62] Although, as usual, Pirckheimer did not name his opponent in his autobiography, what evidence he gave probably points to Lazarus Spengler, the city secretary.[63]

It was this man and his faction, Pirckheimer claimed, that ultimately led him to withdraw permanently from the city council, in 1523. Again with some exaggeration, Pirckheimer recounted the "plots," "ambushes," and "harassments," fostered against him, since he was the one man above all others who opposed this faction's clandestine plans, "useful to themselves, but most dangerous to the republic."[64] Pirckheimer grew tired of this constant irritation and, having a legitimate excuse, his affliction with the gout, applied for and received his discharge from the city council on April 5, 1523. In his autobiography, Pirckheimer claimed that the council, upon the instigation of the hostile faction, also offered him a liberal stipend for work as a consultant, a request that is not documented in the city's sources. This, Pirckheimer said, he refused, but indicated his willingness to give his advice when called upon without financial reimbursement.[65]

This account of Pirckheimer's struggles, which has provided a picture of the discord prevalent among Nürnberg's ruling elite at the beginning of the sixteenth century, suggests several observations about the nature of patrician government in Nürnberg.

It is perhaps a truism that in any government such as Nürnberg's, where the members are elected by an essentially meaningless electoral process, differences of opinion and political ambitions can most likely be resolved only by factional politics and personal animosities of the type witnessed and experienced by Pirckheimer. At the same time, such a carefully controlled government, as Nürnberg's city council frequently demonstrated, had to be careful to avoid any public display that would give evidence of dissension, since that would only endanger its own privileged position, a position resting basically on tradition and effectiveness in government. Such a goal necessitated the ruthless subordination of individual personality to the common good of the state, as was evident in Pirckheimer's affair with Hans Schütz. Finally, it is apparent that the maintenance of a communal government, free of dissension at least for public consumption, required the expenditure of considerable time and effort for the resolution of both serious and petty issues. And this, of course, the ruling patricians of Nürnberg were quite prepared to do.

1. In this year a final closing of the ranks occurred when the *ältere Herren* issued a decree listing those families who were entitled to official invitations to dance in the city hall. This decree effectively limited the membership of the patriciate to forty-three families. The decree is printed in Emil Reicke, *Geschichte der Reichsstadt Nürnberg* (Nürnberg, 1896), p. 103.

2. This brief discussion of Nürnberg's government is based on the sixteenth-century description by Christoph Scheurl, one of the city council's legal consultants. See "Christoph Scheurls Epistel über die Verfassung der Reichsstadt Nürnberg. 1516," *Die Chroniken der deutschen Städte, Nürnberg,* 5 (Leipzig, 1874), 781–804. For a detailed, modern examination of the government structure, see Gerald Strauss, *Nuremberg in the Sixteenth Century* (New York, 1966), pp. 57–115.

3. On Pirckheimer's role in Nürnberg as a city councilor, see the author's article, "Willibald Pirckheimer's Domestic Activity for Nürnberg," *Moreana* 25 (1970): 17–29. Most of the literature on Pirckheimer concentrates on his humanistic activity, religious thought, and his relationship to the Reformation. These were the major concerns of the nineteenth-century works by Paul Drews, Karl Hagen, Rudolph Hagen, and Friedrich Roth. Significant twentieth-century studies of Pirckheimer include a brief biography by Emil Reicke (Jena, 1930); an article by Hans Rupprich, "Willibald Pirckheimer, Beiträge zu einer Wesenserfassung," *Schweizer Beiträge zur Allgemeinen Geschichte* 15 (1957): 64–110; a chapter in Lewis Spitz's *The Religious Renaissance of the German Humanists* (Cambridge, Mass., 1963), pp. 155-96; and a work published on the occasion of the five hundredth anniversary of Pirckheimer's birth by Willehad Eckert and Christoph von Imhoff, *Willibald Pirckheimer* (Cologne, 1970).

4. This autobiography, *Cl. Viri, D. Bilibaldi Pirckheymheri, Senatoris quondam Nurenbergensis, Vita,* was found in the British Museum by Karl Rück; he edited and published it as an appendix in *Wilibald Pirckheimers Schweizerkrieg nach Pirckheimers Autographum im Britischen Museum* (Munich, 1895), pp. 137-52 (hereafter cited as Rück, *Vita*). There is also an edition in Marianne Beyer-Fröhlich, ed., *Aus dem Zeitalter des Humanismus und der Reformation* (Leipzig, 1931), pp. 41–56. Pirckheimer did not specifically mention his enemies

by name in his autobiography. Their identities can, however, for the most part, be ascertained by the information he gives about these men.

5. Pirckheimer to Dr. Thomas von Thierstein (?), Emil Reicke, ed., *Willibald Pirckheimers Briefwechsel*, 1 (Munich, 1940); ep. 51, p. 166 (hereafter cited as *Br* with the volume, letter, and page numbers following).

6. An apparent reference to the criticism of Pirckheimer after Nürnberg's defeat in the battle of the Nürnberg forest on June 19, 1502. See Emil Reicke, "Die Schlacht im Nürnberger Walde am Tage der Affalterbacher Kirchweih 19 Juni 1502," *Fränkischer Kurier, Unterhaltungsblatt.* 1902. Nos. 200, 204, 206.

7. *Br*, 1: ep. 53, p. 176.

8. Pirckheimer indicated that his enemy had been elected to the highest position in the government. Rück, *Vita*, p. 144.

9. StAn RV 352, fol. 6v–7; RV 357, fol. 2r; RV 358, fol. 13r; RV 364, fol. 13v, 17r.

10. Volckamer died of a stroke on February 9, 1505.

11. Rück, *Vita*, pp. 144–45.

12. According to Scheurl, p. 793, the city councilors received for every session they attended a token worth fifty pfennigs. These tokens could then be cashed in at the end of the month. If they came late to a session, they were fined four pfennigs, and if they were absent without excuse they forfeited one of their tokens.

13. The four charges are contained in a writing by Pirckheimer in which he defended himself against them. Although his defense was delivered orally, the work probably faithfully follows the oral defense. The written defense is printed in *Br*, 2: ep. 193, pp. 84–92. The four charges are on pp. 85–86, 88.

14. Ibid., pp. 85–86.

15. Ibid., p. 86.

16. The Ratsverlässe indicate otherwise, although it can be noticed that Pirckheimer was directed to a much greater activity after this affair than before. Compare, for example, RV 526–33, *passim*, with RV 535–41, *passim*.

17. *Br*, 2: ep. 193, p. 87.

18. Ibid., p. 88.

19. Ibid., pp. 88–90.

20. Pirckheimer's service as a legal counsel was henceforth given with the permission of the council. See RV 559, fol. 13r; RB 10, fol. 88r; "Willibald Pirckheimer is permitted to counsel and serve as advocate for Leonhard Grundelfinger's widow before the imperial supreme court in her case against Barbara Sturmer." See also RV 570, fol. 7v; RB 10, fol. 131v.

21. RV 534, fol. 3v4r; RB 9, fol. 235r; printed in *Br*, 2: 92–93. Pirckheimer's defense also contains the substance of the decision. Ibid., pp. 90–91.

22. Rück, *Vita*, p. 146.

23. Ibid., p. 147.

24. On the background to this affair, see Emil Reicke, "Der Sturz des Losungers Anton Tetzel," *Fränkischer Kurier, Unterhaltungsblatt*, 1909, No. 3, p. 15; No. 5, p. 28.

25. RV 535, fol. 24v; RB 9, fol. 243.

26. RV 536, fol. 6r; RB 9, fol. 246.

27. RV 556, fol. 14r.

28. On Hans Schütz, and for a brief account of this affair, see Emil Reicke,

"Willibald Pirckheimer und sein Ehrenhandel mit Hans Schütz," *Jahresbericht des Vereins für Geschichte der Stadt Nürnberg* 24 (1921–22):35–38.

29. *Br*, 2:ep. 302 pp. 341–45. The charges he levied against Pirckheimer are mentioned below, pp. 13–14, in the discussion of Pirckheimer's defense.

30. *Br*, 2:ep. 302, pp. 352–53.

31. His written defense, *Br*, 2:ep. 310, pp. 377–402, probably follows faithfully his oral presentation.

32. Ibid., pp. 377–81.

33. See above, pp. 6–8.

34. *Br*, 2:ep. 310, pp. 381–90.

35. Ibid., p. 390. The *Losunger* at this time were Anton Tucher and Anton Tetzel. The *ältere Herren*, in addition to these two, were Jakob Groland, Hieronymus Ebner, Georg Holzschuher, Martin Geuder, and Leonhard Grundherr. In addition to Tetzel, Pirckheimer was at odds with Holzschuher and Groland.

36. Ibid., pp. 390–92.

37. Ibid., pp. 394–99.

38. In its letter asking Nützel to inform Pirckheimer of Schütz's attack; see above, p. 12.

39. RV 570, fol. 4; RB 10, fol. 130b–131a; the entry is also contained in Prickheimer's written defense, *Br*, 2:ep. 310, pp. 399–400.

40. Ibid., p. 400.

41. StAN BB 72, fol. 101v; *Br*, 2:ep. 311, p. 413.

42. The relevant documents are in the StAN S. I L. 57, No. 13. The drafts for the apology are printed in *Br*, 2:ep. 318, p. 454; ep. 318, pp. 435–36; ep. 318, pp. 437–38.

43. On Tetzel's fall from power, see Reicke, "Der Sturz," No. 9, pp. 51–53.

44. BB 73, fol. 174v; RV 583, fol. 12r, 14r; RB 10, fol. 224v–226v; the Ratsbuch entry is printed in *Br*, 2:ep. 358, pp. 538–42.

45. RV 591, fol. 3v; RB 10, fol. 274r; printed in BR, 2:ep. 373, p. 583, but with incorrect page citation and date.

46. City council to Hans Pauer, BB 75, fol. 43v.

47. City council to bishop of Bamberg, BB 75, fol. 59v.

48. *Br*, 2:ep. 324, pp. 444-46.

49. Stadtbibliothek, Nürnberg. Pirckheimerpapiere, No. 331c.

50. For example, see city council to Duke George of Saxony, Feb. 17, 1517, BB 76, fol. 143r–145v.

51. Pirckheimer's request was in a postscript to his answer to Gregory Schütz's petition to the council printed in Ernst Münch, *Bilibald Pirckheimer's Schweizerkrieg*, p. 286. The original is lost.

52. Gregory Schütz's petition is in ibid., pp. 277–79.

53. RV 616, fol. 22; RB 11, fol. 113r.

54. RV 619, fol. 12r. The exact terms of the agreement are in StAN Amts- und Standbuch, No. 47, fol. 209v.

55. RV 620, fol. 20v. The court of the *Fünf Herren* met three times a week and heard cases involving slander and injury.

56. RV 622, fol. 7r. Pirckheimer's charges are in Pirckeimerpapiere, Nos. 136a, 221.

57. RV 622, fol. 8v.

58. Pirckheimer to city council, Pirckheimerpapiere, No. 136b.

59. StAN Amts- und Standbuch, No. 47, fol. 210 .

60. See reference to such in a letter of Albrecht Dürer to Pirckheimer, *Br*, 1:ep. 118, p. 387.

61. RB 11, fol. 85ᵛ–87ʳ, contains a lengthy discussion of the entire affair; the RV 610, fol. insert between fol. 7 and 8, contains only the council's decision.

62. Rück, *Vita*, p. 149.

63. His discussion of this enemy (ibid., pp. 149–51) gives few tangible clues for identity. Pirckheimer did say that the man was burdened by poverty and a multitude of sons. Although Spengler, as city secretary, was not poor, he did not possess the wealth that most patricians did. In the time period to which Pirckheimer is referring, Spengler had six sons. See Gottlieb Haussdorff, *Lebensbeschreibung eines christlichen Politici, nehmliche Lazari Spenglers* (Nürnberg, 1741), pp. 19–25. The general tenor of Pirckheimer's comments coincides with his other known statements on Spengler. However, the evidence is sketchy enough to warrant some uncertainty regarding the identification. On Spengler, see Hans von Schubert, *Lazarus Spengler und die Reformation in Nürnberg* ("Quellen und Forschungen zur Reformationsgeschichte," vol. 17; Leipzig, 1934); and more recently, Harold J. Grimm, "Lazarus Spengler, the Nürnberg City Council, and the Reformation," in *Luther for an Ecumenical Age*, ed. Carl S. Meyer (St. Louis, 1967), pp. 108–19.

64. Rück, *Vita*, p. 149.

65. Ibid., pp. 150–52.

THE IMPACT OF THE REFORMATION ON SOCIETY

Part 2

THE DYNAMICS OF PRINTING IN
THE SIXTEENTH CENTURY

Richard G. Cole

The typographic revolution was one of the most important and dynamic factors of change in sixteenth-century Germany.[1] The revolutionary impact of printing on Western culture in the sixteenth century is well known and recognized by almost every author of a sixteenth-century monograph or textbook. Relatively few people have attempted to assess just what these revolutionary developments were that resulted from the publication of thousands of pamphlets and books. Elizabeth Eisenstein has suggested several significant procedural changes in the area of scholarship introduced by the printing press. For example, Eisenstein notes the differences between a fifteenth-century humanist who laborously copied manuscripts and his sixteenth-century counterpart who edited works for publication.[2] Writing the preface for an edited book was a significantly different task from the laborious job of a hand copyist. In effect the printing press stimulated the creative processes of traditional scholarship as well as opening up possibilities for writing new materials totally unrelated to the problems of conventional and classical scholarship.

One of the first Reformation leaders to understand clearly the potential for change inherent in the new media of printing was Johann Eberlin von Günzburg. Eberlin, while a member of the Franciscan Observants, reacted vigorously and positively to Luther's famous pamphlets written in 1520. Encouraged by Luther's tracts, Eberlin directed his energy toward writing pamphlets detailing his disenchantment with many levels of German life, the rigidness and inadequacies of his monkish order, the failures of Emperor Charles V in understanding German problems, and what seemed to him to be the generally distressed conditions of German life. Eberlin's work as a religious reformer is relatively minor; his significance for the sixteenth century lay in his clear understanding of the implication for change inherent in the printing press. He believed that the publication of his ideas for a new society could influence public consciousness. Within a year after he left his Franciscan order, he published a series of fifteen pamphlets outlining a wide gradation of reforms ranging from suggestions for practical education of children to the creation of a Lutheran Utopia. He wanted his readers to respond favorably to his positive image for future earthly life.[3] Eberlin, keenly aware of the potential of printing, hoped that large numbers of people would soon learn to read in their native tongue.[4]

Even though astronomers like Regiomontanus in the fifteenth century and reformers like Luther or Eberlin in the early sixteenth century seemed cognizant of the possibilities of printing as an effective tool of scholarship and dissemination, it is only recently that the civilized world has begun to probe the significance of the Gutenberg revolution and the subsequent formation of a book culture. In the 1930s Lewis Mumford suggested some of the changes wrought by the introduction of printing. One obvious result was that print produced an opportunity for a release for an individual from the confines of a local environment. But, writes Mumford, since printed accounts made a stronger impression than the actual event, the reader lost the balance "between the sensuous and the intellectual, between the image and sound, between the concrete and the abstract." Mumford concludes: "To exist was to exist in print; the rest of the world tended gradually to become more shadowy."[5] The invention of printing created a typographic language and gave to print a semblance of authority and accuracy that seemed likely to remain forever.[6]

Many of the religious aspects of the Protestant Reformation had been foreshadowed by Occam, Biel, Groote, and Hus. Why was Luther's impact upon his contemporaries disproportionately greater than his precursors? Luther, whether he was aware of it or not, placed upon the public arena answers to his private questions, answers that were soon rationalized and became of intense public interest. The development of Luther's theology coincided exactly with the period in which European culture moved from the age of manuscripts to the era of printed books. A manifold increase in the availability of books during the early years of the Reformation is well documented; less conspicuous and somewhat puzzling is Marshall McLuhan's observation that the impact of the printed page upon the reader was one that gave a new configuration to his mental processes by narrowing the dimensions of reality (no audio-tactile response and fewer nonlinear images) and at the same time stirred up polemical controversy.[7]

Much of the popular literature illustrating Lutheran, Catholic, or various other sectarian points of view was blatantly propagandistic, alarmist, and frequently vulgar. Reformers and their opponents moved quickly to exploit the new media in order to move information and ideas to wide audiences now exposed and subjected to an informational transmission capability unknown in any era previous to the sixteenth century. Many pamphlets have disappeared in the destruction wrought by war, some were destroyed by zealous censors, and many were thrown away or not passed on to heirs. Although professional archivists showed little interest in pamphlets, with the exception of those bearing Luther's and perhaps Erasmus' name on the title page, many of the "little books" are extant in archives in Europe and in the United States. The survivors represent only a limited part of the original production.[8] Most major cities by the middle of the sixteenth century were sites of at least some printing activity. One of the largest printing firms was the House of Koberger in Nürnberg, which had twenty-four presses and employed over one hundred workers.

More research has to be done to determine the extent and effectiveness of German education in the sixteenth century. Several generalizations with regard to the impact of printing on the formation of attitudes are tenable on the basis of present knowledge. First, literacy rates are higher in urban areas than in rural districts. Second, most people connected with business and trade in commercial centers contribute to the rising pool of literacy. In Germany, it is worth noting that the printing arts developed first in commercial centers and only later in university towns, a development that from the outset placed the production and distribution of books into a close relationship with the average person.[9] Thus, much of the pamphlet literature was written to appeal to the masses of partially educated people. Nonliterate persons enticed by graphically illustrated pamphlets on a variety of topics could easily become book owners. The printing revolution cut across the entire spectrum of society by making it possible for each family unit to own a printed book and to become a part of a common book culture. Startling is the contrast between the age of incunabula and the limited-circulation manuscript culture of medieval Europe.

In some situations the printed media when combined with traditional methods of oral communication through preaching and public oratory became a potent agent of change.[10] An articulate reformer having at his disposal printed tracts from Wittenberg and elsewhere had the best of both of the oral-script culture and the typographical age. A literate reformer who could cite specific tracts or particular chapter and verse of Holy Scripture added a new dimension to normal processes of disputation. A penetrating account of the spoken word based on Luther's written ideas was left by a sixteenth-century Danish chronicler describing the tactics by which his order, the Greyfriars, were displaced from their monastaries in Denmark during the late 1520s and early 1530s. Since public support had to be aroused to disrupt monastic life effectively, the chronicler was particularly sensitive to the efficiency with which Lutheran reformers could preach Luther's doctrines. Of the apostate Danish Greyfriar Claus Bødker, the chronicler writes: "For he, who was a cunning man not unskilled in the counsels of evil, perceived that it was not possible to pour out pure poison to begin with, but little by little, locked up in sweet honey, to drip it into the ears of his audience."[11] As the Greyfriar chronicler demonstrates in the course of his chronicle, the presence of the written word combined with fiery orations was an effective dynamic in the process of change. Minor reformers like Bødker realized that since a relatively low state of literacy existed in his rural audience, more could be accomplished by oral communication than by devoting all his energy to writing pamphlets. The combination of oral methods with printed materials as sources of information created a new "cultural mix" that was essentially a new force in the sixteenth century.[12]

The print culture in some ways affected the development of Protestant theology and religious practices. Allowing for the continuity of values and the imperatives of tradition, especially in the area of religion, the relatively dramatic and swift theological shifts of the Reformation are unprecedented. In a fairly short period of time, although to an uneven degree, many people underwent a basic shift in their relationship to God and the traditional church, a significant cultural change in any period of history. Many of the seeds for a religious metamorphosis were sown in Luther's three famous tracts of 1520: *The Freedom of the Christian, Address to the German Nobility*, and the *Babylonian Captivity of the Church*. Lutheran polemical literature threatened established traditions to a higher degree than intended by the authors, not necessarily as a result of their internal contents but because they were printed. The awesome authority of the printed page contributed to the possibility of misinterpretating pamphlets and books. Abuses stemming in part from a misunderstanding of printed words generated some of the profanation of church property and denigration of worship that Luther had heard about before and witnessed in Wittenberg in 1522 after he returned from the Wartburg Castle.

From the ninth to the sixteenth of March, Luther preached his famous eight sermons designed to reduce the fervor of enthusiasts led by Carlstadt. In an effort to lessen the degree of tumult, Luther, in his second sermon preached on the Monday after Invocavit (March 10, 1522), referred to his published works of 1520 and elaborated on his idea of change and how it should be carried out.[13]

Some of Luther's thoughts rapidly became slogans, and were accepted by some without careful thought and reflection. The idea of a "priesthood of believers," carefully worked out in print by Luther in *The Freedom of the Christian,* stimulated and intensified the feeling of social and political equalitarianism, a result not in the forefront of Luther's thinking.[14] If the flood of printed materials stimulated confusion, additional books and pamphlets served to correct misunderstanding. The catalyst of this theological dialectic was the printing press.

Luther who avidly exploited printing potential was aware of the many liabilities of print. In a letter written to Georg Spalatin in August of 1521, Luther conveyed his concern for errors that careless printers set into his manuscripts—errors that would be perpetuated in many editions of the same work.[15] At one point Luther was quoted as saying: "I'd like all my books to be destroyed so that only sacred writing in the *Bible* would be diligently read." He conceded, however, that if his books were to be preserved, they should be so for the sake of history.[16]

Other reformer-pamphleteers like Eberlin worried over another dimension of print abuse, an indiscriminate printing of materials for the sole purpose of profit making. Eberlin wrote in his satirical pamphlet *Mich wundert das kein Geld im Land ist* (1524), with regard to printers, that it seems as though "the whole world is in the hands of buyers and sellers." He continued by complaining that useful works such as history books, which teach young people useful examples, and other types of decent literature were slighted in favor of sensational and misleading books and pamphlets. To satisfy the voracious needs of the polemical pamphlet wars, printers failed to differentiate between "good and bad, good and better, decent and indecent, for the single purpose of obtaining excess profits."[17]

During the early years of the sixteenth century, the readiness of many people to accept and use the new medium of printing depended in part on one's chronological age. Luther was only thirty-four in 1517, and many of his fellow pamphleteers and coworkers were students under thirty.[18] The young men around Luther who sought to foment change depended heavily on printed sources for communication and transmission of ideas whereas many of the older generation relied on the traditional oral and manuscript culture for authority. A classic example of a "generation gap" related to different uses of media is found in a pamphlet: *A Dialog or Conversation Between a Father and His Son About Martin Luther's Doctrine* (1523).[19] The son, a student at the University of Wittenberg, tries to convince his peasant father of the value of Luther's doctrine. Although the peasant father can read in vernacular as well as in Latin (claimed by the author of the dialogue), he states that he does not often use his reading skill in matters of religion and is content to follow old customs observed by his forefathers. The learned son impresses his father by citing many passages of Scripture giving exact textual locations. The father wants his son to "tell" him more what the Bible says in order that he may memorize it.[20] His son advises that be buy his own copy of the Bible and read it for himself. The father and son argue more about the methods of finding religious truth than about doctrinal issues. In the end the father agrees to buy a Bible, and, according to the anonymous author of the *Dialog*, the printed word of God in this case becomes the path of the older generation to Lutheranism. The oral traditions and customs of his forefathers gave way to a newly formed printed tradition.

A characteristic not uncommon among some of the older generation during the late fifteenth and early sixteenth centuries was a reluctance to part with hand-copied manuscripts of the oral-script culture. A letter written by Trithemius, the abbot of Sponheim, to Gerlach, the abbot of Deutz (printed in Mainz in 1494 as *De Laude Scriptorium Manualium*) reveals on several levels a traditionally conservative yet literate skepticism toward printed books. Trithemius argued that parchment volumes would last five times longer than paper books. Second, he believed many important books would never be printed and would not be recopied since the number of scribes would dwindle as the printing revolution gained momentum; if enough scribes quit work, the intellectual cultivation of later generations would be hindered. Finally, Trithemius noted the poor aesthetic quality of printed works as opposed to the tactile beauty and artistic form of carefully prepared manuscripts.[21] Similar to Trithemius's reservations on printing was the opinion of the Danish archbishop, Jens Brostrup, who in 1494 expressed a fear that since certain letters existed only in printed collections of documents, they could be easily lost, more "easily than if they had existed in a handwritten parchment book."[22]

Much of the popular literature of the Reformation period was intended for extended audiences and for polemical purposes rather than for libraries of scholars and literati. One of the results of the popular nature of the new medium of the pamphlet was that incendiary and vulgar language became commonplace. Few tract-writers surpassed Luther in the use of the rhetoric of violence. In 1520 when commenting on an attack on him by Sylvester Prierias, Luther stated that we should "assault them (the Pope and Cardinals) with all weapons and wash our hands in their blood."[23] A year later Luther wrote, in *Eyn trew vormannung Martini Luther zu allen Christen, sich zu vorhuten fur auffruhr unnd emporung* (1521), "With letters one can do more than enough, neither hewing nor stabbing is necessary."[24] Luther's tendency to contradict himself both in content and in style has made difficult the job of biographers and historians. Explanations for Luther's dissimilarities in style and thought range from an emphasis on his peasant background, or his fiery temper, to an overuse of his creative imagination.

Two aspects of the print culture may serve to point up some of the reasons for the variant and divergent interpretations of Luther and numerous other reformers as well as Reformation movements in general. First, many of Luther's statements refer to specific situations and were printed in many cases only after oral delivery, a condition making it difficult for the historian to reconstruct the setting in which the words were spoken. Second, many of Luther's written statements were published in the nascent period of the typographical age during which the rules for linear consistency were not fully laid down. Moreover, authors in the age of incunabula had little accurate knowledge or experience in the ways printed books and pamphlets affected human behavior. Philip Schaff, writing in the nineteenth century, may have been on to more than he knew when he wrote that the peasant wars of the 1520s were "kindled by inflammatory books."[25] Normally, a simple cause and effect explanation of the peasant wars would be dismissed as a simplistic interpretation ignoring complicated socioeconomic tensions and dynamics of a traditional peasant culture. Yet, in the final analysis, printed Reformation pamphlets altered conditions of reality and facilitated strong reactions among peasant leaders, who spurred on their followers to revolt.

The dynamics of change viewed from the perspective of the impact of printing on the sixteenth century runs its course in a number of directions. The legislative activity of the 1520s resulting in a number of poor laws designed to alleviate problems of widows, unemployed persons, and beggars is connected in a generic way to the spread of the book culture resulting from the printing revolution.[26] Although an exhaustive study of sixteenth-century poor laws and their background is not a primary concern here, it is necessary to survey briefly some of the social flux in Germany at the time of the Reformation.[27] One of the consequences of a gradual shift from a stratified society based upon feudal orders to one resembling a class society was the appearance of poor and newly urbanized peasants seeking a better life. These lower-class elements made increasingly large demands upon rich merchants, guildsmen, and powerful nobles, who dominated politics in many cities and towns.[28] Facts of economic distress are far from complete for sixteenth-century cities, but limited available evidence is suggestive. Tax rolls for the city of Augsburg, which was a scene of unrest and reformation in the 1520s, show that 50 percent of the inhabitants paid no property tax and another 40 percent paid only a minimal tax.[29] A general maldistribution of wealth seemed to be a fairly common phenomenon in German cities.[30] Poverty was not a sudden specter of the sixteenth century. In prior periods, cities and villages depended upon various church orders or upon private donations to alleviate suffering among poor people. By 1517 the willingness and ability of the Catholic church in many areas to operate charities diminished to an extent that it could not continue its welfare responsibilities. The social problem of poverty fell under the aegis of Protestant reformers spurred by biblical injunctions and a general dislike of begging either by clerics or transients. Poor-law legislation was needed to protect the well-being of the commonwealth and at the same time fulfill Christ's demand to serve poor humanity.

Reasons for poor-law legislation are many, but the catalytic factor in fostering a rapid spread of poor laws was the printing press, which allowed the production of easily obtainable models for cities to follow. Within a three- to four-year period similar ideas of welfare reform appeared in a number of cities. First among Lutheran reformers to print plans for a social welfare was Eberlin von Günzburg. Eberlin constructed in 1521 a theoretical model of what he considered to be an ideal society. Part of his construct included provisions for taking care of the poor. He advocated a monthly collection to be taken from those who could afford to pay, the monies received to be given to those with greatest need. If there were any surpluses of gifts in money or kind, they would be given to the common treasury of the city and used at the discretion of secular officials. To prevent cheating among welfare recipients, the poor were all required to carry identification cards.[31] Eberlin felt that, in the ideal society, concern for one's neighbor was imperative; if a prosperous citizen were a remiss giver, he would be publicly punished.[32] It is evident that the basis of Eberlin's social thought is rooted in both the love ethic of the New Testament and the practical idea that the poor man has as much right to physical comfort as the rich person.[33] Eberlin, in his pamphlet *Warnung an die Christen der Burgauischen Mark* (1526), summed up one of the common reasons for Reformation concerns for social welfare by writing that if destitute persons were taken care of, no one would have reason to commit a crime against the common good.[34] An interesting aspect of Eberlin's concern for the poor is the similarity between his statements and the rash of poor laws enacted in the years immediately following the publication of his socially and politically oriented pamphlet series of 1521.

A comparative study of the Wittenberg (1522), Nürnberg (1522), Regensburg (1523), Kitzingen (1523), Leisnig (1523) and Strassburg (1523) poor laws reveals striking similarities to each other and to the ideas of Eberlin. All of the various plans state the necessity of Christians to care for the poor and unfortunate; cite methods of distribution of money and kind; list conditions of distribution; and detail special requirements for welfare recipients, for example, the wearing or carrying of identification tags. The Nürnberg law of 1522, influenced somewhat by Venetian welfare experiments, is the most detailed statement of the conditions and requirements to be met to obtain free drugs from an apothecary.[35] The poor laws of the 1520s were more than a common response to a common prob-

lem; visual, repeatable statements available in printed texts ac-
celerated the process of spreading information and facilitated
poor-law planning. The author of the Regensburg poor law of
May, 1523, literally copied entire sections of the Nürnberg law
of 1522.[36] Welfare ideas similar to those found in city ordinances of the early 1520s appear in "Church Disciplines" written later for cities going through the process of Reformation.
In the ordinance that Johann Bugenhagen wrote for the city of
Brunswick in 1528, widows, waifs, and workers who have suffered misfortune were helped in a manner essentially the same
as in other German cities. Bugenhagen exhorted all those who
had good fortune to contribute money to a common welfare
treasury, "not for ourselves but rather for the common good."[37]
The similarity of Reformation thinking on poor laws in widely
divergent areas indicates the rapidity with which ideas could be
spread and implemented, ideas given a common structure
through the medium of the printing press.

Reformation movements in sixteenth-century Europe are an
immensely complicated series of events. The first decades of Reformation are as chaotic and multifaceted as the various conflicting historical interpretations of that era. If changes wrought by
Reformation movements resemble the prototypes of modern rev-
olutions, they cannot be accurately measured by conventional
definitions of revolutionary social and political upheaval. The
revolution lay in a change of consciousness of society rather than
in the destruction of feudalism, territorial princes, or other institutions. Underlying many of the lasting innovations of the Reformation period is the printing press, which added a new and
revolutionary dimension to the process and method of reform.

1.   Elizabeth L. Eisenstein, "The Advent of Printing and the Problem of the
Renaissance," *Past and Present*, No. 45 (November, 1969):19. See the following
articles by Eisenstein: "The Advent of Printing in Current Historical Literature: Notes and Comments on an Elusive Transformation," *American Historical
Review* 75 (February, 1970):729; and "Some Conjectures about the Impact of
Printing on Western Society and Thought: A Preliminary Report," *Journal of
Modern History* 47 (March, 1968):1–56.
2.   Eisenstein, "The Advent of Printing and the Problem of the Renaissance,"
p. 43.

3. Johann Eberlin von Günzburg, *Sämtliche Schriften*, ed. Ludwig Enders ("Flugschriften aus der Reformationszeit," Vols. 11, 15, 18, Nos. 1–3; [Halle a. S., 1896–1902]). (Hereafter cited as Enders). For the main body of Eberlin's Utopian thought, see his tenth and eleventh pamphlets of his 1521 series: *New Statuten die Psitacus gebracht hat uss em land Wolfaria welche betraffendt reformierung geistlichens stand* (Basel, 1521). For a detailed discussion of Eberlin's Utopia see: Richard G. Cole, "Eberlin von Günzburg and the German Reformation," (Ph.D. diss., Ohio State University, 1963).

4. Enders, No. 2, 69.

5. Lewis Mumford, *Technics and Civilization* (New York, 1963), p. 136.

6. H. J. Chaytor, *From Script to Print* (Cambridge, 1945), p. 7.

7. Marshall McLuhan, *Mass Media: The Extensions of Man* (New York, 1965), p. 178.

8. Friedrich Kapp, *Geschichte des deutschen Buchhandels* (Leipzig, 1886), p. 136.

9. George Putnam, *Books and Their Makers during the Middle Ages*, 2 vols. (New York, 1896), 1: 363.

10. Richard G. Cole, "Propaganda as a Source of Reformation History," *Lutheran Quarterly* 22, No. 2 (May, 1970): 166–71.

11. *Kroniken om Graabrodrenes fordriveleslse fra deres Klostre i Danmark* (Copenhagen, 1967). My special thanks to John Christianson of the Luther College department of history for translating this document from Danish to English.

12. See W. J. Ong's provocative book *The Presence of the Word: Some Prolegomena for Cultural and Religious History* (New Haven, Conn., 1967).

13. *WA*, 13:14.

14. *LW*, 21:354.

15. Luther to Georg Spalatin (August, 1521), in Preserved Smith, *The Life and Letters of Martin Luther* (New York, 1911), p. 124.

16. *LW*, 54:274 and 311.

17. Enders, No. 2, 161.

18. Lewis W. Spitz, "Reformation Youth and Youth Today," *National Lutheran Educational Conference: Papers and Proceedings, 53rd Annual Convention* (January 15–16, 1967), pp. 15–24.

19. "Eynn Dialogus ader gesprecht zwischen einen Vatter unnd Sun dye lere Martin Luthers vnd sust andere sachen des Christenlichen glaubens belangende," trans. Carl S. Meyer in Carl S. Meyer, ed., *Luther for an Ecumenical Age* (St. Louis, 1967), pp. 82–107.

20. Ibid., p. 90.

21. Quoted in *Books and their Makers*, 1:366.

22. Erik Arup, *Danmarks Historie* (Copenhagen, 1932), 2:300. My thanks to John Christianson for bringing this to my attention.

23. Quoted in Eric W. Gritsch, "Martin Luther and the Revolutionary Tradition of the West," *Bulletin of the Lutheran Theological Seminary*, Gettysburg, Penn., 51, No. 1 (February, 1971):4.

24. *WA*, 8:680. See also Chapter three, "Luther's Attitudes on Religious Liberty," in Roland H. Bainton, *Studies on the Reformation* (Boston, 1963).

25. Philip Schaff, *History of the Christian Church* (New York, 1888), 6: 563.

26. See: Robert M. Kingdon, "Social Welfare in Calvin's Geneva," *Amer-*

ican Historical Review 76, No. 1 (February, 1971):50–69; and Richard G. Cole, "Sixteenth-Century Lutherans and Poverty," *Lutheran Standard*, 5, No. 25 (December 14 , 1965):6–7.

27.   For the text of two varient editions of the Nürnberg poor law and texts of poor laws for Kitzingen, Regensburg, and Ypern, see: Otto Winckelmann, "Die Armenordnungen von Nürnberg (1522), Kitzingen (1523), Regensburg (1523), und Ypern (1525)," *Archiv für Reformationsgeschichte*, 10–11 (1913–14):242–80, 1–17. For the original text of the first printed edition of the first Reformation poor law see: *Ain Lobliche ordnung der Fürstlichen stat Wittemberg* (Wittenberg, 1522). A copy of this edition is available in the *Flugschriftensammlung Gustav Freytag* located in the Stadt-u. Universitätsbibliothek in Frankfurt a.M. Cf. *Ordnung von des Bettels und der armen lüth wegen, In der Statt Schaffhusen, Im fünfzehenhundert und vierundzwaintzigisten Jar. angesehen* (Basel, 1524). See Paul Hohenemser, ed., *Flugschriftensammlung Gustav Freytag* (Frankfurt a. M., 1925), 3:28.

28.   In the case of one of the most famous examples of radical action in the sixteenth century, the Anabaptist takeover of Münster, many of the insurgents were newly urbanized peasants from Friesa and Holland. See: *Newe Zeytung von den Widertauffer*, 1535. Microfilm Roll 1300: Foundation for Reformation Research Archives, St. Louis, Missouri.

29.   Norman Birnbaum, "Social Structure and the German Reformation," (Ph.D. diss., Harvard University, 1957), p. 197.

30.   Winckelmann, "Die Armenordnungen," 11:9.

31.   Enders, No. 1, 183.

32.   Enders, No. 1, 124.

33.   Enders, No. 1, 173–75. Cf. *LW*, 45:169–94.

34.   Enders, No. 3, 282.

35.   Winckelmann, "Die Armenordnungen," 10:269.

36.   Compare lines 52–66 (pp. 259–61) of Nürnberg Poor Law (Text A) with paragraph No. 2 in Regensburg Poor Law. Winckelmann, "Die Armenordnungen," 10:9.

37.   Karl Vogt, *Johannes Bugenhagen Pomeranius: Leben und ausgewählte Schriften* (Elberfels, 1867), pp. 300–303.

THE GERMAN REFORMATION
AND THE PEASANTS' WAR

Hans J. Hillerbrand

Our topic seems hardly novel. It has been dealt with many times, from Johann Cochläus in the sixteenth century to Friedrich Engels in the nineteenth and Paul Althaus in the twentieth.[1] None other than Luther himself may be said to have inaugurated this lengthy (and illustrious) line of commentators, for his two famous tracts of 1525, *Ermahnung zum Frieden auf die zwölf Artikel der Bauernschaft in Schwaben* and *Wider die räuberischen und mörderischen Rotten der Bauern*, constituted the first (and biased) effort to relate the peasant uprising and his own sentiment, with his *Sendbrief von dem harten Büchlein wider die Bauern* serving as an apologetic afterthought.[2] The list of modern monographic studies is lengthy.[3] In most instances the focus is on Luther's role, with the demonstration of the consistency of his thought beckoning the scholar rather like the forbidden fruit in the Garden of Eden.

It seems to require, therefore, an uncommon measure of self-confidence on the part of any author to approach the topic once more.[4] But, as a matter of fact, a careful survey of the historiographical data shows that *our* topic, the Reformation and the Peasants' War, has not received much attention at all.[5] Virtually all studies have confined themselves to a rather myopic examination of Luther's role in the peasant uprising, with particular attention paid to his two tracts on the peasant demands. Despite the multiplicity of scholarly studies, so exhausting to the specialist, there are few analyses of the broader issue of the relationship between the Reformation and the peasant uprising in Germany. This relationship is the concern of our essay; Luther, in turn, will receive only modest attention.

There can be little doubt that the convergence of Reformation and Peasants' War opens perspectives of far-reaching import for the understanding of the religious turbulence in the early sixteenth century.[6] This is illustrated by the widely held notion that Luther's involvement in the uprising heralded a marked shift in the popular dimension of the Reformation.[7] I myself have suggested that the evident politicalization of the Reformation should be seen as the result of the Peasants' War, with the formation of political alliances as the secondary aftermath.[8]

In any case, numerous questions arise—the popular dimension of the Lutheran proclamation, the presence of notions of general reform in German society, the ideological literacy of the peasants, the impact of the uprising on the character of the Reformation and on German society. Moreover, since the German uprising was not the only instance of socioreligious restlessness in sixteenth-century Europe, comparisons may be made between the German uprising and the English Pilgrimage of Grace.[9]

The problem is broad and calls for specificity. Several questions pose themselves: Was Luther's religious concern taken over by the peasants? Was the thrust, on the part of Luther and other pamphlet writers, for a general reform of society echoed by the peasants? Were there "revolutionary" tendencies in Luther's proclamation so that it precipitated the actual disruption of law and order by the peasants?

The problem, in other words, extends far beyond the matter of the consistency of Luther's 1525 pronouncements. A whole cluster of questions exists. The intent here is to explore the possible echo of the proclamation of Luther and the other reformers in the writings of the peasants.

The outline of this essay will follow a fairly obvious pattern. We will examine, first of all, the pronouncements, both direct and indirect, of the "reformers" on various social and economic issues before 1524. In particular, we will analyze what the reformers said about the peasants, their plight, their state in society. Needless to say, we must speak, in this connection, about

Luther—though not about the Luther of 1525 and the two famous peasant treatises, but the Luther of the time *before* 1525.
Second, we will examine the peasants' grievances of 1524-25 in
order to discern the echo of the Reformation message in their
statements.

In a way, this broader theme had also been earlier expressed
in Luther's 95 theses, with his assertion of the economic implications of the sale of indulgences. Luther's questioning of the
practice of indulgences also entailed financial ramifications. Accordingly, thesis 86 noted, "Why does the pope, whose wealth
is greater than that of the wealthiest banker, not build a basilica
of Saint Peter from his own means?"[10] Although a peripheral
matter, it clearly enlarged the scope of the controversy. From
the very beginning, religion was not its only ingredient; rather,
a concern for societal issues went hand in hand with the call for
the reform of religion.

Luther himself was one of the voices. One of his tracts from
the early time of the indulgences controversy, the *Sermon von
dem Wucher*, dealt explicitly with an economic issue and included a denunciation of the suppression of "the common people."[11] His *An den christlichen Adel*, of 1520, expressed the dual
concerns of religion and society in a striking manner. It was
more than a theological tract.[12] Probably it was one of Luther's
most popular writings: more than a dozen reprints, together
with a first edition of 4,000 copies, sold within a week, attest to
this popularity. It was replete with references to the need for
reform in social and economic matters. To be sure, at the beginning of the treatise stood the forceful repudiation of what Luther called the (theological) "three walls" of the Romanists
—the notion that the spiritual authorities were superior to the
temporal ones; that only the pope was entitled to interpret
Scripture; that no one except the pope might convene a general
council.[13] The first, which stressed the importance of the laity,
was of particular theological significance since it repudiated the
time-honored distinction between clergy and laity: "Inasmuch as
we are all priests, no one may boast and attempt, without our
agreement and concurrence, to do what is in the power of everyone."[14] But even here were obvious nontheological ramifications.

The assertion of the fundamental religious equality of all men, clerical or lay, was bound to have consequences other than strictly theological ones. The stress on religious equality seemed to imply that men also were equal in other respects.

Still, in order to understand the treatise we must keep in mind that this theological introduction occupied only a modest part; the major portion was devoted to a discussion of various social and economic grievances.[15]

In his discussion of the tasks of a general council, Luther cited several social and economic ills that needed alleviation. Most of them were related to an anti-Romanism that found expression, for example, in the challenge that "every ruler, noble, and town should promptly prohibit their subjects from paying annates to Rome, indeed, should see that they are abolished."[16] The list of Luther's general concerns was a lengthy one. Luther decried begging,[17] called for university reform,[18] denounced costly apparel—"through which so much nobility and people are impoverished"[19]—pleaded for the reduction of the import of spices and the curtailment of luxury, and inveighed against the banking house of the Fuggers.[20]

Two characteristics of Luther's treatise must be noted. His enumeration of various social and political grievances confined itself to a listing and brief discussion of the issues. He did not offer solutions. Talking about usury, for example, he candidly acknowledged that the intricacies of high finance were beyond his understanding (as well as competence) and added, "I turn this matter over to the experts."[21] By the same token, he refrained from offering theological solutions for societal problems.

Secondly, Luther's tract clearly indicated whence, in his opinion, the solution for the ills of society had to come: the authorities (*Obrigkeiten*) were to undertake the various reforms. This was the very point of his "letter," which was not, after all, addressed to the people (it was not a rousing manifesto of change), but to the nobility. Still, Luther's tract indicated that he echoed the sentiment of those who called for broad and sweeping reforms of society. His *Grosser Sermon vom Wucher*, reprinted over twenty times, reiterated the theme of his earlier sermon on the same topic. Similarly, his tract *Von den guten Werken* had harsh words for the abuse and perversion of governmental authority,[22] and the tract *Von der Freiheit eines Christenmenschen* included comments that lent themselves to a broad nontheological interpretation. There was the spectacular assertion on the first page that "a Christian is a perfectly free lord of all, subject to none."[23] "We are the freest of kings," Luther wrote, "every Christian is by faith so exalted above all things that, by virtue of a spiritual power, he is Lord of all things, without exception, so that nothing can do him any harm."[24] In his tract *Von Weltlicher Obrigkeit*, of 1523, Luther devoted a section to a discussion of the proper qualities of a ruler. He was not uncritical of certain abuses, and commented on the ruler's responsibilities, among which he numbered the need for concern for his subjects.[25]

The list of Luther's pronouncements on social issues can be lengthened. He contributed a preface to the *Leisniger Kastenordnung*, which discussed the various uses, social and otherwise, of monastic property. His tract *An die Ratsherren aller Städte deutschen Landes, dass sie christliche Schulen aufrichten und halten sollen*, of 1524, contained a variety of comments about educational matters, such as the advantages of the classical languages.[26] The tract *Von Kaufhandlung und Wucher*, also of 1524, again devoted to the nagging problem of usury, contained sharp invectives against the exploitation of the common people, as against the rulers who permitted it.[27]

Such emphases were marginal in Luther's tracts in comparison with his fundamental religious and theological concerns. But they were present, and those who wanted to find nonreligious emphases in Luther's pamphlets could find the evidence without difficulty.

What shall we make of Luther's involvement? Obviously, religious concerns were primary for him. Luther meant to call his contemporaries to a deepened understanding of the gospel, being little interested in matters of practical ecclesiastical abuse or even societal reform. At the same time, he voiced a concern for the alleviation of economic and social abuses, notably in his *Sendbrief an den Christlichen Adel*. Luther was not silent on the social ramifications of the Christian faith, an emphasis to which such reformers as Calvin and Knox subsequently gave explicit expression.[28] By voicing certain social and economic concerns, Luther was sure to arouse support on the part of those who would not have been otherwise moved. It was a gesture to the gallery, and he was as much aware of it as have been subsequent historians.

Still, the enormous quantity of Luther's writings during those years reduces his relevant comments on social and economic matters to few in number and modest in emphasis. In other words, one must not use a few citations to build a stronger case than the evidence actually allows. More important than Luther's comments is the fact that he did not disapprove of those who advocated comprehensive social change. When he did voice disapproval, as in his *Vermahnung zu allen Christen sich zu hüten vor Aufruhr und Empörung* or his *Brief an die Fürsten zu Sachsen von dem aufrührischen Geist*, it was to speak on behalf of order, rather than to denounce the intermingling of religious and nonreligious concerns.[29] Even the anonymous author of *Karsthans* recognized this, for he had Luther protest in the course of the dialogue, "lieber freundt, es sol von mynet wegen niemant fechten noch todschlagen."[30] Luther's own sentiment, found in the *Vermahnung*, was that "der gemeyne man in bewegung und vordriess seiner beschedigung am gut, leyb, und seel erlitten tzu hoch versucht, und uber alle mass von jhn aufs aller untreulichst beschweret, hynfurt solchs nymmer leydenn muge noch wolle und dazu redliche ursach habe, mit pflegeln und kolben dreyn zu schlagen."[31] The notion that Luther's proclamation entailed civil disturbances was widespread: Henrich Kettenbach thought it necessary to defend Luther against the charge that his "leer macht und schafft unfryd, auffrur."[32] Still, prior to the Peasants' War there was no reason to believe that Luther was not concerned about reform in society as well as in the church, or that he did not sympathize with the aspirations and goals propounded by a loud chorus of voices.

Alongside Luther stood the large number of pamphlet-writers and reformers. Ulrich von Hutten, the *enfant terrible* of early sixteenth-century Germany, deserves the priority of place since he was the first to propound explicitly the connection between religious and social reform.[33] He was violently anti-papal and anti-Roman, and a staunch and emotional German nationalist to boot. Religion was only of peripheral interest to him. Characteristically, his denunciation of indulgences was based on economic considerations (namely, the flow of moneys from Germany to Italy) rather than theological reflections.[34] This orientation did not mean, however, that he did not write about religion. The dialogue *Monitor I* had Luther expound the true nature of the church and bewail the numerous ways in which it had become embroiled in secular affairs.[35] Hutten was especially vehement about canon law, which he wanted abolished.[36] The emperor was to attend to more important matters than the persecution of Luther, such as doing away with robbers and monopolies, restricting luxury, and improving the ancient statues.[37]

Hutten's dialogues *Vadiscus* and *Arminius* similarly propounded a variety of religious and ecclesiastical critiques of the church and offered proposals for the improvement of social, economic, and political conditions in Germany. With respect to ecclesiastical matters, however, he lacked constructive suggestions.[38] In his *Vadiscus*, Hutten informed his readers that all evil came in threes. Thus, Rome did not like to hear of three things: a general council, the reform of the ecclesiastical estate, and open German eyes. Rome abhorred three things: simplicity, moderation, and piety. Rome esteemed three things: beautiful women, stately horses, and papal bulls.[39] Three things kept Germany from knowing the truth: the laziness of its rulers, lack of learning, and the superstition of the common people.[40]

Hutten's repetitious chorus was a vehement denunciation of Rome. "Have any people been treated with more mockery and contempt by Rome than the Germans?"[41] About the fiscal policies of the curia, Hutten remarked: "I fear we Germans will not be able to tolerate this situation any longer. Their unfair demeanor with which they assault us increases daily; their fiscal demands have no end, no decency, no limit."[42]

Hutten was not a religious reformer.[43] His concerns were social and political, and his initial skepticism toward Luther illustrated this. But in the end he did associate himself with the Wittenberg professor and vigorously propounded a program that, alongside his own concerns, echoed Luther's proclamation. In actuality he may never have concurred with (or even understood) Luther's religious thought. At least on the face of things, he gave ample literary evidence that he and the Wittenberg professor were comrades-in-arms. Of this *mariage de provenance*, the title page of Hutten's *Gesprächbüchlein*, of 1521, gave evidence when it showed Luther and Hutten together, the former with Bible, the latter with sword. Accordingly, the forceful presence of such social and political reform concerns, as exemplified by Hutten's *Vadiscus*, added a significant dimension to the controversy associated with Luther's name.[44]

In Hutten's dialogue *Monitor II*, Monitor and Sickingen discused at length the need for reform in Germany. Luther was mentioned repeatedly, as were some of the standard grievances, such as the flow of German moneys abroad.

Hutten did not stand alone in voicing such sentiment. A large number of *Flugschriften* in the early 1520s echoed his notions and advocated a broad reform of society.[45] A random sampling of the materials will illustrate our contention. The tract *Onus ecclesiae* denounced the political authorities and their covetousness for larger incomes.[46] The *Dialogi septem festivi candidi* advocated the common cause of humanism and "Martinianism."[47] Another tract spoke of Hutten and Luther as "protagonists of Christian and German liberty."[48]

Other writings that ostensibly supported Luther's cause addressed themselves to various social and economic issues.[49] Hartmuth von Kronberg, a German knight, published a series of "letters" that expressed a comprehensive reform concern, one based on the principles of the newly "discovered" gospel.[50] Then there was Johann Eberlin von Günzburg, whose *15 Bundtgenossen* proved to be an immensely popular work.[51] The first of these *Bundtgenossen* was a direct appeal—"ein klägliche Klag"—to Hutten and Luther, the "two messengers of God," who were related to Reuchlin, Erasmus, Wimpfeling, and Oecolampadius.[52]

Eberlin's eminent concern was ecclesiastical reform, and he acknowledged that Luther provided the stimulus for his literary

work. Several of his *Bundtgenossen* (specifically those numbered III, IV, VII, IX, and X) dealt with issues of reform of
monasticism and the clergy. The title of number XV expressed
the widespread (among the reformers) notion that their teaching was old—and that of the Catholic church new: "To each
and every Christian a salutary warning to take heed against new
and pernicious teaching." Alongside the religious themes, social
and economic concerns also were present. Eberlin complained
about high prices. He spoke in favor of the classical languages,
pleaded for a revision of judicial procedure, economic practices, and public luxury, and wanted military pursuits altered.[53]

In two *Bundtgenossen* (X and XI) Eberlin sketched the picture of a "utopian" society, which he called "Wolfaria." (The
name was derived from "wohl fahren"—where one "fares
well.") The two titles explicitly expressed this comprehensive
concern for reform, for they referred to the "reformation of
the ecclesiastical estate" and the "description of a new order
for the secular estate." Günzburg's description indicated that he
was concerned about pointed, indeed radical, change. The number of festivals was to be reduced. Worship was to be altered
and the Sabbath rigidly kept. The specific social and economic
proposals ranged all the way from stipulations concerning the
price of bread to detailed recommendations concerning education.[54] Several of Eberlin's proposals expressed a democratic
notion for the restructuring of society.[55] Eberlin's tract *Mich
wundert, kass dein Geld im Land*, of 1523, a somewhat simpli-
cistic attempt to explain the inflationary trend of the time,
brought the exploitation by the clergy into direct relationship
with the economic state of society.[56] Eberlin denounced the greed
of the clergy and scorned the lavish church expenditures.

In addition to Eberlin, there were still other pamphlets and
pamphleteers. Jakob Strauss, minister in Eisenach, wrote two
tracts on usury, the *Haubtstuck und Artickel Christlicher leer
wider den unchristlichen wucher*, of 1523, and *Das Wucher zu
nemen und geben unserm Christlichen glauben und bruderlicher lieb . . . entgegen ist*, of 1524.[57] The former denounced as unbiblical insurrection or use of force for the realization of religious goals; but its economic pronouncements were

radical.[58] Thesis 29 was a challenge to refuse the payment of interest.[59] In Eisenach some people followed Strauss's suggestion and did not pay their debts.[60] The tract *Von der Gült*[61] had a peasant inveigh against the usury of a "rich" burgher and a priest.

The dialogue *Cunz und der Fritz*, of 1521, essentially devoted to a discussion of religious matters, noted that "he who has many benefices opposes Luther . . . but the poor folk esteem him highly."[62] The *Gesprech-Buechlin Neuw Karsthans*, written by Martin Bucer, stressed the responsibility of the political authorities for a "truly evangelical reformation," scored the impoverization of the common people, and affirmed the unwillingness to accept ministers who did not teach evangelical doctrine and did not live pious lives.[63] The peasant Karsthans implored his friend Franz—the reference obviously was to Franz von Sickingen—to put himself at the head of a reform movement. Actually, not much was said about specific details, and, indeed, the main thrust of the *Buechlin* was religious; Karsthans announced that "after I return home, I shall buy all the Lutheran books."[64] The very fact, however, that the ebullient Sickingen was seen as the leader of a movement of reform clearly indicated the convergence of religious and general reform concerns.

Balthasar Stanberger, the author of the tract *Dialogus Zwischen Petro und eynem Bawren*, of 1523, explicitly dealt with economic issues. Thus, he charged that "the pope's teaching is concerned about the money and blood of the poor."[65] His solution was simple: "[T]he peasants should gather, convene a peasants' council . . . if the people rule, the clerics will not be in a good position. . . . The peasant must judge the matter, give the priests a beating; then will he be able to bring up his children."[66] Heinrich von Kettenbach, a friend of Eberlin von Günzburg, concluded one of his tracts with an "appeal to the German nobility": "Let this my grievance touch your heart."[67] The call for reform of German society, both church and state, was related to the scourge of the Turks.[68] The cities in particular were to do their share to save German society.

Hans Sachs, the Nürnberg meistersinger, in addition to contributing tracts explicitly Lutheran, wrote his *Dialogue Con-*

cerning Greed in 1524, in which once again the new faith and certain economic principles were brought together. The opposition was against the wealthy businessman—and the Lutheran burgher expressed the hope that the preaching of Christian truth would bring about a change.[69]

The Zurich reformer Ulrich Zwingli propounded his program of ecclesiastical change within the setting of political and social concerns, seeing theological and political-social reform as intimately interwoven.[70] He dealt with problems of poverty and inveighed against the rich, whom he warned, "What with angry demands you have taken from the poor must angrily be taken from you."[71]

Last, but not least, a comment must be made about Thomas Müntzer, who enjoys the dubious honor of being widely credited as the signal cause of the peasant uprising in central Germany.[72] Although this involvement is not so ironclad as the scholarly consensus would suggest, the fact remains that Müntzer did connect economic and religious suppression.[73] Even as in Luther, the assessment of Müntzer's place in the course of events must be based upon his writings published *before* the uprising in central Germany. His fiery pronouncements during the Thuringian rebellion are significant (and worthy of their own investigation), but of little import when it comes to establishing connections between his thought and the ideology of the peasants.

It is not beside the point to recall that Müntzer was, ever since August, 1524, a victim of the "establishment." His expulsion from Allstedt at that time clearly indicated a division within the ranks of the reformers, even as Luther, in contrast to his silence with respect to the pamphlet literature, had clearly indicated his views of the "archdevil of Allstedt." Luther's *Brief an die Fürsten von Sachsen von dem aufrührischen Geist* also indicated where he saw the difference—Müntzer's proclamation of insurrection. At the same time, even Luther's treatise did not address itself to the incisive characteristic of the pamphlets, namely, the convergence of religion and social concern. That issue, in other words, was left open.

About Müntzer's pre-1525 pronouncements it must be said

that they did not exactly abound in references to social and economic needs. If anything, such references are rare.[74] If Müntzer's 1524 pronouncements thus said less about specific social or economic ills than did the pamphlet literature—and even less, as a matter of fact, than did Luther—it is clear that his writings contained the same juxtaposition of religion and socioeconomic considerations as did the pamphlets.[75] His *Ausgedrückte Entblössung*, of the fall of 1524, spent most of its space talking about "true faith."[76] But it also talked about the "armen, elenden pauren,"[77] about the "grossen Hansen" whom God rejects,[78] though his point was to bewail the *religious* (rather than economic) plight of the common people, notably of the peasants, who had been woefully misled by the "scribes."[79] In Müntzer's last tract, the *Hochverursachte Schutzrede,* the theme is the same, but the expression slightly different. Müntzer chided Luther for his disregard of the common people with his characteristic notion, "I warn you, the peasants might take a stand against you."[80]

Our survey has sampled only a slight portion of the evidence that is, in actual fact, far more extensive. We ought to establish that there existed a stream of pamphlet writings between 1518 and 1524 addressed to the questions of reform and whose task was conceived in a broader context than merely that of ecclesiastical or theological change.[81] In so doing, some writers connected earlier calls for reform—one thinks of the German *gravamina*, which were discussed at the Diet of Augsburg in 1518 and again at the Diet of Worms in 1521—with the proclamation of Martin Luther. This was done initially (and most spectacularly) by Ulrich von Hutten, and subsequently by others as well.

What conclusions can be drawn from the evidence? In one respect our observations have surely belabored the obvious. The existence of the prolific pamphlet literature, with its vague though ubiquitous Lutheran ring, is well established in Reformation scholarship and hardly needs additional verification. But four additional observations may be made. The first of these has to do with the character of this literature. Whatever the

extent of religious content in the pamphlets (or, for that matter, the extent of authentic Lutheran notions), it is clear that
religion and politics were *both* present. Reform of the church
(and of theology) was seen as inseparable from notions of reform of society. Neither was particularly specific, and they
amounted more to vague propositions than to a specific program.
Luther's theology, for one, was portrayed only in simplified and
fragmentary form. The centrality of the Word of God was
stressed and work-righteousness rejected. There also was a vehement anticlericalism. But that was all.

The "Lutheran" propensity of these tracts was thus a far cry
from a full and sophisticated representation of the reformer's
thought, though in making this statement we need to keep in
mind that not all of Luther's writings necessary for such a representation were easily accessible at the time. Important theological notions were only found in his (unpublished) academic
lectures, and others were in Latin and thus hardly widely known.
Most accessible were those in German, and they had a way of expressing their "Lutheran" stance only vaguely. In other words,
the pamphlets conveyed in this setting an authentic, if partial,
understanding of Luther. After all, at the time the "Lutheran"
movement lacked any confessional cohesiveness. A multitude of
local preachers and partisans of Luther's cause offered their own
versions of the new evangel, so that even Luther's tracts were
also read *sub specie* to the local proponents. No normative proclamation existed.[82]

Second, it was characteristic of many pamphlets that what had
been marginal emphases in Luther's own writings became central concerns. Luther's essential openness toward the social and
political issues of his day was modified so that these issues assumed a definite priority over those pertaining to religion. Questions of societal reform, of judicial change, or of economic equity
became important. One must not posit discontinuity between
Luther's pronouncements and those of the pamphlet-writers, especially since Luther himself never protested against the intriguing variants of his own teaching propounded by the *Flugschriften*. But there was a difference of emphasis that could not but
create uncertainly and misunderstanding as to the real meaning of the "Martinian" movement.

There can also be little doubt that there seemed to be (or actually was) an anti-intellectual impulse in the pamphlets. Although their concerns and emphases varied in a thousand different ways, they did share the notion that the status quo was unsatisfactory. With this premise it was not difficult to indict the intellectual establishment as well. The common denominator was the insistence on a dramatic reversal of values. The learned and powerful had failed to understand the authentic meaning of the gospel; it was given to the simple to understand it. The theologians and doctors did not know the true faith; it was the simple "artisan" and "peasant" who had grasped the authentic meaning. In the tract *Karsthans*, a peasant was called upon to decide the theological disagreement between Luther and his Catholic opponent Murner—and (not surprisingly) opted for the former.[83] In the tract the term *einfältig lai*—simple layman—occurs several times[84] and it is meant as a word of commendation rather than derision.

A third point is related to the fundamental premise of reform. How was it to be accomplished? Luther had addressed his major "political tract" to the German nobility. In a similar fashion, his treatise on the establishment of schools was addressed to the councils of the German cities. Clearly, he appealed to those in authority.[85] The authors of the pamphlets, on the other hand, did not so restrict themselves. Indeed, they singled out the "common man" as the embodiment of their concerns. And in so doing, they echoed in an intriguing way a theme found in Luther's writings. Luther himself had propounded egalitarian notions when he argued that the comprehension of the gospel was not to be confined to the few, but was open to the simple as well. He had virtually posited a dichotomy between the ignorance of the learned and the learnedness of the ignorant. "Whoever comes from baptism can boast to have been consecrated priest, bishop, and pope already."[86] The very title of his *Auslegung des Vaterunsers* "für die einfältigen Laien" is a case in point. The "peasant" was depicted as the paradigm of the authentic understanding of the gospel.[87] There was a glorification of the illiterate man whose very simplicity seemed to assure the authenticity of his faith. The pamphlets discussed the multitude of socioeconomic questions, always from the perspective of the common man, and even the peasant. "The poor people must pay for all this," observed the author of the *Neuw Karsthans*.[88] In the *Gesprächbüchlein von einem Bauern, Belial, Erasmo Rotterodam und Doctor Johann Faber*, of 1524, a peasant discussed learnedly religious matters with the famous personages and concluded with "Ade, ein kue bescheis dich!"[89] The *Beclagung aines leyens*[90] spoke of "wir armen hautwercksleüt oder Gauleüt.

A fourth characteristic of the pamphlet literature was its specific concern for the plight of the peasant. One must be careful here not to take a few isolated passages and consider them typical of the pamphlets as a whole. If anything, the citations show less the explicit connections between the Lutheran proclamation and the plight of the peasant (which they seem to make) than the *possibility* of such a connection.

We may note a few references. Thus, the tract *Der Curtisan und Pfründenfresser* observed that "und schint die bauern ganz und gar / das in bleibt weder haut noch har"; and the tract *Neu Karsthans* wrote, "Dass blut und schrein der armen lüt / so üppiglich werd verzert."[92]

The tract *Ein kurzer Begriff von Hans Knüchel*[93] had the congregation replace its absentee priest by one of their own number, and the tract *Die Göttliche Mühle*, of 1521, included a title-woodcut that depicted Luther confronting the pope—with a peasant twirling a threshing stick in the pope's direction.[94] That, of course, was ominous.

Having thus established the "spirit" of the pamphlet literature, we need to turn to the second major focus of this paper: What were the concomitant characteristics of the peasant pronouncements? What were the abuses and grievances enunciated and enumerated by the peasants? More specifically, were there any echoes of the pamphlets in the peasant statements? The answer to these questions directs us to the relationship between Reformation and peasant uprising.

We can begin with a fairly obvious statement. The overwhelming bulk of the peasant pronouncements dealt with economic and social issues. If we take one peasant document at random—and as a case in point—we find that this particular grievance had to do with such matters as the free use of fowl and water; the free right to arms and crossbows; freedom from spreading manure for their lords; freedom from taxes and other obligations, except those imposed by law; freedom from property confiscation in case of suicide; inheritance by relatives rather than the lords; free pouring of wine in one's own house.[95] If the peasant grievances generally tend to be seen in a different light, then that is not because the dominance of economic and social concerns is not clearly established, but rather because of the religious ornamentation provided by the most famous peasant document, the Twelve Articles.[96]

Reading the Twelve Articles in a superficial way, one might suspect that they were the product of Luther's pen. There were several dozen scriptural references in the margin of the document; there was the explicit acknowledgment, in the introduction, that the uprising of the peasants was charged against the new teaching; there was the stress of the first Article that ministers should be appointed by the congregation; there was, finally, the sentiment of the Twelfth Article, "if any one or more of these articles should not be in agreement with the Word of God, which we do not believe, we will willingly recede from such article when it is proved to be against the Word of God by a clear explanation of Scripture."[97] These were words and phrases right out of the Lutheran vocabulary—and it is not surprising that Luther felt intimately involved by the document and ventured forth with his famous, if infamous, response.[98]

The real sentiment of the Twelve Articles is another matter. The ten complaints (omitting the first and the last already cited above) pertained to such topics as tithing, serfdom, woodcutting, use of the waters, new laws, and communal pastures. Luther had never commented on them in the way the Twelve Articles suggested; indeed, one would even be hard put to find extensive references to them in the pamphlet literature.[99] It was primarily the scriptural ornamentation of the Twelve Articles that seemed to demonstrate a "Lutheran" propensity and thereby implicate the Lutheran movement.

But what about the other peasant documents? They were voluminous, filling several volumes, though we need to keep in mind that none of them actually saw the printer's ink. They were all handwritten grievances, restricted to the local situation and its peculiarities. They complained, rather than reflected.[100] Still, the question is whether the atmosphere conveyed by the Twelve Articles finds its duplication in the peasant documents.

The answer seems to be in the affirmative. No doubt, the slogans of the Reformation—or, better, those of the pamphlets— had seemingly found an echo among some of those who purported to speak for the peasants. Religious slogans and ornamentation are unmistakably present. Specifically, three types of statements may be distinguished. There were, first of all, religious references or terminology. These were either general in tone, or Lutheran. Thus, the peasants at Bildhausen affirmed "das ewangelium und wort gotts und die gerechtickait zu hanthaben und etlich beschwernus armer leut abthun nach christlicher ordnung."[101]

Second, there were statements that combined economic or social grievances with a religious principle.[102]

A third type of statement was characterized by its explicit reference to the new (Lutheran) teaching in order to justify the same juxtaposition of religious and secular concerns.[105]

The most significant expression of such sentiment probably was the emphasis on the right of the congregation to appoint (and dismiss) its minister—if this may be called a "secular" concern. To be sure, it was hardly a fundamental Lutheran notion, though it had been voiced by Luther in 1523 in his tract entitled *Dass eine christliche Versammlung oder Gemeine Recht und Macht habe, alle Lehren zu urteilen und Lehrer zu berufen*, of 1523[106] and so must be considered part of Luther's proclamation. Michael Gaismair's "Landesordnung" also must be mentioned, for "the gospel constitutes its firm frame of reference."[107]

Two general observations may be made at this point. Basically, we have to keep in mind the paucity of statements in all three categories, but especially in the second and third. These, in turn, would be of incisive importance for establishing a causality between Reformation and Peasants' War. The new teaching was indeed cited by the peasants, but by no means frequently, intensely, or with determination. The actual number of citations is astoundingly small, as our table demonstrates.[108] Other than the Twelve Articles, with their explicit invocation of the "new teaching," (and those peasant documents obviously copying them), the incidence of juxtaposition of religion and secular grievances is virtually nonexistent. On the other hand, in no instance did the peasants invoke the old religion in support of their program and goals.

Second, we must mention the geographic distribution of what we may call "Reformation" sentiment among the peasants. Clearly, such sentiment was restricted to certain locales. It clustered especially in South Germany—Baltringen, Meran, Salzburg. Here the imitative effect of the Twelve Articles must be noted, even as it is necessary to keep in mind that with respect to Salzburg, for example, it was an ecclesiastical territory so that denunciations of ecclesiastical shortcomings were virtually automatic.

A summary of peasant grievances may be made as follows (see Appendix for detailed tabulation):

Total number of grievance documents examined	90
Total number of grievances	1,510
Total grievances dealing with religion (or having religious terminology)	73
Total grievances dealing with relations between church and society	53
Grievance documents without religious material	29
Grievance documents with multiple religious material	16
Grievance documents with religious material	61
Specific grievances:	
Free preaching of the Word of God	27
Free appointment of minister	33
Repudiation of serfdom	9
Religious terminology	9

Before attempting an assessment of the evidence garnered, we must note that the charge of disruption of law and order was raised by Catholic protagonists against the Lutheran move-

ment well before 1524. There may have been two reasons for
this: the generally unsettling implications of the Lutheran proclamation and the actual disturbances that occurred at a few
places, where images were forcibly destroyed or Catholic shrines
were dismantled. The significance of these Catholic charges—
whether authentic or not—can hardly be overestimated; it indicates that the identification of Luther as the cause of insurrection existed well before the peasants ever took to arms. Accordingly, an explanation for the "cause" of the peasant uprising
was available when the storm broke loose. The introduction to
the Twelve Articles took note of this when it spoke of "the
many Antichrists who on account of the assembling of the peasants cast scorn upon the gospel, and say: is this the fruit of the
new teaching?"[109]

Jacob Fugger observed that "the new preachers proclaim that
one should not observe man-made commandments."[110] In a
similar fashion, Elector Joachim of Brandenburg accused the
Erfurt city council of tolerating ministers who perverted the gospel and preached insurrection.[111] Such was also the attitude of
Ferdinand, who noted, as early as August, 1524—when the uprising was still confined to the Black Forest area—that the "Lutheran sect" was the cause.[112] Other evidence for such immediate Catholic denunciation of the Lutheran movement as the
cause of the uprising is not hard to come by. A prominent spokesman for such sentiment was Duke George of Saxony, who never
tired of reiterating it.[113]

That the identification of the Lutheran movement with civil
disturbance antedated the actual outbreak of the uprising obviously limits its value. At the same time, there is some evidence,
albeit indirect, for the connection between the Lutheran proclamation and the agitation of the peasants.[114] Zurich was quite
willing to relate certain turbulence in Waldshut to the new
teaching.[115] Moreover, ministers were variously identified as agitators. (How modern!) Although their religious propensity
must by no means be automatically labeled Lutheran, it does
stand to reason that this is what they were (or at least took
themselves to be; there was a difference). In the Alsace it was
reported that a Lutheran preacher "ist gewichen, und hat etlich
Pauern . . . mit werhafter Hand nahend bey Bass zu zie-

hen."[116] A chaplain in the town of Sangershausen reportedly preached the doctrine of Luther "so das die pfarrekirchen gar verwüstet werden, durch wilche seine predigte das volk zu ungehorsam gereitzet und aufruhr dienende."[117] The minister of Dipperz in Hesse was executed for his involvement in the uprising.[118]

What, then, are our conclusions?

Above all, there can be little doubt that the famous Twelve Articles convey an utterly erroneous picture of the relationship between the Reformation and the peasant uprising. The bulk of the peasant documents does not echo the sentiment of that document. The majority of the grievances are concretely economic or social. If our own tabulation is fairly representative, roughly one-third of the grievances contain no religious complaint (or religious terminology involving secular complaints) whatsoever. One may put the situation even more dramatically: of a total of 1,510 specific grievances in 90 statements, only 73 (or less than five percent) have to do with religion or exhibit religious terminology.

These figures should, moreover, be interpreted in light of the fact that some of these grievances appeared *after* the publication of the Twelve Articles and thus may merely be taken as their plagiarized echo. Of course, the matter is touchy, for such plagiarism (though indicating a lack of creativity) does not obviate identity of sentiment—and that is what counts! In any case, statements with a distinctly Lutheran or religious ring are rare. But they do exist, and, whether perceptive appropriations or thoughtless plagiarism, they indicate that a connection could be made, at times rather glibly (and thoughtlessly): at Rothenburg intricate grievances pertaining to the baking of bread were boldly related to the teaching of the gospel.[119]

The connection between the Lutheran proclamation and the peasants' grievances was possible. Undoubtedly, there was an awareness of this connection on the part of all astute observers, even beyond, one suspects, what in actual fact appears in the sources. The Lutheran agitation, especially as found in the pamphlet literature, had created a climate of general anticipation of reform which encompassed the peasants.

This takes us to what may well have been the incisive factor in the entire situation. German society had been made restless and turbulent through Luther's proclamation. It would have been surprising if the peasants had not been affected by this turbulence, and this all the more so in view of the long tradition of restlessness that was theirs.

Historians have long recognized that the Reformation constituted only one of several causes of the Peasants' War. The findings of this essay would confirm this and underscore, moreover, the limited impact of Reformation ideas upon the peasants. They would suggest, above all, that we should view the Reformation not so much as a cause—not even one of several —but as the catalyst of the war.

1. See Johann Cochläus, *Historia Martini Lutheri* (Ingolstadt, 1582); Fr. Engels, *The Peasant War in Germany* (English translation, New York, 1926); P. Althaus, *Luthers Haltung im Bauernkrieg* (Tübingen, 1952).

2. Luther's tracts are found in *WA*, 18: 291–334, 357–61.

3. I note, of the most recent ones, H. Mackensen, "Historical Interpretation and Luther's Role in the Peasant Revolt," *Concordia Theological Monthly* 35 (1964); M. Greschat, "Luthers Haltung im Bauernkrieg," *ARG* 56 (1965): 31–47, and H. Lehmann, "Luther und der Bauernkrieg," *Geschichte in Wissenschaft u. Unterricht* 20 (1969):126 ff. The task of the Marxist interpreter of the Reformation is to show the existence of socioeconomic class struggle in the early sixteenth century and then demonstrate that the protagonists of the Reformation were identical with the progressive class, bourgeoisie or early bourgeoisie. The disagreements among Marxist historians (Cajkovskaja, Smirin, Macek) indicate that no definitive Marxist interpretation has, as yet, been offered.

4. For a general introduction to the problems of the peasants' uprising, see K. Sessions, ed., *Reformation and Authority: The Meaning of the Peasants' Revolt* (New York, 1968); still useful is the older work by J. S. Shapiro, *Social Reform and the Reformation* (New York, 1909). G. Franz, *Der deutsche Bauernkrieg* (Munich, 1935) remains the basic monograph. His distinction between "old law" and "divine righteousness" as the two categories informing the peasant grievances has been widely accepted. A Marxist demurrer is offered by G. Günther, " 'Altes Recht" und 'Göttliche Gerechtigkeit,' " *Wissensch, Zeitschrift d. Karl-Marx Universität, Gesellsch.-und Sprachw. Reihe.* 14 (1965):427 ff. Of the Marxist contributions I mention M. M. Smirin, *Die Volksreformation des Thomas Münzer und der grosse Bauernkrieg* (Berlin, 1952) and M. Steinmetz, "Über den Charakter der Reformation und des Bauernkrieges in Deutschland," *Wissensch. Zeitschrift d. Karl-Marx Universität, Gesellsch.-und Sprachw. Reihe* 14 (1965):389 ff., both very valuable.

5. E. Fabian, *Die Entstehung des Schmalkaldischen Bundes und seiner Verfassung* (Tübingen, 1962), has rightly called attention to the doubtful accuracy of the term "peasants" war in that a great deal of the uprising occurred, in actual fact, in cities. With his demurrer in mind, we will employ the term "peasant" occasionally in the relatively broad sense of encompassing the artisans as well.

6. There are perceptive comments in H. J. Grimm, "Social Forces in the German Reformation," *Church History* 31 (1962):3–13.

7. For a recent restatement of this notion, together with the ascription of the label "Fürstenreformation" for the period after 1525, see E. Iserloh, *Reformation, Katholische Reform und Gegenreformation* (Freiburg, 1967), p. 145. This "most persistent of Luther legends" was repudiated by F. Lau: "Der Bauernkrieg und das angebliche Ende der lutherischen Reformation als spontaner Volksbewegung" (*Luther-Jahrbuch* 26 [1959]):109–34. Although this essay precludes a consideration of this issue, the following (random) citations show that this "legend" was taken as authentic as early as 1525: F. Gess, ed., *Akten und Briefe zur Kirchenpolitik Herzog Georgs von Sachsen* (Leipzig 1905–17), 2:405, "dor durch her [scil. Luther] och in abgunst des armen gmenen folks gfaln"; W. P. Fuchs, ed., *Akten zur Geschichte des Bauernkrieges in Mitteldeutschland* (Berlin, 1923–42), 2:437, "Doctor Martinus ist pei dem gemeinen volk und auch pei gelarten und ungelarten in grossen abfall."

8. Hans J. Hillerbrand, *Landgrave Philipp of Hesse: Religion and Politics in the Reformation* (St. Louis, 1968).

9. In effect, this essay seeks to do for the German scene what the article by A. G. Dickens does for England: "Secular and Religious Motivation in the Pilgrimage of Grace," *Studies in Church History* 4 (Leiden, 1967):39–64.

10. *WA*, 1:237.

11. Ibid., 6:7: "Hei wirt das gemeyn volck heymlich aussgezogen und schwerlich unterdrugkt."

12. The text is in ibid., pp. 404 ff.

13. Ibid., pp. 407–15.

14. Ibid., p. 408.

15. Luther followed notions of Ulrich von Hutten in long stretches: for a list of parallels see W. Köhler, *Die Quellen zu Luthers Schrift An den christlichen Adel deutscher Nation* (Halle, 1895), pp. 309 ff. P. Held, *Ulrich von Hutten: Seine religiös-geistige Auseinandersetzung mit Katholizismus, Humanismus, Reformation* (Leipzig, 1928), pp. 132 ff., acknowledged Luther's "literarische Anregung durch Hutten" and saw the relationship characterized by Luther's utilization of Hutten's argumentation: "Damit gewann Huttens Schrift zwar keinen wesentlichen Einfluss auf Luthers eigene geistige Entwicklung, wohl aber auf den Fortgang der Reformation."

16. *WA*, 6:427: "das ein yclicher Furst, Adel und Stat, in yhrem unterthanen frisch an vorpiet, die Annaten genn Rom zu geben, und sie gar abthue."

17. Ibid., p. 450.

18. Ibid., p. 457.

19. Ibid., p. 465.

20. Ibid., p. 466.

21. Ibid., pp. 3–8, 36–60.

22. Ibid., 7:21.

23. Note, for example, ibid., 6:29: "seyn gantz knecht wordenn der aller untüchtigsten leuth auff erden."

24. Ibid., 11:245 ff.

25. Ibid., 15:36: "Ich weiss leider whol, dass wir Deutschen müssen immer Bestien und tolle Tier sein und bleiben, wie uns denn die umliegenden Länder nennen und wir auch wohl verdienen. Mich wundert aber, warum wir nicht auch einmal sagen: Was sollen uns Seide, Wein, Würze, und die fremde aus

läncische Ware, so wir doch selbst Wein, Korn, Wolle, Flachs, Holz und Steine in deutschen Lande nicht allein die Füller haben zur Nahrung, sondern auch die Kur und Wahl zu Ehren und Schmuch?"

26. Ibid., 15:313: "Könige und Fürsten sollten hier dreinsehen und nach gestrengem Recht solches Wehren. Aber ich höre, sie haben Kopf und Teil darab, und geht nach dem Spruch Jessaiä 1, 23: 'Deine Fürsten sind der Diebe Gesellen worden.' Dieweil lassen sie die Diebe hängen, die einen Gulden oder einn halben gestohlen haben, und hantieren mit denen, die alle Welt berauben. . . . Was wird aber zuletzt Gott dazu sagen? Er wird tun, die er durch Hesekiel spricht, Fürsten und Kaufleute, einen Dieb mit dem andern ineinander schmelzen wie Blei und Erz, . . . dass weder Fürsten noch Kaufleute mehr seien, wie ich besorege, dass es schon vor der Tür sei."

27. Ibid., 15:293–322.

28. The social and political concerns of John Knox are noted in the recent biography by P. Janton, *John Knox (ca. 1513–1572), L'Homme et l'oeuvre* (Clermont-Ferrand, 1967).

29. *WA*, 15:220–21.

30. O. Clemen, *Flugschriften aus den ersten Jahren der Reformation.* 4 vols. (Leipzig, 1907–11), 4:95; Luther, in turn, recognized the sentiment of that tract—and rejected it, *WA*, 8:676.

31. *WA*, 8:679.

32. O. Clemen, *Flugschriften*, 2:189.

33. On Hutten, see H. Holborn, *Ulrich von Hutten and the German Reformation* (New York, 1964), and G. Ritter, "Ulrich von Hutten und die Reformation," *Die Weltwirkung der Reformation* (Munich, 1959).

34. Ulrich von Hutten, *Opera Omnia*, ed. E. Böcking (Leipzig, 1859), 4:99: "Da meinen diese elend betrogenen Weiblein, keine Sünde zu tun, wenn sie ihre Männer plündern, ihre Kinder verkürzen und das Haus leeren, um jenen Possenkrämern zu geben. Wo doch in Wahrheit das recht Frömmigkeit und Barmherzigkeit wäre, die von den Predigern verkündet werden sollte, die weibliche Keuschheit rein zu bewahren, die Kinder fromm und rechtschaffen zu erziehen, die eheliche Treue zu halten."

35. Ibid., 4:339.

36. Ibid., p. 343.

37. Ibid., p. 358.

38. L. W. Spitz, *The Religious Renaissance of the German Humanists* (Cambridge, Mass., 1963), p. 120.

39. *Opera Omnia*, 4:178 ff.

40. Ibid., p. 220.

41. *Gesprächbüchlein* (Dresden, 1905), p. 81.

42. Ibid., pp. 79 ff.

43. See here the evaluation of L. W. Spitz, *Religious Renaissance*, p. 128.

44. See here P. Held, *Ulrich von Hutten* p. 146: "Er kann auch nicht das religiöse Problem sehen, ohne zugleich dessen sittliche Folgerungen und politische Auswirkungen aufzugreifen."

45. The *Flugschriften* are listed in A. Kuczynski, *Thesaurus Libellorum Historiam Reformationis illustrantium* (reprinted, Leipzig, 1960). Reprints of some are found in O. Schade, ed., *Satiren und Pasquille aus der Reformationszeit.* 3 vols. (repr. Hildesheim, 1966), and O. Clemen, *Flugschriften*.

46. See H. Herner, "Die Flugschrift "Onus ecclesiae" (1519)" (dissertation, Giessen, 1901), pp. 30 ff.

47. See A. E. Berger, *Die Sturmtruppen der Reformation* (Leipzig, 1931), p. 28.

48. Quoted in M. Gravier, *Luther et l'Opinion Publique* (Paris, 1942), p. 239.

49. A. E. Berger, *Die Sturmtruppen*, p. 37.

50. E. Kuck, ed., *Die Schriften Hartmuths von Cronberg* (Halle, 1859), pp. 154 f.; see also W. Bogler, *Hartmuth von Kronberg* (Halle, 1897), p. 21, who finds "ein kräftiger sozialer Zug" typical of Kronberg.

51. On Eberlin, see the literature cited in K. Schottenloher, ed., *Bibliographie zur deutschen Geschichte im Zeitalter der Glaubensspaltung* 7 vols. (Stuttgart, 1966), 7:65.

52. A. E. Berger, *Die Sturmtruppen*, p. 127; see also ibid., p. 131: "hie zwischen lasen wir, was Hut und Luther geschrieben haben oder schrieben werden, jn hoffnung, es soll bald der romanisten ärger list also an tag kummen."

53. Ibid., pp. 134, 145 f.

54. Ibid., p. 155: "So vyl brot soll man umb ein helblin geben, als vil ein starck man vff ein imbiss mag essen"; also, p. 157: "Alle kind, magdlin und knablin, soll man im dritten jar irs alters zu schul thun, biss sie archt jar alt werden. . . . Kein oberhand soll gewalt haben etwas zu thun on hylff und rat deren, so vom hauffen der underthan darzu gesatz oder geordnet sind."

55. Some actually recurred in 1525 in the *Twelve Articles of the Peasants*, of 1525, but Eberlin denied any connection with the rebellious peasants. Ibid., p. 54.

56. Ibid., p. 261: "Got und alle seine heiligen send betler worden und tragen all unser gut, ehr, leib und leben nit allein auss dem land, sonder auch auss diesser werlt."

57. On Strauss, see J. Rogge, *Der Beitrag des Predigers Jakob Strauss zur frühen Reformationsgeschichte* (Berlin, 1957). The quotations in the next two footnotes are from the appendix (unpaginated) of this book.

58. Thesis 34: "Der gewalt dir uffgeladen wider Gottes wort besteet nit lang, musz mit den ersten Tyrannen wider Christum mit dem geist seines munds erlegt werden"; thesis 40: "Du hast dich Gott gelobt und seinem wort mag kein verschreibung diner eltern oder von dir beschehen, den wucher zu bezalen, dich bezwingen."

59. "Sol er umb kein gebott noch gewalt den wucher bezalen."

60. See J. Rogge, *Jacob Strauss*, p . 74.

61. O. Schade, *Satiren und Pasquille*, 2:73 ff.

62. A. E. Berger, *Die Sturmtruppen*, p. 55.

63. A good introduction to the tract is found in A. Goetze, "Martin Butzers Erstlingsschrift," *ARG*, 4 (1906):1–64.

64. O. Schade, *Satiren und Pasquille*, 2:16.

65. Ibid., p. 209.

66. Ibid., p. 214.

67. O. Clemen, *Flugschriften*, 2:146: "Sehet an, wi ir an ewern gutern syt verarmet und verdorben. . . . Wann ewer einer wil etwas verkeuffen oder versetzen, so lauffent jr seltenn zu einem weltlichen hern oder Edelman, sunder zu den Stifften, clöstern, Apteyen."

68. Ibid., p. 226.

69. A. v. Keller, *Hans Sachs* 6 vols. (Tübingen, 1870), 5:63 ff.

70. This is instructively shown by S. Rother, *Die religiösen und geistigen Grundlagen der Politik Zwinglis* (Erlangen, 1956), and by E. Wolf, "Die Sozialtheologie Zwinglis," *Festschrift Guido Kisch* (Stuttgart, 1955), pp. 167–88.

71. See A. Rich, "Zwinglie als sozialpolitischer Denker," *Zwingliana*, 13 (1969):67–89, with the extensive literature and sources cited.

72. Good introductions to Müntzer are the two historiographical surveys, by A. Friesen, "Thomas Müntzer in Marxist Thought," *Church History*, 34 (1965):306 ff., and J. M. Stayer, "Thomas Müntzer's Theology and Revolution in Recent Non-Marxist Interpretation," *MQR*, 43 (1969):142 ff. The comment of M. Steinmetz, "Das Ebe Thomas Müntzers," *Zeitschr. F. Geschw.*, 17 (1969); 1118, "Müntzer [hat] alle damaligen Möglichkeiten des revolutionären Kampfes um eine Neugestaltung . . . voll ausgeschöpft," may be said to epitomize Marxist historiography.

73. Note, for example, his early comment, Günther Franz, ed., *Thomas Müntzer, Schriften und Briefe* ("Quellen und Forschungen zur Reformationsgeschichte," Gütersloh, 1968); p. 27: "Die grundtsuppe des wuchers, der dieberey und rauberey sein unser herrn und fürsten."

74. Scholars have recognized this paucity by suggesting a dramatic development on Müntzer's part, extending from early 1524 to early 1525; see C. Hinrichs, *Luther und Müntzer* (Berlin, 1952).

75. I take it as indirect confirmation of this point that a South German list of possible arbiters, which includes Luther, Melanchthon, and Jacob Strauss, does not mention Müntzer: G. Franz, ed., *Quellen zur Geschichte des Bauernkrieges* (Munich, 1963), p. 150.

76. For example, *Thomas Müntzer, Schriften und Briefe*, p. 287: "das die recht, theüre weyssheyt Gottes, der recht christenglaub, verunehret und geschmecht ist worden."

77. Ibid., p. 294.

78. Ibid., p. 299.

79. This is Müntzer's explicit comment; ibid., p. 294.

80. Ibid., p. 337.

81. K. Schottenloher, *Der Münchener Buchdrucker Hans Schobser* (Munich, 1925) finds "revolutionary" tendencies in just about every pamphlet.

82. See the pertinent comments of O. Seitz, *Die Theologie des Urbanus Rhegius* (Gotha, 1898), p. 27.

83. O. Clemen, *Flugschriften* 4:110: "Luther, meins bedunken, tausentmal geschickter ist in gemeinem natürlichen verstand von der geschrifft zureden dann der Murner."

84. Ibid., pp. 95, 98.

85. See, for example, Luther's comments in *WA*, 2:178, on the removal of abuses with respect to processions.

86. Ibid., 6:408.

87. See P. Böckmann, "Der gemeine Mann in den Flugschriften der Reformation," *Deutsche Viertelj. f. Literaturwiss. u. Geistesgesch.*, 22 (1944), esp. 195 ff., and K. Uhrig, "Der Bauer in der Publizistik der Reformation," *ARG*, 33 (1936): 70 ff., 165 ff.

88. O. Schade, *Satiren und Pasquille*, 1:8.

89. O. Clemen, *Flugschriften*, 1:334.

90. Ibid., 1:351.

91. O. Schade, *Satiren und Pasquille*, 1:8.

92. Ibid., 2:9.

93. O. Clemen, *Flugschriften*, 1:227 f.

94. O. Schade, *Satiren und Pasquille*, 1:19.

95. The "Artikel der Bauern auf dem Schwarzwald," G. Franz, ed., *Quellen*, pp. 96 f.

96. The full text is found in G. Franz, *Der deutsche Bauernkrieg*, pp. 174–79.

97. As quoted in H. J. Hillerbrand, *The Protestant Reformation* (New York, 1968), p. 64.

98. Luther had been cited by the South German peasants as arbiter in the dispute: see G. Franz, *Der deutsche Bauernkrieg*, p. 151.

99. The exception pertains to the reference to tithing, where Zwingli's position was a bit more "innovative."

100. See the appropriate comment of A. Waas, *Die Bauern im Kampf um Gerechtigkeit 1300–1525* (Munich, 1964), p. 7: "Die meisten dieser Beschwerden bleiben bei der Schilderung des tagtäglich auf den Bauern lastenden Druckes in seinen Einzelerscheinungen haften."

101. W. P. Fuchs, *Akten*, p. 35. From Hildhausen also comes the affirmation, ibid., p. 381: "das gottlich wort zu erhalten und dabei zu stehen, pleiben und halten." Similarly also, ibid., p. 511: "geschworen haben, bei dem heiligen ewangelium und dem wort gottes zu bleiben." H. Schreiber, *Der deutsche Bauernkrieg* (Freiburg, 1863), 1:139: "wollen wir uns . . . götlich Rechtens und Ustrags beflissen." Ibid., 2:4: "auch uns . . . bei dem göttlichen Wort und Gerechtigkeit bleiben lassen."

102. Schreiber, *Der deutsche Bauernkrieg*, p. 140: "dwil sie nichts dann das götlich Recht begeren."

103. G. Franz, *Der deutsche Bauernkrieg*, p. 169: "dass uns Christus all mit seinem teuren Blut erloset und erkauft hat, den Hirten gleich sowol als den Kaiser"; ibid., p. 176: "ist der Brauch bisher gewesen, das man uns für ir aigen Leüt gehalten haben, wölchs zu erbarmen ist, angesehen das uns Christus all mit seinem kostparlichen Plutvergüssen erlösst und erkauft hat, den Hirten gleich als wol den Höchsten kain ausgenommen."

104. *Thomas Müntzer, Schriften*, p. 468: "wer hat dich zu einem fursten des volks gemacht, welichs Got mit seinem theuren bloet erworben hat?"

105. Thus, the peasants at Bildhausen remarked, W. P. Fuchs, *Akten*, 1:62: "Nachdem das götlich wort und evangelisch lere lang zeit gefangen gewest und durch verhindernus etlicher und furnemlich gaistlicher obrickait nit hat ledig werden mögen . . . zuletzt untregliche beschwernus und burden von der obrikait und herschaft wider götlich und christlich ordnung und geschrift"; see also, ibid., p. 266: "unangesehen das etliche gotlose das evangelium zu schmehen ursach nemen sagent, das sint die frucht des neuen evangeliums, niemant gehorsam sein. Dan unser her Jhesus Christus . . . wil seine glaubige kinder us der Babilonische gefenknus foren."

106. *WA*, 11:408–16.

107. This is the judgment of J. Macek, *Michael Gaismair* (Berlin, 1965), p. 370; Macek also acknowledges the influence of Zwingli upon the formation of Gaismair's thought (ibid., p. 375) and cites approvingly O. Vasella, "Ulrich Zwingli und Michael Gaismair, der Tiroler Bauernführer," *Zeitschr. f. Schweiz. Geschichte*, 24 (1944). The various influences on Gaismair are summarized in J. Macek, "Das Revolutionsprogramm des deutschen Bauernkrieges vom Jahre 1526," *Historica*, 2 (1960):136.

108. See p. 26.

109. As cited in H. J. Hillerbrand, *The Reformation*, p. 64.

110. As quoted in G. F. v. Pölnitz, *Anton Fugger* (Tübingen, 1967), p. 600.

111. W. P. Fuchs, *Akten*, p. 505: "Nachdem ir etliche prediger bei euch hettet, die das wort gottes und heilige evangelion etlicher mas verkerlich und zu aufrur predigen teten." See also, ibid., p. 697: "imands, ehr sei geistlich ader weltlich, wormerken . . . mit worten, die zu ufrur oder ungehorsam dienen."

112. Schreiber, *Der deutsche Bauernkrieg*, p. 7: "so sich daselbst in vorder Landen an ettlichen orten der Luttrischen sect halber bissher erzeigt"; see also, ibid., p. 12: "sich dann seine unterthanen daselbst zu Stühlingen, so der luttrischen sect anhangen und sich wider ihn empörn.

113. W. P. Fuchs, *Akten*, 2:237: "dasselbig in einem guten schein (als ob es allein zu sterk und underhaldung des gotlichen worts und heiligen evangelion geschehe)."

114. See note 111 above.

115. Schreiber, *Der deutsche Bauernkrieg*, p. 91: "dieser Handel, dwyl er vom Gotteswort und Verkündung des heiligen Evangeliums entspringt und herkumpt." Similar is the comment on the situation near Zürich, ibid., p. 116: "dwyl dise Uffruren allenthalben zu gutem Theil von wegendes Gottsworts und der heiligen Evangelien (wie die jetzt klarlich an Tag gelegt worden) offerstanden."

116. Schreiber, *Der deutsche Bauernkrieg*, 2:61.

117. W. P. Fuchs, *Akten*, p. 39.

118. Ibid., p. 441.

119. F. L. Baumann, *Quellen zur Geschichte des Bauernkrieges aus Rothenburg* (Stuttgart, 1878), p. 107: "wans prots gerrynnt in dem brothaws, so muss ain yeder ain pfund geben, das ist wider gott und das hailig evangelium."

Appendix: A Tabulation of Peasant Grievances

Place	Total Number of Articles	Articles Dealing with Religion*	Content†	Source‡
1. Königshofen	19	1	A	F I,35
2. Bamberg	10	1	A	F I,69
3. Fulda	13	1	A	F I,123
4. Münnerstadt	18	4	A, B	F I,149
5. Lauenheim	12	0		F I,282
6. Ilmenau	17	1	B	F I,341
7. Unterpörlitz	16	0		F I,343
8. Seckbach	19	1	B	F I,405
9. Sleusingen	23	1		F I,427
10. Geisenheim	24	1 (+1)		F I,431
11. Gersgereuth	24	1 (+1)		F I,432
12. Rappelsdorf	21	1 (+1)		F I,433
13. Neundorf	13	1 (+1)		F I,433
14. Thambach	24	1 (+1)		F I,433
15. Kamberg	12	0		F I,523
16. Schwarza	30	1	B	F II,125
17. Six villages	5	1	B	F II,126
18. Rudelstadt	16	1	A, B	F II,127
19. Neustadt	12	1	B	F II,139
20. Ichtershausen	12	1	A	F II,144
21. Several towns	27	1	B	F II,151
22. Frankenhausen	14	1	A	F II,168
23. Osterhausen	12	0		F II,169
24. Apolda	16	0		F II,183
25. Stolberg	23	1	A	F II,194
26. Merseburg	19	0		F II,205
27. Pfarre in Halle	26	Several	A, B, schools	F II,216
28. Erfurt	28	1	A	F II,250
29. Sangerhausen	16	0		F II,265

Place	Total Number of Articles	Articles Dealing with Religion*	Content†	Source‡
30. Wolkenstein	5	1	A	F II,315
31. Ziegenrück	9	0		F II,330
32. Joachimsthal	17	0		F II,388
33. Königsee	29	1	B	F II,112
34. Rudolfstadt	30	1	B	F II,110
35. Stadtilen (?)	31	1	B	F II,108 ff.
36. Arnstadt	27	1	A	F II,101
37. Blankenburg	28	1	A	F II,113
38. Wimpach	21	0		F II,114
39. Dornfeilt	27	1	B	F II,115
40. Plane	14	2	Ceremonien "wie in schrift" Tiere "frei wie in schrift"	F II,116
41. Mombach	19	0		F II,117
42. Espenfeldt	6	1	"was ein andern christen- menschen in wasser und wilder gemein ist"	F II,118
43. Gräfenroda	9	0		F II,118
44. Elleben	15	1	A	F II,119
45. Hasseloben	7	1	B	F II,120
46. Kerernburg	16	1	B	F II,121
47. Wullersleuben	19	1	B	F II,122
48. Angstedt	25	1	B	F II,123
49. Doersdorf	9	0		F II,123
50. Seberg	10	1	B	F II,124
51. Basel	24	2	A, B,	S III,13 ff.

	Place	Total Number of Articles	Articles Dealing with Religion*	Content†	Source‡
52.	Wygersheim	9	0		S II,197
53.	Rothenburg	7	1	C	Bm 77
54.	Rothenburg	10	0		Bm 110
55.	Rothenburg	9	1		Bm 119
56.	Rothenburg	10	0		Bm 121
57.	Rothenburg	11	0		Bm 125
58.	Rothenburg	14	0		Bm 127
59.	Rothenburg	17	0	O	Bm 130
60.	Schwarzwald	16	0		Fr 96
61.	Stühlingen	62	0	O	Fr 101 f.
62.	Martinszell	12	1	Marriage	Fr 133
63.	Baltringen	11	1	A, C	Fr 152
64.	Baltringen	2	1	C, O	Fr 153 f.
65.	Baltringen	1	1	A	Fr 153 f.
66.	Baltringen	4	1	C, O	Fr 153 f.
67.	Baltringen	9	0		Fr 153 f.
68.	Baltringen	2	0		Fr 153 f.
69.	Baltringen	15	0		Fr 153 f.
70.	Baltringen	2	1	C	Fr 153 f.
71.	Baltringen	13	0		Fr 153 f.
72.	Rettenberg	23	2 (+5)	Sacraments	Fr 163
73.	Schussenried	12	1	C	Fr 164
74.	Augsburg	6	0		Fr 165
75.	Allgäu	11	2	A, B, O	Fr 166
76.	Memmingen	10	2	A, C	Fr 169
77.	Langenerringen	16	2 (+2)	A, B	Fr 201
78.	Rheinfelden	5	1	12 Articles	Fr 224
79.	Klettgau	43	0		Fr 226
80.	Neuburg	7	2	B, C	Fr 238
81.	Solothurn	12	1	A, O	Fr 265
82.	Meran	62	1 (+8)	B	Fr 272
83.	Salzburg	24	1 (+7)	C, O	Fr 295

Place	Total Number of Articles	Articles Dealing with Religion*	Content†	Source‡
84. Forchheim	5	0		Fr 315
85. Amorbach	12	1	B	Fr 342
86. Sulzbach	29	1	A, O	Fr 410
87. Württemberg	16	2	A, B	
			12 Articles	Fr 420
88. Rheingau	31	1 (+2)	A	Fr 445
89. Mainz	29	1 (+3)	A	Fr 453
90. Frankfurt	45	2 (+5)	A, B	Fr 455
Total	1,510	73 (+37)		

*Includes economic or social grievances presented with religious rationale. The numbers cited in parentheses refer to additional articles that may be said to deal with religion either *evasively* or *in a broad definition*, such as the repudiation of serfdom.

†A = demand for preaching of the Word of God
B = demand for right to appoint minister
C = rejection of serfdom as in conflict with Scripture
O = religious terminology

‡Bm = Baumann, *Quellen*
F = W. P. Fuchs, *Akten zur Geschichte*
S = Schreiber, *Der deutsche Bauernkrieg*
Fr = G. Franz, *Quellen zur Geschichte*

CHRISTIAN HUMANISM AND FREEDOM
OF A CHRISTIAN: JOHANN EBERLIN VON
GÜNZBURG TO THE PEASANTS

Kyle C. Sessions

Late in the summer of 1526, Johann Eberlin von Günzburg published a pamphlet written to the South German peasants of the margravate of Burgau.[1] He was addressing kinfolk and countrymen, for he had been born, probably in 1470, in a village a few miles from the province's capital town. This is Günzburg, in the center of the tiny margravate that straddled the Danube about twenty miles downstream from Ulm.[2] Most of the district's limited area lay below the south bank, around the junction where the Günz River ends a short flow northward from its origins in the Allgäuer Alps.[3]

Eberlin wrote to the peasants of Burgau for a special reason, to admonish them not to break out in revolt. They for the most part had abstained in the huge Peasants' Revolt the year before even though districts in the immediate vicinity had been the very focal points of rebellion. Memmingen, birthplace of the Twelve Articles, was scarcely twenty kilometers away in the next valley.[4] Discontent still smoldered in the area, making the margravate seem a likely candidate for renewed peasant outbreak.

The province answered to the description of a typical locale of revolt. That which had taken place generally in South Germany had taken place there as well in recent times. The vital substance of the medieval political order had been leached out by the infusions of a reviving capitalistic, commercial economy, leaving only the skeletal frame of feudalism. Manorialism as well had more or less dissolved as most agricultural activities had become capital enterprises conducted within one or another form of free tenure, and only vestiges of serfdom still remained in evidence. Although change had altered customs or usages and had eviscerated servile systems from the social corpus, the captions still remained and the regulations were still formally in force. Many lords still retained some real power in the exercise of justice, and with that tool in hand they characteristically tried to resurrect the lost, stringent feudal and manorial conditions.[5]

The local nobility of Burgau labored under another liability, as well. They were a client nobility of an absentee ruler. Their province was the westernmost of the many scattered Hapsburg family possessions. The local magnates, restrained from above by distant authority and constrained from within by obsolescence, progressively declined in fortune and utility. Their response was to tighten up the operation of the system.

In the view of the peasant, his lord's acts of survival were wrong both under the law and under God. The law was immutable, born out of timeless custom. Man lived under it and applied it to circumstances, but did not alter it. To attempt to do so was a violation. Such assault on the law also contravened the peasants' tradition that the law is born out of God's intentions for his creation. The law was both ancient and divine. To impose drastic distortions upon the law, as the lords were venturing to do, was not only unjust, it was unrighteous.[6]

In a general manner, these sentiments and conditions that had stimulated local outbreaks in such profusion in 1525 as to create the Peasants' Revolt still remained to trouble the Burgau peasants a year later. It was in light of his homeland's susceptibility to revolt in 1526 that Eberlin penned his *True Warning to the Christians in the Margravate of Burgau, That They Should Guard Themselves Against Revolt and False Preachers.* The pamphlet numbers among the last of his known writings (he died in 1533) and reveals him in full possession of his mature powers.

Eberlin von Günzburg according to the received tradition was an evangelical preacher and a social reformer. The writing at hand to the peasants seems to reveal something more of Eberlin. It is well established that the evangelical Reformation found expression in him as a representative Lutheran. The address to the peasants suggests that the Renaissance in the North also found voice through him as a Christian humanist.

Eberlin's proficiency as a humanist had begun early in his up-bringing, and had been built upon during his student years in the Universities of Basel and Freiburg.[7] Particularly at Basel, where he entered the university in 1489, he encountered a rich growth of learning and scholarship in the humanistic bent. Skilled and learned persons from numerous walks of life—jurists, historians, theologians, printers, and others—formed a march back into classical and biblical antiquity with the objective of service to the Christian church. These men at Basel, Christian humanists such as Johann Amerbach, Heinlin vom Stein, Geiler von Kaisersberg, and Sebastian Brant,[8] left an indelible imprint on Eberlin. They endowed his thinking lifelong with the traditions of humanism in the North, wherein late medieval Christian learning was animated by Renaissance concern about man.[9] His subsequent interests mirrored this legacy, for he came to see his learning as best directed toward Christian scholarship and his human concern best occupied with the needs of Christian society. His writings emerged in the form of treatises on Christian doctrine and on the ideal society in Christendom.[10]

Following his university training (he graduated Magister Artium, Basel, 1490, and Freiburg, 1493), Eberlin entered the monastery of the Observant Franciscans at Heilsbronn; and by the time of the appearance of Luther's ninety-five theses, he was a regular monk and an ordained priest. In 1521 he left the monastery. Circumstances surrounding his departure are not clear in the record, but they appear not to have been cordial or brotherly.

A variety of experiences he could have encountered have been advanced as sources for his exposure to Luther's teaching. These include a meeting with Philip Melanchthon. One biographer has attributed Eberlin's motive for leaving to the ambivalence between his classical-humanistic knowledge of the gospel and the self-abnegation and world-denial incorporate in his monastic life.[11] He later professed himself to have experienced justification by faith while in the monastery. Whatever may have been the course of his metamorphosis during years that were crucial for Luther as well, Eberlin embraced the evangelical gospel and subscribed to Luther's reforms about the time of the Diet of Worms. His conversion stimulated disciplinary measures within the order, initiated by the nuncio Aleander and the imperial confessor Glapio. He preached his farewell sermon on the feast of Peter and Paul (June 29, 1521). The months between 1522 and 1524 saw him in Wittenberg on two occasions.[12]

Eberlin's education and experience before 1526 had endowed him with humanism and evangelism. His competence in Lutheran theology had been established by then in his evangelical and reform writings. Through them he had gained a mark as especially knowledgeable on freedom and justification. His skills of persuasion were well founded in the late-medieval practices of rhetoric that had carried over and largely informed Renaissance humanism.[13]

His Franciscan career as a wandering preacher had honed his public address to a keen edge even before his exposure to Luther's teaching. Indeed, it may have been during a preaching tour in South Germany that Eberlin first encountered the Reformer's doctrines.[14]

Humanism and evangelism as components of his thinking are strongly evident in the address to the Burgau peasants. Thus the pamphlet of 1526 offers a unique opportunity to observe the interplay between German humanism and evangelical doctrine. A situation of crisis real enough to stimulate the concern of a kinsman provides the chance to consider a Christian humanist who is using techniques of Renaissance persuasion to expound Reformation doctrine. As a humanist he utilized three skills: adroit rhetorical argumentation, masterly biblical scholarship, and an eloquent style. As a reformer he employed his humanism to advance a single doctrine: Luther's teaching on the freedom of a Christian.

Eberlin's first task in his *True Warning* is to validate himself to his audience—to establish his credentials. To this end he offers several recommendations, including being a native son, a kinsman, and even a concerned neighbor. The last embellishment was somewhat artful, for he was a neighbor by literary license at best. He was living at the time in Wertheim, a small duchy on the confluence of the Tauber and the Main, directly but considerably north of the Günz and the Danube. Wertheim was Franconian, and Burgau was Swabian, yet both were South

German and lay in locales of exceptional violence the previous year. Eberlin's concern also might have arisen from his Wertheim employment as pastor and superintendent for Duke George II, a ruler who seems to have been more sympathetic than most in his time toward social and intellectual pressures for reform in all aspects of life.[15]

Seeking more substantial rapport with the peasants, Eberlin next executes a rhetorical exercise in which he proves first that they should listen to him and then that he is one of them.

Rumors are about that revolt is brewing again. He condemns it as conspiracy inspired by Satan.[16] So much for conspirators, but most of the citizenry was peaceable. Even so, among the peaceable are many who do not attend God's Word nor fear his justice. Innocence by itself is not enough because only active propagation of the gospel will bring the way of our Lord. Those who don't are earning the promise of Proverbs 26: "A whip for the horse, a bridle for the ass, and a rod for the fool's back."[17] Eberlin's hope is that all the peasants will hear him. To that end

> I have told you plainly and at length—for it is always necessary to proceed thus with simple people—what moves me to write to you, how useful my warning is for you, and how necessary it is that you take it and turn it toward your hearts.[18]

But what gives him the right to instruct the common man? Rhetorically, he poses to himself the challenge, "You don't know about the misery of the poor; you are flattering the lords and being useful to them!" In refutation he can announce knowledge firsthand among the poor as a youth, constant preaching in their behalf as a mendicant monk, and a career of exposing bad rulers and bad conditions since discovering the gospel.[19] His writing and preaching have worked solely for the benefit of the poor. He validates himself, we see, with the rhetorical exercise of appeal to personal authority. Personal authentication will come to be his handiest rhetorical tool.[20]

> Now let's get down to business. All the defects among you and bad counsel given to you come from the fact that either you don't have the gospel or you don't understand its use. In truth, you don't know

the gospel at all. You truly don't know what to look for from the gospel, and so you do yourselves more harm than if you didn't have any gospel.[21]

In these blunt words opening the main body of the address, Eberlin sets out his first hypothesis, that his hearers have an imperfect knowledge of the gospel. The need for peace is real but it is also incidental. The important thing to achieve is correct understanding of the gospel. Revolt may be the direct work of Satan, but misunderstanding the gospel is their own failing. It has led them to the common misconception that reform of religion means reform of society:

> You have heard the gospel and read it. So watch yourselves that you don't let it get you thinking that it will release you from the everyday world (as has been suggested). Or that through the gospel there will be no inequality in property—none richer nor poorer—and that goods will be divided equally. Or that we'll all be in equal classes, none more nor less powerful, since all are saved with the blood of Christ and all are children of one Father. Or even that no wicked person will go unpunished or remain in public office. In short, don't think that all will be like what Germans talk about as *Schlaraffenland* [approximately translated, land of milk and honey], or the poets as the "blessed isles" [*insulis fortunatis*], or the Jews at the time of the Messiah; that is, even as what some of the disciples thought to be the kingdon of Christ, Matt. 20, Luke 22, Acts.1.[22]

The principal stratum in the bed of unrest, lying just below the surface worked by Satan, is misunderstanding of the gospel. Thus the main vein in Eberlin's address is to be his instruction in the gospel. The doctrine concerning freedom of the Christian is the particular issue, and Eberlin is about to put across its main argument. This he does, when he declares that the realm of the Christian is not the natural world. The righteousness of the Christian takes effect in the realm of God. "Christ told Pilate his kingdom is not of this world. . . . From that a Christian surely realizes that he may not take over the turning or the authority of the world. The faithful preach the world its sin and manifest their faith in suffering the pain of the world. They pray deliverance by God and thereby amplify themselves in the gospel."[23]

The argument is unsatisfying at best and abstruse at least, which Eberlin must have recognized, for his next step was to construct a vivid reinforcement through allegory on Scripture. All of us, Adam's kin, are like a prisoner, he writes, condemned to a damp and musty dungeon, hungry, thirsty, and quite uncomfortable, without hope for any future but execution! What hope could he have? But then he hears of the mercy—boundless mercy—of the judge's son such that he comes himself to take the place of the prisoner. The son's life will satisfy the prisoner's sentence. How could he now measure his joy? The meaning of the allegory is apparent and need not be drawn, though Eberlin did so, speaking simply to simple people. Let us pass directly to the crux of his lesson: Take the judge as your friend and have faith in the son. He who does will not know "death, hell, hunger, thirst, and injury (Rom. 8). Rather what joy, thankfulness, peace, and happiness will be in him. He will author no murmuring or impatience in the midst of his suffering and death, "for the essence of suffering and the power of death —namely sin—are taken away and in place of them the gift of eternal life is promised us, though cloaked still with the appearance of suffering and death. . . . Christ's spirit works in us a willingness to endure all that God metes out to us and to thank him for making us like His son. . . ."[24]

This is Eberlin's main point. The freedom of the Christian commissions him to live the gospel, not to confound it with disturbance, creating even more suffering. To authenticate this point, the humanist appeals once again to his personal authority. They need to know the gospel that he heard, he says, at the source. At Wittenberg he learned from Luther, Melanchthon, and Bugenhagen. "Now," he says, "God grant me grace that I may follow and comply with what I have learned. The more we thus grasp the true use of the gospel the more we will recognize the function in ourselves which we need in all life's circumstances. We will gladly hear and read these exhortations and admonitions of the Word by pious people teaching us what is conformable to the Spirit of Christ. And God is well pleased that we do admonish one another in speaking, writing, and Scripture [sound humanistic media]. God's Spirit, needing that for our salvation, makes it all become alive and effective in our hearts.''[25]

Wittenberg also provides Eberlin with a rhetorical appeal to remote authority, in this case the reformer Johann Bugenhagen. "Not to be writing only my own words, [he says] I will set down a true and ringing witness, John Pommern." Eberlin, preoccupied with what corrupts proper behavior in a hierarchical society, cites his mentor: "Some who would be called gospel preachers can't do anything except denounce papistry: the monks and the priests, the fasts and the Fridays, the holy water, the useless services, the decorations. And so on, from which we are supposed to be well taught." They know how to stop error by denouncing it but not how to start preaching the gospel that could save their listeners. They renounce all authority, even God. Such is the gospel, they say.[26]

Such is not the gospel, of course. The gospel truly understood makes the Christian free and enables him to accept his world. To understand it otherwise is to deny the gospel; to act otherwise is to thwart it as well. "For good reason," he concludes, "I have written this somewhat longer than would have been necessary just for the use and comfort of pious preachers and listeners.''[27]

Eberlin's evangelical conclusion on truly understanding Christian freedom points him toward his next objective, a humanistic one, which is to cause freedom to be truly lived in Burgau. If he is to persuade citizens to that goal in any meaningful degree, he needs to enlarge the circle of those who must listen to him. Ideally, all the citizenry should act like Christians. But up to this point, he had made only some of the Burgau peasants liable to his instructions. Some of his readers were pious preachers and listeners—were Christians. Others were false preachers and impious listeners and had done many of the bad things he had attacked. But the Burgau peasants mostly were doing nothing, and he had yet to touch the people in general. In the segment following, Eberlin makes an audience of these passive peasants and pins his lesson squarely on them all. Proving that doing nothing constitutes failure to live the gospel, he makes their inertia an active, positive wrong through the rhetorical device of metaphor. Along the way, he displays an astute ken of human nature.

"Now let it be known," he wrote, "that the devil in his lair has built a bellows to blow a fire that will burn and destroy all Germany." One side of the instrument is Satan and his ambitions. The other side is the ignorant zeal of unknowing mankind made up of two types of person, each with a distinct flaw that the devil knows and exploits when he can.

The first type has all the right instincts, Eberlin explains. He would do no harm or wrong knowingly. But he also lacks true knowledge of how to serve God faithfully. "Saul of Tarsus was one of them before his conversion. . . ." The devil works on this person accordingly. He can be persuaded that a few heads regrettably must be knocked together, or knocked off, to make preaching true and the gospel free. Private faith notwithstanding, how much better it is for one to have public concern, about widows and orphans, perhaps. For the exaltation of these unfortunates, priests are driven out (an end to witchery) and tithes are quitted (an end to thuggery).

If ignorant good will is the flaw in the former type, it is self-serving ill will in the latter that Satan exploits. This person feels that others are injuring him, so do not cross him lightly. He is in a large group that includes "the angry empty ones who haven't anything to show for themselves and the others who are honorable or dishonorable according to their own good opinion and self esteem."[28] He is persuaded easily of the need to eliminate tyranny and tyrant rulers, all for the gospel, of course. With both types of men being led by Satan, Eberlin reveals that it is only preaching the gospel that cools down the disaster.

> Without that, the cost and toll of last summer would be incalculable. . . . It is a wonder that when such great hordes of ignorant, grim people came to demand so much from so many unready lords, so little actual damage was done. In truth, true Christians cried truly to God to stay the rebels—men like the pious M. Luther in his book to the peasants.[29] . . . And God did intervene, though we heard it said that the Christians had caused the revolts.[30]

Eberlin has captivated his audience now. It has no choice but to receive his lesson. His rhetoric up to this point has been modulated to achieve that goal, to secure as his own an audience that largely was not guilty of those acts that ostensibly occasioned the writing. After introducing and authenticating himself, he argued that his readers were victims of bad preaching in two ways. First, they had not really heard the gospel, but second and more serious, they had not understood the gospel concerning their freedom. Satan exploited their lamentable condition either by corrupting their ignorant good will or by perverting their selfish ill will. In the outcome none were right, all were wrong, and all suffered. Only the earnest prayers of Christians crying to God restored peace.

The conclusion is inescapable. All rebellion is wrong but to remain quiet is not enough. If only preaching and prayer mitigated the disaster, then the gospel must be taught rightly, understood by all, and fully lived. These peaceable peasants in the margravate of Burgau, these kinsmen and countrymen, are all fit subjects for his true warning. Rightly to them all is he addressing the gospel message of their own freedom.

With his audience in hand, Eberlin devotes several pages to a full-force sermon expounding the correct way for the Christian to enact his freedom.[31] The faith that makes the Christian free is the means to consolation and strength equal to any suffering. This understanding the author characteristically demonstrates wholesale with citations from Old and New Testaments.[32] Next Eberlin tells how the Christian acts: that he endures all suffering himself while protecting his neighbor against all harm. The alternative, Eberlin wrote, is

> those who rampage under the banner of the gospel, who run in a gang or place hope in the great mobs with spears and armour, who look only to themselves for trust and protection and crucify the opposition, who do nothing less than deny God's Word and say to God, "Get away from us; your way doesn't satisfy us. . . . So who wants to bear the cross forever?" And they fall from a lesser to a greater evil. They are afraid of frost and they let the snow fall all over themselves. . . . To them Christ doesn't say, "I will save you." Rather, he says, "All they that take the sword shall perish by the sword," Matt. 26 and Ps.

36. . . . Mark you how much of a false understanding of the gospel everyone had last summer who gladly would have enforced God's Word with the sword. All they did was bring misfortune on themselves, go against God, hinder his work, and prepare a feather bed for the devil.[33]

Such is the whole doctrine of the freedom of the Christian. His justification by faith frees him in this world as it assures him the next. Yet it also totally obligates him in this world to care for his neighbor through Christian service. To instruct his compatriots in these meanings has been his intent throughout as an evangelical preacher with a past record of social concern. The remainder of the writing, some ten octavo pages, contains humanistic rhetoric like the previous twenty, embellishing the teaching.

The freedom of the Christian empowers him to suffer and obliges him to love here even as he is wholly exonerated from suffering and is wholly loved beyond. Yet the concept seems unsatisfactory because it seems devoid of present hope. Is change in the natural order never possible? Is the character of Christian life in this world entirely apart from the present conditions of Christian living?

We would want the answer to be, "No!" from a man moved by Eberlin's concerns. For the two reasons of Christian freedom and Christian humanism that have structured his writing, we would hope for assurance that the order of the world is mutable. First, we would anticipate that Eberlin the evangelical preacher would offer consolation and hope from within the gospel. And he does. Second, we would expect that Eberlin the Christian humanist would endow man's work in this life with the capacity to enhance the condition of man. And he does.

First is the reassurance of the gospel. He sets out a quick rhetorical question and answer showing that the lower orders consoled and peaceable makes way for God's judgment on rulers. "You ask, who can endure eternally such madness and skinnings from tyrants and extortionists. Answer: only the Christian. . . . God will give the Christian hair that is longer and skin that is deeper than all that the tyrants may take with their fleecing and flaying," but meanwhile, the verdict and the pun-

ishment on the oppressors may be delivered only by God.[34]
". . . God now works a mighty work stronger than all power in
the world.[35] He causes the work to move along over and beyond
our will and help, except for preaching the Word of God. God
alone will have the prize. He won't have anyone putting his
hand on it, for then someone would say that his power had
helped."[36]

Second is the humanist's plea for reason. Eberlin must prove
that pursuit of the freedom of the Christian actually can affect
the world of man. He does so in the final few pages, the perora-
tion of this warning to the Burgau peasants, by showing that
the true way of the Christian does wield influence among men.
Drawing evidence from his own experience, he writes autobiography, applying the device of appeal to personal authority. His
narrative meanwhile is splendid chronicling, full of human
drama, triumph, humility, bravery, and poise. And as is to be
expected of a humanist, it is good, gleaming prose that con-
vinces through the havoc of time and translation. Let us conclude with the words of Eberlin the Christian and humanist:

> In order to let lords and commoners note how I have dealt truly
> with both sides often and plenty, I will relate just one story out of
> many. I went to Erfurt in Thuringia in the year 1524 and preached
> there for a whole year. At the outset I declared, as I do at this time,
> what is set forth in Paul and Peter. I taught very distinctly that there
> is more to being a Christian than censuring priest eating meat, or re-
> fusing mass and confession. I scolded the gluttony, drunkenness, whor-
> ing, usury, cursing, lying and more, of these vicious, so-called gospel
> hordes.
>
> Yet I read the lords their charge too, in four points: They shall
> punish the cruel, angry, willful mob or God would decree that they
> themselves be punished by the mob. They shall truly take unto them-
> selves the poor widows and orphans, humbly hear them and be seri-
> ously concerned about them, but not bend the law for them never-
> theless, even as they won't for the rich. They shall look out for the
> sick in the community hospitals and sanitoriums and see that they
> really receive care, for in a Christian realm such people are not just
> cast-offs. They shall see to it that no damage comes to the people's
> needs because of them or through their neglect; in short they shall
> behave so that they might stand up before God or before pious in-
> nocent people. Lest their rulership be like that of some ordinary

boob or fool, they shouldn't rely much on force, for whoever serves a community must expect to have a lot of work and very little thanks. But God will reward him amply.

I maintained this direction without let up, preaching before all kinds of groups. One would praise me and another would scold me. I taught in all my preaching the simple Christian hope that they would not make themselves useless by disobedience toward their lords, or the wealthy people, or others by whom they felt themselves unjustly injured. I brought forth cases and examples like those in this little book. Indeed, if any of my loyal hearers in Erfurt will read this pamphlet, whether because of my name or because of the title, they will say that this surely is Eberlein's preaching.

At that time a copy of the Twelve Articles of the Peasants in Swabia was brought to me and I warned the people of it like death itself. But in the event, not every man clearly grasped that I had denounced such articles. I labored in great concern, since the uprising in Erfurt seemed bound to come. It need never have come had not the devil stirred up false men who for false causes aroused the peasantry of the Erfurt area and led them some four thousand strong on the city.

Early one Friday morning [It was Friday, April 28, 1525, and Eberlin was appearing before the city council to respond to charges of preaching outside the pulpit.[37]] I was going on some business to the authorities at the city hall. As I was taking my leave they all rose and bade me loudly and earnestly that I join and counsel them. When I asked what was bothering them they replied that they had just received news that now people of the city were in riot at the Augustine Bridge. Herr Hans Kock, council member from the farther Saint Gilgen district, said, "Sir, we know you to be a trustworthy man; you probably can help us."[38]

I replied that when the populace rises up against legitimate authority, I pledge my very life and limb to restoring peace. "However," I asked, "Our distinguished president of the city council, Herr Adularius Hüttner, is not here. Now how can we know his pleasure?"[39]

Whereupon Herr Adularius sought me out (in conference outside the council chamber) and bade me extend my utmost energy and help. I selected to accompany me Herr Christoffel Milwitz, Herr N. Rindtflaisch (and this year both were reelected to the council) Herr Mattes Schwengenfeld, and others.[40] They went with me to the Augustine tower to meet the mob. And good men will know the fear these companions were in until we gained its attention. I said to the people that I was there as a friend and that they should admit me into their midst. The others and I reached a barricade. [This was a fortification known as the Augustine Wall. Still discernable, it lies south of the city, running easterly from the Weimar gate.] I mounted, crying to the people, "Look upon me as your friend! Listen to me in peace!"

As the crowd became still, two of their preachers came forward. Seeing them I said, "Dear friends, you know how I have preached the gospel to you for a whole year, and how I have counseled you to be patient and obedient and peaceful. Some of you have seen the good in my teachings and have praised them, while I have hoped that God's word alone would have held you in peace. But (God have mercy) I see you today in such a state that it is impossible for me to think that God is still among you. If you don't stop this, you will plunge yourselves into fearful danger before God and the world. My dear friends, think twice! Follow me, dear people. Have I not always proven true to you in your need? I will always be true to you henceforth. My God! What disgrace you are bringing to the gospel.

"You can't think that I would be hypocritical about your lords, just so I could get you on my side. No sir! I haven't been two-faced in the past and I won't be two-faced now or in the future. I go along with authority only up to the point that it has sufficient power for the common need; that much is given all authority. So what I am worrying about now is how to bring you and your lords together in a seemly and just peace. Our common city needs that and that's why these others are with me, etc. If you are my friends and if my teaching pleases you, give me a sign by lowering your battle standard."

Soon they put it down. I took heart from that and said, "Now all kneel down and pray for mercy. Then I'll talk a bit more."

This they did and then I told them in substance what is in this pamphlet. I said: "Dear friends, by my teachings, I will die (God willing) upon the cross of the faithful, still remaining patient toward the authorities and bringing grief to no man. Now all who will follow me raise a finger." All in the assembly raised up their fingers with a cry, "We too, we too!" Whoever was happier then than I and my councilmen?

I continued then, saying: "Dear friends, I see that your robbing has been more of a devilish, passing deception than a genuine act of will. Because of that, the sooner you repent through God's word, the sooner God and your lords will appreciate you. Yet if there is a person here who knows any better how to preach; let him do so."

Then Dr. Johann Lang, the preacher, raised his hand. (He was one who had come up as I was speaking.) He said, "My friends, as surely as God is in his Heaven, so has our lord and brother Johan Eberlain taught correctly. Follow him!"

And so with peace in the city I went directly with my gentlemen and preached in the fields to the peasants, saying in meaning the same as above. And every man there went down on his knees.

After I had been speaking a while, some one called out that there were better things to do than be preached at. It wasn't hard for me to figure out where this barb came from, and it wasn't from the peasants.

In fact, I challenged them to tell me who it was who had stirred them up and told them that they should break into the monasteries, the houses of priests, and the residence of the Archbishop of Mainz (who is the church boss of Erfurt) and his jailhouse and armory. [Erfurt was in the ecclesiastical jurisdiction of the Archbishop of Mainz.] I knew for sure that such things were not called for in the articles of the peasants, since Master Mahy the councilman had read those articles to the community.[41]

God will not allow those louts who deceived the simple people to go unpunished. However much we may think it no surprise that the city did not receive any extensive damage, still it is no joke, either. It may be eqully no wonder that a dreadful shedding of blood could have taken place. The common people are quick to rise up and slow to calm down.

The people in the city were so peaceful as to cause wonderment. No citizen received any damage to his property. Daily I made my way from one lodging to the next (as did other very energetic preachers) and cautioned the people to be patient and obedient. Several hundred peasants were occupying the Carthusian monastery and I brought them the same teaching as above. Dr. Johann Lang publicly gave them witness of my teachings. Herr Hans Müller, the tanner who was a councilman, [and had been put forward by the city mob for leadership of the council][42] had seen my energy and concern at work in the Charterhouse because some agitators had infiltrated the simple peasants and got them stirred up. Whoever they were, these deceitful bums told the simple people that they should march on the city hall, that their lords were untrue. And so they drew themselves up in the street in front of the monastery. I stilled that mob, God be praised, under great danger to the lives of all of us.

Now I was preaching every day in the high altar of Our Lady Church, to all the people, burgher and peasant. To all classes I preached God's Word and how there was no hope in rioting. Then one day Herr Adularius Hüttner, president of the city council, served me a document in the name of the joint commission of the council, the community, and the peasantry, declaring that I was dismissed from Our Lady, along with my four assistants. [Eberlin had been named pastor of Our Lady and given four assistants, apparently in appreciation for his services in the Peasants' Revolt.] Twice I publicized this command to all the people and said that I could not and would not obey it. But that was the only pulpit I ever had in Erfurt.

A couple hundred peasants over in nearby Saint Petersburg sent for me. Accompanied by two worthy citizens, I went and met them in a great hall. They demanded counsel from the Bible on how they should fashion their articles. There before them all I declared that their articles were wrongful and that the gospel couldn't help them at all.

At the time elections were being held for a new [Erfurt] city council, I was called from my pulpit (as I was preaching in the main altar) to the city hall, along with several other preachers. When I heard them carrying on, I opposed them with all my might. Dr. Johann Lang, Herr Andres Zum Propheten, [a conservative anti-Reformation member of the council], Master Chon [Cohon (Kune), named in letters of Mutian and related to Nicholas Engelmann noted below], Herman Sachsen and others must verify this. When it was proposed to put the nuns out of the nunnery and let them go free, I opposed it as being useless. So strenuously did I speak before all those newly elected people that this one and that one became alienated. Then I proposed that we should deal with the papists in a friendly fashion; thus might people notice that we seek not their treasure but their souls. Thus had Martin Luther counselled in the admonition to the people at Leisnig.[43] And so I went to the nuns' convent and told them that they were safe and that no one was going to drive anyone out. . . . Actually if someone hadn't sent two messages into the convent of Saint Andreas with the intent of enticing the nuns to come out, virtually none would have been frightened into leaving regardless of how much Herr Adularius Hüttner made noise that they would not be allowed to remain inside.

In a way I was helpful to priests and monks through my work. And because they had experienced a great deal, I protected the steward [Nicholas Engelmann] and the vicar of the bishop of Mainz and guaranteed their security with the peasants. For this they were extremely gratefull.

So in conclusion, the peasants were put off from all damage to the city and no violence had been done except to religious houses and the bishop's place. The persons who did those deeds, let me tell you, had nothing to do with Christ; indeed, He will see to it that these false leaders are punished.

So I say, follow me now and you will not regret it. For none may honestly refute my story told above. . . . Everything is such public knowledge that many thousands know it to tell.

So I pray, dear Christians, that you won't give way to any revolt but rather will combat against it with word and prayer, that on the judgment day we may be found secure in peace. Pray God for my sake. The grace of Christ be with you all. Amen.

Your brother, Johan Eberlein von Gintzburg[44]

1. Johann Eberlin von Günzburg, "Ein getrew War/nung an die an die Christen, in der Bur/gawischen marck, sich auch furo/hin au hutun vor aufrur,

/unnd vor falschen/predigern" [1526], *Sämtliche Schriften*, ed. Ludwig Enders ("Flugschriften aus der Reformationszeit, Vol. 18, No. 3; [Halle a. S., 1902]), 253–87. Probably written after August 27, 1526; see below, n. 35. Hereafter cited as Eberlin, "Warnung."

2. *Wenschow-Atlas für Höhere Lehranstalten* (Munich, Chicago, 1950), pp. 4–5.

3. Dr. Karl von Spruner, *Historisch-Geographischer Hand-Atlas; Part Two* "Geschichte der Staaten Europas vom Anfange des Mittelalters bis auf die Neueste Zeit" (Gotha, 1846), No. 18, p. 20.

4. The area along the Danube from Ulm to Leipheim (just west of Günzburg) was the center of the revolt after its origins around Lake Constance. Leipheim was the site of an early major victory of Georg Truchsess von Waldburg against the rebels. Memmingen is just south of there. Cf. Günther Franz, *Der Deutsche Bauernkrieg*, 4th ed. (Darmstadt, 1952); and Wilhelm Zimmerman, *Grosser Deutscher Bauernkrieg*, ed. Wilhelm Blos (Stuttgart, 1913).

5. Cf. Hajo Holborn, *A History of Modern Germany*, 3 vols. (New York, 1959-69), 1: *The Reformation*.

6. Franz, *Bauernkrieg*, pp. 1–3, 41–43, 80–87, 89–91.

7. Lewis W. Spitz, "Johannes Eberlin," *New Catholic Encyclopedia*, 17 vols. (New York, 1967), 5:28–29.

8. Johann Amerbach (1444–1514), highly educated printer at Basel after 1475; specialized in humanist writings and editions; Mülhbrecht, "Johann Amerbach," *ADB*, 1:398.
Heinlin von Stein [Johann Heynlin] b. 1425 (?) at Stein bei Schaffhausen; educated mainly at Paris; brilliant *via antiqua* scholastic and beloved preacher; at Basel, 1470; entered Carthusian order, 1484; d. Basel, 1496; Prantl, "Johann Heynlin," *ADB*, 12:379.
Johannes Geiler von Kaiserberg, b. 1445 at Schaffhausen, educated at Freiburg i. B.; to newly founded Basel University, 1471, dean of philosophy faculty, 1474; 1476 to Strassburg, where most of life spent; orator and forensic humanist-reformer; career peak as court preacher to Maximilian I; d. 1510 at Strassburg; E. Martin, "Geiler," *ADB*, 8:509–18.

9. Julius Werner, *Johann Eberlin von Günzburg, der evangelisch soziale Volksfreund* (Heidelberg, 1889), p. 3. In 1526 Eberlin published a translation, somewhat edited, of Tacitus, *Germania*, and other classical authors on the Germans: Popiscus, Eutropius, Procopius; title was, *Ein zamengelesen buchlin von der Teutschen Nation gelegenheit, Sitten und gebrauchen, durch Cornelium Tacitum und ettlichen andere Verzeichnet.* Cf. Bernhard Riggenbach, *Johann Eberlin von Günzburg und sein Reformprogramm; Ein Beitrag zur Geschichte des sechszehnten Jahrhunderts* (Tübingen, 1874; repr. Neuwkoop, 1967), pp. 247–48.

10. Enders' edition reproduces twenty authenticated pamphlets, of which the Burgau warning is the last, and two unverified. The most well-known are those comprising the series of critical social treatises, "Die 15 Bundgenossen."

11. Werner, *Eberlin Volksfruend*, p. 6.

12. Ernst Deuerlein, "Johann Eberlin von Günzburg," *Lebensbilder aus den bayerischen Schwaben*, 5 (1956):75, 77. Bernhard Riggenbach, "Eberlin, Johann," *ADB*, 5:575–76. Ernst Wolf, "Eberlin," *Neue Deutsche Biographie*, 7 vols. (Berlin, 1953–66), 4:247–48.

13. For Renaissance rhetoric see Charles Sears Baldwin, *Ancient Rhetoric and Poetic* (New York, 1924; repr. Gloucester, Mass., 1959), chap. iv; Charles Sears Baldwin, *Medieval Rhetoric and Poetic* (New York, 1928), pp. 237 ff; and Jer-

rold L. Seigel, *Rhetoric and Philosophy in Renaissance Humanism* (Princeton, N.J., 1968), pp. xiii, 205 ff.

14. Deuerlein, "Eberlin," pp. 73, 71–72.

15. Riggenbach, *Eberlin und sein Reformprogramm*, p. 246.

16. Eberlin, "Warnung," pp. 256–57.

17. Ibid., p. 257.

18. Ibid., p. 258.

19. Ibid., p. 259.

20. Baldwin, *Ancient Rhetoric*, p. 66, establishes in Quintilian that one of the basics of rhetoric is the moral and philosophical authority of the speaker. Quintilian's was the principal pedagogic of rhetoric absorbed by humanism.

21. Eberlin, "Warnung," p. 260.

22. Ibid.

23. Ibid., p. 261.

24. Ibid., pp. 263–64.

25. Ibid., p. 265.

26. Ibid., pp. 266–67; Eberlin is abstracting from Bugenhagen's, *De conjugo episcoporum et diaconorum ad ven. Doct. Reissenbusch* (1525); ibid., p. 371.

27. Ibid., p. 268.

28. Ibid., pp. 268–69.

29. *Admonition to Peace, A Reply to the Twelve Articles of the Peasants in Swabia*, 1525.

30. Eberlin, "Warnung," p. 271.

31. The rhetoric of the medieval and humanist sermon is perceptively treated in Marshall McLuhan, "The Ciceronian Program in Pulpit and in Literary Criticism," *Renaissance and Reformation* ("University of Toronto Renaissance and Reformation Colloquium and Victoria University Center for Renaissance and Reformation Studies," 7, No. 1 (Toronto, 1970): 3–7. See also Baldwin, *Medieval Rhetoric*, pp. 237 ff.

32. Eberlin, "Warnung," pp. 272–73: Isa. 55, 58; Acts 9; 1 Pet. 2; Job 9; Matt. 2; Ps. 17, 91, 44.

33. Ibid., pp. 273–74.

34. Ibid., pp. 279–80.

35. Probably refers to new adherences to the Lutheran movement consequent to the favorable Recess of the Diet of Speyer, August, 27, 1526.

36. Eberlin, "Warnung," p. 281.

37. Riggenbach, *Eberlin und sein Reformprogramm*, pp. 233–35.

38. Hans Kock, representing the town quarter behind Saint Aegidius (=Gilgen), had his house burned during the "Priests' Riot," June 10-12, 1521: it is reported in the poem of that title written by Gotthard Schmalz. Cited in Eberlin, "Warnung," pp. 372–73.

39. Adularius Hüttner, youngish president of the city council for 1525, was favorably disposed toward the religious and political reformation in Erfurt. He sought to exploit the Peasants' Revolt as a means to forward both, but the failure of the revolt discredited him and wrecked his political career. He died in 1566. Schumm, "Adularius Hüttner," *Mitteilung des Vereins für Geschichte von Erfurt*, 5:132; cited in Eberlin, "Warnung," p. 373.

40. Christoffel Milwitz was a conservative member of the city council opposed to Reformation and political reforms. F. W. Kampschulte, *Die Universität*

Erfurt in Ihrem Verhaltnis zu dem Humanismus und der Reformation, 2 vols. (Linz and Trier, 1856–60), 2:165; cited in Eberlin, "Warnung," p. 373.

41. M. Mahy was president of the council in 1514, 1519, 1521, and 1527. Eberlin, "Warnung," p. 373.

42. Ibid.

43. *Preface to the Ordinance For A Common Chest* (1523), *LW*, 45: 176–94.

44. Eberlin, "Warnung," pp. 282–87.

THE TWO SOCIAL STRANDS IN ITALIAN ANABAPTISM, CA. 1526–CA. 1565

George H. Williams

INTRODUCTION

Sixteenth-century references in Italian and Latin to Anabaptists are numerous, covering sectarian conventicles, bands, and leaders from Sicily to the French, German, and Slavic frontiers, but most abundantly for the region from the Papal States to the German and Slavic frontiers. To be sure, for the same time and region there are numerous references to Lutherans; and we know that such references are mostly to Protestants or dissenters in general rather than to devotees of the distinctive precepts of Martin Luther. By analogy, many scholars have raised the question whether or not those called in the Italian and related sources "Anabaptists" are really of the same spiritual stock as the Germanic Anabaptists.

It is a fact of Christian history that the insistence on believers' baptism and then the repudiation of infant baptism and finally the espousal of rebaptism (anabaptism) has been a recurrent phenomenon in church history.[1] The fact that in sixteenth-century Italy many were called and even sometimes called themselves Anabaptists is of itself no sure proof that they were genetically related to the much more amply documented German- and Dutch-speaking Anabaptists, contemporaneous with them. Moreover, there were some characteristics of the Italian Anabaptists that might seem to set them apart more as analogues to rather than as kinsmen of those to the north. The most notable difference between the northern (Germanic) and the southern (Italian) Anabaptists was the much more clearly marked tendency by 1550 among the Italians to be programmatically antitrinitarian while concurrently humanizing Jesus either as the adoptive Son of God or as the hidden and prospective Messiah or sometimes as but the greatest of the prophets —in all three cases as the son of both Mary, not necessarily perpetually virgin, and of Joseph. However, this fully unraveled Triadalogy (leading to Unitarianism) and the lowered Christology were not common to all Italian Anabaptists even by 1550. And the first references to Italian Anabaptists, beginning in 1526 are to people very much like those to the north who spoke German or Dutch, that is, they were not explicitly Nicene or Chalcedonian in their terminology, although, within a largely scriptural vocabulary, the earlier Italian like the German Anabaptists were traditional in their Triadology and Christology, unaware of any break on this matter with their Catholic past. It was in the pan-Italian Anabaptist synod of Venice of 1550 that the second more radical phase of development was consolidated; and thereafter the unitarian Josephite Anabaptists, as they can be called, seem to have come to prevail over the theologically more conservative groups.

The defection of one of the major Anabaptist apostles, the former priest Peter Manelfi, in 1551, and his exposure at inquisitorial hearings in Bologna and then Rome of numerous Anabaptist names and meeting places all over north-central Italy brought the movement in Italy almost to an end, although documentation of Italian Anabaptism continues in ebbing strength until circa 1580.[2] During the whole period of documentation in Italy from circa 1526 to circa 1580, Italian Anabaptists, whether christologically traditionalist or radical, are clearly distinguishable from true Lutherans, as in Venice; from self-conscious Calvinists; and also from various exponents of two thrusts that, among the German radicals, have been called contemplative and prophetic-revolutionary Spiritualism. To a certain extent, Italian Anabaptists during this period can also be distinguished from the Evangelical Rationalism (Socinians and their predecessors), although the two groups had shared some episodes and even some personalities as part of a common past. The difference between Spiritualism of various kinds and Evangelical Rationalism is that the former assigned a preeminent role to the ongoing work of the Holy Spirit in the interpretation of Scripture, whereas Evangelical Rationalism, like Anabaptism remained very close to the Scripture, particularly the New Testament, using reason in the context of a special vocation for tolerance—the last due possibly to the distinctive Evangelical Rationalist setings of Italian humanism, of Polish gentry politics and culture, and of Transylvanian pluralism under Muslim suzerainty.

In any case, in Italy, representatives of all these three radical tendencies (Anabaptism, Spiritualism, Evangelical Rationalism) mingled more freely and mutually supportively with classical (magisterial) Protestantism than in the north where, of course, Lutheranism and Calvinism were established territorial versions of the Reformation, sanctioned by the state. The turncoat Anabaptist Manelfi, for example, could list *en passant* in his deposition some true Lutheran leaders and conventicles along with Anabaptists because, over against the Catholic-Humanist world, all these dissenters came into some sympathetic contact with each other as they sought protection and concealment in the same receptive interstices of Italian society.

Usually distinguishable, nevertheless, from Italian Lutherans (very few) and Calvinists, from Italian Valdesians and other Spiritualists, and from Italian Evangelical Rationalists, the Italian Anabaptists of whichever strand were wholly pacifistic (unlike some of their northern counterparts), given to mutual aid and group discipline, devoted to Scripture study, prayer, preaching, prophecy, and evangelization through sustained missions, interpreting the Lord's Supper as a commemoration of Christ's suffering and a solemnly joyful anticipation of his eschatological return and vindication. These dauntless men and women nevertheless also differed among themselves. Manelfi himself quite readily referred to "the old" and "the new" strands in Italian Anabaptism.[3] Thus there still remains some uncertainty in modern scholarship as to how to perceive and classify Italian Anabaptism, whether new or old, and how to relate it to its counterpart and namesake to the north and to other movements.

In the historiography of Italian dissent in the Reformation Era, the sometime Communist Delio Cantimori (d. 1968)[4] holds a place of preeminence. Aware of the two strands in Italian "heresy," as he commonly referred to all anti-Catholic movements, whether classical Protestant or sectarian, namely, that of the lower classes (mostly Anabaptism) and that of the aristocratic and cultured classes (true Protestantism running into Socinianism), Cantimori took immense satisfaction in this earlier contribution of heretics or reformers in Italy in having brought theory and practice close together and especially in their having combined the ethical and social-reformatory concerns of the lower classes with the antidogmatic and humanistic proclivities of the upper classes (concerned to preserve amid change their intellectual freedom).[5] Cantimori did not in his most influential works make a distinction between Anabaptism, which characteristically gave attention to group discipline, and Spiritualism, which commonly spiritualized the sacraments and gave itself over to eschatological hopes.[6]

The American Mennonite scholar Henry A. DeWind,[7] moving in the fresh currents of Mennonite scholarship to repossess the sixteenth-century norms of the heritage, argued that most Italian Anabaptists, except for a few from the Venetian Republic who became Hutterites in Moravia, should be more accurately classified as "spiritual reformers." I myself in *The Radical Reformation* (1962) sought to bring the Italian and German Anabaptists under the same heading; and Antonio Rotondò, Marxist historian at the University of Turin, one of the four editors of the new *Corpus Reformatorum Italicorum,* in a review essay involving my book among others,[8] defended the essential unity of the international Anabaptist movement. The Polish Marxist, W. Urban, an authority on the Polish peasantry in the Reformation era, in dealing more specifically with Italian dissenters settling in Moravia,[9] came to the conclusion that the Tyrolese Anabaptists who constituted the core of the Moravian Anabaptist colonies (Hutterites) only gradually repossessed the traditional doctrines of the Trinity and of Christology around 1565, partly in clarifying their position over against both the unitarianizing Polish Brethren (who unsuccessfully sought to establish fraternal relations with them) and the more radical Italian Anabaptist immigrants in the same region; but that

originally there would not have been much difference in social
origin or ethical aspiration or theological-scriptural formulation
as between the Italian and the German Anabaptists.

Two recent studies of the Catholic scholar Aldo Stella, based
on the archives primarily of Venice, have greatly advanced our
knowledge of Italian Anabaptism, *Dall'Anabattismo al Socin-
ianismo nel Cinquecento: Ricerche storiche* (Padua, 1967) and
*Anabattismo e Antitrinitarismo in Italia nel XVI Secolo: Nuove
ricerche storiche* (Padua, 1969).[10] The two works, incorporating extensive new archival material strewn *in extenso* through
the notes and fully exploited in the main analysis and narrative,
overlap each other, the second book in part a supplement to the
first, in part a revision and substantial extension. The titles are
indicative of the shift in the author's point of view amid his
researches. In the first he presupposes the research of Cantimori
and follows the progression from authentic Tyrolese Germanic-
Italian Anabaptism to the onset of Socinianism, appropriating
as helpful my own terminology for the latter, and for antecedent groups: *razionalismo evangelico.* Basic to Stella's first book
is his admirable appropriation of the findings of the Czech Marxist scholar Josef Macek, *Der Tiroler Bauernkrieg und Michael
Gaismair* (in Czech: Prague, 1960; Berlin, 1965). Stella ex-
pands the documentation for the involvement of Italian-speaking denizens of the lower valleys of the county of Tyrol (and in
the prince-bishopric of Trent) in the *guerra rustica* under the
Zwinglian Michael Gaismair in the last and constitutionally
most ambitious phase of the German Peasants' War. Stella, noting that there were several copies of peasant articles in Italian
in the archives of the former Republic of Venice bordering on
the Tyrol and the Rhaetian Confederacy, was convinced that
Italian Anabaptists in Veneto and adjacent territories, were of
the same social stock and sociopsychological experience as the
Germanic Anabaptists who likewise after the war, recoiling from
their great effort at participatory politics and reform, withdrew
into separatist and pacifistic conventicles. From these palpably
authentic war-related Italian Anabaptist conventicles, Stella
proceeded to follow the evolution of some toward Socinianism,
rehabilitating *en passant* the Collegia Vicentina (Vicenza),

which survive in Socinian tradition as notable colloquies in 1546 on Venetian territory among persons who later became identified respectively with the Polish Brethren and the Hutterites.[11]

In his second book Stella is less certain of a natural progression from Anabaptism to Socinianism (Evangelical Rationalism). His first of three chapters is indeed entitled "From Spiritualist Radicalism to Antitrinitarianism," at the center of which is the sometime Neapolitan Bendictine Abbot, Jerome Busale, student of Hebrew at Padua, who was elected bishop of the two kinds of Anabaptists in Padua, those of Tyrolese-Venetian and those of Neapolitan-Sicilian origin. As the title of the second book suggests, sensitized to the distinction between Anabaptism and Spiritualism, and in any case quite clear about the distinction between the groups he has his scholarly eye on and Italian representatives of classical Protestantism, Stella rehabilitates the term "Antitrinitarianism" to cover a thrust in Italian heresy that he clearly detects to be distinguishable from Tyrolese-Venetian Anabaptism of the Germanic type, namely, a dissolution of the doctrine of the Trinity and a humanizing of Jesus as son of Joseph.

In both books Stella is aware of the difference between the earlier northern Anabaptism, central to his first book, and the Neapolitan-Sicilian unitarianizing Anabaptism that seemed to issue from the Valdesian circle in Naples. For the first time in the scholarship in the field, Stella glanced at the possibility that it was more than Valdesian influence that made the movement from the south unitarian; namely, Marranism.[12]

The Marranist component is not easily identified; otherwise, this explanation would have long before been advanced. There are no references in the sources to Marranos as such; and surely after the institution of the Roman Inquisition of 1542 the spiritual officials would have brought out in the hearings any suspicion of Jewish or Marranist antecedents in the heretics on trial. Yet there is a Judaizing thrust in southern and eventually in almost all Italian Anabaptism, which is not merely that of Italian dissenters moving toward Judaism but that also of Jewish Catholics (Marranos) moving into radical Protestantism.

As the thesis of Marranist influence from the south has yet to be proved, it must suffice to put forward in a schematic way its plausibility. The evidence for an authentically Germanic type of Italian Anabaptism following upon the extension of the Peasants' War into the Tyrol has already been sufficiently marshaled by Stella, especially in his first volume. After hypothesizing reasons for a Marranist component in the southern strand in Italian Anabaptism, we shall proceed to rehearse the history of Italian Anabaptism in a succinct narrative account with due attention to both Tyrolese and Neapolitan ingredients.

THE PLAUSIBILITY OF MARRANIST INFLUENCE
IN SOUTH ITALIAN ANABAPTISM

Throughout its entire history in Italy up until the racial laws under Benito Mussolini and the Nazi collaboration-occupation, Jewry in the peninsula never went through the most brutal and destructive forms of Christian anti-Semitism that befell Jewish communities elsewhere in Western Christendom, as in England, France, Spain, and Germany.[13] The peninsula had in the sixteenth century several distinguishable kinds of Jews, often with their own quarters, synagogues, rites, customs, and even vernaculars: Sicilian Jews who still used some Arabic and Greek; Neapolitan Jews of the whole peninsular region south of the Papal States; older Italian communities farther north; Germanic Ashkenazi Jews seeking refuge from northern European persecution, settling as far south as Rome; Spanish and Portugese Jews who had fled from the Iberian Peninsula in 1492–97; and finally, Levantine Jews from the Ottoman Empire doing business in Italian ports.

Although conditions for Jews varied considerably in Italy, the Papal States in general being the most favorable and the Spanish-controlled territories being after 1492 the most difficult, it may be said that the Renaissance era was in general a high point in congenial Jewish-Gentile relations on the peninsula up to the infamous bull *Cum nimis absurdum*, July 12, 1555, of Pope Paul IV, Caraffa. This restrictive measure represented the climax and implementation of the preaching of the friars, particularly of the Franciscans, and notably of Giovanni di Capistrano against the Jews in favor of the Catholic poor, who suffered the most from losses in Jewish pawn shops and banks. Already in 1516 the Jews of Venice, except for the Levantines, were obliged to resettle in the New Foundry (*Ghetto Nuovo*) and shortly thereafter the Levantine Jews, despite their *condotti* (renewable contracts with the council), were required to move into the Old Foundry (*Ghetto Vecchio*). Soon the Venetian term *ghetto* was everywhere adopted as Jews throughout Italy were generally obliged after 1555 to live in sectors apart from the rest of the town population with strict regulations as to entry and egress.

The first quarter of a century, however, of Italian Anabaptism, roughly 1526–51, coincides with the to date most open and integrated phase in the history of Italian Jewry and *a fortiori* of the Marranos.

In Italy in this same quarter-century the Marranos were of varying degrees of Christianization.[14] It is commonly assumed by Jewish and non-Jewish scholars alike that Marranos were by definition crypto-Judaic. But that is to generalize as a universal fact the suspicions of the Spanish Inquisitors. Undoubtedly many Marranos retained Jewish customs and Jewish convictions under the guise of Catholic conformity. But they all had by definition at least a superficial knowledge of Christianity by reason of their regular attendance at the services of the dominant religion. Moreover, there were many differences among *conversos* as produced in Spain, Portugal, and Italy itself. The Portuguese Marranos were but recently and harshly forced into compliance with Catholicism (1497), and those who reached Italy would easily revert. The conversion of Spanish Jews went back to an earlier date and many of them were sincere Christians, even when they found themselves in the relative freedom of the Italian mosaic of small or diminutive sovereign territories. A Jewish authority on the Spanish Marranos has even concluded: "Assimilation, Christianization and anti-Jewishness were indeed the foremost symptoms of [the dominant Spanish] Marranism."[15] But besides Iberian Marranos there were native Italian *Neofiti*. It is inconceivable in the Renaissance atmosphere of Italy, with two religio-political events of such enormous potential as the

Lutheran Reformation in Germany and the Muslim advance on Western Christendom under Suleiman I, the Magnificent, that some Marranos in Sicily and the kingdom of Naples would not have been caught up in the messianic and the other expressions of eschatological fervor and speculation that stirred others—Jews, friars, conventicular radicals.

It is of some interest that the Portuguese and Spanish Marranos were ordered from Veneto on July 8, 1550, just a few months before the Judaizing Anabaptist synod in Venice in September, 1550. It was charged against the Marranos that they were heretics or relapsed Jews pretending to be Catholics and that, while controlling much of the commerce with the Levant and Spain, they were disturbing the faithful of Veneto.[16] The deposition of Manelfi in 1551 twice refers to Anabaptists working or living in Venice "in getto vecchio," which would have meant in the quarter of the Levantine Jews and Marranos.[17] To be sure, this is the only nearly direct evidence thus far chanced upon to prove incontrovertibly some Jewish-Marranist-Anabaptist connection.

But the indirect or circumstantial evidence is ample. A change of name is much more common among the Italian than among the Germanic Anabaptists, a Marranist (but of course, also a monastic) practice. Many Italian Anabaptists fled to renowned Jewish and Marranist centers under the Ottoman Empire: Thessalonica,[18] Alexandria, and Damascus. In one important case a Neapolitan-Paduan Anabaptist bishop (Jerome Busale) is said to have gone to Alexandria "where he had relations."[19] The Anabaptists of "the new opinion" "doctrine" as distinguished from "the old"[20] were almost unaccountably concerned to press for a swift unitarianization in contrast to the agonizing devolution by way of Arianism, tritheism, binitarianism, and Christ-adorant Unitarianism among the Evangelical Rationalist Polish Brethren (who were also proponents of believers' baptism). Italian Anabaptists of "the new opinion" also pressed for a complete humanization of Jesus, even to the elimination of the first and second chapter of Matthew and the first, second, and part of the third chapter of Luke as prejudicial to Joseph's paternity. On this they insisted at the synod of Venice in 1550.[21]

Only Christians of Jewish stock or Marranist inspiration would have had a motivation in vindicating in Christian terms the unity of the Godhead and the full humanity of Christ. To challenge as an addendum the beginnings of two gospels was to impugn the authority of a portion of Christian Scripture that no other Anabaptists in their struggle alike with Protestantism and Catholicism elsewhere would have felt drawn to do. Moreover, there is evidence that the southern Anabaptists were particularly concerned with the Hebrew text of Scripture and with close scrutiny of the prophetic books. It is perfectly plausible to assume that a number of Marranos, having lost contact with Judaism, and having been as nominal or even as devout Christians part of a community still held suspect even in Italy, would have espoused the Reformation and especially its more radical and conventicular form as a repudiation of their ancestral conformity to the dominant religion. They could have done this in the prospect of some eschatological vindication of the radical evangelical version of that religion and as incorporating what was for them residually valid in a moral, Judaic messianism. Moreover, prospective Anabaptists from the ranks of truly Catholic Marranos and Neofiti will have carried memories of the substitution of female proselyte ablution for circumcision among crypto-Judaic Marranos; and this "spiritual circumcision" by water could easily have become assimilated to the practice of believers' baptism (i.e., anabaptism) coming south from Tyrol and Switzerland. It is quite possible that this circumcision-ablution-baptism would have seemed to the Marrano or part-Marrano converts to a radical Christianity both a sign of conversion and reconversion as they became members of a still persecuted but now eschatologically hope-filled minority, the socially lower-class Anabaptists. Prudential Marranos will have, for economic reasons or personal relief from harrassment, continued to conform to the dominant religion in Italy; but the conscientious, especially among the humbler class of Marranos, will have plausibly made common cause either with Jews by reversion despite the often capital hazard of being declared relapsed heretics (about this choice most literature to date on the Marranos concentrates exclusively) *or* they will have by baptismally signified conversion identified themselves with a new form of Christianity in a now non-oppressive, pacifistic, mutually supportive dispensation. Finding in Anabaptism all that they could hope for in rebelling against the distortions and oppressions and even hypocrisies of established Christianity as they would surely have judged the Catholic church to be, such Marranos would understandably have proceeded to change even the Germanic type of Tyrolese-Tridentine-Venetian Anabaptism ("the old opinion") into antitrinitarian Josephite Anabaptism that would carry all before it in the synod in Venice ("the new doctrine").

ITALIAN ANABAPTISM FROM 1526 TO 1565

The County of Tyrol, 1525–26: Michael Gaismair[22]

In May, 1525, the peasants in the Black Forest were able to force Freiburg to capitulate—the last success of the peasant forces in the main theaters of the Peasants' War (1524–25).

In the same month began in Tyrol the attempt of a petty burgher in alliance with peasants, miners, and artisans to establish an Alpine workers commonwealth, to be in power comparable to the Swiss Confederation or the Rhaetian League but in constitution more radically egalitarian. Incidentally, these two partly Protestantized confederations (Swiss and Rhaetian) contained within their southern boundaries the only native Italian populations to enjoy magisterial toleration or even support in espousing the Reformation. On May 9, 1525, one Peter Pässler, a rural rebel perhaps unfairly condemned to death in the prince-bishopric of Brixen (Bressanone), was rescued by a Tyrolese band, which thereafter constituted itself a new revolutionary organization. With the help of the city's artisans, the insurgents occupied Brixen and sacked the convent of Neustift. They thereupon elected Michael Gaismair (ca. 1490–1532) their commander.

Born near Sterzing (Vipiteno), Gaismair had presumably studied at the episcopal school and become successively the amanuensis of the burgrave of Tirol (the castle whence the county received its name) and at once secretary to, and tax collector for, the bishop of Brixen. Under the impress of Gaismair's genial vision, insurgency spread south into the prince-bishopric of Trent and north to Innsbruck, elaborating a series of sixty-two articles presented to the county diet as Merano (Meran) May 30–June 8, 1525. These were in turn submitted for deliberation at the Diet of Innsbruck. The Hapsburg King Ferdinand, as count of Tyrol (1520–64), protracted the discussion (resulting in enlargement of the Merano articles to ninety-six) and also promoted a division of the insurgents between organized miners and propertied peasants on the one side and on the other day laborers and others without holdings. Ferdinand refused to countenance any of the Merano Articles respecting religious reform. Gaismair was imprisoned. To the limited concessions the more advantaged insurgents and especially those in North Tyrol agreed.

The poorer insurgents especially in the south, including Italian-speaking peasants in the dioceses of Brixen and Trent, arose again in revolt. In the meantime, Gaismair escaped to Zurich, and he apparently held secret conversations with Zwingli in a common concern for a Reformed anti-Hapsburg Tyrol. Establishing himself thereafter in Prättigau for reflection, Gaismair worked from February into March, 1526, on his revolutionary *Landesordnung*,[23] going well beyond the Merano articles. The sixth article, for example, called for the abolition of pictures, statues, and non-parochial chapels. Animated more than ever by a Zwinglian concern for social justice in a unitary state, Gaismair demanded social equality to the point of insisting in article five that all city walls be razed to equalize the rich burghers and the peasants (like the Swiss forest cantons; cf. Prov. 18:11). Gaismair had clarified his vision of a peasants and miners commonwealth with the public management of mines and commerce. With all his enthusiasm for equality he still left a place for the prince as head of state (cf. Thomas Müntzer), but the lesser nobles and ecclesiastical princes and their domains were to be eliminated to make way for a workers' republic on the crossroads of European trade.

After an unsuccessful attempt to rally the peasants of Tyrol and also Salzburg to his grand design, especially in the Pinzgau and the Puster Valley, Gaismair withdrew to Venetian territory, seeking aid. He became a pensionary of the republic, resident in Padua. Until his assassination (1532) by two Spaniards a year after the death of Zwingli, Gaismair strove tirelessly for an Anti-Hapsburg coalition of Venice, Rhaetia, Switzerland, and France to realize his Tyrolese utopia. Two of his sons became Anbaptists.

Anabaptists in South Tyrol and the
Venetian Republic, 1526–1533

The rise of Italian-speaking Anabaptists can best be followed in the region of the headwaters of the Adige River (Alto Adige, Südtirol). The Adige flowing into the Adriatic south of Venice and the Inn flowing into the Danube constituted the principal river systems of the county of Tyrol. Anabaptism in the Inn Valley and its tributaries was an important regional variant of Germanic Anabaptism.[24] Of special interest is the extension southward of this movement from the upper, German-speaking valleys of the Adige (Etsch) and its principal tributaries, the Eisack (Isarco) and the Rienz (Rienza), because the descent of the valleys into Italian-speaking regions, and notably into the religiously most tolerant of Italian territories, the Venetian republic, meant that originally Germanic Anabaptism would, before the close of the last phase of the Tyrolese Peasants' War, have its Italian counterpart not only in South Tyrol but also on the Lombard Plain.

Italian- and Ladin-speaking peasants, miners, and petty burghers in the upper Noce Valley and in the Adige Valley from Trent down to Nogaredo and over into the upper valley of the Brenta (Val Sugana) fully participated in the Tyrolese Peasants' War.[25] Adapted Italian versions of the Merano Articles of 1525 and of the twenty-three peasant articles of Rettenberg in the archives in Brescia[26] testify to Italian participation in the constitutional program of Michael Gaismair. And after his flight to Padua under Venetian protection, Anabaptists in Brixen, for example, in 1527 eagerly awaited his return to carry out his grand design for social justice.[27] It is noteworthy in trying to visualize the onset of Italian Anabaptism that the vivid chronicler George Kirchmair, writing from the vantage point of pontifical Brixen below the Brenner Pass, first mentioned the rise of Anabaptists of whatever stock in the paragraph immediately following an entry on the ten thousand "walisch Petler" streaming into his region from Venetian territory in May, 1528.[28] These Italian beggars, as he loftily called the wretched war refugees following the sack of Rome, would readily have yielded to radical preachers of social justice. As in Germany, so in the episcopal territories of Brixen and Trent and in South Tyrol, despair at the failure of an in part religiously motivated peasants' uprising with constitutional as well as economic demands would lead to further social alienation even more intensely religious, manifest in Anabaptist withdrawal into disciplined conventicles for mutual aid.

The valleys of Tyrol were the most prolific spawning grounds of the whole South German Anabaptist movement. Coming downstream with the Inn to the Danube, we need but recall the names of such German-speaking Anabaptist leaders as John Schlaffer martyred at Schwaz, Leonard Schiemer martyred at Rattenberg, and Pilgram Marpeck converted at Rattenberg—all about 1528. Coming downstream with the Adige and its tributaries toward the Adriatic, we evoke equally important Anabaptist names. George Blaurock, who baptized Conrad Grebel in Zurich in January, 1525, was born in Bonaduz just over the mountains in Rhaetia from the headwaters of the Adige, and was put to death in 1529 on his mission in Guffidaun (Gudon) on the Isarco well south of Brixen, in a martyrdom witnessed by the youthful Peter Walpot, destined to become the head of the Hutterites. Jacob Hutter himself, converted in 1526, was born near Bruneck (Brunico) on the Rienza. Ulrich Stadler was born in Brixen and was a mine official in Sterzing (Vipiteno) before his conversion.

We do not have the names of the first Italian- and Ladin-speaking Anabaptists, only geographical references to conventicles in the upper Adige in 1525, in Merano and Bolzano in 1529, in the diocese of Trent in 1530, whence they fled up the Val di Fiemme and into Venetian Territory.[29] It is natural that these

Italian Anabaptists would eventually think of Hutterite Moravia[30] as a place of refuge as did their German Tyrolese confreres further up the valleys.

The first Italian Anabaptist of whom the name and particulars survive was not, so far as is known, a Tyrolese. Master Anthony Marangone was a carpenter of the Rialto district of Venice, tried at the beginning of May, 1533, and sentenced to life-imprisonment June 2, 1535.[31] The title *master* may have more to do with his headship of a school than his status as a carpenter, and vaguely suggests Waldensian usage. He comported himself with dignity throughout the year's hearings. One associate was a certain twenty-five-year-old "foreigner, red, ingenious person, strong Lutheran."[32] Saxon Lutherans would never have acknowledged Anthony as their own! Venetian philo-Protestants in high places appear to have been sympathetic with his cause; and in any case the abundant testimony from Anthony, his humble followers (whom he instructed sometimes in front of his booth up to as many as fifty), and the parochial clergy provide invaluable documentation of the transition in an Italian conventicular atmosphere from "Lutheranism" to Anabaptism. One of the distinctively Lutheran marks of Anthony's German-derived Anabaptism was firm adhesion to the doctrine of predestination and salvation by faith alone without free will.[33] Most other Italian Anabaptists defended the freedom of the will. Anthony defended in interesting ways the priesthood of all believers and held that Saint Peter was the only pope. He eschewed infant baptism and then espoused adult rebaptism[34] as a sign of withdrawing from Rome. Spiritualizing, Anthony apparently believed in the possibility of spiritual Communion at the parish mass.[35] He denied purgatory and apparently held that souls go straight to paradise or to hell.[36] He indirectly disavowed the Trinity.

Northern Italian Anabaptists outside Rhaetia, 1533–1551: Giacometto Stringaro, Il Tiziano, and Peter Manelfi

Italian Anabaptism was said by two relapsed Anabaptists to have been derived from Camillo Renato (ca. 1500–ca. 1575).

A sometime Franciscan from the south of Italy, active as an exponent of theological and social reform in Ferrara, escapee from prison in Bologna, Renato (having successively changed his name: born Paolo Ricci, then Lisia Fileno) found refuge in Caspano near Chiavenna in Rhaetia and became in due course a correspondent of Henry Bullinger, defending "the rite of Caspano," which included an ample agapetic meal for the refugees and the poor. Although, indeed, Renato soon came to espouse believers' baptism in a lost *Adversus baptismum . . . sub regno Papae atque Antichristi* (1548), he was more a precursor of Socinianism.[38] The fact is that Renatian and other outcroppings of Anabaptism in the Italian- and Ladin-speaking lower fringes of the Rhaetian Confederation and the subject confederal territory of the Valtellina (none of which region had directly experienced the social turmoil of the Peasants' War, as had the Tyrol and some of the Swiss cantons) tended to be more of a congregationalist reformation of the (Rhaetian) Reformation than a separatist and conventicular sociopolitical protest. Lower Rhaetia, however, as a readily accessible and congenial place of refuge among native Italians, remains a continuous point of reference in our narrative.

The first Italian Anabaptist of whom we have a writing of his own is Giacometto the Stringer (*stringaro*), a haberdasher of Vicenza and "bishop and minister of the church" thereof. He is reported to have rebaptized many in Vicenza. In 1547 he addressed an epistle to his "brethren in Christ," in effect a semiliterate but scripturally discerning tract entitled *La rivelatione*, wherein he was principally concerned to clarify his Triadology, Christology, and soteriology on the basis of Scripture, notably John, Romans, and Hebrews. On some points he came very close to views later to be expressed by Faustus Socinus. Since Stringaro's is, apart from Renato's, the earliest articulation of Italian anabaptist, adoptionist, psychopannychist theology on the boundary between Evangelical Rationalism and Anabaptism, it should be quoted at some length:[39]

> It has appeared to me [i.e., been revealed] to write down how we understand and have the knowledge of God our Father and of his

Son. . . . Someone may say: I find in the Scripture that God is Christ. Now we come to this. If you understand these words to say this [John 14:19], "Who sees me sees the Father"—if you wish to understand thereby a visible sight—that would not be able to stand with these other words [cf. John 1:18; 1 John 4:12], "No man seeth me." And consider that other word in St. Paul [1 Cor. 13:12], "then shall we see face to face," and in St. John [I John 3:2], "and then we shall *see* him as he is." And Christ says [Matthew 5:8]: "Blessed are the pure in heart for they shall see God." If we do not have yet to see *in another manner* than when Christ says [John 14:19]: "Whoever *sees* me *sees* the Father also," these words above cited would be false, because the apostles and more than five hundred brethren had seen Christ resurrected and ascending into heaven and Paul saw him; nonetheless they say that we ought to see him, God, one day and avow that they have not seen him although they have indeed seen Christ. Accordingly, of necessity another person this is than Christ, and another essence and presence and sight is that of the Father, speaking of the sight of the eyes. It is necessary, accordingly, to understand that this seeing of the Father in seeing the Son is in the knowledge and perception of the *will* of God: Whoever sees the wisdom of Christ sees the wisdom of God and thus the Power [citing Heb. 1:3 and Col. 1:15]. . . . [C]oncerning the saying [cf. John 5:17, 36; 10:25], "The Father who stands in me it is he who does the works," we understand this in power and virtue, giving to him the spirit of this wisdom and power. And we say that Christ is created by the Father, indeed generated, indeed—if you will—born or even "procedured," as the Holy Spirit says in diverse ways. We say this also according to the Spirit; and we say that Christ does not have life by himself but that God has given it to him.

Going on to make God's election of Christ for a mighty purpose paradigmatic of each man's salvation, Giacometto continues:

[T]hus as God has made the sons of Adam from earth and they by sin are sick and sons of wrath, ignorant and corruptible, so the same [God] can and does make spiritual sons, holy and eternal, of the same nature and character: God could make of stones sons to Abraham [Matt. 3:9], that is through blessing and honor and glory and sanctification. Nothing remains but this that we all be made good by God; and we understand that Jesus [himself] was made by God neither more nor less than we others . . . having father and mother like us, a true man, son of Adam subject to the law. And we understand that Christ was "born" [Son] when God sent the Holy Spirit into the man [Jesus at his baptism at Jordan], not that the Holy Spirit

is not eternal in God but in a similar way as used in Scripture, understanding that the one Son of God was "born" when God sent his
Spirit in this renewing of the will. . . . [F]or we understand that
God has sanctified Christ and washed him, that is, baptized him. . . .
[A]nd as God lives so does he give life to men to whom he will, God
having given life to Christ in resurrecting him, restoring him from the
evil of death in complete perfection both in spirit and in body; and
God wishes to perform this in one in order that all the others would
have [reason] to believe that God will do with them as he has done
with him. . . . We understand that Christ is the true Son of God
and is not God.[40]

Giacometto goes on to distinguish in Jesus Christ his suffering
humanity common to all mankind and his Spirit. The flesh of
Christ was not generated by God in conception and gestation,
but was infused with the Spirit at baptismal regeneration, and
then "generated" definitively at the resurrection—reference being made to the sermon of Paul at Antioch in Pisidia, Acts
13:33: "God hath . . . raised up Jesus again, as it is also written. . . . 'Thou art my Son, this day have I begotten thee.' "
And on the basis of Rom. 8 (especially verses 9, 11, 26, 29),
Giacometto suggests that in the resurrection community (the
Church), in which the Spirit that raised up Jesus dwells (v. 8),
Christ and the Spirit might well be one. In any case "we would
not adore and honor him [a Messiah and Redeemer] if the
Father had not commended him; but, in obeying him we do not
obey him for himself but for having the commission and the
power of the Father; and we say that this Christ will be subject
to God, God having placed all things under him [1 Cor. 15:28]."
Nowhere in so brief a compass and at so early a moment could
we overhear so many of the convictions of a man and movement
that were clearly Anabaptist but also proto-Socinian.

A major but mysterious Italian Anabaptist leader was Il Tiziano (often in the monographic literature and in the sources confused with Lawrence Tizzano, see below).[41] It is possible that
the persistent indisposition of Il Tiziano to disclose his real or
full name was due to his former prominence as a cleric in the
court of an unnamed cardinal in Rome where he first began to
imbibe Lutheran doctrines. Thence he had fled to Geneva and
after visiting "some Lutheran places" returned to Italy from

Germany, "a messenger sent of God." Il Tiziano's claim to have his apostolic authority "from Germany" could have meant that he was commissioned for the Italian mission by some Anabaptist group in German-speaking territory as close as Graubünden (Grigione, Rhaetian Republic) or the Tyrol.[42] His closest associate, Joseph Sartori, had connections with Saint Gall.[43]

Il Tiziano apparently first established himself as an Anabaptist pastor in Rhaetia, where he was expelled from the Reformed synod by the federal government in August, 1549.[44] He had two children, one of whom he maintained in the house of an Anabaptist in Rovigo, the other in a villa of another Anabaptist three miles out from Vicenza. In many towns in northern Italy he is documented between 1549 and 1553 as a major Anabaptist apostle and organizer of conventicles. He baptized Bruno Busale, presumably in Padua. It is possible that it was in Ferrara that he approached Giammaria Ciocchi Cardinal del Monte (later Julius III), seeking to convert him to the radical evangelical cause![45]

Il Tiziano's most fateful action, however, was to convert Peter Manelfi in Florence and to rebaptize him in Ferrara circa 1549. Peter Manelfi, born in San Vito (near Urbino), a priest in Ancona (a Marranist center), he was moved circa 1540 ("ten or eleven years ago") in a "Lutheran" direction by the preaching of Bernardino Ochino and was helped to find his further way into Protestantism by Ochino and two other Capuchins. He read two works by Luther and one by Melanchthon. He gave up his priestly duties; but moving in Lutheran circles, he was instituted *ministro della parola* by the Lutherans in Padua and traveled extensively as a Lutheran evangelist. It was in this capacity that in Florence he was prevailed upon to consider the Anabaptist version of evangelical Christianity by Il Tiziano along with Joseph Sartori of Asolo and Lawrence Niccoluzzo of Modiana.

Manelfi believed that Il Tiziano was responsible for the introduction of Anabaptist teachings into Italy. Il Tiziano's teachings consisted of six or seven points of which the most distinctive were rebaptism and pacifism.[46] Six months later, on submitting to rebaptism at the hands of Il Tiziano in Ferrara,

Manelfi helped found many Anabaptist conventicles, going first to Vicenza. He and Benedict del Borgo of Asolo in one case bribed the guards at a prison in Venice and persuaded one of the Lutheran prisoners, Peter Speziale of Cittadella, to undergo rebaptism at their hands.[47] In other cases they helped prisoners to escape. Theirs was a well-organized underground network and communication system.

Valdesian and/or Marranist Antitrinitarian
Anabaptism from the South to 1550

We turn from the merchant republic of Venice, largely tolerant toward local manifestations of Protestant and sectarian ferment, to the kingdom of Naples under Spanish authority. Here an Erasmian-Valdesian Evangelicalism moved within the context of monastic reform and aristocratic lay devotional circles with philanthropic concern for the poor and the vision of a new "church of the poor." Some of these conventual and lay circles, inspired by John de Valdés (1490–1541), himself quite possibly a Marrano, became theologically and socially radical. Indeed, Valdés, who would review the night before the draft of any sermon of Ochino preached in Naples, had with the great Capuchin evangelist a vision of the incoming *regno di Deo*, of which the devout in villa, convent, and among the parish poor were already faithful subjects.[48] With this Valdesianism came philo-Judaic, universalistic, and prophetic impulses that in some way surely derived from Spanish and Portuguese Marranos and their South Italian counterparts, the *Neofiti*. Proponents of both moderate and radical versions of Valdesianism found their way into numerous centers in the north, priests and friars among them settling down as Reformed ministers in Rhaetia and as conventicular leaders in other parts of the peninsula.

To the larger circle of Valdés belonged, at one time or another, Lady Julia Gonzaga and Lady Isabelle Breseña (Bresegna); the proto-Protestant Peter Carnesecchi and Peter Martyr Vermigli;[49] and the radical viceregal official John de Villafranca, Abbot Jerome Busale, and the Cistercian brothers Lawrence Tizzano[50] and John Laureto.[51] Alike concerned with the poor, some of them became interested in the Hebrew Scriptures. Already while still in Naples some of them moved to an adoptionist, anabaptist, millennialist radical Valdesianism. A defector was later to distinguish as many as eight groupings or types in the larger movement.[52]

The radicalization of Valdesianism, with the possible incorporation of Marranist concerns, and its merging into Anabaptism may be followed in representative detail in the circle around Abbot Jerome Busale.

After the death of Valdés, the Benedictine Abbot Jerome Busale (Buzzale),[53] with his brothers Matthew and Bruno, left Naples and ended up at the University of Padua studying Hebrew and philosophy. Here he appropriated two views closely associated with Paduan intellectual and popular religious circles: (1) that saints and sinners sleep until the day of resurrection and last judgment and accordingly that there is thus neither a heaven nor a purgatory, and (2) that Jesus was born of the seed of Joseph. Already in 1530 in Padua the Franciscan Jerome Galeato (born in Venice circa 1490; died in prison 1541) had been sentenced for life for holding that the souls of the saints sleep until the general resurrection.[54] As for Ebionitism in Padua, its origins are obscure. By 1551 Bullinger in a letter to Calvin would be alarmed about it: "In Padua the horrible heresy of Ebion teems again, that Jesus Christ was born of the corruptible seed of Joseph. In order to affirm this they must deny a good part of the gospels."[55] One cannot but surmise that Marranos from Spain and Portugal and then the kingdom of Naples, resettled in towns up the peninsula, would have been the Judaizing influence, whether from inside or outside the heretical fellowships. The Anabaptist community in Padua in the same year as Bullinger's letter would be apprised of a whole group at Naples who thought Jesus to have come first as a prophet, to return as the Messiah.[56] The Neapolitan circle even held that Paul had misunderstood the prophecies of the Old Testament, mixing in inventions "of the Greeks and Gentiles." This view penetrated the Paduan circle. It is of interest that Busale's group in Padua met first in the home of the Spaniard John de Villafranca and then after the Spaniard's death, in the residence of the abbot himself.

John de Villafranca (d. 1545),[57] sometime official under the viceroy in Naples and a friend of Lady Isabelle Breseña, may have been a Marrano. He was in any case a fount, alike in Naples and then in Padua, of the inspiration leading to adoptionist, anabaptist, psychopannychist, millennialist Valdesianism. He came to hold that Jesus as Messiah would come to rule his elect saints for a thousand years on earth and then deliver his kingdom to the Father (cf. 1 Cor. 15:24).

Into the new Paduan circle of Villafranca and Busale came the two Neapolitan Cistercians, Lawrence Tizzano and John Laureto di Buongiorno. Both of them monks of Santa Maria di Monte Oliveto, they had joined the movement of John Valdés, concerned with the new theology and especially with charity toward the poor. Tizzano came to Padua to study medicine; Laureto, via Genoa and Vicenza, to study Hebrew. From radical Valdesianism they moved through Anabaptism into Jewish Christianity and in the case of Laureto into outright Judaism. Their peregrinations are recounted in their hearings before the Inquisition after they separately turned themselves in (in 1553) with the hope of clemency.

Lawrence Tizzano, who had entered the monastery circa 1533, left circa 1539 with the consent of his superiors to serve as a priest with various charges, for about nine years as chaplain to Lady Catherine Sanseverino (sister of the prince of Bisignano). Hearing of the renown of Valdés, he visited him at his villa and had further contact with his writings through Villafranca. He left for Padua circa 1548 to study medicine, and finding there a certain Neapolitan who could have informed on him, he changed his name to Florio Benedetto. In the two decades between his departure from the Cistercians and his uncoerced resubmission to Catholicism, Tizzano-Benedetto acknowledged having passed through three heretical phases: Lutheran, Anabaptist, and "diabolic." The first phase might better be styled Protestant Valdesianism, for it went beyond Valdés himself in disallowing the papacy but it was no more distinctively Lutheran than Calvinist. Tizzano connected his entering the Anabaptist phase with the influence of Abbot Jerome Busale, Villafranca, and a certain Fra Mattheo Francese while he was living with "Lutherans" as a medical student. As he characterized his

Anabaptist phase, the distinctive mark thereof concerned Joseph's paternity of Jesus without any mention of baptism; but Tizzano may well have said something about it in an earlier confession in Padua, where he first presented himself, as distinguished from his confession in Venice, from which we are drawing; but in any case a Neapolitan associate of Tizzano both in Naples and Venice, Ambrose de Apuzzo, who confessed views otherwise like those of Tizzano in his Anabaptist phase, expressly declared "that baptism should be given to adults and when given to infants should be repeated."[58] For entering what Tizzano called his "diabolic" phase, he inculpated Matthew Busale and especially the former Capuchin Francesco Renato. He expressly says that Bruno Busale, however, and an Anabaptist bishop of the Tyrolese type, Marc Anthony d'Asolo of Treviso, did not countenance his entering this third phase.

"Diabolism" was, in effect, Marranist messianic, evangelical Christianity. Tizzano, who "had the Hebrew language," now held that Jesus was only a prophet, born of Joseph and Mary, perhaps the greatest prophet, for he "may well have had more spirit and gift of God than the other prophets"; that he came as the herald (*Nuntiatore*) of the will of the Father and of the evangelical law; that, although he was not resurrected from the dead, he "will come as the Messiah"; and that then God will resurrect his elect, and Jesus Christ will "restore the Kingdom of Israel and he will reign with all his elect for a certain space of time and thus will be fulfilled that [prophecy] of the prophet [Isa. 2:2]: 'They will beat their swords [into ploughshares]', [after which] . . . there will be the Universal Judgment and he will return the Kingdom to the Father [1 Cor. 15:28]." Tizzano had come to hold that "when the body is dead the soul dies also but that God, blessed be He (*Dio Benedetto*), will resuscitate His elect who have died in the hope of the resurrection, have been good men, and have died in the Communion (*unione*) of the faithful." Tizzano apparently based his extreme view on such texts as Psalms 1:5, "Therefore the wicked will not stand in the [last] judgment"; Isa. 26:14, 19; and Ezek. 37:3.[59] Tizzano reported in Padua that there were many in Naples who went even further and denied "the whole New Testament and say it is the invention of Greeks and Gentiles and that Paul understood nothing of the Old Testament, especially concerning justification and the resurrection, because he says justification is through the blood of Christ and the [Old] Scripture says justification is through the mercy of God." Not far from this extreme even in Padua was the Neapolitan lawyer Julius Busalù, who, holding "that the Hebrew religion is true," could believe "only that which is in harmony in the one and the other law, that is, the Hebrew and the Christian."[60]

John Laureto di Buongiorno della Cava, born circa 1518, had at about the age of seventeen made, like Tizzano, his vows as a Cistercian monk at Monte Oliveto in Naples and was at length also ordained a priest. About 1543, without permission, he donned lay garb and left. Attaching himself at length to the Austin Canons of Sant'Annelo in Naples, he resumed daily mass for a while. He made the friendship of a Spaniard in the service of the viceroy of Naples, who introduced him to Lutheranism and gave him books, promising to take him with him to Germany to learn more. To this end they sailed circa 1544 together to Genoa; but Laureto, who again cast off his priestly garb, got sick and had to stay behind. He contacted Lady Isabella Breseña,[61] whom he had come to know as a Valdesian in Naples, now wife of the governor of Piacenza under Charles V.

Apparently Lady Breseña had called Jerome Busale thither primarily into her spiritual services, but nominally as secretary for what proved to be two years.[62] Busale openly expressed doubt about the divinity of Christ, and he urged Laureto to pursue the study of Greek and Hebrew like himself in order to get "at the truth." Busale prudently left his employment with Lady Breseña to study philosophy at Padua. Laureto, after the arrest of a local Lutheran, his friend, presently followed Busale to Padua.

While Laureto was studying Hebrew there, several Anabaptists came to town and, after discussion, persuaded both Busale and Laureto to submit in 1549 to rebaptism, Laureto at the hands of Benedict del Borgo of Asolo, Jerome Busale at the hands of Nicholas d'Alessandria of Reviso.[63]

Jerome Busale had by now moved from Benedictine monasticism, through Adoptionist Valdesianism, to antitrinitarian Anabaptism. Busale himself proceeded to rebaptize for about three months. He remained, however, subject to harsh judgment from some Anabaptists of a different social background in that still "he ate the blood of the Beast" in retaining the revenues of his abbatial benefice, however generous therewith; and under Anabaptist pressure for apostolic simplicity, he renounced them.[64]

The divergence between a christologically conservative Anabaptism of the Tyrolese type and a Josephite or Ebionite Anabaptism necessitated a conclave that met in Busale's home opposite Saint Catherine's in Padua in January, 1550. Present were representatives from Treviso, headed by Julius Gherlandi; from Rovigo, headed by Francis della Sega (both of the latter of Hutterite connections); from Vicenza, headed by Julius Callezaro; along with Jerome Busale, Il Tiziano, and Manelfi.[65] The most extreme position at the conclave seems to have been taken by the Judaizing Marc Anthony da Prata of Asolo, an earlier associate of Il Tiziano. Prominence in the discussion was given to Deuteronomy 18:15: "The Lord your God will raise up for you a prophet like me from among you, from your brethren—him you shall heed."[66] We can well imagine that Hebraist Busale was among the most forceful in pressing for a Judaizing Christology.

Thereupon Busale became the bishop of the Anabaptists of both the northern and the southern types resident in Padua.[67] Bishop Benedict del Borgo, former notary of Asolo, concurred in this arrangement before setting out to organize the conventicle of Polesine in November 1550. The fact that Busale "was a very learned person and had the Hebrew language" was a factor in his elevation to the dignity of bishop for all Anabaptists in Padua.[68] Busale was thus emerging as a major figure throughout the movement. Moreover, several leaders of the northern type began appropriating the more radical views being formulated in Padua, thus creating theological tension among Anabaptists throughout the north-central region of Italy.

The Anabaptist Synod in Venice, 1550

To settle the still disputed points in a wider context, it was decided to hold a synod in Venice[69] with two delegates from

each congregation. Il Tiziano and Joseph Sartori of Asolo re-
cruited the delegates from refugee conventicles in Rhaetia and
Switzerland. Manelfi claims to have had part of the responsibility for seeking funds and providing housing for the delegates.
Some sixty persons, all Italians and representing around thirty
conventicles, gather in September, 1550. Francis Negri may have
come from Chiavenna. There was even a delegate from Saint
Gall. Jerome Busale and Benedict of Asolo were present. They
met for forty days, opening their sessions with prayer. The
Lord's Supper was three times observed.

Manelfi was apparently very forceful in moving the synod to
adopt as their own a nearly unanimous statement of ten disputed
points, strongly supporting the kind of theology represented by
Camillo Renato, Francis of Calabria, and Lawrence Tizzano.
The ten points can be condensed thus: Jesus was not God but an
exceptional man, the natural child of Joseph and Mary; Mary
had other sons and daughters after Jesus; human seed has the
God-given power to produce both body and soul (traducian-
ism); the elect are justified by the eternal mercy and love of God
rather than the merits of Christ's death; the "benefit" of Christ
consisted solely in his giving instruction in the good life and in
his self-sacrificial testimony to the love and justice of God. There
are no angels but, rather, human messengers of God. There is no
devil other than human prudence. The latter claim, possibly a
Waldensian note, is based on Rom. 1:18–23 and the general
biblical observation that "we do not find anything in the Scripture created by God as his enemy except human prudence." They
agreed that the souls of the wicked die with their bodies; that
for the unrighteous, there is no hell except the grave; and that
after the death of the elect their souls sleep till the day of judgment. This point represents a muting of Renato, Tizzano, and
Busale's starker conception of the expiration of the souls, even of
the saints, pending the resurrection.

For those who were most radical at the Synod of Venice, the
Josephite Christology embodied in articles 1 and 2 involved al-
so the rejection of the first and second chapters of Matthew and
Luke as spurious.[70] On the basis of a letter of Saint Jerome to
Pope Damasus,[71] they argued that a false genealogy had been
introduced, which did injustice to the motherhood of Mary and

the fatherhood of Joseph and which was not in conformity with the Old Testament prophets.

The delegates of the Anabaptists of Cittadella refused to accept all the Venetian Articles as did those in Vicenza, both groups continuing with the "old doctrine"; but for the most part, the Venetian synod clearly represented a general triumph of the new doctrine, of radical unitarian Italian Anabaptism over the older Tyrolese type.

At the conclusion of the synod, several participants were designated as "apostolic bishops" to bring the synodal decisions to the constituent and related congregations. They moved about in pairs reminiscent of the Waldensian bards. Manelfi, with Marc Anthony of Asolo, for example, traveled to Vicenza, Padua, Treviso, and Istra. With Lawrence Niccoluzzo of Modiana he visited the Romagna, Ferrara, and Tuscany.

In Rovigo, apostolic bishop Benedict del Borgo of Asolo was apprehended for preaching Anabaptism and, on March 16, 1551, having refused to abjure his faith, was put to death.[72] In Friuli, Nicholas d'Alessandria and his fellow evangelist Giacometto, a tailor, both of Treviso, converted the sisters of Saint Clare in the local Franciscan convent that happened to house, among many daughters of noble families, the sister of sometime Bishop Peter Paul Vergerio. But when the converted sisters prepared to submit to rebaptism, Nicholas refused except on condition that they leave.[73] This only partly successful penetration of a distinguished convent for women indicates the social and vocational coverage of the Italian Anabaptist mission in the period leading to, and immediately following, the synod of Venice— from Milan to Venetian towns down the Istrian coast to Pirano (Piran)[74] and Castelnuovo (Podgrad) and into Slovene territory as far as Ljubljana,[75] and from Brunico[76] to Perugia. Nevertheless, a schism had developed between the congregations willing to accept the Ten Venetian Articles and those which, like the original standout, Cittadella, held to a more moderate course.

Manelfi in September, 1551, was asked by the brethren in Verona to explain the Ten Venetian Articles of agreement. A Sunday meeting broke up in disagreement over his defense of the Venetian article that Christ was merely a prophetic teacher, but some twenty-five converts were baptized by him in a secluded spot.

The Defection of Manelfi, 1551, and of Laureto and Tizzano, 1553

Suddenly, on October 4, 1551, Manelfi decided to return to the Catholic church and told his companion of his startling decision. In Bologna he turned himself over to the Inquisition and on October 17 made his first deposition, describing his "aberrations," disclosing the deliberations of the synod in Venice, and recounting the history of the movement from radical "Lutheranism" to radical Anabaptism during the preceding decade. He said: "We maintain union with Anabaptists in Germany and the Grigioni."[77] The case was transferred, because of its obvious importance, to Rome, where Manelfi prepared three more statements, enabling the Inquisition very shortly thereafter to wipe out most of the Anabaptist movement in Italy. In a deposition of November 12, he gave further details about his work as bishop. He pointed out that the stress on Christ's sole humanity had not been so prominent in the conventicles until his own urging of it in Venice. On November 13, he provided further information about the synod and named several participants and some of the other apostolic bishops. Manelfi also listed as many members of the sect as he could recall and added the names of a number of Lutherans in Veneto. In his final deposition on November 14, he described the several occasions on which he and other evangelists had narrowly escaped capture and how they had entered prisons to comfort fellow believers, winning also new converts.

The Inquisition moved swiftly against the Anabaptists and related nonconformists. The orders for the arrest of the persons named by Manelfi were sent to the authorities at Padua, Vicenza, Treviso, and Asolo. Arrests and recantations followed. The fate of Manelfi, the informer, is not known.

Giacometto Stringaro fell into the hands of the Inquisition in 1552.[78] Busale for his part decided to return to Naples and asked Laureto to accompany him on the road. Busale talked as they walked about the prophecies of Amos, applying them to contemporary Italy, which would soon be chastized by God for the persecution of Anabaptists. Laureto challenged his claim to be speaking through the Holy Spirit. When Busale decided to leave Naples for Alexandria,[79] where he had "relations,"[80] he refused to let Laureto accompany him. Laureto had indeed suggested the trip to spare Busale's mother and some of his brothers from the hazards of his preaching doom locally.

Laureto went back to Padua via Rome and for four months studied Hebrew in company with Bruno Busale and Lawrence Tizzano. During this brief sojourn, presumably, Laureto was excommunicated by Nicholas d'Alessandria of Asolo from the Paduan Anabaptist community for his having criticized them for superstitiously confining their reading to the Bible. About Christmas, 1551, Laureto and Tizzano went to Venice and then to Ferrara and there separated, Laureto to Vicenza. He then sailed to Thessalonica, where he found a large number of Anabaptists under the headship of his excommunicator, Nicholas. Preferring by now the company of the Sephardic Jewish community, the better to continue his study of Hebrew, Laureto finally submitted to circumcision,[81] but he did not accept the proffer of a Jewish wife. The more he studied under Jewish tutelage, the more "superstitious" and "erroneous" post-biblical Judaism appeared to him; but to get away, he had to feign a desire for more advanced studies in Constantinople before being able to establish a school.

In his heart he had already decided to return to Roman Catholic obedience; sailing by way of Heracleon (Candia), he reached Venice and turned himself over to the inquisitorial authorities to recant and recount in 1553 his extraordinary spiritual peregrinations.

In the same city at the same time, his erstwhile companion, first in Monte Oliveto in Naples and then in the Judaizing Anabaptist conventicle in Padua, made a similar confession, which we have already used to recount his life to date. Lawrence Tizzano-Florio Benedetto, alarmed by the arrest of the Lutherans with whom he had been living as a medical student, left Padua, as just noted, in the company of Laureto for Venice and then Ferrara. Separating, Tizzano went to Genoa with a view to returning to Naples; but getting sick there and without any acquaintances, he decided to go back to Padua. It was there that he turned himself in to the inquisitor, whence his hearing was transferred to the capital.[82]

Il Tiziano, of German Anabaptist inspiration, for his part escaped the consequences of the defection of Manelfi in the relative security of Rhaetia, from which he had been banished in 1547. His preaching brought him a renewed following. Thereupon in June, 1554, the authorities at the federal capital, Chur, had him imprisoned and questioned about his beliefs. He answered in ambiguous language, claiming to be guided only by the Holy Spirit. Fear of capital punishment moved him, however, to sign in the presence of assembled elders and others a confession prepared by Philip Gallicius, pastor at Chur.[83] This confession implied that Il Tiziano denied the Trinity and the divine nature of Christ (as an Ebionite), had suspected a tendentious corruption of the genealogies and nativity narratives by Jerome (as a Helvidian), had placed the authority of the Holy Spirit above that of the Bible, had rejected infant baptism, and had said that Christians might not serve as magistrates. After his recantation, Il Tiziano was driven by rods from the town, exiled (a second time) from the Rhaetian republic. Gallicius, in his letter to Bullinger, felt obliged to justify his relative leniency in the treatment of Il Tiziano by pointing out that a recantation would be demoralizing for his followers, whereas another martyrdom (Gallicius refers to the martyrdom of Michael Servetus) would but raise their devotion to a new pitch.

Camillo Renato, for his part, had found that not even two recantations could dampen the ardor of his followers. He was captured by the constables in Bergamo in September, 1551, just a year after the Anabaptist synod in Venice. Cardinal Innocenzo del Monte, a secretary to Pope Julius III, was almost at once in possession of the information that the notorious "Sicilian heresiarch" had been captured; and he sought, through the papal nuncio in Venice, to gain possession of the escapee from the inquisitorial prison in Bologna—but in vain. With the aid of "powerful supporters who are able to use shields of gold," and with a formal renunciation once again of all his heretical views, Camillo returned to Rhaetia, where as a "poisonous bladder" (Bullinger's phrase) he began to "contaminate the whole of the Valtellina with his poison" (Vergerio's report). Camillo Renato even made bold to seek the headship of the evangelical school in Sondrio as a counterweight to the seminary in Chur. "Here Camillo reigns," wrote Vergerio with alarmed exaggeration.

The principal document surviving from this period is Camillo's long, flamboyant, passionate indictment of Calvin for burning Servetus. The *Carmen*, composed in Traona in September, 1554, for the anniversary of the execution, mingled biblical and mythological language in highly mannered, humanistic verse.[84] It was a great plea for religious toleration. Distinguishing between the two dispensations, that of the New and that of the Old, Camillo associated the Roman priesthood with that of the Hebraic covenant, since both stressed law and sacrifice; and he appealed for a gentler conception of religion as proclaimed and practiced by Jesus himself, who healed, who forgave, and who was slow to anger. Nowhere else do we have in Camillo's writings such stress upon the apostolic ban as the only means of force allowable to Christians. He laments the fact that in the so-called Reformed church the wholesome apostolic ban has itself been banned.

Mention can be appropriately made to an implementer of Camillo's tactics on the Rhaetian scene during the lifetime of the heresiarch. Michelangelo Florio, father of John Florio (translator of Michel Montaigne's *Essais* into English), was a native of Tuscany, a converted Jew who became a Franciscan and then a Protestant (ca. 1541). In 1550 he had fled from Rome via Naples, Venice, and Lyons and reached London, where he served the Italian congregation affiliated with the Strangers' Church. In England, 1551–54, he had taught Italian to Lady Jane Grey, of whom he later wrote a life in Italian. His *Apologia di M. Michel Agnolo Fiorentino* (Chamogasko, 1557) is a major source for his interesting career.[85] Much-traveled Michelangelo Florio, with four other Italian refugee pastors, perpetuat-

ing some of Camillo Renato's teachings, widened the schism in
the Italian Reformed community of Rhaetia and renewed the attack on Reformed orthodoxy in Chiavenna.

Italian Spiritualists: George Siculo[86]

The nearest counterpart in Italy of such disparate Germanic
Spiritualists as Sebastian Franck, Caspar Schwenckfeld, and
Thomas Müntzer was perhaps George Siculo.[87] A former Benedictine monk, Siculo was a prophetic preacher. A hostile Italian refugee in Rhaetia said of him that he had satanically
combined Papism and Anabaptism and contributed to the establishment of a third sect.[88] He repudiated all the sacraments,
holding that true baptism consisted in having faith in Christ, in
repentance and in receiving the Spirit, not water, as did the apostles at Pentecost.[89] He was a traducianist rather than creationist,
holding that God directly created only the soul of Adam; he
denied the existence of purgatory and hell, and held that souls
at death go flying into the air until the Last Judgment.[90] He considered Father, Son, and Holy Spirit as "tre signori et no un solo
signore." He had strong convictions on social order, holding that
temporal lords should not amass wealth or impose unfair taxes
or services and that Roman and common law should give way
to the Law of Moses. All this George Siculo believed was revealed to him by Jesus Christ in person,[91] who had made him his
"legate" to restore true Christianity after its lapse for more than
a thousand years. In company with most Germanic Anabaptists
in opposition to classical Protestants, Siculo believed in the freedom of the will unto salvation and took the occasion of the bacil-
lation and then the execution in Padua of the Protestant jurisconsult Francesco Spiera to compose a doctrinal *Epistola* that
was printed in Bologna in 1550. It contained in substance what
Siculo had preached for forty days at Riva di Trento. He had
gone there, possibly with the hope of preaching before the Council of Trent, convened a bit farther up the Adige, of exhorting
it prophetically to turn from predestinarian Protestantism (!)
and to the true catholic and apostolic tradition. But he was denounced and summoned before the magistrates of Riva. The

same year he was again in Ferrara, where he enlisted a number of followers, still preaching against the Luthern predestination and bondage of the will. The Inquisition at Ferrara was well aware that his opposition to Luther shielded a heresy even more dangerous. Siculo was in prison by the beginning of April, 1551. On May 23 he was hanged, having once recanted and then disavowed his abjuration. His followers were numerous. He was so much appreciated by some of the Italian residents in Geneva that Calvin wrote against him, saying of his books and ideas "Passing swiftly throughout Italy, they corrupt many people."

Italian Anabaptists, 1553–1565:
Relations with the Hutterites

Three important survivors of the first wave of persecution caused by Manelfi's desertion of the Anabaptist cause in 1551 were the Venetians Julius Gherlandi, Francis della Sega, and Anthony Rizzeto. All three had moved in the antitrinitarian direction, but could be called moderates; and Gherlandi in the end completely repudiated the more extreme of the Ten Articles of the Synod of Venice.[92] All of them sought asylum with the Hutterites in Moravia and led many of their followers thither.[93] Around them can be told much of the remainder of the Anabaptist story in Italy.

The first notice of Italian Anabaptist contact with Moravia dates from well before the intra-Italian Anabaptist schism, namely, 1540. A "Rechenschafft der Brueder zu Trüest," preserved in a Hutterite *Chronicle*, records the faith and the martyrdom by drowning of certain Anabaptists in Trieste.[94] The "community of the saints" in Moravia continued to draw large numbers of Italian Anabaptists to their commonwealth.[95] We turn to the three later martyrs of whom we have notable particulars.

Julius Gherlandi (also, in Hutterite records, Klemperer) was born circa 1520 near Treviso in Veneto and was intended by his father for the Catholic priesthood. He was troubled in conscience by the contradiction between his Christian professions and his own actual achievements and failings. It is quite possible that he belonged for a season to the circle in Vicenza and that his memory was preserved in Socinian records as "Julius of Treviso."[96] In reading Matt. 7:15 f. about false prophets and bad fruit trees, he was led to break from the Roman church to join the Anabaptists. He was baptized about 1549 by Nicholas d'Alessandria of Asolo. He baptized several persons himself. We have already encountered Gherlandi with Francis della Sega at the conclave in Padua in 1550. After the defection of Manelfi, Gherlandi, on learning about the Hutterite colonies, journeyed to Moravia and was admitted to the Bruderhof at Pausram (just west of Auspitz). Despite involvement in the unitarian, adoptionist thrust of Italian Anabaptism, he was not required to be rebaptized. Gherlandi engaged in his new craft of making lanterns, but soon asked permission to bring the message of the Hutterites to his former associates in Italy.

In March, 1559, Gherlandi arrived with two companions from the Hutterite community bearing a letter from della Sega (who had settled there in the meantime) to a fellow believer in Vicenza, as well as a general letter of introduction from the Hutterites to the Italian Anabaptists.[97] The letter describes Hutterites as communitarians and makes clear that only those Italian Anabaptists would be welcomed as members whose minds were not contaminated with false doctrines about the seed of Joseph, the resurrection only of the saints, and other matters (in obvious reference to the articles approved by the Venetian synod of 1550). Gherlandi also carried a list of more than a hundred Italians living in over sixty localities in Hungary, northern Italy, Trentino, and Rhaetia.[98]

On March 21, 1559, Gherlandi came to official attention when on arriving in Venice he refused, as every other Anabaptist did, to swear by oath: in this instance, to the port authorities that he had no disease! On being released, he appeared a few days later in his native Treviso, publicly criticizing the Roman church. He was arrested and examined at Treviso and was then transferred to prison in Venice, from which he managed to escape and return to Moravia.

He was back in Italy by Christmas of 1560, and in October, 1561, was captured once again near Treviso and imprisoned at

San Giovanni in Bragora in Venice. From his prison he wrote, October 4, 1561, a letter[99] to Bishop Leonard Lanzenstiel in Moravia. He had on his person a German scriptural concordance. The letter explains his predicament and breathes a courageous spirit, firm in the faith: "Do not for a moment doubt that there will be given to me in the hour, according to the true divine promise, wisdom against which all the adversaries shall not be able to prevail." A few days later, Gherlandi prepared a comprehensive confession of faith, recounted the reasons that had prompted him to leave Catholicism and eventually to join the Hutterites as for him the best exemplification of the holy nation, a peculiar people (1 Pet. 2:9), reborn in the Spirit and together in Christ overcoming the sin of Adam. He closed thus: "That is my simple confession. I ask that it be accepted with indulgence, for I am no orator, writer or historian, but only a poor lantern-maker—I am however not truly poor, since I am indeed content with my fate." On November 16, 1561, Gherlandi was examined by three theologians. The issue between the inquisitors and the Hutterite concerned the relative authority of church, tradition, and the Scriptures. The Catholics found that he remained "obstinate in the crime of heresy," and he was left to languish in the prison, where he sought to convert his fellow prisoners. When admonished by a priest to beg pardon from the court for proclaiming his gospel in prison, he replied, "To God alone ought I to bend the knee and not to worldly men."

It is at this point that we pick up the story of the already mentioned Francis della Sega.[100] Della Sega was born at Rovigo in 1528. He studied civil law in Padua. Stricken with illness brought on by his carefree life as a student, and chided by a pious craftsman, he turned to the New Testament, determined to model his life on that of Christ. His conversion was complete. He abandoned law and became a tailor, incurring the ridicule of family and friends. He joined the Anabaptist movement. He, too, is remembered in the Socinian tradition, as among the refugees in the Grisons after 1551.

Around 1557 he was in Vienna and then traveled with a Hungarian friend through Hungary and Slovakia. Learning of the Hutterites from their Moravian servant, he visited several communities in Moravia. He was admitted to membership, perhaps first in Slovakia, but later in Pausram in Moravia. There he married an Ursula from the Engadine and settled down as a tailor. He was ordained a Hutterite *Diener* and preached in both Italian and German.[101] On receiving news of his father's death, della Sega returned to Italy to see about his inheritance. Once again he tried to convert his mother from a religion of "wood and stones." Everywhere he carried word of the Hutterite way of life to friends and prospective converts.

In August, 1562, on one of his missions, in the company of one Nicholas Buccella, a surgeon of Padua, and of Anthony Rizzetto of Vicenza, della Sega was leading to Moravia some twenty-one or so members of the Cittadella conventicle. A large part of this group had not assented to the Venetian Ten Articles. The company were overtaken at Capodistria just as they were embarking for Trieste,[102] betrayed by a fellow believer who desired to recover his investment. The *podestà* sent the band of Anabaptists to the Inquisition at Venice for further examination. Della Sega was found to be carrying the names and addresses of other recruits, several of them in the Piedmont region earlier turmoiled by the Tyrolese Peasants' War.[103] They were put in the prison where Gherlandi was being held. The two Italian Hutterites quickly made contact and were able to reinforce one another in the difficult weeks ahead. Della Sega must have made use of Gherlandi's German concordance or have had one of his own, for most of his surviving documents composed in prison are scripturally replete (though he complained several times of not having a good memory).

On October 15, 1562, the court sentenced Gherlandi to be drowned. When informed of his fate, he prepared a last work of greeting to the Moravians. It was necessary first to degrade him formally from his rank as ordained subdeacon of the Roman church before turning him over to the secular arm. Under the cover of darkness his boat set forth into the *Laguna* to meet another one that was waiting for it. A plank was thrown between the two boats, he was tied upon it and weighted with stones, and the boats thereupon grimly returned separately to their ports. The martyrdom of Gherlandi in Venetian waters took place sometime after October 23, 1562.

Our third representative, Anthony Rizzetto,[104] is as interest-

ing a personality as Gherlandi and della Sega. He had been rebaptized about 1551 in Vicenza by the apostle Marc Anthony of
Asolo, sometime companion of the renegade Manelfi. Rizzetto
and Bartholomew of Padua, the latter with wife and daughter,
chose to flee persecution by taking ship to Thessalonica. When
Bartholomew died, Rizzetto married the widow; and, after returning to Italy, he too visited the Hutterites. It was on his return trip from Moravia to bring back his wife and family that
he had joined della Sega's company and had been overtaken with
him by the *podestà* at Capodistria.

During the imprisonment, there was a series of examinations
conducted by the Jesuit theologian Alfonso Salmerón, among
others. Throughout, della Sega and Rizzetto stressed their devotion to Scripture and the rights of conscience uncoerced by the
Roman church or the Venetian state. Both della Sega and Rizzetto prepared statements, reflecting these encounters. The
Memoriale of della Sega, circa November 3, 1562, is a moving
account (from which we have already drawn) of his student
days in Padua, his conversion, and his discovery of the true
church among the Hutterites.[105] He then turns to the particular
points on which the inquistors had pressed him: baptism, Communion, and confession. Having affirmed his acceptance of the
Apostles Creed, he feels drawn to specify his faith in God the
Father and Creator, Jesus Christ his Son and Lord and Savior,
and the Holy Spirit, as though to clear himself of the more extreme views formulated at Padua and then at the Venetian synod
and from which he had turned back while among the Hutterites.

Baptism he then deals with at length. He denies having himself ever baptized anyone, holding that only those with proper
authority may do so. Baptism is for believers who can receive the
gift of the Holy Spirit and do things meet for a Christian within the Ark of Noah, the church of the sanctified. As for children, he notes that Jesus bade them come unto him but never
spoke of their being baptized. He is inclined to hold that Christ's
sacrifice was for the whole world and that in wiping out the
guilt of Adam and hence original sin, Christ cleansed all infants
everywhere even beyond the reach of the gospel. One has only
to confess one's own sins and to be prepared for a new disci-

plined life in love to receive baptism. As for Communion, della Sega recognizes its great mystery and diverse meanings, a recollection and an anticipation, with always the danger that one might participate in it to one's hurt, like a Judas. In remarking that it should be observed not only once a year, he must be alluding to what at some point became Hutterite usage. With this he presumably did not agree and in any case would not wish to have his Catholic examiners know about this Hutterite peculiarity. As for confession, he recognizes its Dominical origin, but shifts the action from sacramental confession in the presence of a priest to varying degrees, within the fellowship of earnest believers, of repentance and reprimand up to the ban. He then turns to eschatology with a resurrection and Last Judgment (in the idiom of the Synoptic Apocalypse: Matt. 25:31–46)[106] of both the righteous and the wicked, eschewing the mention of psychopannychism. In fact, the sleep of the soul and resurrection of the saints only (cf. the Venetian synod) are not mentioned in any of the della Sega's rather substantial literary remains.

Early the next year, della Sega directed a letter to Bishop Leonard Sailer Lanzenstiel, Peter Scherer Walpot, and the whole community in Moravia. Unlike the one written earlier by Gherlandi, it was delivered. Of exceptional interest, it transmits Gherlandi's last words and speaks movingly of his martyrdom. It breaths a purified faith and devotion to Christ:

> I would not [writes della Sega] let the occasion pass while I am yet in this tabernacle of desiring for you the grace of salvation of the omnipotent God. I have loved you all sincerely; but I love you even more now that I have been deprived of your presence, which deprivation is a great tribulation to me. And when the end comes, I will love you with the love that I have through Christ himself, because you are of his flesh, yea, bone and limbs of Christ. And you have loved me sincerely. Through you I have received of God innumerable benefits for which I have not repaid you, and thus I remain your debtor. But I desire to bear this my humiliation with patience, for love of you; yea, I would bear being rejected and cast out and finally led to execution on account of my love of you.[107]

Della Sega exhorts the pastors and the community as a whole, and has special words for his fellow Italians who, in Christ, had been so hospitably received by the Hutterites. The doctrinal section of the letter suggests that della Sega had not entirely abandoned his earlier triadological and soteriological views. He looks forward to the delivery by Christ ("the Son of man," "the first born") of his Kingdom "of those reborn and renewed by the Holy Spirit" to the Father "that God may be for eternity all in all" (cf. 1 Cor. 15:28).[108] He closes with greetings to his friends in Moravia, to his beloved and loyal wife, Ursula, and to his mother-in-law.

A decree of the Venetian Council of Ten, issued April 7, 1564, providing for the mere expulsion of heretics,[109] momentarily raised in della Sega and Rizzetto the hope that it might apply to them. Della Sega wrote the inquisitors and the patricians respectively on July 18 and 20, 1564,[110] praising the authorities for what seemed an enlightened policy, reminding them that Jesus would have approved of allowing such alleged heretical tares as the Hutterites to grow up until the harvest, and asking release from imprisonment to return to his wife and family in Moravia.

The second and by far the longer communication (to the irritation of the divines) is to the lords temporal, a moving and cogent marshaling of scriptural and other arguments in what amounts to a small treatise on religious toleration. Della Sega fully recognizes the God-ordained role of magistracy, but contends that the Roman church through the arrogations of her canonists and theologians has converted the church of Christ itself into a rival kingdom or principality of this world, citing Matt. 10:42–45 (and parallels), and insisting that the priestly theological inquisitors should be the servants instead of the masters of all. He argues that a Christian magistracy and *a fortiori* a Christian ministry should not be involved in anything so heinous as capital punishment for alleged heresy, citing, in addition to many scriptural passages concerning free will and against coercion in the realm of faith, a number of Fathers: Ignatius of Antioch (*Epistle to the Philadelphians*), (Pseudo-) Dionysius (supposedly bishop of Corinth, then Paris: *Epistle VIII* on kindness in religion), and Augustine, twice (*Commentary on Matthew 13; Epistle CXXVII* to the Proconsul Donatus).[111] He reminds the Venetian Council that Jews and Muslims under

Venetian jurisdiction enjoy religious toleration and insists that those like himself who are trying to follow the express commandments of Jesus, the Apostles, and the Fathers should be accorded the same privilege or at least the lesser punishment of exile.

The eloquent arguments were ignored, perhaps because Rome itself was rebuking Venice for its relative leniency. In November, the inquisitor Fra Adriano reported the case, listing the chief heresies of della Sega and Rizzetto—namely, their rejection of the Roman church, of infant baptism, and of confession to priests, and their union with the Hutterites as the allegedly true church. An interrogation of December 12, 1564, showed della Sega and Rizzetto still firm in their faith despite the abjuration of their companion, Dr. Nicholas Buccella, and his efforts on December 7 to help them moderate their views.

This Dr. Buccella,[112] a popular anatomist of the medical faculty in Padua, had been an Anabaptist. Though for awhile austere, steadfast, and frank, preparing a confession of faith modeled on the Apostles' Creed, he had finally yielded to the importuning of his solicitous brothers and the sympathetic counsel of a consultor in the hearings and had agreed to try in turn to persuade Rizzetto and della Sega, with some temporary effect on the latter. Dr. Buccella was thereupon released and required only to stay in Padua and its environs for three years under surveillance. (He later shows up as a friend of Faustus Socinus in Cracow.)

Della Sega recovered his resolve and addressed in December, 1564, a letter or testament to his Catholic mother and brothers. This undelivered message is remarkable in being directed to next of kin who had disowned him and would do nothing to relieve the anguish and physical wretchedness of one who for his faith was enduring the dank, sunless squalor in nearby Venice. He lovingly reproached them for ignoring his efforts to bring them to see the spiritual light and concludes:

> Now, if this letter should not please you . . . I know nought else to say, for God will not save you by force. It remains to me, in this case, to ask you only to pass this letter to some other who may have

the desire to do good and to live far from sins like a good Christian according to the will of God.[113]

Sentence was passed on della Sega and Rizzetto on February 8, 1565. Della Sega again wavered momentarily. When the executioner told this to Rizzetto, the latter replied: "Unhappy soul! But if he has lost his soul, I do not want to lose mine. What I have said, I have said."[114] Della Sega still appeared undecided in the presence of Salmerón, and he was reproved for his indecision; but in the end he remained true to his faith. The two Hutterite heretics were spared the usual fiery punishment[115] for heresy that prevailed beyond the confines of watery and more clement Venice. At ten o'clock of the night of Monday, February 26, 1565, after refusing to kiss the crucifix pressed to their lips, they were cast, weighted, from planks into the depths of the sea. "But the sea will give up its dead at the Judgment Day of God," the Hutterite *Chronicle* reminded its readers.[116]

When word came to the Italian Anabaptists in Moravia of the deaths of the two Italian Hutterites in Venice in 1565, there would have been, to summarize the observations of the Italian merchant-seeker Marcantonio Varotta,[117] in that land of refuge a dozen or so sectarian groupings of predominantly German or Czech speech. Among them there were many Italian communitarian Anabaptists (Hutterites, *Cappellari*) and Josephites (*Giosepitti*); also Samosatenes (e.g., Nicholas Paruta). The Josephites were clearly Italian antitrinitarian Anabaptists. Whether there were Italians among the Sabbatarians mentioned by Varotta is less certain; but it is in any case clear that even in Moravian exile the two main social and possibly ethnic strands in the Anabaptism of the peninsula remained distinguishable.

CONCLUSION

Italian Anabaptism displayed the same mobility as the German. Its devotees as missionaries or refugees covered indeed a much greater geographical range, showing up in the surviving documents everywhere from Sicily through Rhaetia and Moravia to Lithuania; from London, Lyons, Chiavenna, to Koloszvár, Thessalonica, and Damascus!

Because, to be sure, representatives even of the classical Protestant Reformation (Lutherans, Calvinists) as well as of the three thrusts in the Radical Reformation (Anabaptists, Spiritualists, Evangelical Rationalists) in Catholic Italy (after 1542, the seat of the Papal Inquisition) all had to be on the move continuously and convene in secret, distinctions among these movements and phases in the individual careers of their leaders and followers are not so easy to keep sorted out at any one moment or in any given conventicle as with their counterparts in Germanic lands. Moreover, the pre-history of what later became Socinianism in Poland and Unitarianism in Transylvania, namely, Evangelical Rationalism (which in any case was preeminently a distinctive Italian amalgam but little represented in the Radical Reformation in Germanic lands) overlapped in part with that of antitrinitarian Anabaptism.

Italian Anabaptism had two or three major foyers: the southern Tyrolese and Rhaetian valleys, Neapolitan Valdesian salons, and Bible study circles in the homes of town artisans south and north. Conventual, priestly, artisan, petty burgher, humanist, and almost certainly Marranist seeker types prevailed over peasants and other rural types in contrast to the social types in German Anabaptism (mostly peasants and artisans). Italian Anabaptists counted proportionately more learned people than the Germans; and on the whole also more defectors or outward conformists (Nicodemites: a Marranist reflex); but they were all authentic Anabaptists, even if an increasing proportion of them did come to expound ever more explicitly what the German and Dutch Anabaptists (except notably for Louis Haetzer and Adam Pastor) for the most part did only implicitly, namely, the unacceptability of the Nicene and Chalcedonian formulations in concentration on, and devotion to, *Christus pauper*, who they expected would soon return as the benign comforter and vindicator of his faithful flock.

The overall impression is very strong in both Anabaptism and Evangelical Rationalism in Italy that Marranism or even messianic or Cabbalistic or spiritualizing Judaism played, especially in the south and among immigrants from the south to the cities of the Papal States and the sovereign territories further north, a formative role in the devolution of the doctrine of the Trinity and in the lowering of Christology up to the complete human-ization of Jesus as the son of Joseph. Clearly, these theologically provocative thrusts served no soteriological or other purpose, ex-cept as they made the evangelical reformation of Catholic Chris-tianity more acceptable precisely to those whose ancestors had been presumably forced into Christianity. In the era of universal Reformation and high eschatological and even interfaith ecu-menical hopes, it would appear that some Marranos, being them-selves already acquainted with persecution or harassment even as would-be conforming Catholics, were apparently confident that there was more meaning in advancing into a radically new Christian way of life than in reverting to Judaism. And it is of interest that Nicodemism or nominal conformity was a great temptation that beset all kinds of evangelical Christians in Catholic Italy from the crypto-Calvinists pilloried by Calvin to no less a Socinian than Faustus Socinus himself, who lived un-obtrusively for a decade at the court of the grand duke of Tus-cany.

Despite the eventual predominance of antitrinitarian Ana-baptism, the awareness of confessional, social, and perhaps even regional-ethnic differences persisted among Italian Anabaptists in the vast diaspora, most notably and demonstrably in Moravia, where so many of them congregated as refugees seeking the promised land of the true evangelical church. There the south Tyrolese and Tridentine types and their conservative confreres, whose major experiential background had been the sociopolitical upheaval in the Tyrolese extension of the Peasants' War under Gaismair, commonly joined the Hutterites. In contrast, other Italian Anabaptists whose major experiential background had been in some obscure way related to the persecutions of Jewish Christians (Marranos) or to the spiritual frustration of Valde-sians remained apart in Moravia, many of them known as Jo-sephites, Samosatenes, and so forth.

Nevertheless, the regionalist, possibly ethnic, and surely con-fessional variations in Italian Anabaptism do not justify any fundamental separation of it from the larger international Ana-baptist movement as an evangelical option over against both classical (magisterial) Protestant and Catholic establishments. Indeed, it is noteworthy that Italian Anabaptists were everywhere without exception strictly pacifistic and almost without a trace of that vindictive eschatology which long adhered to certain *ad interim* pacifistic German Anabaptists, like the followers of Hans Hut or Melchior Hofmann. To be sure, Italian Anabaptism was sometimes susceptible to interfaith ecumenicity, open to Islam as well as "evangelical" Judaism. But then there was some of this also among German Anabaptists.[118] It had less of the communal discipline of the ban than in Germany. One hears far less of women in the conventicles than in Germany. Italian Anabaptism seems to have had many fewer martyrs. It had nothing of that intense national self-consciousness that informs German-speaking reformers from Martin Luther to Jacob Hutter. Italian Anabaptism created very little surviving literature. Most of it speaks to us from the inquests and hearings. But the Italian Anabaptists of both northern and southern provenance were truly Anabaptists. Surely there were as many regional and even confessional differences among Swiss, Saxon, Upper Tyrolese, Moravian, Alsatian, Hessian, Dutch, and Westphalian Anabaptists as among any of the groupings we have seen in Italian Anabaptism.

Its story remains to be more fully told, as new source materials and monographs become available. Only in Italy was evangelical Christianity in the form of Anabaptism bold enough to hope to convert professors, pontiffs, and physicians as well as the common people and to present to Islam and Judaism a new and winsome Christian face.

---

1. Anabaptism was an issue in the pre-Constantinian period as between rigorists and laxists; it persisted in the struggle between Donatists and Catholics in North Africa; it cropped up in medieval sectarianism and had its monastic analogue in the monastic vow. It was a major phenomenon in the Reformation era, constituting the common bond of most of the contingents in the Radical Reformation, including the Polish Brethren, despite the stand on this particular point taken by Faustus Socinus. It cropped out in the Baptists among the English separatists in the seventeenth century. It reappeared in New England, in the eighteenth century, in protest against the Congregationalist establishment.

The author has traced the history of Anabaptism as an international movement from 1525 to 1575 with reference to certain medieval antecedents and analogues in *The Radical Reformation* (Philadelphia, 1962), hereafter cited as *RR*. The present essay goes, however, beyond what he therein was able to say about Italian Ananaptism. In *RR* and in the earlier *Anabaptist and Spiritual Writers*, Library of Christian Classics, vol. 75 (Philadelphia, 1957), he defined and described Anabaptism as one of three thrusts in the Radical Reformation, the others being Spiritualism and Evangelical Rationalism, the latter best represented in Socinianism. He set the Radical Reformation over against both the Magisterial or Classical Protestant Reformation, dependent upon magistrates, and the Counter-Reform.

2. The invaluable hearings of Manelfi, with his summary of the Ten Articles (pp. 34 f. of the Anabaptist Synod of Venice of 1550), have been edited by Carlo Genzburg, *I costituti di don Petro Manelfi* (Florence and Chicago, 1970), hereafter cited as Manelfi, *Costituti*.

3. Manelfi, *Costituti*; see below, note 20.

4. See Leandro Perini and John Tedeschi, "Bibliografia degle scritti di Delio Cantimori," in *Rivista Storica Italiana* (hereafter cited as *RSI*) 79 (1967):1173–1208, with 553 items.

5. Delio Cantimori, "Anabattismo e neoplatonismonel XVI secolo in Italia," Reale Accademia Nazionale dei Lincei, *Rendiconti della classe di scienze morali, storiche e filogiche*, (Florence, 1939), hereafter cited as Cantimori, *Eretici*; and idem, *Prospettive di storia ereticale italiana del Cinquecento* (Bari, 1960).

6. Cantimori's view prevails in the *Corpus Reformatorum Italicorum*, the first volume of which, edited by Antonio Rotondò, is devoted to the works of the proto-Socinian Camillo Renato.

7. " 'Anabaptism' and Italy," *Church History* 21(1952):20–38; "Italian Hutterite Martyrs," *MQR* 28(1954):163–85; "Anabaptists in Thessalonica?," *MQR* 29(1955):70–73; *Mennonite Encyclopedia* 3 (Scottsdale, Ariz., 1957):55 f.

8. "I movimenti ereticali nell' Europa del Cinquecento," *RSI* 79(1966): 137–39.

9. "Z dziejow włoskiej emigracji wyzaniowiej na Morawach," *Ocrodzenie i Reformacja w Polsce* 11(1966):esp. pp. 58 f.

10. Stella has written a number of other related works. These two, however, containing as they do abundant documentary material, will be frequently cited as Stella, 1 and Stella, 2.

11. The confreres of Vicenza included Laelius Socinus, Bernardino Ochino, Niccolò Paruta, Valentino Gentile, Francesco della Sega of Rovigo (later a Hutterite martyr). The reference to the conventicle in Vicenza occurs in connection with the entry on Laelius Socinus in Christopher Sand (Sandius), *Bibliotheca Antitrinitariorum* (Amsterdam, 1684); offset reprint with introduction and index by Lech Szczucki (Warsaw, 1967), pp. 18 f.; and in Stanislas Lubieniecki, *Historia Reformationis Polonicae* (Amsterdam, 1685), p. 39. The proto-Socinian-Anabaptist academy-conventicle of Vicenza has been dissolved into a phantom by a succession of scholars (see, among others, Earl Morse Wilbur, *A History of Unitarianism: Socinianism and its Antecedents* [Cambridge, Mass., 1954], pp. 80–84); but Stella has adduced reasons for again taking the tradition seriously (with which I concur), 1:55–61.

12. It is really only a guarded surmise in the form of an analogy between Marranist and Spiritualist Antitrinitarian aspirations, Stella, 2:31, notes 47 and 81.

13. The history of Jewry in Italy is related most comprehensively in Cecil Roth, *The History of the Jews of Italy* (Philadelphia, 1946) and Attilo Milano, *Storia degli ebrei in Italia* (Turin, 1963); Milano has also done a succession of

comprehensive bibliographies: *Bibliotheca Historico Italo-Judaica* (Florence, 1964), items 1-1597; *Supplemento 1954–1963* (Florence, 1964); "Bibliografia degli studi sulla storia degli ebrei in Italia (1964–1966)," *La Rassegna di Israel* (1966). Hayim Hillel Ben-Sasson, dealing mostly with the Ashkenazi world beyond Italy, "The Reformation in Contemporary Jewish Eyes," *Proceedings of the Israel Academy of Sciences and Humanities*, 4 (1970):314, concludes: "Since Judaism has nurtured the vision of *Tiqqun*—gradual improvement leading to ultimate Messianic perfection—many came to feel that partial reform of the prevalent social and religious situation in the Church was one more step in the right direction . . . welcomed with so much genuine Jewish joy."

14. Cecil Roth, *A History of the Marranos* (Philadelphia, 1959). Roth's chapter on "The Religion of the Marranos" is unique in the literature; but it and the book in general are based largely on materials outside of Italy (Portuguese, Netherlandish, and Mexican Marranos being frequently adduced). Salo Wittmayer Baron deals with the Marrano diaspora with substantial references to Italy in *Inquisition, Renaissance, and Reformation*, chap. 56, vol. 12, *A Social and Religious History of the Jews*, 2d ed. (New York and London, 1969). Louis Israel Newman, with scarcely a reference to Anabaptism, notes the persistence from the ninth century of an Italian group of Judaizers centered in Milan, called obscurely Passagii: *Jewish Influence on Christian Reform Movements* (New York, 1925–66), pp. 255–303.

15. B. Netanyahu, *The Marranos of Spain from the Late XIVth to the Early XVIth Century, According to₁ Contemporary Jewish Sources* (New York, 1966), p. 205.

16. David Kaufmann, "Die Vertreibung der Marranen aus Vendig im Jahre 1550," with five documents, *Jewish Quarterly Review* 13 (1900–1901):520–32; Cecil Roth, carrying his account well beyond 1550, "Les Marranes à Venise," *Revue des Etudes Juives* 89 (1930):201–23. Both these writers assumed that all the Marranos of Veneto were Judaizers; but the documents adduced by Kaufmann suggest that the authorities were having some difficulty defining the Marranos they insisted on driving out and that many Marranos dressed and passed themselves off as Christian and lived outside the two ghettos.

17. Manelfi, *Costituti*, p. 67, lines 733, 735.

18. Joseph Nehama deals with Jews and with Marranos who reverted to Judaism (often with some rabbinical resistance) under Muslim protection in *L'Age d'or du Sefaradisme salonicien (1536–1593)* in *Histoire des Israelites de Salonique* 3 (Thessalonica and Paris, 1936). There are several studies of Anabaptists in Thessalonica: DeWind, above, note 7, and Robert Friedmann, "Christian Sectarians in Thessalonica and Their Relationship to the Anabaptists," *MQR* 29 (1953):54–69.

19. See below at note 80.

20. The words are used by Manelfi, *Costituti*, pp. 66, 67, 74, 78, 79.

21. Points 1 and 2; Manelfi, *Costituti*, p. 34; see also p. 64.

22. See Josef Macek, *Der Tiroler Bauernkrieg und Michael Gaismair* (Berlin, 1965); also the review article by Leandro Perini, "La guerra dei contadini nel Tirolo," *Studi Storici* 7 (1966):388–400; also the forthcoming study of Walter Klaassen of Conrad Grebel College, Waterloo, Ontario, "The Religious Views of Michael Gaismair."

23. Edited by A. Holländer, *Schlern-Studien* 12 (1932):375–83, 425–29.

24. See *RR*, chaps. 7.5.

25. Macek, *Der Tiroler Bauernkrieg*, map 6.

26. "Gravimenti deli comuni di paesani del conta de Tirol," June, 1525;

Acta Tirolensia, 3, in *Quellen zur Geschichte des Bauernkriegs in Deutschtirol 1525,* ed. Hermann Wopfner (Innsbruck, 1908), 1:47–50. Cf. Stella, 1:13, n.8. The Rettenberg articles in Italian and the Venetian dialect are published by Paolo Guerrini, "I Postulati della Riforma nell'Alta Italia," *Rivista di Storia della Chiesa in Italia* 1 (1947):292 f. The full identification is by Perini, *Studi Storici,* 7:398. C. Giuliani published in Latin, Italian, and German for the territory of the bishop of Trent, "Documenti per la guerra rustica nel Trentino," *Archivio Trentino,* 3 (1884):95–116 and thereafter in 6, 8, 9, and 40 (1893).

27. Diocesan archives of Brixen, noted by Stella, 1:17, n. 20.

28. "Denkwürdigkeiten seiner Zeit, 1519–1553," ed. Thomas Georg Karajan, *Fontes Rerum Austricarum,* Abt. I., Scriptores, 1 (Vienna, 1855):481 f.

29. Eduard Widmoser, "Das Tiroler Täufertum," *Tiroler Heimat,* 15 (1951): Pt. 1, pp. 60 f. Without giving the exact date, Stella, 1, p. 21, mentions also Caldaro and Egna as early having Anabaptist conventicles.

30. Jarold Knox Zeman in the most recent and detailed account of Anabaptist colonists in Moravia chose not to deal with the Italian immigrants: *The Anabaptists and the Czech Brethren in Moravia 1526–1628: A Study of Origins and Contacts* (The Hague, 1969), pp. 19 f.

31. Mastro Antonio Marangone was in the Venetian dialect called "cormorant" = carpenter. The extensive documentation of his case, some of it stemming from the papal nuncio sent to Venice in March, 1533, Girolamo Aleandro, is edited by Franco Gaeta, "Documenti da Codici Vaticani per la Storia della Riforma in Venezia," *Annuario dell'Istituto Storico Italiano per l'Età Moderna e Contemporanea* 7 (1955):3–53, hereafter cited as Gaeta, "Documenti"; Stella, I:26–8.

32. Anthony's hearing, doc. 2, the testimony of the priest of Holy Trinity, Gaeta, "Documenti," p. 33. The redheaded Lutheran is called "un *altro* forastier." This need not mean more than that both the "red" Lutheran and Anthony were not of Venero.

33. Anthony's heresies, doc. 19, arts. 6, 7, Gaeta, "Documenti," p. 40: 6, "Non habet homo liberum arbitrium," and 7, "Bona opera non sunt meritoria prescitis, nec mala demeritoria predestinatis."

34. Ibid., doc. 20, p. 41, where Anthony is pressed with the charges against him: "An credat pueros debere baptizari; An sciat aliquem dogmatizare quod non pueri sed adulti dumtaxat baptizandi sint et quod hac ratione velit rebaptizari." Anthony only withheld his children from baptism; he is not known to have himself submitted to rebaptism.

35. Ibid.: "An aliquando dixerit quod . . . astantes communicantur sacramentaliter, precise sicut ille [sacerdos]."

36. Ibid., doc. 21, p. 42.

37. Ibid., doc. 19, art. 12: "Non est Spiritus Sanctus, sed unus solus Deus."

38. His career, essential to the prehistory of Socinianism and fairly important also for Italian Anabaptism, cannot be repeated here. See my "Camillus Renatus Called Also Lysias Philaenus and Paolo Ricci (c. 1550–c. 1575): Forerunner of Socinianism on Individual Immortality," *Harry Austryn Wolfson Jubilee Volume,* ed. Saul Lieberman (Jerusalem, 1965), 2:833–70, expanded as "Camillo Renato c. 1500–c. 1575," *Italian Reformation Studies in Honor of Laelius Socinus (1562–1962),* University of Siena, Collana di Studi Pietro Rossi, vol. 4 (Florence, 1965), pp. 103–83, 195; *The Proceedings of the Unitarian Historical Society* 14, Parts 1 and 2 (1962–63):103–83, 195. The *opere* of Renato have been critically edited by Antonio Rotondò as *Corpus Reformatorum Italicorum,* 1 (Florence and Chicago, 1968).

39. Venetian Archives, Sant'Uffizio, Processi, busta 9, fascicolo iv, f. 10. The

most important parts of the testimony and documentation have been printed and interpreted by Stella, 1:67–71, with much of the original transcribed *verbatim* in the long notes.

40. Ibid., p. 69, n. 19.

41. I distinguished the two Anabaptists in *RR*, p. 564, n. 19. Stella, 1:37 f., was disposed to identify the two as one; but in 2, although still noting the interchangeability of spelling in some Venetian records, effectively treats Il Tiziano and Tizzano as distinct and theologically disparate Anabaptists, dealing with Il Tiziano esp. pp. 47–58, 69–72. He wrote before he had the advantage of using the critical edition of a major source: Manelfi, *Constituti* (1970). The editor thereof, Ginzburg, (without the advantage of Stella, 2) in his preface, pp. 18–25, reinforces the distinction. The evidence adduced by Stella, 2, and Ginzburg is complementary and therefore all the more convincing.

42. For the German authorization of Il Tiziano's Anabaptist mission (testimony of Bruno Busale), see Stella, 1:72; pp. 53 f; Ginzburg, ed. Manelfi, *Costituti*, p. 20, n. 21.

43. Stella, 2:56, esp. n. 126.

44. Reported by August Mainardo of Chiavenna, August 7, 1549, Bullinger's *Korrespondenz mit den Graubündern*, ed. Traugott Schiess (Basel, 1904), 1: No. 110, hereafter cited as *Korrespondenz*. Letter, Peter Paul Vergerio to Bullinger, January 10, 1553; *Korrespondenz*, 1: No. 199.2. For the extrusion, see n. 25. Here Vergerio says that two Italian Anabaptists have returned "to the purity of our doctrine" and that they admit that they were seduced by Camillo Renato. One of these could have been Il Tiziano.

45. The conjecture of Ginzburg, ed., Manelfi, *Costituti*, pp. 17–21. Cardinal del Monte, as papal legate and first president, opened the Council of Trent in 1545. (He was pope from 1550 to 1555.) It is noteworthy that the Benedictine Spiritualist, George Siculo, appealed in like vein to the whole Council. See below, Section 7.

46. Manelfi, *Costituti*, 1551, p. 63.

47. Peter Speziale in 1542 claimed that he had grasped the Reformation principle of salvation *sola fide* before Luther, in 1512. Unpublished treatise, *De gratia Dei*, Bk. vi, chap. xi, Biblioteca Marciana, Venice. Noted by Philip McNair, *Peter Martyr in Italy: Anatomy of Apostasy* (Oxford, 1967), p. 8, n. 1.

48. See Salvatore Caponetta, "Origini e caratteri della reforma in Sicilia," *Rinascimento* 7 (1956):219–330; McNair, *Peter Martyr in Italy*, has an introductory chapter, "The Environment of Evangelism." For Valdés and the Marranist background, see Edmondo Cione, *Juan de Valdés: La suo pensiero religioso*, 2d ed. (Naples, 1963), and Jose Nieto, *Juan de Valdes and the Origins of the Spanish and Italian Reformation* (Geneva, 1970), esp. pp. 41 f. A major source for the radical Valdesians become Anabaptists is the documentation from Venice provided by Domenico Berti, "Di Giovanni Valdes e di taluni suoi discepoli," Accadamia Nazionale dei Lincei, *Memorie della classe di scienze morali, storiche e filologiche*, 34th ser. (Rome, 1877–78), 2:61–81, including nine documents.

49. Alfredo Casadei, "Donne della Riforma Italiana: Isabella Bresegna," *Religio* 13 (1937):6–63.

50. The testimony of Tizzano is published by Berti, "Di Giovanni Valdes," esp. Doc. 1; conveniently reprinted in large part by Franceso Lemmi, *La Riforma in Italia e i Riformatori Italiani all'estero nel secolo XVI* (Milan, 1939), pp. 65–83. Tizzano is extensively discussed by Stella, 1:36, where he considers him, however, identical with Il Tiziano, and in 2:35–40, where on reconsideration he rightly distinguishes between Tizzano and Il Tiziano.

51. The testimony of Laureto, when about thirty-five years old, is published by M. Pommier, "L'itinéraire Religieux d'un moine vagabonde italien au XVIe siècle," *Mélanges d'archéologie et d'histoire* 66 (1954):317–32, preceded by an interpretation of Laureto as a representative spiritual wanderer, pp. 293–317, hereafter cited as "Laureto."

52. Julius Basalù in 1553; Casadei, "Donne," p. 53. In group viii were those who, besides the previously mentioned views, held to the "reiteratio . . . baptismatis in laudem religionis Hebraicae."

53. Stella, 1:33; Stella, 2:chap. i.

54. Emilio Comba *I Nostri Protestanti*, (Florence, 1895), chap. ii, hereafter cited as Comba, *Nostri Protestanti*; Antonio Rotondò, "Per la storia dell'eresia a Bologna nel secolo XVI," *Rinascimento*, 2d ser., 2 (1962):136.

55. Letter of March 25, 1551; in Calvin, *Calvini opera quae supersunt omnia* (Brunswick, 1875), vol. 14, no. 1472, col. 87. There are no clues as to Jewish influence on Christians in Antonio Ciscato, *Gli ebrei in Padova (1300–1800): Monografia storica documentata* (Padua, 1901), or in the comparable work for Ferrara, Andrea Balletti, *Gli ebrei e gli Estensi* (Reggio Emilia, 1930). Between 1517 and 1619 there were eighty Jews matriculated as students in the medical faculty. In this capacity they were not required to wear the distinctive Jewish garb.

56. The communication from Naples in September, 1551, is discussed by Stella, 1:81 f., Manelfi, *Costituti*, p. 69.

57. Concerning Villafranca, the following gave testimony: Marcantonio Villamarina, Naples, July 1552; Stella, 1:101; Tizzano, Venice, 1553 in Berti, "Di Giovanni Valdes," pp. 69–71, or in Lemmi, *La Riforma in Italia*, pp. 65 ff.; Matthew Busale, Naples, May, 1555; Laureto, Venice, 1553, p. 319.

58. The testimony of Ambrose appears as item 17 in Doc. 6 in the same collection edited by Berti, "Di Giovanni Valdes," p. 77, where besides Tizzano's principal testimony, Doc. 1, and the fifteen inquistorial queries from Rome to Venice, Doc. 2, to which Tizzano gives replies seriatim, there is the further signed statement of Tizzano, Doc. 4; and then there are testimonies from Antonio de Alessio of Naples, Doc. 5; the already cited Doc. 6 from Ambrose e Apuzzo; Matteo de Aversa, Doc. 7; from Bruno Busale concerning Tizzano, Doc. 8. The testimony of Tizzano at his first hearing in Pauda is not available.

59. Combined here in a series of quoted phrases is the testimony of Tizzano himself or about him by others, in order: of Marc Anthony del Bon of Asolo in Stella, 2:37; of Tizzano himself, Doc. 1, Berti, "Di Giovanni Valdes," p. 70; of Mattheo de Aversa, Doc. 7, ibid., p. 78; of Manelfi, *Costituti*, p. 69; of Mattheo Busale, Doc. 8, Berti, "Di Giovanni Valdes;" and of Jerome Capece of Naples, Stella, 1:101.

60. Manelfi reporting Tizzano, *Costituti*, p. 69; Stella, 1:34 and 82, n. 54. Cf. above, n. 52.

61. Casadei, "Donne," p. 63. For the general religious background, see Frederico Chabod, "Per la storia religiosa dello Stato di Milano durante di Carlo V, Parte Seconda: La Riforma," *Annuario dell'Istituto Storico Italiano per l'Età moderna e contemporanea*, 2-3 (1938): 81–164, with documents; for a brief survey of the inquisitorial records of Milan bearing on religious emigration, including both Anabaptists and Antitrinitarians, see Mario Bendiscioli, "Aspetti dell'immigrazione e dell'emigrazione nelle carte dell'inquisizioni anti-ereticale di Milano nie secc. XVI-XVII," *Archivio Storico Lombardo*, 9th ser., 1 (1961):65.

62. Stella, 2:35.

63. Laureto, 1553, p. 319. On Nicholas see further, Stella, 1:92 ff., and Au-

gusto Serena, "Fra gli eretici trevigiani [Benedetto da Borgo d'Asolo et Nicolo d'Alessandria]," *Archivo Veneto-Tridentino*, 3 (1923):169–202; 182 f.

64. Manelfi, 1551, *Costituti*, pp. 45, 68; Stella, 1:75; cf. Laureto, 1553, p. 319. Bruno Busale was baptized by Il Tiziano: Manelfi, *Costituti*, p. 20.

65. Manelfi, 1551, *Costituti*, p. 34, places the conclave in Vicenza; Laureto, 1553, p. 319; Stella, 1:91.

66. Stella, 1:75 f.

67. Stringaro; Stella, 2:51.

68. Laureto, 1553, p. 319; Stella, 2:73.

69. Emilio Comba, "Un sinodo Anabattista a Venezia anno 1550," *Rivista Cristiana* 13 (1885): 21–24, 83–87; idem., *Nostri Protestanti*, chap. 13; Karl Benrath, *Geschichte der Reformation in Venedig* (Halle, 1866); idem, "Wiedertäufer im Venetianischen um die Mitte des 16. Jahrhunderts," *Theologische Studien und Kritiken* 58 (1835):9–67; Stella, 1:76–83; Stella, 2:64–72, where he draws attention to the discrepancies between Manelfi's account (*Costituti*, pp. 34 f. with the Ten Articles) and other archival testimony.

70. Manelfi, *Costituti*, p .64; Il Tiziano, below at note 83.

71. Possibly Jerome, *Epistola* 19, misconstrued; *Patrologiae cursus completus, series latina*, ed. J. P. Migne (Paris, 1865), 30, col. 294 f.

72. Stella, 2:79; documents from the trial quoted at length, pp. 74–78.

73. Stella, 1:93; Comba, *Nostri Protestanti*, p. 512, citing an additional source; and L. De Biaso, thesis, "Fermenti ereticali in Friuli nella seconda metà del secolo XVI," Padua, 1967.

74. Stella , 1:28, 81, 94; Stella, 2:68, 86.

75. Stella, 2:94, 162, 204 f.

76. Gherlandi's list, 1559; Stella, 2:106, n. 79; cf. p. 3, n. 88.

77. Cf. Manelfi, *Costituti*, pp. 65 f.; Stella, 1:72, n. 25. In confirmation of this assertion from another quarter, there is an adoptionist Anabaptist devotional book in the seminary library of Treviso dated 1557, which is an Italian translation from German of a children's prayer: ibid., p. 107, n. 80.

78. Stella, 1:96.

79. Laureto, Testimony, p. 320. Stanislas Lubieniecki, *Historia Reformationis Polonicae* (Amsterdam, 1685), p. 39, reporting the earlier lost History of Laelius Socinus by Stanislas Budziński, says that Busale went to Thessalonica with forty companions and thence to Damuscus, where he died. Budziński has probably confused Busale and Nicholas d'Alessandria. Cf. above, note 11. See also Cesare Cantù, *Gli Eretici d'Italia*, 3 vols. (Turin, 1865-67), 3:167; Stella, 2:31.

80. Laureto, Testimony, 1553, p. 320.

81. Ibid.

82. Ibid.; Tizzano, Doc. 1, Berti, "Di Giovanni Valdes," p. 68.

83. Letters to Bullinger, June 2 and 25, 1554; *Korrespondenz*, 1, No. 261:1, 2.

84. The *Carmen* is translated by Dorothy Rounds, *Studies in Honor of Laelius Socinus*, ed. John Tedeschi, pp. 184–95.

85. Frances Amelia Yates, *John Florio; The Life of an Italian in Shakespeare's England*, 2d ed. (New York, 1968), chap. 1. The location of the Apology is Camogasco (Ladin), Campatsch (German), near Scuol (Schuls) in the Lower Engadine.

86. Stella, 2:22, 29, 34, 57, 220.

87.   Cantimori, *Eretici*, 8; Bartolomeo Fontana, *Renata di Francia* (Rome, 1893–99), 2:279; 3:155 ff.; and Carlo Ginzburg, "Due Note sul profetismo cinquecentesco," *RSI*, 78 (1966):184–227, which deals with the sect of George Siculo, with the identification of the Benedictine Benedict (Fontana) of Mantua, compiler of *The Benefit of Jesus Christ Crucified for Christians* (Venice, 1543), and with the followers in Venice of Benedict "Corazzaro." Ginzburg, basing his study on the abjuration of a follower of the Georgian Sect, Antonio da Bozzolo, 1555, printed as Doc. 1, pp. 212–17, discusses Siculo, pp. 188–90.

88.   Giulio da Milano in "Esortatione al martirio" (Poschavio, 1552), p. 145; Comba, *Nostri Protestanti*, p. 309; Cantimori, *Eretici*, p. 60; Manelfi, *Costituti*, p. 23.

89.   Bozzolo's abjuration, art. 2; Ginzburg, *RSI* 78:213.

90.   Ibid., p. 216.

91.   Ibid., art. 1.

92.   De Wind in several works cited regarded the three as the only true Italian Anabaptists.

93.   Domenico Caccamo gives a good comprehensive picture of all Italian groups in Moravia, *Eretici Italiani in Moravia, Polonia, Transilvania (1558–1611)* (Florence and Chicago, 1970), chap. 2, and prints the very revealing confession of Marcantonio Varotta (Undine, January 21, 1567) as appendix 8, pp. 194–216.

94.   Joseph von Beck collection, State Archives of Brno; noted by Stella, 1: 25, n. 52. Beck edited *Die Geschichts-Bücher der Wiedertäufer in Oesterreich-Ungarn* (Vienna, 1883).

95.   Stella, 1:104–12; Stella, 2: 11 ff. passim.

96.   See above, n. 11.

97.   The letter to the antitrinitarian Anabaptists of Italy, written in one version by him (and another by della Sega) in the name of the Brethren in Pausram in March, 1559, is printed in full, Stella, 2, Doc. 3, pp. 245–48.

98.   The localities are listed by Stella, 1:106, n. 79; the whole list is published by Stella, 2, as Doc. 4, pp. 249–51. Of interest is the name of a German-speaking Tyrolese living in Venice, one Christina fio!a de Osbolt calegaro da Pursterstol [Pustertal], p. 251. Cf. Stella, 1:111, n. 88.

99.   It was never delivered and is now in the archives of Venice: Stella, 1:108, n. 82; Stella 2, Doc. 5, pp. 252 f. The quotations of the remainder of the paragraph are, however, from De Wind.

100.   Stella, 1:esp. pp. 110–19; 2:esp. pp. 156–59; 165–71; 268–72; with seven substantial letters and other writings or records of della Sega. Docs. 1, 2, (3), 6–10. He recounts his life in Doc. 7, *Memoriale*, ca. Nov. 3, 1562.

101.   Stella, 1:114 at n. 93.

102.   The episode leading to the arrest of della Sega and Rizzetto is told by Benrath, "Wiedertaüfer," pp. 16 f.; Stella, 1:114 f. The betrayer was Alessio Todeschi of Bellinzona, who had sojourned in Moravia. In his testimony Todeschi spoke of the Hutterite commonwealth as consisting of thirty thousand from many lands: Germans, Poles, Hungarians, Paduans, et al. Della Sega wrote to him in anguish: Stella, 2, Doc. 6, pp. 254–57.

103.   Stella, 1:91; 2:esp. 165–69.

104.   Stella, 2, Doc. 7, pp. 258–68.

105.   Della Sega preferred the simp!e Dominical separation of the sheep from the goats to the more martial eschatology of Revelation.

106.   The Italian original is lost. The most commonly cited German version

is that of 1618 among the Hutterite Codices in Bratislava. Stella 1:114, n. 92; 115, n. 95, supplies plates and a partial transcription of a German version of 1563, preserved in Esztergom, Hungary.

107. Benrath, *Theologische Studien und Kritiken*, 58:49; De Wind *Mennonite Encyclopedia*, 4:495 f.

108. Stella, 1:115 ff. and n. 95, moderating the view of W. Urban, *Odrodzenie i Reformacja w Polsce*, 11, who argues that della Sega remained essentially proto-Socinian in his theology even in the Hutterite context. Stella shows, however, that at least the "Einigkeit" of the 1618 version, which Urban stresses, is "Ewigkeit" (as in I Corinthians 15:28) in the 1563 version. On this particular point, see also Caccamo, *Eretici Italiani*, p. 62, n. 80.

109. Stella, 2:271, n. 17.

110. Della Sega's letters are printed by Stella, 2: Documents 8 and 9; Benrath, *Theologische Studien und Kritiken*, 58:64–67.

111. The patristic references are in Stella, 2:respectively on pp. 277; 278; and 276 f. and 280 f. He also cites the apocryphal Judith 8:2.

112. Stella considers Bucella a representative figure passing from Anabaptism to Socinianism, 1:121–44, 191–93; 2:esp. 175–82, and more fully with documents in "Intorno al medico padovano Niccolò Buccella, anabattista del 1500," *Memorie dell' Accademia Patavina di scienze, lettere ed arti*, 74 (1961–62):333–61.

113. This whole testamentary letter was characterized by Benrath, *Theologische Studien und Kritiken*, 58:49, as "one of the most moving documents to come out of the whole Anabaptist movement." Printed by Stella, 2, Doc. 10, pp. 290–300.

114. De Wind, *Mennonite Encyclopedia*, 4:346.

115. The adjustment of the sentence "for special reasons" is signed by the bishop of Vercelli in his capacity as papal legate, by the patriarch of Venice, and by the inquisitor general. Benrath, *Theologische Studien und Kritiken*, 58:53.

116. A. J. F. Zieglschmid, *Die älteste Chronik der Hutterischen Brüder* (Philadelphia, 1943), p. 413. The specific reference to the Last Judgment is to the previous drowning of Gherlandi.

117. Confessione, Udine, January 21, 1567; printed in full by Caccamo, *Eretici Italiani*, Appendix 8, pp. 194–216. On Varotta, see also Henry A. De Wind, "A Sixteenth-century Description of Religious Sects in Austerlitz, Moravia," *MQR* 29 (1954):44–53.

118. See George H. Williams, "Sectarian Ecumenicity: Reflections on a Little Noticed Aspect of the Radical Reformation," [Baptist] *Review and Expositor*, 64, no. 2 (1967):141–60; idem, "Erasmus and the Reformers in Non-Christian Religions and *Salus extra Ecclesiam*," *Essays in Memory of E. Harris Harbison*, ed. by Theodore K. Rabb and Jerrold E. Siegel (Princeton, N.J., 1969), pp. 319–70.

JOHN FOXE AND THE LADIES

Roland H. Bainton

The Actes and Monuments of John Foxe offer a vast amount
of material for the social history of the Reformation in England.[1] The term *social* is usually applied to the class status of
the adherents of a particular confession. On that score he has
much. The occupations of the men are usually enumerated. *Social* may also apply to political relations, as for example those
of the guilds and the municipal councils or of the imperial cities
to the empire in Germany. In England the political problem
arose because, when the king was the supreme head of the
church, disobedience to his decrees in matters ecclesiastical could
be interpreted as treason. There are many echoes of this dilemma
in Foxe's pages. Still another aspect of social history derives
from the most basic division of the human race, that between
men and women. No source gives us more information about the
role of women in the English Reformation than does the great
work of John Foxe.

One has the feeling that he derived a special relish from relating the tart, smart, pert, audacious, and superbly defiant words
and deeds of these women to illustrate the point that the weaker
vessel, when filled with the Holy Spirit, is powerful enough to
pull down strongholds. He reports with gusto the retort of a
woman who, when asked what she thought of the See of Rome,
replied that it was "a sea for crows, kites, owls and ravens to
swim in."[2] A woman, shedding tears at the burning of a martyr,
was asked why she wept for a heretic, and answered that actually she saw more reason to weep over the priests attending the
execution.[3] One woman dared to call Queen Mary a Jezebel.[4]

Another asked why she would not let Saint Nicholas into her house at Christmas replied, "Saint Nicholas is in heaven."[5] There was one who instead of absenting herself from mass, attended and did everything contrary. When the congregation rose she sat, when they sat she rose.[6]

Mistress Dolly said to her servant John Bainton (I am going to look him up in the heavenly places if I ever get there) that prayer in her chamber had as much merit as going on a pilgrimage to Walsingham. The women, said she, go and make offerings to the saints to show off their fine gear, and the people go on pilgrimages more "for the green" than for devotion. Images are a "carpenter's chips."[7] An image in the rood loft was dubbed "Block Almighty."[8] A woman in the early days of Henry VIII got into trouble for knowing too much Scripture. How delightful was the version she learned! "Blessed be mild men for they shall weld the earth."[9]

Whenever the available documents sufficed, Foxe reported examinations *in extenso* for women as well as for men. The questions put to the accused became stereotyped. There is a neat summary of the points of nonconformity that led to the stake in the letter of one awaiting execution to a woman suggesting that she should reject all practices that Christ did not observe. Christ, said he, ought to be regarded as a heretic because he never "went in procession with cope, cross or candlestick: he never censered images, nor sang Latin services. He never sat in confession: He never preached on purgatory; nor on the pope's pardons. He never honored saints nor prayed for the dead: He never said mass, matins, nor evensongs; he never commanded Friday fast, nor vigil, Lent, nor Advent: he never hallowed church nor chalice, ashes, nor psalm, candles, nor bells."[10] The references to the mass covers also the doctrinal points that the mass is not a sacrifice and that Christ's body and blood are not substantially present in the bread and the wine.

Now let us turn to the examinations. The records for our purpose are here considerably abridged and slightly paraphrased. The first is that of Anne Askew, a woman born of such stock that she might have lived in great prosperity. She suffered in the year 1546 during the "Tudor reaction" of the last days of Henry

VIII. Among the examiners were Wriothesley, the chancellor, Gardiner, bishop of Winchester, a priest named Shaxton, who had recanted and tried to persuade her to do the like, and others who need not be enumerated. The report of her examinations comes from her own pen.[11] The first was in March, 1545. Here is an abridgement:

I [Anne Askew] was asked how I interpreted the passage in the Book of Acts which says that God dwells not in temples made with hands. I replied that I would not cast pearls before swine. Acorns are good enough. Did I say that five lines out of the Bible are better than five masses? Yes, I get something out of the Bible, nothing out of the masses. I was accused of saying that if an evil priest administers the sacrament it is of the devil. I never said anything of the sort. I said that without faith I cannot receive worthily. What did I think of confession? I replied that to confess one's faults is salutary. Do private masses profit the dead? I answered that it is idolatry to trust to masses more than to Christ. I was sent back to prison for eleven days. Only a priest visited me.

At the next examination I was asked whether if a beast ate the sacrament it would eat God. I told the examiner to answer himself. He said it was not the custom of the schools for the questioner to answer the question. I told him I was not versed in the custom of the schools. My cousin came to bail me out. He was told that the consent of a churchman was necessary and I was, therefore, taken to the bishop of London. He set the hour for three o'clock and then sent sudden word that I should come at once. I sent word that friends were coming with me at three and three it should be.

I was asked why I was in trouble, and replied, You tell me. It is because of that book you have written by a man already burned. I told him that 'such unadvised hasty judgment is a token of a slender wit.' I showed him the book and he could find nothing wrong with it. The bishop of London told me to bare my conscience. I told him there was nothing to bare. I was asked to interpret a text of Paul. I answered that a woman should not presume to interpret Paul. I was accused of making mock of the Easter Communion. Produce the accuser, said I. I was asked, If Scripture says that the bread and wine are the body of Christ will you believe it? I replied that I believe Scripture. If Scripture says they are not the body of Christ will you believe it? I replied that I believe Scripture. I believe all things as Christ and the apostles did leave them. I was asked to sign a confession that the body and blood of Christ are in substance in the mass. I said, in so far as Holy Scripture doth agree unto.

At the third examination she was told that the king's pleasure was that she should open her mind to the examiners. I will answer to the king. They replied that he is too busy to be bothered. I answered that Solomon was not too busy to be bothered with two women. I was asked to say that the sacrament is the flesh, blood and bone of Christ. The bishop asked to speak familiarly with me. I told him that was the way Judas betrayed Christ. He would like to speak alone with me. I said that the truth is established out of the mouths of two or three witnesses. I was threatened with the fire and answered that Christ and the apostles put no one to death. God would scorn their threatenings. I asked to be allowed to speak to Dr. Latimer and was refused. I wrote out for them my confession of faith: The sacramental bread was left to us to be received with thanksgiving, in remembrance of Christ's death, the only remedy of our soul's recovery; and that thereby we also receive the whole benefits and fruits of his most glorious passion. I told them that if the bread is left in a box for three months it will be mouldy, so it cannot be God. I wish neither death nor fear his might: Shaxton tried to persuade me to recant as he had done. I told him it were better he had never been born.

I was moved to another prison. An attempt was made to compel me to inform on others. The chancellor and another took off their gowns and racked me 'till the bones were almost plucked asunder. I had to be moved in a carriage.

At the stake she had to be chained up to keep her limp body from sagging. The chancellor sent her a pardon if she would recant. She refused to open it saying, "I did not come here to deny my Lord and Master." Three men suffered with her and were "boldened by her invincible constancy."

While in prison she had composed a poem of which this is the first verse:

> Lyke as the armed knyghte
> Appointed to the fielde,
> With thys worlde wyll I fyght
> And fayth shall by my shielde.

Our second example is the examination of Elizabeth Young in the year 1558.[12] She was the mother of three children and had gone to Holland to bring back for sale Protestant books there printed in English. One of the books was entitled *Antichrist*. Of her thirteen examinations nine have been recorded. Here is an abridgement. The examiners are not differentiated in this summary.

First Examination

EXAMINER: Where were you born and who were your father and mother?

ELIZABETH: This has nothing to do with the case. Come to the point.

EXAMINER: Why did you leave the country?

ELIZABETH: For conscience.

EXAMINER: When were you last at mass?

ELIZABETH: Not for three years.

EXAMINER: And before that?

ELIZABETH: Another three years and another three years.

EXAMINER: How old are you?

ELIZABETH: Forty and upwards.

Second Examination

EXAMINER: What are the books you brought from over the sea? I hear you won't swear. If you are stubborn you will be racked by the inch, you traitorly whore and heretic.

ELIZABETH: I don't know what it is to swear. As for the books you have impounded them.

EXAMINER: Yes, and you have sold some of them already. We know every place where you have been. We are not fools.

ELIZABETH: No, you are too wise for me.

EXAMINER: I'll make you tell to whom you sold those books.

ELIZABETH: Here is my carcass. Do with it what you will. You cannot take more than my blood.

Then the examiner gave order that Elizabeth should be given bread on one day and water the next.

ELIZABETH: If you take away my meat, I hope God will take away my hunger.

Third Examination

EXAMINER: Give me the names of those in exile on the continent or you will be racked.

Elizabeth gave no answer.

Fourth Examination

She was sent to the bishop of London, who told her that the refusal to swear was the mark of an Anabaptist. One present, seeing her courage, bet twenty pounds she was a man.

ELIZABETH: I am not a man. I have children.

He was evidently convinced, for he called her a whore. She was examined as to her belief with respect to the sacrament of the altar and declared:

ELIZABETH: I believe in the holy sacrament of Christ's body and blood. . . . When I do receive this sacrament in faith and spirit I do receive Christ.

EXAMINER: Nothing but spirit and faith, is it? Away with the whore.

She was told that being a woman she should stick to the distaff and spindle and not meddle with Scripture.

Fifth Examination

EXAMINER: What is your belief? Do you believe that Christ's body is present really, corporally, substantially?

ELIZABETH: I don't understand really and corporally and if by substantial you mean his real human body I say that he is at the right hand of God and cannot be in two places.

EXAMINER: If you don't have this faith you are damned.

ELIZABETH: Can you give me this faith?

EXAMINER: No, only God can do that.

ELIZABETH: Well, he hasn't. "The spirit gives life, the flesh profits nothing." [John 6:63].

Sixth Examination

EXAMINER: You accept only what is in Scripture? How about the seven sacraments? Is marriage a sacrament?

ELIZABETH: No, it is a holy estate.

EXAMINER: What about purgatory? You have only skimmed the Scriptures. The doctrine of purgatory is there.

ELIZABETH: Sir, that could never be found in Scripture.

EXAMINER: If you accept only what is in Scripture what about the Sabbath? In Scripture it is Saturday.

ELIZABETH: Is there anything in Scripture to prove that it cannot be Sunday?

EXAMINER: You know so much about Scripture you must be a priest's woman or wife.

ELIZABETH: I am not a priest's woman or wife.

EXAMINER: Have I touched your conscience?

ELIZABETH: No, you'd better look after your own.

Seventh Examination

EXAMINER: Do you believe that the pope of Rome is the supreme head of the Church?

ELIZABETH: No, Christ is the head.

EXAMINER: Haven't you prayed that God deliver you from the tyranny of the bishop of Rome and all his detestable enormities?

ELIZABETH: Yes, I have.

EXAMINER: Aren't you sorry?

ELIZABETH: Not a whit.

Now came some who offered to go surety for her.

Eighth Examination

EXAMINER: Are you any wiser than last time?

ELIZABETH: I haven't learned much since.

Ninth Examination

The two women who came to offer surety were asked whether they also "did not smell of the frying pan of heresy." This they denied. Then why did they come? "Because," said one, "she has three children who are like to die. I got a nurse for one. I'll have to look after her children and that's why I want her out."

The death of Queen Mary brought about her release.

Foxe was by no means inhibited from telling ghastly tales both of routine and of wanton cruelties. Mother Seaman, aged three score and six, for refusal to go to mass had to sleep in bushes, groves, and fields or sometimes in a neighbor's house. Her husband, eighty years old, fell sick. With no regard for her safety she came and nursed him to the end and shortly followed. She was denied Christian burial, and her friends had to lay her in a pit by the moat's side.[13] Elizabeth Folkes, when she came to the stake, took off her petticoat to give it to her mother, who came and kissed her, but the gift was not permitted.[14] Alice Benden, about to be delivered up by her own husband, to save him the shame went of her own accord. The sheriff allowed her to be taken to prison by a lad. There she lay without change of raiment for nine weeks, and when she was cleansed, the skin peeled off.[15] Joan Waste of twenty-two years had been blind from birth. She had learned to "knit hosen and sleeves and to turn ropes." She had saved enough to buy a New Testament and from listening had learned portions by heart. Refusing to confess that the bread and wine on the altar were the body and blood of Christ, she was told that she was blind not only in body but also in soul and that her body would be burned with material fire and her soul with fire everlasting. None should be permitted to pray for her. During her execution the bishop dozed.[16]

In the case of Rose Allin, a certain Master Tyrrell had come to arrest her parents. The mother thereupon felt sick and asked for a drink. Rose took a stone pitcher in one hand and a candle in the other to fetch water. But Tyrrell interrupted her, saying that she should instruct her parents. She answered that the Holy Ghost would do that. He perceived that she was of their mind and told her she would burn, too, "for company's sake." "For Christ's sake," she corrected him. To show her how she would burn, he grasped her wrist, took the candle and burned crosswise over the back of her hand "until the very sinews cracked asunder." Rose reported, "I had the stone pot in the other hand and might have laid him on the face with it. I thank God I did it not."[17]

After the recitation of such cases one can understand why Foxe should gloat over calamities that befell the persecutors. He had behind him a venerable tradition in this regard. In the days of Constantine, Lactantius had written his *De Mortibus Persecutorum, On the Deaths of the Persecutor*, and Tertullian thought that one of the delights of the martyrs would be to look down from heaven on the torments of their persecutors. Foxe relates instances of divine retribution: In the days of Henry VII, at the instance of Chancellor Whittington, a woman was burned for heresy. A great concourse assembled to witness her death, among them Chancellor Whittington. Now while she was being burned, a butcher was slaying a bull, and being less adept in slaughtering beasts than papists in murdering Christians, struck too low. The bull with a mighty lurch broke his tether and rushed out as the crowd was coming from the burning. The people parted. The bull paid no heed but went straight for the chancellor "and, pricked with sudden vehemency, ran full butt, gored his paunch and careened through the street with the entrails on his horns, to the great admiration and wonder of all that saw it." Some might attribute this to chance, but who can be so dull "which seeth not herein a plain miracle of God's mighty judgment?"[18]

Another instance occurred in the first days of Mary's reign when a curate continued to use the Prayer Book of Edward VI. As he was so engaged, a bailiff seized him in the pulpit, saying, "Will you not say Mass, you knave? or by God's blood, I will sheathe my dagger in your shoulder." The curate set himself to saying mass. As the bailiff was on his way home a crow, sitting in a willow tree, flew up directly over his head, cawing, "Knave! knave!," and let go a dropping, which falling on his nose, ran down over his beard. "The scent and savor so noyed his stomach that he never ceased vomiting till he came home, where he got him to bed" and in a few days desparately died without repentance. This story, we are assured, was testified by credible witnesses.[19]

But Foxe derived greater satisfaction from deliverances than from retributions. He relates the case of Agnes Wardell. She and her husband were suspect. He went to sea. She, left with a babe and a maid, took in a woman and child as tenants. The queen's men came by night to arrest Agnes, who was asleep. At the first and second knocks the tenant did not answer. At the third she called to know who was there. Why had she not responded sooner? "Because," said she, "there are spirits and if one answers to the first or the second knock there is peril." They laughed but would not be put off. Let her open. "There is no candle," said she. "Open, or we'll take off the door." During this stalling the maid had wakened Agnes, who came down in a buckram apron and was locked in a closet in the parlor. The queen's men, having obtained a candle from a neighbor, were admitted and began the search, first in the tenant's room. "The bed's warm. Who's been in it?" "The child and I." "None other?" "None other." Then they came into the parlor. "There's a fair cupboard," said one, "She may be in it." "Yea, she may," agreed another, but they did not pry. In the yard they found a horse eating shorn grass. "Whose horse is this?" they asked the maid. "Hers. She came in before night and went away again. I know not whither." They took the maid in to custody and went to search the grounds.

In the meantime Agnes, in the closet, began to think burning would be preferable to suffocation and asked the tenant to let her out. "Where are the keys?" "In the hamper." The lock would not yield. "Then break the door." The tenant went for a chisel and hammer but found none. "Try again with the key. I trust God will give you the power to open it." He did. Agnes slipped out into the garden, pushed back two loose pales on the fence, threw herself into a ditch of nettles, and at the approach of searchers concealed herself beneath the buckram apron. Thus she escaped.[20]

But where to? And what became of the babe, and the maid, and did she ever find her husband again?

Another instance of deliverance was the case of one Crossman's wife. Her own name is not even known. For not going to mass she was sought in her own home by the constable. She hid herself with a babe in arms alongside of a chimney. The child, though wailing before, did not cry, and she was saved.[21]

Babes more than once proved a convenience. There was the case of Moon and his wife. The bishop said, "Is this your wife, Moon?" "Yea, my lord." "O good Lord, how may a man be deceived in a woman!" The wife broke in. "None can charge me with dishonesty of body." "No, not that," quoth the bishop; "Better to have given your body to twenty sundry men than to pluck the king and the queen's majesties out of their royal seats." Then Moon yielded, and his wife followed. Hearing her child crying below, she must leave to give suck. The bishop granted permission on condition that they report again on the morrow; but he was called away, and they were not again summoned.[22]

Highly gratifying was an act of restitution when Elizabeth became queen. The wife of Peter Martyr had died during Edward's reign and had been buried in the cemetery of Corpus Christi College at Oxford. On Mary's accession complaint was made to Cardinal Pole that the bones of this heretic should not be allowed to repose in holy ground. Sufficient evidence could not be produced to warrant the burning of her remains. Nevertheless, the cardinal would not suffer them to lie in close proximity to the relics of Saint Frideswide. Madam's bones were disinterred and left on a dunghill. On Elizabeth's accession they were restored and so mixed up with the relics of the saint that if any future cardinal were so mad as to move them again, he would not know which were which.[23]

One is amazed at the measure of communication between

those in and out of prison, both men and women. In the case of the women this was chiefly by way of visitation and the supplying of material needs, in the case of the men by way of correspondence.

We have Latimer's letter of thanks to a Mrs. Wilkinson of London, who, prior to her own exile, did much to supply the needs of the bishops in prison under Mary including Hooper, the bishop of Hereford, Coverdale, Cranmer, and Latimer, who wrote: "If the gift of a pot of cold water shall not be in oblivion with God, how can God forget your manifold and bountiful gifts, when he shall say to you, 'I was in prison, and you visited me?' God grant to us all to do and suffer, while we be here, as may be to his will and pleasure. Amen."[24]

We have a letter in like vein from a William Tyms who suffered in 1556. He was really a lay preacher, though called a deacon, ministering to a congregation in the woods. When the owner learned that his woods were polluted by sermons to as many as a hundred, the preacher was apprehended. In a garment white above and sheep's russet below, he was brought before Winchester, who thought his attire did not resemble that of a deacon, to which Tyms retorted that it more nearly resembled that of a deacon than the bishop's did the attire of an apostle. Tyms had children and a wife brought again to bed during his captivity. To the women of his parish he wrote:

> Dear sisters, I have me most heartily commended unto you, thanking you for the great kindness showed unto me in this time of mine imprisonment, and not only unto me, but also unto my poor wife and children; and also for the great kindness that you show unto all the living saints that be dispersed abroad, and are fain to hide their heads for fear of this cruel persecution. . . . I do believe that when the Lord shall send his angel to destroy these idolatrous Egyptians here in England, and shall find the blood of the Lamb sprinkled on the doorpost of your hearts, he will go by you, and not hurt you, but spare your whole households for your sakes.[25]

We have an instance of a man visiting a woman prisoner in grave disturbance of mind. Agnes Bonger was not permitted to die with her fellow prisoners because her name had been misspelled as Bowyer, and the jailer required confirmation of her identity. She was grieved because she had made herself a smock for the occasion and had already engaged a wet nurse for her babe. The man consoled her that God accepted Abraham's readiness to sacrifice his son, though excusing him from doing it. "Yes," she objected, "But it's not my son. It's me." "And your babe," he reminded her. Thereat she began "to stay herself" by reading and prayer until the time of her offering up.[26]

Great was the distress of those guilty of recantation, whether men or women. Elizabeth Cooper made amends by going to Saint Andrew's church while the people were at their "popish service" and renouncing her recantation, for which she suffered accordingly.[27] Agnes Glascock had gone to mass under pressure from her husband and now reproached herself bitterly. A letter of assurance came from John Careless lying in prison:

> Your foot hath chanced to slip forth of the way, to the great discomfort of your soul, and the heaviness of your heart. But, my good sister, the Lord will raise you up again, and make you stronger than ever you were. For if you had not by this proved the experience of your own strength, or rather your own weakness, you would have stood too much in your own conceit, and have despised and condemned other weak persons that have committed the like offence. Do not think that God will cast you clean away. It is a greater sin to mistrust the mercy and goodness of God than to commit the greatest offence in the world. Know for a surety that all your sins be utterly forgiven you for Christ's sake, be they never so many, so grievous and so great. The thing that is done cannot be undone, and you are not the first that hath offended. There is with the Lord "mercy and redemption." He maketh backslidings many times to turn to profit, as doubtless, dear sister, yours shall do, if you put your whole faith, hope and trust, only in his infinite and eternal sweet mercies.[28]

When she visited him in prison he wrote some verses in her book with the concluding lines:

> And think on me, I do you pray,
> The which did write this for your sake.
> And thus to God I you betake,
> Who is your castle and strong Rock;
> He keep you, whether you sleep or wake;
> Farewell, dear Mistress A. Glascock![29]

Here are a few lines written from prison by Ralph Atherton to
Agnes Smith, widow.

> We are spoiled of our labors. The holy sanctuary of God's most
> blessed word, is laid waste and desolate, so that the very foxes run
> over it. Yet it is the food of our souls, the lantern of our feet, and
> a light unto our paths, and where it is not preached the people perish.[30]

Richard Woodman wrote to Mistress Roberts of Hawkhurst:

> For when I have been in prison, wearing onewhile bolts, other-
> while shackles, otherwhile lying on the bare ground; sometime sitting
> in the stocks; sometimes bound with cords, that all my body hath been
> swollen; much like to be overcome for the pain that hath been in my
> flesh; sometime fain to lie without in the woods and fields, yet for
> all this I praise my God. All this that hath happened unto me hath
> been easy, light and most delectable and joyful of any treasure that
> ever I possessed. Fear hath painfulness, but perfect love casteth out all
> fear; which love I have no mistrust but God hath poured it upon you
> so abundantly, that nothing in the world shall be able to separate you
> from God. Neither high, nor low, rich nor poor, life nor death, shall
> be able to put you from Christ; but by him I trust you shall enter into
> the new Jerusalem, there to live forever.

There are many tributes to women. Here is one to Mother
Benet, who was not allowed to be buried in a churchyard. Her
benefactions were so great that her husband chided her and said
she might have saved him a hundred marks. She answered, "I
could not firkin up my butter and keep my cheese in the chamber and wait a great price, and let the poor want." Foxe comments, "This good woman, of that vice of covetousness, of all
that knew her was judged least to be spotted of any infirmity
she had."[31]

Protestants and Catholics would have marriage only within
the faith, and this insistence tended to break down the system
of family-made marriages in favor of unions grounded in conviction. The above mentioned John Careless wrote to his wife
that when the daughters came of age, he hoped they might be
provided with husbands "as fear God, and love his holy word.
I charge you take heed that you match them with no papists,
and if you live and marry again yourself (which thing I would

wish you to do, if need require, or else not) good wife, take heed how you bestow yourself, that you and my poor children be not compelled to wickedness."[32]

This same John Careless sent the following counsel to a friend about to embark upon matrimony:

> First and above all things you must be very circumspect to keep the band of love, and beware that there never spring up the root of bitterness between you. If at any time there happen to rise any cause of unkindness between you (as it is impossible always to be free from it), see that you weed up the same with all lenity, gentleness and patience; and never suffer yourself, nor your wife, to sleep in displeasure.
>
> If you have cause to speak sharply, and sometimes to reprove, beware that you do not the same in the presence of others, but keep your words until a convenient time, and then utter them in a spirit of meekness, and the groaning spirit of perfect love; which you must also let sometimes to cover faults, and wink at them if they be not intolerable. Whatsoever loss and mischance shall happen unto you, take it patiently, and bear it merrily; and though the same should come partly through your wife's negligence, yet let it rather be a loving warning to take heed in time to come, than a cause of sorrow for that which is past and cannot be holpen. I know by mine own experience, that we are in this life subject to many inconveniences, and that of nature we are prone to displeasure, and ready to think unkindness of every little trifle, and specially with our own best friends, yea soonest with our loving wifes, which be most loath to displease us. But let us beware of this cankered corruption, and consider that we ought most of all in love to bear with them, according to Christ's example.[33]

1.   The title of this essay is taken from a forthcoming volume by Roland H. Bainton, *Women of the Reformation*, volume 2, to be published by the Augsburg Publishing House. This essay has been revised by the author for inclusion in this volume. All of the references are to John Foxe, *Actes and Monuments*, 8 vols. (New York, 1965). An instructive chapter is devoted to Foxe by Helen C. White, *Tudor Books of Saints and Martyrs* (Madison, Wis., 1967).

2.   John Foxe, *Actes and Monuments*, 8:391.

3.   Ibid., p. 429.

4.   Ibid., p. 493.

5.   Ibid., p. 579.

6.   Ibid., p. 553.

7.   Ibid., 4:239.

8.   Ibid., p. 243.

9.   Ibid., p. 225.

10.   Ibid., 8:115–6.
11.   Ibid., 5:537–50.
12.   Ibid., 8:536–48.
13.   Ibid., p. 467.
14.   Ibid., p. 382.
15.   Ibid., p. 327.
16.   Ibid., p. 247.
17.   Ibid., p. 385–6.
18.   Ibid., 4:128.
19.   Ibid., 8:633.
20.   Ibid., p. 219.
21.   Ibid., p. 556.
22.   Ibid., p. 224.
23.   Ibid., p. 296.
24.   Ibid., 7:517.
25.   Ibid., 8:113–4.
26.   Ibid., p. 422–3.
27.   Ibid., p. 381.
28.   Ibid., p. 193–6.
29.   Ibid., p. 195.
30.   Ibid., p. 414.
31.   Ibid., p. 467.
32.   Ibid., p. 174. Cf. 7:117.
33.   Ibid., p. 197.

WITTENBERG BOTANISTS DURING
THE SIXTEENTH CENTURY

Karl H. Dannenfeldt

In reviewing the botanical renaissance of the first half of the sixteenth century, George Sarton correctly observed that "this revival was not only German but also Lutheran."[1] In support of this statement it might be pointed out that of the outstanding herbalists and botanists of the period, Jerome Bock (Hieronymous Tragus, d. 1554), an early convert to Lutheranism, was pastor at Hornbach when he published his *New Kreütter Buch* at Strassburg in 1539. Leonhard Fuchs (1501–66), educated at Erfurt and Ingolstadt and later professor of medicine at the new Lutheran university at Tübingen, was a Lutheran when he published his great herbal *De historia stirpium*, in Basel in 1542. This well-written and beautifully illustrated book is the outstanding early work on botany. In addition to these examples, a large number of other early botanists were identified with Lutheranism.

Although the fact that these German botanists were also Lutheran may be coincidental, it is interesting to examine the attitude of Luther himself toward plants and also the role of the University of Wittenberg in educating in whole or in part a number of botanists during the first half of the sixteenth century, when botany as a science had its hesitant beginnings. The University of Wittenberg is here used as a *focal point* for the study of this transitional phase of a science.

Luther, whose personal emblem was the rose, was a keen observer of nature and a lover of flowers and plants. He was also an enthusiastic gardener, who found recreation from his busy life by growing plants and trees in his gardens at Wittenberg and on other plots of ground purchased at various times. He took particular interest in fruit trees and, like the botanists of the day, exchanged plants with others. On September 4, 1538, he wrote the Duchess Elizabeth of Brunswick that at her request for unusual plants he was sending her "some slips of mulberry and fig trees, the only rare things I have at present."[2]

Besides the recreational and aesthetic interest in plants, Luther's love of nature also had a theological basis. Only a few examples can be given here. In his commentaries on Genesis, for example, the Reformer emphasized that when God created the earth, he adorned it with plants before creating the firmament, fish, fowl, animals, and man. Because of Man's Fall, however, the earth was cursed so that it produced such things as "darnel, wild oats, weeds, nettles, thorns, thistles." And this curse was made more severe after the Flood when harmful herbs and insects increased.[3]

Luther marveled at the immutability of the species as shown in the recurring miracle of plant reproduction:

> Now, indeed, everything is produced from seed of its own kind. But the first creation without seed was brought about simply as a result of the power of the Word. However, the fact that seeds now grow is also a work of creation full of wonderment. It is a unique property that a seed corn which falls on the ground comes up in due time and brings forth fruit according to its kind. A sure proof that the creation was not fortuitous but the exclusive work of divine foresight is the fact that similar plants are brought forth from similar plants in uninterrupted sequence. . . . Perpetually the same inherent character, the process of development, and the nature of the individual kinds are preserved unimpaired.[4]

To Luther, the entire botanical creation taught man much about God and life. Plants are constant reminders of God's mercy: "Thus you must be ashamed of yourself when you look at the sun which preaches this to you every day, ashamed even when you are in a field and you look at a little flower or at the leaf of a tree. For this is written all over the leaves and grass."[5] We must reproach ourselves for our lack of love for God and our neighbor when we consider how much God does for us through his creatures. Indeed, "the little flowers in the field, which cattle trample and eat, are to become our theologians and masters and embarrass us still further." However, man does not learn the theological lessons that nature provides, and remains greedy and selfish despite the fact that "to our eternal shame and disgrace each individual flower is a witness against us to condemn our unbelief before God and all creatures until the Last Day."[6] A flower might cheer us by its beauty, but it also reminds us of our tragic life, for "it is also a phase of life's misery that the petals of the flower so soon fall to the ground and wither and that it cannot preserve its color and distinctive fragrance."[7]

Luther used the term *physiologia* to denote the study of nature and natural forces. While he complained that the experienced peasants of his day knew more about natural sciences than was taught in the universities, he admitted that each person knew some facts about nature: "I know, for example, that dog's tongue [*Cynoglosum officinale*] is healing for wounds . . . and so forth; one person knows more than the other about nature, but only a small part; so now reason is so inquisitive and wants to know more and more; therefore, the study and investigation of nature has been intensified."[8] Luther also observed that an interested person could perceive that there was still much secret activity in nature, "and whoever is able to apply this performs more wondrous deeds than those who do not possess this skill."[9]

Only through the eyes of faith can God's creation be correctly seen, and Luther rightly boasted that the Reformation had awakened a new interest in the creatures of this world:

> We are now living in the dawn of the future life; for we are beginning to regain a knowledge we had forfeited by the fall of Adam. Now we have a correct view of the creatures, more so, I suppose, than they have in the papacy. Erasmus does not concern himself with this. . . . But by God's mercy we can begin to recognize his wonderful works and wonders also in the flowers when we ponder his might and goodness. Therefore we laud, magnify, and thank him. In his creatures we recognize the power of his work. By his Word everything came into being. This power is evident even in a peach-stone. No matter how hard its shell, in due season it is forced open by a very

soft kernel inside it. All this is ignored by Erasmus. He looks at the creatures as a cow stares at a new gate.[10]

When founded in 1502, the University of Wittenberg was organized with a philosophical, or arts, faculty and the graduate schools of law, theology, and medicine. That a number of Lutheran botanists received botanical instruction at Wittenberg was due to the presence of this medical school and the inclusion of some classical botanical works in the arts curriculum.

In the sixteenth century the study of botany was an integral part of a medical education, for most of medical physic was derived from plants. The pharmacopoeia was predominantly botanical. The physician had to know the properties of beneficial plants in order to prescribe remedies, and the apothecary needed the herbal in order to identify and stock the plants traditionally considered medicinal. Thus, the physician or anyone else who took notice of plants was usually less interested in the materials of a science than in what practical and beneficial results could be obtained from plants in the treatment of diseases or other infirmities. Traditionally, this botanical knowledge was derived from the classical authors, and Renaissance humanism had enhanced the authority of such medical herbalists as Pliny, Dioscorides, Theophrastus, Apuleius Barbarus—all of whom had described the useful plants of the Mediterranean areas.

At the University of Wittenberg, the distinguished Martinus Polich von Mellerstadt, one of the founders, was a physician and taught medicine as well as theology. However, the first medical professor apparently was appointed in 1508.[11] For years the medical faculty consisted of two *ordinarii*, but in the reorganization of 1536 a third member was added to the faculty. The medical instruction was divided among these, with the primary and oldest professor teaching the books of Galen and Hippocrates, the second teaching the Arab physicians Rhazes and Avicenna, whose works incorporated much on the medicinal plants of the Near East, and the third instructing in anatomy.[12] In Melanchthon's reorganization of the faculty in 1546, provision was made for an instructor in the philosophical faculty to teach Aristotle's *Physics* from the original text, Dioscorides' *De materia medica*, and to point out the plants found therein.[13]

The electoral library at Wittenberg was humanistically oriented and supported the instruction in medical subjects, including botany, with a wide variety of classical and medieval works, 545 in number. In a catalog of 1536 about 150 "Medici Latini" are listed, with the works of Galen and Avicenna being most numerous. Other authors important to the study of plants, usually in a number of editions, included Dioscorides, Rhazes, Pliny, Aetius of Amida, and the famous *Hortus sanitatus.* Several German *Kraüterbücher* (herbals) were also available.[14]

In the first half of the sixteenth century a number of instructors in the arts faculty taught "physics," or natural science. In the winter of 1517–18, the distinguished and aged Johann Rach (Rhagius; Aesticampianus) came to Wittenberg to teach Pliny, a classical author held in great respect by Luther, who hoped to use the Roman scientist as a counterfoil to Aristotle and his scholastic interpreters. The learned Aesticampianus had earlier taught Pliny at Cologne and on his arrival in Wittenberg published an edition of this author. He was promoted to doctor of medicine in September, 1518. Aesticampianus, however, soon turned to lecturing on the Church Fathers. He died in May, 1520, and the recently arrived Philip Melanchthon took up the instruction in Pliny.[15]

Caspar Cruciger (1504–48), professor of theology and Hebrew at Wittenberg after 1529, was very interested in botany and industriously collected all kinds of plants. He lectured on Dioscorides and established two botanical gardens outside the city in which he planted unusual plants of native and foreign origin. Using Galen and Hippocrates as guides, he sought to discover the healing qualities of plants and even mixed his own medicines. He saw in nature a sovereign God who "had placed in each plant an exclusive and preventive power for every kind of illness, which is in this time still hidden from the eyes of the scientific investigator."[16]

Paul Eber (1511–69) came to Wittenberg in October, 1532, and was promoted to *magister artium* on April 27, 1536, at the same time as Georg Joachim Rheticus, the famous mathematician. In April, 1537, he was received into the arts faculty. After a period of absence, he returned to Wittenberg in 1547 and

lectured on science, including mathematics, astronomy, and botany. In his lectures on Dioscorides he used for demonstration
the plants growing near the city, beginning with those eaten by
man. He thought it a shame that everyone did not know the
nature and names of the cereals and vegetables that were used
for meals. To Eber, who later went over to theology, plants were
a manifest and wonderful witness to God's omnipotence. In
Wittenberg, in 1556, he published his *De vita et scripta C. Pli-
nii. Quaedam praefationis loco recitata a Paulo Ebero Auspicante
explicationem secundi libri Naturalis Historia*.[17]

Melanchthon, the young Greek scholar, arrived in Wittenberg in August, 1518, from Tübingen, where he had acquired
his classical orientation and a religious attitude toward the natural sciences from his teacher, Johann Stöffler. In his inaugural
address he described the students of Wittenberg as fortunate in
that they were taught Pliny, other classical authors, and the classical languages. Melanchthon's view of the natural sciences was
grounded in the *theologia naturalis*: all creation showed God's
presence, wisdom, and goodness. His view thus differed from
that of the humanists of his day in that he saw much more in the
natural sciences of his classical sources than a philological exercise. He also realized in a historical way that the classical works
formed only a base for later and current expansion of knowledge in the natural sciences.[18]

Just as Luther was responsible for a new theological orientation of the University of Wittenberg, Melanchthon was primarily responsible for a new emphasis on the humanities and the
natural sciences. In the areas of medicine and botany, Melanchthon, oriented to the classics as he was, criticized quackery and
folk-medicine. He was especially interested in Hippocrates and
Galen and even contributed a preface to the Greek edition of
the latter's works published at Basel in 1538 by Joachim Camerarius, Leonhard Fuchs, and Hieronymous Gemusaeus.[19] He also
gave a number of declamations on medical subjects, and in one
of these, *Laus artis medicae*, he wrote (1529 or 1530) that the
study of medicine turned one

> to the contemplation of the boundless kinds of herbs, there to tarry
> long and to become acquainted at closer hand with their marvelous

and clearly divine powers and riches. These are so manifold, so extraordinary, and so unbelievable that there is in fact nothing in nature herself more deserving of esteem or more beautiful to investigate, or more delightful to understand. It seems to have been the object of nature herself to conceal and hide in the inmost pith of herbs rare things, the gifts of her kindness, an extraordinary power for good, in order to spur good, zealous men on to investigation, and to repay their zeal and labor with bountiful rewards.[20]

He corresponded with the botanist Leonhard Fuchs, whom he knew from his days in Leipzig and whose works he greeted with enthusiasm.[21] On several occasions (1559) he discussed the sycamore tree and cited Dioscorides and Theophrastus.[22] He went on botanical expeditions himself,[23] and included medicinal herbs in medical recipes he prepared against the plague.[24] In 1544 Melanchthon sought the correct identification of a plant popularly called "Jelängerjelieber" (*Ajuga chamaepitys*). He examined the classical texts and wrote an inquiry to his friend Joachim Camerarius, Sr. He showed in this case that he realized that the Greek and Near Eastern plants described by the classical authorities did not necessarily grow in Germany, as many of his contemporaries held. He even painted a picture of the plant, including the root system as was the custom in plant depiction of the day, and sent it to his friend Christoph Pannonius, who was also asked to identify the plant.[25]

The most prominent of German botanists to be associated with the University of Wittenberg was Valerius Cordus.[26] He was born on February 18, 1515, at Erfurt, the son of the gifted and scholarly Euricus Cordus, a Lutheran botanist, poet, and professor of medicine at Marburg.[27] His father carefully educated Valerius. A later biographer, Walther Hermann Ryff, recorded that "Valerius Cordus was imbued with an incredible zeal for learning thoroughly not only medicine, but also the correct recognition of plants, to which latter his father, Euricius, a physician and also an illustrious poet, urged him by both precept and example; for he reared the child even from the cradle in the midst of herbs and flowers."[28]

The young Valerius received his baccalaureate in medicine at the University of Marburg at the age of sixteen. From 1531 to 1543, when he left for Italy, Cordus based his activities at the

University of Wittenberg. He spent some time with his father at Marburg and also with an uncle, Joachim Johann Ralla, an apothecary in Leipzig. It was probably while at Leipzig that he wrote his famous *Dispensatorium pharmacorum omnium,* which was compiled at the request of his uncle. He finally officially enrolled at the University of Wittenberg during the winter semester of 1539–40.[29] Crato von Krafftheim, later physician to three emperors, recorded that he and Cordus heard Melanchthon lecture on Nicander's *Alexipharmaca* in 1539.[30] Cordus was apparently both a student and an instructor at the same time, for he lectured three times on Dioscorides during the next years with considerable success. Among those in attendance were Johann Aurifaber, later professor of theology at Rostock and Königsberg, Johann Placotomus (Plachetius), later a physician at Danzig, and Viet Winshemius (Ortel), who was later a professor of medicine and a frequent rector at Wittenberg.

Important for his personal fame and that of the University of Wittenberg and for the history of botany was the fact that Valerius Cordus was an early innovator in the use of botanical field trips. This novelty was indicative of a change from classical medical herbalism to the study of nature from a truly scientific viewpoint and method. Before the sixteenth century the medical herbalists had been primarily concerned with classroom instruction or with the issuance of manuscripts or printed editions and commentaries on ancient Greek and Near Eastern botany as found in Pliny, Dioscorides, Theophratsus, Rhazes, Avicenna, and other classical and Arabic writers on medicinal herbalism.

Already in the first century A.D., Pliny the Elder had observed that "little by little experience, the most efficient teacher of all things, and in particular of medicine, degenerated into words and mere talk. For it was more pleasant to sit in a lecture-room engaged in listening, than to go into the wilds and search for the various plants at their proper season of the year."[31] Even the great works of Brunfels (1530) and Fuchs (1542) were devoted almost entirely to classical and medieval medical botany, describing little new and reproducing, with some correction of gross errors, only the standard descriptions and therapeutic applications of earlier authors. Hieronymous Tragus was the first botanist to actually make original verbal descriptions of German plants in his *New Kreüter Buch* (1539).

From his father, Valerius Cordus had learned that many of the plants found in Germany were far different from those named and described by the ancient authorities.[32] Now as a member of the faculty at Wittenberg, he gave evidence of the new scientific approach to botanical studies by his field trips. Many of these trips were made with students in the region about Wittenberg, but others were farther afield. A major botanical expedition was made from the spring to the autumn of 1542. This included, among others, the regions about the Erzebirge, northern Bohemia, Carlsbad, Königsberg, Auerbach, Nürnberg, Regensburg, Passau, Augsburg, Salzburg, Tübingen, Speyer, Frankfurt am Main, Stolberg, and Seeberg.[33] At Tübingen he undoubtedly visited with Leonhard Fuchs, whose great herbal had just been published in Basel.[34]

In 1543 Cordus and several companions left Wittenberg for a botanical expedition in Italy, a trip that was probably financed, at least in part, by Cordus's older brother, Philippus. One of the members of the group was Hieronymous Schreiber (Scribonius) of Nürnberg. He had matriculated at Wittenberg in the summer semester of 1532 at the same time as Georg Joachim Rheticus, the future mathematician. On September 15, 1541, while Rheticus was dean, he became a member of the arts faculty.[35] In the summer semester of 1542, while Rheticus was on leave, Schreiber took over his courses in mathematics.[36] Schreiber's detailed account of the Italian expedition and of the death of Cordus was printed in Gesner's edition of the works of Cordus at Strassburg in 1563 and at Nürnberg in 1751 in Gesner's *Opera botanica*.

The party paused at Nürnberg, Schreiber's home city, and it was probably while there that Cordus revised the manuscript of his *Dispensatorium*, preparing it for the press. Cordus was well received at Venice, and the travelers then went to Padua, where the University was noted for its medical school and the famous professor Giambattista Montanus. In the spring of 1544 Cordus left for Ferrara while Schreiber remained at Padua. At Ferrara, Cordus met the noted physician Antonius Musa Brassavola. At Bologna, where he remained a month, Cordus conversed with Lucas Ghini, who is credited with being the first to attach plants to paper and thus form an herbarium (*hortus siccus*).[37] Cordus explored the environs of Bologna in the company of Cornelius Sittard, a young physician of Cologne.[38] Cordus then left for Rome in the company of Sittard, a servant, and the Prussian Nicolaus Friedewald, who may have come with Cordus from the University of Wittenberg, where he was a student.[39] They traversed the areas where Pliny had observed plants and visited Florence, Pisa, Lucca, Livorno, and Siena. Then they turned to the seacoast.

At one of the inns where they stayed, Cordus received a kick on his leg from a horse. The summer heat, the injured leg, and the difficult terrain soon took their toll. The servant fell ill and was left at Ronciglione, between Viterbo and Rome, while the feverish Cordus and his ailing companions entered Rome with great difficulty. Physicians were called, and Schreiber joined the group on September 5. The condition of Cordus grew worse for a time, but when he seemed to improve, Schreiber and Sittard left for Naples. When Cordus again worsened, the attending physician demanded that he commune. A German priest was found, but because Cordus, a Lutheran, wanted to commune under both elements—the administration of which would have meant imprisonment and burning at the stake for the priest—it was decided that Cordus should receive absolution without Communion (*Crede et manducasti*) and the priest reported the patient too weak to receive the consecrated wafer. Because of the dangerous hostility of some monks who threatened to throw the German into the Tiber, Cordus received the sacrament of extreme unction from another priest before he died on the night of September 25, 1544. After some difficulties, he was buried in the Church of Santa Maria dell'Anima, which Hadrian VI had built for Germans and Lowlanders. Schreiber and Sittard returned too late to attend their dying friend.[40]

The news of the death of Cordus caused widespread grief. Melanchthon wrote Leonhard Fuchs on December 25: "We have lost an ingenious youth, an exceedingly diligent investigator of all nature." He also wrote Joachim Camerarius the Elder in December, lamenting the death of the twenty-nine year old botanist: "et res litteraria magno detrimento affecta est."[41]

Cordus published nothing during his brief life—that task was reserved for his friends and especially Conrad Gesner, the Swiss naturalist, who had never met Cordus but who recognized his genius. The first work to appear was the *Dispensatorum pharmacorum omnium quae in usu potissimum sunt,* which was published in Nürnberg in 1546 under the auspices of the council of that city.[42] The work, the earliest official pharmacopoeia to appear in print, was often reprinted. In 1549 his *Annotationes doctissimae in Dioscorides de medica materia libros,* designed as an aid to physicians, was published in Frankfurt am Main as an appendix to Walther Ryff's edition of Dioscorides. This edition of the *Annotationes* was based on notes taken by a student who attended the first lectures of Cordus on Dioscorides.

A collection of works by Cordus, edited by Gesner, appeared in a volume published in Strassburg in 1561. The prefatory letter dedicated the volume with high praise to the "renowned and notable" medical faculty of the University of Wittenberg. Included is a second edition of the *Annotationes* based on a copy with corrections by Cordus himself up to Book II, Chapter CVIII. These changes had resulted from his extensive tour through Germany in 1542. This copy Gesner received from Johann Placotomus, a physician of Danzig, who had obtained the manuscript for Joachim Ralla, the uncle of Cordus.[43]

Gesner had two manuscripts for Cordus's *Historiae plantarum libri IIII,* which was included in the 1561 collection. The first manuscript was the original, which Cordus had written about 1540 and which Gesner obtained also from Placotomus. It contained annotations by Georg Aemylius (Oelmer). Aemylius, though no botanist himself, contributed much to the scientific efforts of his friends who were practicing botanists. Aemylius studied theology at Wittenberg, where he matriculated in the winter of 1532. He was regarded with esteem by Melanchthon and Luther and became a close friend of Cordus at Wittenberg, where his own love of plants originated. During the leisure hours of his later life at Siegen and Stolberg, Aemylius maintained his interest in botany. He corresponded with, and sent plants to, such botanists as Johann Thal and Conrad Gesner and maintained his own botanical garden with many unusual plants.[44]

Gesner also had a second copy of the *Historiae*, with annotations, which he received from Hieronymous Herold (d. 1566), a physician of Nürnberg. Gesner included in the collection a letter that he wrote to Herold describing the preparation of the *Historiae* for the press. Herold, originally from Leipzig, had matriculated at Wittenberg on November 15, 1540, and was thus probably well acquainted with Cordus and Schreiber.[45] Herold visited Gesner in July, 1558, and signed his host's *Liber amicorum*. To Herold's signature Gesner added the comment: "Most expert in the science of herbs."[46] On January 27, 1565, Gesner wrote Herold thanking him for some unusual plants he had received from him and begged him to send plants, or at least full descriptions of such plants, that he had observed on a trip to North Germany.[47]

The *Historiae plantarum* of Cordus has been described as the "most important of the early German herbals of the sixteenth century."[48] It was a landmark in descriptive botany, for Cordus, a keen observer, described the plants from nature and did not deal with their therapeutic applications. He described over 500 plants, timbers, and resins. J. P. de Tournefort credits Cordus as having been "the first of all men to excel in floral description,"[49] and Albert Haller says the Wittenberg botanist was "the first to teach men to cease from dependence on the poor descriptions of the ancients, and to describe plants anew from nature."[50] Gesner supplied 270 woodcuts of plants of which about 220 are correctly associated with the plants described.

Gesner's collection also included Cordus's *Sylva observationum variarum*, printed from a manuscript received from Placotomus and consisting of observations on animals, minerals, and plants. Also printed here were the three parts of Cordus's *De artificiosis extractionibus*, which gives us the first clear account of the preparation of ether from sulphuric acid and alcohol. A fifth book of his *Historiae plantarum*, containing descriptions of 25 plants seen on his Italian expedition, was printed at Strassburg in 1563 and reprinted by C. I. Trew and C. C. Schmiedel in Gesner's *Opera botanica* (Nürnberg, 1751).

Among the associates of Cordus at Wittenberg was the celebrated French naturalist Pierre Belon du Mans (1517-64). Attracted by the reputation of Cordus, he came to the University of Wittenberg in 1541, bringing with him a number of rare plants from the garden of the bishop of Touvoie. Belon, who worked closely with Cordus for a period of twelve months, described his friend as having a large number of students to whom he gave "demonstrations and interpretations of the plants of Galen, Theophrastus, and Dioscorides."[51] Belon matriculated, *gratis*, at the university in the late summer of 1541.[52] Later, he gave thanks to the "late Duke John Frederick," who "made provisions for foreigners to be able to maintain themselves as students at little cost."[53]

Belon found Cordus, his teacher "a gracious person and modest . . . of great gaiety and sincere kindness." With ten German students, including Hieronymous Schreiber of Nürnberg and Caspar Naeve of Chemnitz, Belon accompanied Cordus on his major field expedition in Saxony, Thuringia, Pomerania, and in the forests of Germany and Bohemia. They also visited mines, such as those of Joachimstal, and botanized "for four months throughout every region of Germany, sometimes frequenting theologians and sometimes associating with doctors, until they finally reached lower [northern] Germany." But, Belon adds, "since time alters all, there is no relationship, however close, which does not dissolve," and he left for England, "where there was as yet no change in religion."[54]

In 1542 Belon was in Paris. Later he was in Bern, where he visited Benedict Aretius, the professor of theology, Greek, and Hebrew and an accomplished Alpine botanist, whom he named as having been one of his "fellow students at Wittenberg."[55] In 1544 Belon decided to rejoin Cordus, who was then on his Italian botanical expedition. This association, near Leghorn, was brief, for Cordus went on by way of Siena to Rome and his death.

Belon eventually returned to France and in 1547 sailed for the Near East. He and Cordus had often planned botanical trips during their association at Wittenberg, and Cordus expressed his own strong desire to visit Egypt, with its unusual plants and mummies. These discussions had stimulated Belon to travel to the Near East.[56] The trip resulted in his famous book, *Les observations de plusieurs singularitez et choses memorables trouvées en Grèce, Asie, Judée, Egypte, Arabie, et autres pays estranges, redigées en trois livres* (Paris, 1553). This work, and the others he wrote, mark Belon as a botanist of considerable stature, and part of his training and experience as a botanist had been secured at Wittenberg.

A number of other students who studied at the University of Wittenberg made contributions to the development of botany as a science. Belon named Caspar Naevius (Nephius) as a member of the botanical expedition in Germany led by Cordus. This student, born in Chemnitz in 1514, matriculated at the University of Wittenberg in May, 1534.[57] Later he was the physician of the Elector Augustus of Saxony and then became professor at the University of Leipzig, where he died in 1580. In 1556 and 1558 he exchanged letters on *materia medica* with Pietro Andrea Mattioli, the famous editor and commentator on Dioscorides.[58]

More important for this study were the botanical activities of his older brother, Johann, who was born at Chemnitz in 1499 and who graduated from the University of Leipzig. He entered the University of Wittenberg in November, 1519, and on January 24, 1521, was promoted to master of arts at the same time as Johann Lonicer and Janus Cornarius, both mentioned below.[59] Before returning to Leipzig he visited a number of Italian universities and obtained his doctor of medicine degree at Ferrara. George Agricola included Johann Naevius as one of the two "doctissimi et clarissimi medici" who conduct the dialogue that forms the basis for his *Bermannus, sive de re metallica dialogus* (Basel, 1530). In this work, Naevius is the spokesman for matters dealing with the works of Dioscorides, Pliny, Galen, and other ancient authors. Johann Naevius corresponded with the famous botanist Mattioli, who acknowledged with thanks that

Naevius had sent him a considerable sum of money to defray the expenses he had incurred with his botanical work on Dioscorides.[60]

Janus Cornarius (Johann Hagenbutt, 1500–1558) of Zwickau came to the University of Wittenberg in 1520 after receiving his baccalaureate degree at Leipzig. In January, 1521, he was promoted to the master's level with Johann Naevius and two years later received his licentiatus in medicine. Later he traveled in England, the Lowlands, and France, and was with Erasmus in Basel for a year. He practiced medicine in Nordhausen, was *Stadtphysicus* (city physician) in Frankfurt am Main, professor of medicine at Zwickau (1542–46), and finally taught at the universities of Marburg and Jena.

Cornarius's fame rests primarily on his Greek edition of Hippocrates (Basel, 1538), but his Greek edition of Dioscorides (Basel, 1529) is important in the history of botany. Conrad Gesner praised his Latin translation of Dioscorides, with its valuable vocabulary, which appeared in Basel in 1557. In his struggle to promote Greek medical authorities against the Arabists, he also edited, among others, the works of Galen, Aetius of Amida, and Paul of Aigina. These contained valuable botanical information, largely borrowed from Dioscorides. By publishing editions of these authors, Cornarius contributed much to the spread of Dioscoridean botany and to the Hellinization of medicine in general. In 1540 Cornarius also published an annotated edition of the *De viribus herbarum* or *Macer Foridus* under the title *De materia medica libri V*. This well-known herbal, in verse, was probably written by Odo Magdunensis in the eleventh century, who used Pliny, Galen, and Dioscorides as his sources. Books One and Two concern *De herbis ac plantis vulgaribus;* Book Three is *De plantis perigrinis*.[61]

Among the graduates of the University of Wittenberg who contributed to the development of botany was Johann Lonicerus (Lonitzer; 1499–1569). He had been educated at Erfurt and became an Augustinian monk before coming to Wittenberg.[62] In April, 1519, he secured his baccalaureate degree as "Frater Ioannes Lonecerus Eisslebensis Augustinianus." In January, 1521, along with Johann Naevius and Johann Cornarius, both mentioned above, he received his master of arts degree.[63] After positions at Freiburg and Strassburg, he went to the University of Marburg in 1527, where he became professor of Greek and Hebrew and eventually a doctor of theology.

In 1531 he published Nicander's poems on animal and vegetable poisons and antidotes, *Veteris poetae et medici Theriaca et Alexipharmaca, cum scholiis* (Cologne). Not being a physician, he employed a philological approach in his annotations in which he drew heavily on the botanical works of Dioscorides, Pliny, Oribasios, Apuleius Barbarus, and others. In 1543 his learned *scholia nova* were printed in the Frankfort edition of Walter Hermann Ryff's comments on the translation of Dioscorides by Jean Ruel. Conrad Gesner lists this work of Lonicerus among those written on Dioscorides.[64] The same scholia were appended to the translation of Dioscorides by Marcellus Vergilius, the Florentine (Marburg, 1543). In his scholia, which appeared "cum nomenclaturis Graecis Latinis Hebraicis et Germanicis," Lonicerus wrote against the medieval interpretations from the Arabic writers on medicine and referred to Hippocrates, Galen, and especially Dioscorides, condemning the emendations then being made in the text of the last-named botanical authority.[65]

Johann Moibanus of Bratislava (1527–62) matriculated at Wittenberg in the summer of 1544, and on February 7, 1548, while Melanchthon was dean of the University of Wittenberg, he was promoted to the rank of magister.[66] Later he taught at Nürnberg and, while there, became acquainted with Cornelius Sittard, the doctor who had accompanied Valerius Cordus on the latter's Italian botanical expedition. Moibanus and Sittard carefully studied the descriptions of herbs in the ancient Greek authors, especially in Dioscorides.[67] From Nürnberg, Moibanus toured Italy, and settled in Augsburg upon his return to Germany. It was probably during this period that he visited the famous naturalist Conrad Gesner in Zurich.[68] When he died in 1562, Moibanus was working on a Greek edition of Oribasios' *Euporista ad Andramachum*, incorrectly attributed to Dioscorides, which concerned herbal medicine largely drawn from

Dioscorides and Galen. The work, including a Latin version, was completed by Gesner and Achilles Pirimius Gasser and published in Strassburg in 1565.[69]

A Lowland "Lutheran" botanist educated in part at Wittenberg was Carolus Clusius (Charles de l'Ecluse, 1526–1609). Born in Arras, his early education was gained at Ghent, Louvain, and Marburg, where he became a Lutheran while studying law.[70] Encouraged by his teacher Andreas Hyperius, professor of theology at Marburg, to study under Melanchthon, Clusius matriculated at the University of Wittenberg on July 3, 1549.[71] Soon after his arrival, he informed Hyperius that he planned to study medicine. These studies he began at Wittenberg with the intention of later going to France. He botanized in the vicinity of Wittenberg and in later works recorded several plants he had found there.[72]

Early in 1550, Clusius left Wittenberg and after a visit to Marburg, Frankfurt am Main, and Switzerland, he enrolled at Montpellier in the autumn of 1551. He remained there until January, 1554. A long trip through Spain and Portugal lead to the writing of his important *Rariorum aliquot stirpium per Hispanias observatarum historia* (Antwerp, 1576), and his botanical observations in Austria and Hungary were printed in Antwerp in 1583. During his stay at Vienna he resided at the home of Dr. Johann Aicholtz, professor of medicine at the University of Vienna. Aicholtz had received his medical education at Wittenberg, where he matriculated in May, 1543.[73] He aided Clusius in his botanical studies and furnished examples of plants from his own outstanding botanical garden.[74]

A major contribution to the spread of botanical knowledge was made by Clusius in the form of translations of botanical books. In 1557 he published his French translation of the Dodonaeus (Remberg Dodoens). In 1579 his Latin translation of Belon's *Les observations* appeared at Antwerp, and ten years later his Latin translation of another botanical work by Belon, *Les Remonstrances*, was published at the same place. He also made Latin translations of the Portuguese herbal of Garcia da Orta and of the Spanish book by Christoval Acosta, both works dealing with the plants of India. His Latin abbreviation of the Spanish work on Indian plants by Nicolas Monardes was printed in 1572. The genus *Clusia* was named in his honor.

Another German Lutheran botanist educated in part at the University of Wittenberg was Joachim Camerarius the Younger (1534–98), son of the reformer and scholar Joachim Camerarius the Elder. The young Camerarius matriculated at Wittenberg on July 21, 1558, and resided at the home of Melanchthon, the close friend of his father.[75] Camerarius received his medical education at Wittenberg and at Leipzig. He then traveled in Italy, studying with a number of famous botanists and obtaining his doctorate in medicine at Bologna in 1562. On his return in 1564 to his birthplace, Nürnberg, he practiced medicine and established a botanical garden of rare and foreign plants at the gates of the city. These plants are described in his well-illustrated botanical work *Hortus medicus et philosophicus* (Frankfurt, 1588). Other botanical works are Latin and German (with Georg Handsch) editions (1586) of Pier' Andrea Mattioli's commentaries on Dioscorides, the *Symbolorum et emblematum centuriae tres, quibus rariores stirpium, animalium et insectorum proprietates complexus est* (1590), and his *Plantarum tam indigenarum quam exoticarum icones* (1591). In 1581 he obtained the botanical legacy of Conrad Gesner, but unfortunately he did not have the opportunity to publish this. He was a close observer of nature, and the genus *Cameraria* commemorates his contributions to botanical knowledge.[76]

On November 6, 1556, Leonhard Rauwolf of Augsburg, the future botanist of the Near East, matriculated at the University of Wittenberg.[77] Four years later he entered the medical school at Montpelier, where he heard the lectures on plants by the noted Guillaume Rondelet. He also went on field expeditions and began the collections of his outstanding herbarium. After obtaining his medical degree from the University of Valence, Rauwolf made an extensive field trip, gathering specimens throughout northern Italy, Switzerland, and southern Germany.[78] He practiced medicine at Augsburg and in 1573 set out on a lengthy field trip to the Near East that took him as far as Baghdad. It was his intention to discover and identify the plants and herbs described by Theophrastus, Dioscorides, Avicenna, Serapion, and other classical and Arab botanists.

Rauwolf returned to Augsburg early in 1576. Six years later appeared the first edition of his *Aigentliche beschreibung der Raisz so er vor diser zeit gegen Auffgang inn die Morgenländer . . . selbs volbracht* (Laugingen, 1582), in which he described his journey and the many plants he saw and collected. Forced out of Augsburg because of his refusal, as a Lutheran, to support the change to the Gregorian calendar in 1588, he located at Linz until 1596, when he joined the Austrian troops fighting the Turks. He died at Waitzen in September, 1596. His name is perpetuated in the genus *Rauwolfia*, the plant from which modern scientists have isolated the alkaloids that have become the basis for tranquilizers.

A part of the growing scientific study of plants, as distinguished from herbs and drugs, was the use of herbaria, a sixteenth-century innovation. Rauwolf began his herbarium in 1560 while at Montpellier. Upon his return from his trip to the Near East, during which he carefully collected many unusual specimens and preserved these between paper, he reorganized his herbarium into four volumes. These are still preserved at the University of Leyden and contain 834 plants collected from southern France, northern Italy, Switzerland, Tripoli, Aleppo, along the Euphrates River, and on Mount Lebanon.[79]

Another early German botanist to preserve plants on paper was Caspar Ratzenberger of Saalfelden, who matriculated at Wittenberg on April 24, 1548.[80] Early in November, 1560, he entered the University of Montpellier with Rondelet, the great botanist, as his adviser.[81] Rauwolf had preceded him by only two weeks. Other than the date of his death, 1603, little else is known of Ratzenberger. His collection of dried plants is his monument. One herbarium of 746 plants is in the museum at Cassel; another, in four volumes and completed in 1598, is at Gotha.[82]

In summary, the contributions of the faculty and "alumni" of the University of Wittenberg to the development of botany in the sixteenth century are impressive. These contributions center on a number of paths that lead away from herbalism to the study of plants for purposes other than medicine and drugs, important as vegetable *materia medica* was to remain. The religious atmosphere that pervaded all instruction at the Lutheran University of Wittenberg influenced the study of botany as evidence of God's continuing creativity and goodness. Melanchthon's orientation toward the classics and natural science provided a stimulus to many student generations in their quest for more knowledge of God's Nature. It has been rightly stated that "at no other university did mathematics and the natural sciences bloom as at Wittenberg."[83]

The use of botanical field trips by Cordus was a major innovation to the instruction of botany. His own expeditions and those of Rauwolf, Belon, Clusius, and other botanists educated in part at Wittenberg resulted in a new and valid phytography of flora indigenous to Europe and the Near East. New species and varieties were thereby identified, and the descriptions and identifications of the classical authors were verified. This latter development could only reinforce the growing awareness that many of the plants described by classical and Arabic authors did not grow in Europe, especially beyond the Mediterranean Sea littoral.

The emphasis upon the Greek authors and especially upon Dioscorides, who had described about 600 plants, was an important development in furnishing a basis, untarnished by Arabism, for the scientific study of plants. Dioscoridean botany gradually moved from philological studies to scientific observation. The lectures on Dioscorides at Wittenberg by such instructors as Cordus and Eber, the commentaries on Dioscorides by Cordus and Lonicerus, the Greek edition of Oribasios' *Euporista* by Moibanus, the Latin edition and the German translation by Camerarius of Mattioli's commentaries on Dioscorides, and especially the Greek and Latin editions of Dioscorides by Cornarius were all of great importance in establishing the Greek botanist as an excellent platform on which to base the developing science of botany.

Also important in the identification and description of European and Asian flora were the herbaria of Rauwolf and Ratzenberger. The herbarium of Rauwolf, for example, was later used by such botanists as Caspar Bauhin, Jacob Breyn, Robert Morison, Leonard Plunkenet, and Jacob Bobart.[84] Besides the dried plants preserved in herbaria, a number of the Wittenberg "alumni" maintained botanical gardens: Rauwolf at Augsburg, Camerarius at Nürnberg, Aicholtz at Vienna, Cruciger at Wittenberg, and Aemylius at Stolberg.[85] Rauwolf even attempted to acclimatize some plants from seeds brought back from the Near East. The plant *Poterium spinosum* L., raised from seeds from Mount Lebanon, grew but died in the winter, "as exotic plants are not likely to survive here." He was more successful with plants raised from the seeds of the *Tordylium syriacum* L.[86]

Also of value for the spread of botanical knowledge was the exchange of botanical information and plant specimens among the "alumni" of the University of Wittenberg. Gesner, the famed encyclopedist and polyhistor of natural science, thanked the "most learned and renowned Dr. Rauwolf" for sending him some unusual seeds and plants.[87] Gesner's extensive correspondence reveals the exchange of botanical information with many other botanists who had some association with Wittenberg. Clusius recorded that in 1584 he had sent some bulbs and seeds to Rauwolf with whom he freqently corresponded.[88] Camerarius received from Rauwolf some seeds of a plant found on Mount Lebanon, and his *Hortus medicus* acknowledges Rauwolf's many contributions.[89] The exchange of plants and botanical information between Gesner and Aemylius and Herold has been mentioned before.

In all, the University of Wittenberg through its faculty, students, and graduates form an interesting focal point through which to examine some of the first steps in the development of botany as a modern science.

---

1. George Sarton, *Six Wings. Men of Science in the Renaissance* (Bloomington, Ind., 1957), p. 136. Otto Brunfels, one of those named by Sarton, can hardly be called a Lutheran, although he had some indirect associations with Luther and Melanchthon. He openly supported the reformed branch of Protestantism.

2. *WA Br*, 8:285–86.

3. *LW*, 1:36; *WA*, 42:27–28 and 152–53.

4. *LW*, 1:36–7; *WA*, 42:27.

5. *LW*, 21:126; *WA*, 32:404.

6. *LW*, 21:199–200; *WA*, 32:464–65.

7. *LW*, 13:103; *WA*, 40 (3):530.

8. *WA, Kirchenpostille*, 10,1,1:562, 563, 565. Early botanists like Brunfels, Euricus Cordus, and Anton Schneeberger acknowledged their debt to the peasants: Agnes Arber, "From Medieval Herbalism to the Birth of Modern Botany," *Science, Medicine, and History* 1 (London, 1953):317–18.

9. *WA, Kirchenpostille*, 10, 1, 1:560.

10. *WA, Tischreden*, 1:1160.

11. Johann C. A. Grohmann, *Annalen der Universität zu Wittenberg. Erster Theil* (Meissen, 1801), p. 107.

12. Walter Friedensburg, *Geschichte der Universität Wittenberg* (Halle a. S., 1917), p. 181.

13. Ibid., pp. 216–17; W. Friedensburg, *Urkundenbuch der Universität Wittenberg, Teil I* (Magdeburg, 1926), p. 267; *CR*, 10:1010.

14. Ernst Hildebrandt, "Die kurfürstliche Schlosz- und Universitätsbibliothek zu Wittenberg," *Zeitschrift für Buchkunde* 2 (1925):157–88; M. J. C. Mylius, *Memorabilia bibliothecae Academicae Ienensis* (Jena, 1746), pp. 184–88; E. G. Schwiebert, "Remnants of a Reformation Library," *Library Quarterly* 10 (1940): 494–531.

15. Friedensburg, *Geschichte der Universität Wittenberg*, pp. 113–14.

16. Theodore Pressel, *Caspar Cruciger. Leben und ausgewählte Schriften der Väter und Begründer der lutherischen Kirche* (Elberfeld, 1862), p. 9; Julius Köstlin, *Die Baccalaurei und Magistri der wittenberger philosphischen Facultät, 1518–37* (Halle, 1888), pp. 21, 24; *CR*, 11:836; Melchior Adam, *Vitae germanorum medicorum qui seculo superiori, et quod excurrat, claruerunt* (Heidelberg, 1620), p. 283. Luther's son, Paul, received his doctor of medicine degree at Wittenberg in 1557 and was very interested in the chemical distillation of plants (M. Adam, *Vitae germanorum medicorum*, pp. 338–42).

17. T. Pressel, *Paul Eber. Leben und ausgewählte Schriften der Väter und Begründer der lutherischen Kirche* (Elberfeld, 1862), pp. 17–18; Köstlin, *Die Baccalaurei, 1518–37*, pp. 23, 26; *ADB*, 5:529–31.

18. Wilhelm Maurer, "Melanchthon und die Naturwissenschaft seiner Zeit," *Archiv für Kulturgeschichte* 44 (1962):199–226; W. Maurer, *Der junge Melanchthon zwischen Humanismus und Reformation*, 2 vols. (Göttingen, 1967), 1:129–70.

19. *CR*, 3:490–95; Viktor Fossel, "Philipp Melanchthons Beziehungen zur Medizin," in *Zwanzig Abhandlungen zur Geschichte der Medizin. Festschrift für Hermann Baas* (Hamburg and Leipzig, 1908), p. 34.

20. *CR*, 11 and 12; 11:192–93: Fossel, "Melanchthons Beziehungen zur Medizin," p. 35.

21. *CR*, 2:718; 3:411, 606–7, 1210–12, 1246; 4:18–19, 554; 5:555–56.

22. *CR*, 9:740–41, 784–86.

23. *CR*, 5:446; Letter to Camerarius Senior, July 23, 1544.

24. Ernest Wickersheimer, "Les recettes de Philippe Melanchthon contre la peste," *Janus* 27 (1923):1–7.

25. *CR*, 5:447–48; Jacob Caro, "Anekdotisches zu Melanchthon," *Theologische Studien und Kritiken* 70 (1897):805–11. Pannonius (Preuss von Springenberg), a philologist, received his master's degree from Wittenberg in 1538; C.

G. Joecher, *Allgemeines Gelehrten-Lexicon,* 4 vols. (Leipzig, 1750–51), 3:1766; Köstlin, *Die Baccalaurei, 1538–46* (1890), p. 10.

26. See especially Edward Lee Greene, *Landmarks of Botanical History, Part I. Prior to 1562 A.D.* (*Smithsonian Miscellaneous Collections,* vol. 54; Washington, D.C., 1909), pp. 270–314; T. A. and M. S. Sprague, "The Herbal of Valerius Cordus," *Journal of the Linnean Society of London* 52 (1939):1–113; J. F. T. Irmisch, *Ueber einige Botaniker des 16. Jahrhunderts welche sich um die Erforschung der Flora Thüringens, des Harzes und der angrenzenden Gegenden verdient gemacht haben* (Sonderhausen, 1862), pp. 10–34; M. Adam, *Vitae germanorum medicorum,* pp. 42–49; *Biographische Skizzen verstorbenen Bremischer Ärzte und Naturforscher* (Bremen, 1844), pp. 32–35; August Schultz, "Valerius Cordus als mitteldeutscher Florist," *Mitteilungen des Thüringischen botanischen Vereins,* N. S., 33 (1916):37–66; and Otto Beszler, "Valerius Cordus und der medizinisch-botanische Unterricht," *450 Jahre Martin-Luther-Universität Halle-Wittenberg* (Halle, 1952), 1:323–33.

27. His major botanical work, *Botanologicon,* was first published in Cologne in 1534; Greene, *Landmarks,* pp. 263–69; *Biographische Skizzen,* pp. 13–31.

28. Preface to the first edition of Cordus's *Annotationes in Pedacii Dioscoridis Anazarbei de medica materia libros V* (Frankfurt, 1549) and reprinted in the Strassburg (1561) edition of Cordus's work as edited by Conrad Gesner, fol. b3ᵛ.

29. C. E. Foerstemann, ed., *Album academiae vitebergensis,* 3 vols. (Leipzig-Halle, 1841–1905), 1:178.

30. Letter (1559) from Crato to Gesner in V. Cordus, *Annotationes* (1561), fol. b2, b3ʳ.

31. Pliny, *Historia naturalis,* 24:vi, 11.

32. Greene, *Landmarks,* pp. 266–67, 273.

33. Irmisch, *Ueber einige Botaniker,* pp. 13–17.

34. The preface to Fuch's *De historis stirpium* contains praise for the young Cordus and his father: "sed quod parenti per ipsa fata non fuit interum perficere, hoc filius, quem post se reliquit, Valerius Cordus, optimae spei juvenis et incredibili quodam cognoscendarum stirpium studio amoreque flagrans, nisi dii quoque, quod longe absit, illi vitam longiorem invideant, cumulate praestabit. Cum enim nunc paternis vestigiis strenue insistat, non est cur velit quasi in medio cursu gradum sistere."

35. Foerstemann, *Album,* 1:146; Köstlin, *Die Baccalaurei, 1538–46* (1890), pp. 13, 21.

36. On the relationship between Rheticus and Schreiber, see Karl H. Burmeister, *Georg Joachim Rhetikus, 1514–1574,* 3 vols. (Wiesbaden, 1967–68), 1:33, 70–72, 82, 85.

37. Sarton, *Six Wings,* p. 149.

38. M. Adam, *Vitae germanorum medicorum,* pp. 43, 121, 268. Sittard was later a physician in Nürnberg, where he died in 1555. Melanchthon mentions Sittard in a letter to Schreiber, July 3, 1543; *CR,* 5:138–39.

39. Foerstemann, *Album,* 1:192 (Oct. 24, 1541). Wolfgang Meurer (1513–85), who studied at Leipzig and who became professor of medicine there in 1549, apparently joined Cordus "on the highest mountain tops, crawling about studying plants" (M. Adam, *Vitae germanorum medicorum,* p. 253).

40. Petrus Forestus (Pieter van Foreesti, 1522–97), the future medical historian, was at the deathbed of Cordus and later sent plants he had collected with Cordus in Italy to Jacobus Sylvius, professor at Paris. He must therefore have

been a member of the expedition for a time (M. Adam, *Vitae germanorum medicorum*, pp. 328–30).

41. *CR*, 5:546–47, 555–56.

42. On May 4, 1543, the council ordered 100 copies printed and distributed to physicians and apothecaries. In October, 1543, the council paid "Doctor" Cordus 100 gold gulden for the book (documents in Chauncey D. Leake, "Valerius Cordus and the Discovery of Ether," *Isis* 7 [1925]:20).

43. Placotomus (Brettschneider, 1514–76/77), a friend of Melanchthon, received his master's degree in 1541 and later his doctor of medicine degree at Wittenberg. His *Compendium pharmacopoeae* was published at Antwerp in 1560 (Köstlin, *Die Baccalaurei, 1538–46*, p. 13; *Allgemeine deutsche Biographie*, 21:220).

44. Foerstemann, *Album*, 1:147; Irmisch, *Ueber einige Botaniker*, pp. 34–39. Gesner praises his botanical garden in "Horti germaniae" (V. Cordus, *Annotationes* [1561], fol. 239).

45. Foerstemann, *Album*, 1:185.

46. Richard L. Durling, "Conrad Gesner's *Liber amicorum*, 1555–1565," *Gesnerus* 22 (1965):140, 150.

47. Gernot Rath, "Die Briefe Konrad Gesners aus der Trewschen Sammlung," in *Gesnerus* 8 (1951):198–201. In 1559 Herold and Pietro Andrea Mattioli, the eminent Italian botanist, exchanged letters on plants (P. A. Mattioli, *Epistolarum medicinalium libri quinque* in *Opera quae extant omnia* [Frankfurt, 1598], pp. 121–24, 126–27).

48. T. A. and M. S. Sprague, "Herbal of V. Cordus," p. 1.

49. J. P. de Tournefort, *Institutiones rei herbariae* (Paris, 1700), 1:6.

50. Albert von Haller, *Bibliotheca botanica* 1 (Tiguri, 1771):282.

51. Paul Delaunay, "L'aventureuse existence de Pierre Belon du Mans," *Revue du seizième siècle* 9 (1922):256.

52. Foerstemann, *Album*, 1:192.

53. Delaunay, "Belon," p. 257.

54. Ibid., pp. 257–58; Belon, *De admirabili operum antiquorum* (Paris, 1553), fol. 27ᵛ, 36ʳ, 42ᵛ; Belon, *De arboribus coniferis* (Paris, 1553), fol. 24ᵛ.

55. Delaunay, "Belon," 259, 263–64. Aretius was educated at Bern, Strassburg, and Marburg. He taught logic at Marburg and traveled to Cologne and Wittenberg before taking the position at Bern. His *Stokhorii et Nessi Helvetiae montium, e tnascentium in eis stirpium descriptio* was published by Gesner in the 1561 edition of the works of Cordus. Gesner named a plant *Aretia* after this botanist. Cf. Herzog and Hauck, *Realencyklopädie für protestantische Theologie*, 22 vols. (Leipzig, 1896–1909), 2:5–6. See also C. Gesner, *Epistolae medicinales, libri III* (Zurich, 1577), fol. 115 ff. for correspondence between Gesner and Aretius.

56. Belon, *De admirabili operum antiquorum*, fol. 36 ; Irmisch, *Ueber einige Botaniker*, p. 19.

57. Foerstemann, *Album*, 1:153; M. Adam, *Vitae germanorum medicorum*, pp. 219–22.

58. P. A. Mattioli, *Epistolarum medicinalium*, pp. 110–11, 115–16; see also indications of Mattioli's respect for both Caspar and Johannes Naevius, pp. 119–20.

59. Foerstemann, *Album*, 1:86; Köstlin, *Die Baccalaurei, 1518–37*, pp. 10, 18; M. Adam, *Vitae germanorum medicorum*, pp. 222–23.

60. P. A. Mattioli, *Opera quae extant omnia*, prefatory letter by Mattioli, dated 1565; C. G. Joecher, *Allgemeines Gelehrten-Lexicon*, 3:803. On both Casper and Johannes Naevius, see August Hirsch, ed., *Biographisches Lexikon der hervorragenden Äerzte aller Zeiten und Völker*, 2d ed., 2 vols. (Berlin and Vienna, 1930–32), 2:318.

61. Köstlin, *Die Baccalaurei, 1518–37*, pp. 10, 18; M. Adam, *Vitae germanorum medicorum*, pp. 85–90; Gesner, "Qui nam scriptores Dioscoridis de medica materis libros et quomodo explicauerint," in Cordus, *Annotationes* (1561), fol. a4r–bv.

62. Foerstemann, *Album*, has no entry for Johannes Lonicerus.

63. Köstlin, *Die Baccalaurei, 1518–37*, pp. 7, 18.

64. The edition was praised by Gesner; Cordus, *Annotationes* (1561), fols. a4r–bv.

65. *ADB*, 19:158–63.

66. Foerstemann, *Album*, 1:211; Köstlin, *Die Baccalaurei, 1548–60*, p. 6.

67. M. Adam, *Vitae germanorum medicorum*, pp. 120–27.

68. Durling, "Gesner's *Liber amicorum*," pp. 142, 153. Moibanus is frequently mentioned in Gesner's *Epistolae medicinales*.

69. The title reads: *Euporista Ped. Dioscoridis . . . ad Adromachum, hoc est De curationibus morborum per medicamenta paratu facilia, libri II. Nunc primum et Graece editi, partim a Joanne Moibanus . . . partim vero post hujus mortem a Conrado Gesnero in linquam latinam conversi; adiectis ab utroque interprete symphoniis Galeni aliorumque graecorum medicorum*. The work includes letters to Gesner from Gasser and Johann Crato von Krafftheim, both former students at the University of Wittenberg.

70. See especially F. W. T. Hunger, *Charles de l'Escluse (Carolus Clusius), nederlandsch kruidkundige, 1526–1609*, 2 vols. (S-Gravenhage, 1927–42).

71. Foerstemann, *Album*, 1:247.

72. Hunger, *Charles de l'Escluse*, 1:15–17, 397–98.

73. Foerstemann, *Album*, 1:204.

74. Hunger, *Charles de l'Escluse*, 1:127, 139, 143, 167, 343, 350, 354.

75. Foerstemann, *Album*, 1:348.

76. Adam, *Vitae germanorum medicorum*, pp. 344–56.

77. Foerstemann, *Album*, 1:324. On Rauwolf, see Karl H. Dannenfeldt, *Leonhard Rauwolf: Sixteenth Century Physician, Botanist, and Traveler* (Cambridge, Mass., 1968).

78. Early in May, 1563, Rauwolf visited Gesner; Durling, "Gesner's *Liber amicorum*," pp. 138, 144, 155.

79. Dannenfeldt, *Rauwolf*, pp. 228–30; J. F. Gronovius, *Flora orientalis* (Leyden, 1755).

80. Foerstemann, *Album*, 1:245.

81. Marcel Gouron, *Matricule de L'Université de Médecine de Montpellier, 1503–99* (Geneva, 1957), p. 150.

82. Sarton, *Six Wings*, p. 149; Lynn Thorndike, *History of Magic and Experimental Science* 6 (New York, 1941):266.

83. Ferdinand Cohrs, *Philipp Melanchthon, Deutschlands Lehrer* Schriften des Vereins für Reformationsgeschichte, vol. 14, No. 55 (Halle, 1897), p. 44.

84. Dannenfeldt, *Rauwolf*, pp. 229–30.

85. The botanical garden of Didymus Obrecht, a former student at Witten-

berg, is among those Gesner praised; Cordus, *Annotationes* (1561), fols. 239, 243; Foerstemann, *Album,* 1:254.

86. Dannenfeldt, *Rauwolf,* p. 218.

87. Gesner, *Epistolae medicinales,* fol. 59–61.

88. Ludovis Legré, *La botanique en Provence au XVIᵉ siècle: Léonhard Rauwolff, Jacques Raynaudet* (Marseilles, 1900), p. 101.

89. J. Camerarius, *Hortus medicus et philosophicus* (Frankfurt am Main, 1588), p. 67 and fig. 16. For his correspondence with Clusius, see Hunger, *Charles de l'Escluse,* 2.

LUTHER'S SOCIAL CONCERN FOR STUDENTS

Lewis W. Spitz

Less than a year after the posting of the ninety-five theses, with the Dominicans already threatening death for heresy by burning, Luther expressed deep concern not for himself but for his students. Soon after October 14, 1518, he wrote to his friend Georg Spalatin in the service of Elector Frederick the Wise to ask whether the elector could be moved to write the pope that his affair should be decided on German soil, not because he cared about his own miserable self, but because he was concerned about "our university" and did not wish the studies of the most excellent youths wonderfully eager to learn the Sacred Scriptures to be sacrificed already in the tender stage.[1] Luther's relations with the students in his academic role as professor and his ideas on education have inspired much research and many teachers, for he set a personal example of conscientious preparation, lively teaching, and humane examining.[2] He realized the critical role to be played by these very students in carrying the evangelical movement forward. But Luther always saw man whole, and his concern for his students went well beyond the intellectual and theological to include their personal problems and social well-being. Moreover, his interest in the students did not end with their graduation, for he continued to correspond with alumni and to intervene with the authorities on their behalf.

The study of Luther's correspondence, eleven volumes in the Weimar edition containing 4,211 letters, reveals his astonishing preoccupation with the physical and social well-being of the students. Luther once complained that he could not get to his scholarly work because he had to write letters all day long. Many of these letters had to do with financial aid for students, with their physical and psychological health, their personal relations, love life, families, vocations, calls, and placement, with follow-throughs for alumni. His involvement in such an array of problems is reminiscent of Calvin and suggests that the magisterial reformers had more than their theology in common.

Even a statistically unsophisticated and merely approximate analysis of these letters may be somewhat informative. The numbers are imprecise because where several letters have to do with the same matter, they are not all added into the totals; because single letters often deal with several matters, and a judgment as to their main thrust must be made; because it cannot in all cases be established when a youth ceased being a student and became an alumnus; and because of the hurried impatience of this statistician who fancies himself more a humanist than social scientist. Letters of an occasional nature, moreover, scattered all through central Europe, were more apt to be lost than continued correspondence with specific individuals or letters addressed to notables. It is obvious that the letters of this nature included in the *Briefwechsel* are but a small fraction of the total number, for many of the letters, written by others, imply previous correspondence from Luther on behalf of students. But for what the numbers game may be worth, during the decade and a half from 1517 to 1531 Luther wrote some 18 letters, still extant, to or in behalf of students, of which 6 represented efforts to gain financial support for them and 12 had to do mainly with other problems. During the three lustra from 1532 to 1546 Luther wrote some 57 letters, still extant, to or on behalf of students, 31 seeking financial aid for them and 26 dealing with their other social problems.

Two explanations for the notable difference between the first and the second half of Luther's professional career during the thirty years between the posting of the theses and his death suggest themselves. During the early years of nearly constant crises he was preoccupied with such great matters that he was less able to devote himself to the personal problems of students. During the later years, with his authority established, he became an elder statesman, even a dean for a term, known and respected, so that he was appealed to by many and persuasive with most. Moreover, the enrollment at Wittenberg University was very much larger during the last decade and a half. In 1520 the enrollment reached a new high, but fell again during the 1520s, only to rise to new heights during the 1530s and early 1540s. Specifically the enrollment climbed from about 300 in 1508 to around 2,000 in the years just before and after 1522. In the years 1501 to 1505, 1,204 students matriculated at Wittenberg compared with 1,674 at Cologne and 576 at Heidelberg. In the years 1541 to 1545, in contrast, 2,928 enrolled at Wittenberg compared with 430 at Cologne and 493 at Heidelberg.[3] Luther lectured to as many as 400 students in a class. The larger student body naturally made greater demands upon the reformer, but the numbers alone did not depersonalize his relations with the students as one might expect.

Approximately half the letters that Luther wrote on behalf of students over the course of thirty years sought financial aid for them. Even then universities were replacing the mendicant orders in begging for support. The extent to which students attended the universities with publicly financed scholarships is surprising indeed. Luther believed that in general the poorest student usually proves to be the best student and showed a certain disdain for those "aristocratic fellows who carry heavy purses and provisions and do not study."[4] Some of the students were former monks, especially Benedictines or Augustinian canons, who came with nothing. Others were sons of poor craftsmen, miners, or peasants with poor families. During his last years a good many belonged to the first generation of preachers' children, that steady source of intellectuals for centuries to follow.

Luther turned most often for student aid to the elector of Saxony, either petitioning directly or through Georg Spalatin, secretary to the Elector Frederick the Wise. The first such letter requested a stipend for Georg Major, who took his A.B. and M.A. at Wittenberg and later became Luther's colleague.[5] Only one such *Bettelbrief* is extant addressed to Elector John, asking for a two year extension of the 20 gulden payment of support for a poor student, Magister Georg Prenner.[6] But Luther fairly

inundated the young Elector John Frederick, who was deeply
devoted to the reformer and on much more intimate terms with
him. He asked him for another year's subsidy for Konrad Leimbach of the Benedictine monastery in Mönchröden, to whom the
elector had been giving 24 gulden for three years of study.[7] Together with Justus Jonas and Melanchthon he asked for stipends
for two poor students, Nikolaus Peuschels and Andresz Jungandres.[8] He persuaded the elector to give an annual prebend of
30 gulden to the two sons of a Hans von Canitz, who had died,
so that the two, Wolf and Ulrich, could continue their studies
at Wittenberg.[9] Occasionally Luther asked him not only to extend but even to enlarge the stipend of an unusually worthy student, such as Andreas Funius, characterizing him as pious and
learned.[10] The elector sometimes bestowed an outright gift, as
the 40 gulden he presented to Hieronymus Weller, who was taking his doctorate at Wittenberg.[11] Luther asked the elector to
rescue the poverty-stricken son of a Protestant parson, Johann
Schreiner, pastor in Grimma, who needed aid to study at Wittenberg. The father seemed to be compensating for centuries of
clerical celibacy by fathering eight living children, although unable to support and educate them properly.[12] These were all
individual grants, but Elector John Frederick supported large
numbers of students at the university that was the pride of Electoral Saxony. In 1544 he provided stipends for 70 students who
were sons of nobles, burghers, and preachers from Jena, Gotha,
and Weida with money derived from church endowments in
Altenburg, Gotha, and Eisenach.[13]

As the fame of Wittenberg grew, students came from nearly
all parts of the empire, and eventually every tenth student was a
foreigner. The network of support Luther sought to draw on
grew apace. He wrote to Duke Heinrich of Mecklenburg in behalf of Matthäus Roloff of Quassow, who showed signs of promise but would have to abandon his studies because of poverty, a
special pity since he had come such a long way![14] Luther and
Melanchthon turned to Margrave George of Brandenburg for
a supplementary prebend for Petrus Faber (Schmidt) of Kitzingen, whom they described as an orphan with three brothers
and two sisters, a lad of unusual *ingenium*, who had taken his

A.B. in three quarters of a year, distinguished himself in disputations, and would be a useful citizen. The margrave a year later granted the 20 gulden supplement, and Petrus subsequently returned home to serve as deacon.[15] Duke John Ernest of Saxony promised to support two former monks for another academic year.[16] Luther turned to Prince George of Anhalt for a stipend for Magister Johann Zerbst, a "fine, talented person, who will be useful to the church and otherwise."[17] Luther even knelt as a suppliant at royal thrones. In 1541 King Gustav of Sweden wrote that at Luther's request he was instructing his councilors to provide support for a young student at Wittenberg.[18] King Christian III of Denmark, who introduced the Reformation to Denmark and called Bugenhagen there, supported several students through the years.[19]

Social historians have become increasingly aware of the place of the cities in the Reformation movement and specifically of the role of the city councils in resisting or eventually introducing the evangelical reform. The pre-Reformation proprietary church arrangements meant not only that the princes and lesser nobility had a great amount of control over the church in their domains but also that the city councils exercised real authority over the parishes and foundations within their walls and territories, a situation that frequently led to friction and ruction between the cities and the bishops. In the case of student support, Luther turned often to the city councils to ask for aid for a "native son" studying at Wittenberg who would in all likelihood return some day to serve his home town.

Nürnberg was one of the earlier cities to introduce the Reformation, over the opposition of some conservative patricians to be sure. In 1524 Luther wrote the Nürnberg council to ask aid for a poor student named Philipp Gluenspiesz.[20] He wrote to the council of Memmingen to request 10 or 12 gulden for the M.A. graduation of Johann Schmelz, presumably to cover fees charged on that occasion.[21] In 1532 he repeated a petition to the council of Torgau for a stipend for Erasmus Krautheim, to be taken from the community chest. If they do not assist this poor boy, he wrote, he will leave to go into some kind of manual labor, and there is a dire need for preachers.[22] A year later he was back for help, this time for Johann Dachau, whom he called "ewr Stadtkind."[23] Where Luther had a connection in a city, he used such a contact, as when he asked his friend Nicholas von Amsdorf, the reformer of Magdeburg, to arrange a stipend for Johann Busmann.[24] He made a special plea for a stipend for Georg Snell to the mayor and council of Rothenburg ob der Tauber, telling them that they owed something to their *Stadtkind* and that the need for teachers and preachers was acute.[25]

Not infrequently it was the student who asked Luther to intervene in his behalf, as in the case of Laurentius Stengel, who asked him to request the proper official and the council of Bayreuth for a stipend so that he could continue study. He was not suited for handicrafts, Luther observed, like someone with frozen hands, but was honorable and praiseworthy and could be useful in a church office. The council made a good investment, for Stengel upon graduation returned to serve as a schoolteacher in Bayreuth.[26]

Luther expressed his surprise and his admiration for the many students who struggled along in poverty on bread and water. He expressed dismay that the shortage of rooms in Wittenberg, a small university town of only about 3,500 people, often kept or drove students away. The year 1539 was a particularly bad year, when the high price of bread—exploitative, Luther thought—forced many students to leave the university. One student driven away by hunger had no travel money whatsoever, so Luther asked the city council of Wittenberg to provide *Reisegeld*.[27]

In his *Sermon on Keeping Children in School* Luther concluded: "Therefore let everyone be on his guard who can. Let the government, when it sees a promising boy, have him kept in school; if the father is poor, let it help him with church property. Let the rich make their wills with this work in view, as some have done who have endowed stipends; that is the right way to bequeath your money to the church."[28] The most generous of the private donors to aid the Wittenberg students with a very sizable gift was Dorothea Jörger, a wealthy widow in Keppach. In 1533 she sent Luther 500 gulden for student stipends. Luther decided that rather than distributing it all at once, it would be wiser to use it to aid two students or so each year according to need and promise. But later he wrote to her that he would not have believed himself how many pious and able youths live on bread and water all year, and suffer frost and cold, in order to study Holy Scriptures. He therefore had already distributed half of her gift in 2,3,4, and 10 gulden grants to needy students. The good lady was moved to make gifts in subsequent years, and Luther even turned to her in July to extend a stipend for a certain Andreas Hügel to Easter.[29]

As a member of the theological faculty, Luther was primarily interested in aid for students in that professional school; but on occasion he sought financial assistance for students in medicine or law, as well as for the many at the arts level before they entered the professional schools. In 1527 he sought a stipend for a medical student, and in 1536 he even wrote several letters to the mayor and council of Saalfeld urging them to give a stipend to a student who wished to continue to study law with the jurists rather than taking up theology. Since the young man was skilled at law, Melanchthon had counseled him to go on with it because there was a need for good lawyers who would eventually serve their city.[30]

When the candidates finally received their doctorates, Luther often personally arranged the festive dinner, the *Doktorschmaus*, and asked the elector for provisions and money to cover the graduation expense. The first of these was the graduation and celebration for the prior of the Carmelites in Bamberg, Johann Frosch. Luther wrote Spalatin to remind Elector Frederick of his promise to cover the costs and urged that he supply wild game for the feast.[31] From 1523 to 1533 the university granted no doctorates, since the faculty suspended the disputations as being too closely associated with scholastic learning. But when they were resumed in 1533, the Elector John Frederick graced the ceremonies with his presence. When Hieronymous Weller and Nikolaus Medler received their doctoral degrees in 1535, the elector sent venison and seven quarts of the best wine, Justus Jonas supplied poultry, and Catherine Luther prepared the banquet.[32] When Jakob Schenk, court preacher to Duke Henry in Frieberg, received his degree in 1536, Duchess Catherine paid the costs, including a splendid meal, and the Wittenberg city council contributed eight litres of Rhine wine and four quarts of cider.[33] Luther had a fine time twitting at least one candidate with an exaggerated deference for his great learning and high honors![34]

In a charming letter Baron Friedrich II of Dohna wrote from Bohemia in 1531 to thank Luther for his humaneness and for the hospitality and company he had given to his son. He expressed the hope that his son would return home not merely ornamented with letters but distinguished also by Christian piety.[35] Luther was indeed concerned with the health and welfare as well as with the education of the students. He often referred to the problem of sickness and death among the students in his correspondence, especially when the plague or English sweat hit the overcrowded town and struck down the weak and undernourished students. He wrote touching letters of comfort to the parents of boys who died while in study at Wittenberg, telling them what fine students their sons had been and what comfort the hope of the resurrection should bring them. He recalled with feeling how one lad had spent many evenings in his home singing, and how fine, modest, and studious he was. Luther and all sorrowed for him and wished they could have kept him with them, but God loved him even more and wanted him home with Him.[36]

Less obvious than the physical effects of the plague were the psychic ills that often afflict the spiritually sensitive or intellectual. Having struggled personally with *Anfechtungen*, Luther knew the torments that attend the lows that follow the ebullient highs. He discussed the problems of those afflicted with *accidia* often in his *Table Talks*, and addressed many letters of encouragement to students suffering from depression. The Weller brothers, Hieronymus and Matthias, for example, seem to have been regularly afflicted with melancholy, and the advice Luther gave them was typical. Hieronymus had been moved by one of Luther's sermons to leave the study of law for theology and had lived in Luther's home for a year, so Luther knew him well. Luther warned that too much solitude induces melancholy and urged social contacts as a cure. You must not dwell on your own thoughts but listen to what others have to say to you. Relax with others, get angry, play the lute and find refuge in music, joke, play games, drink a little more, pray, learn to despise the devil and to trust God, for the very temptation is a sign that you believe in Christ and that God is merciful.[37] To Conrad Cordatus, a former student at Wittenberg and a table companion in Luther's house, now a preacher in Niemegk near Wittenberg, the reformer wrote:

> I thank God that your health is being restored. But I pray you curb your suspicion that you are assailed by who knows how many diseases. You know the proverb, "Imagination produces misfortunes." Therefore, you ought to take the pains to divert rather than to entertain such notions. I too must do this. For our adversary, the devil, walks about, seeking not only to devour our souls but also to weaken our bodies with thoughts of our souls in the hope that he might perhaps slay our bodies, for he knows that our physical health depends in large measure on the thoughts in our minds. This is in accord with the saying, "Good cheer is half the battle," and, "A merry heart doeth good like a medicine: but a broken spirit drieth the bones." I give you this advice although I confess that I do not take it myself.[38]

Luther was not always sympathetic with ailing students and could be sharp with those who misbehaved. In the summer of 1535 when students were joyously leaving their studies in order to flee the plague, Luther wrote Elector John Frederick about the situation and commented wryly:

> I observe that many students have heard the cry of pestilence gladly, for some of them have developed sores from their schoolbags, some have caught colic from their books, some have scabs from their pens, others caught gout from their paper. Many have found that their ink has become moldy. Others have also devoured their mothers' letters and have acquired heartsickness and homesickness for their home town.

And perhaps there are even more kinds of such weakness than I can relate.[39] Luther wrote to Margrave George of Brandenburg, who supported many students at Wittenberg, that the students seemed to be doing well. There was less tearing around in the streets and less noise at night than was true some time back. The margrave could count on it that when he discovered someone acting that way he would in short order describe him to the margrave and send him home, as he had done with several. What is done secretly he could not judge, and it is possible that he did not learn of everything; but publicly everything is well ordered with all diligence.[40] Luther wrote to Justus Jonas that he had written coldly (*frigide scripsi*) in behalf of a student Mulmann (Mühlmann?) because he had heard shameful and unworthy things about him from two reliable people.[41]

Luther's interest in the social life of the students extended even to their love life. He growled that with so many young men at the university, from many different lands, the girls in town had become bold, ran after the boys into their rooms and chambers, and offered them their love free. He had heard that many parents had ordered their sons home and charged that when they sent their sons for study "we hang wives around their necks and take them away from their parents."[42] He argued strongly as *Seelsorger* against secret engagements of couples without the knowledge and consent of their parents. He even preached a sermon on the theme "that Parents Should Neither Compel Nor Hinder the Marriage of Their Children and That Children Should Not Become Engaged without Their Parents Consent, 1524."[43] He once twitted a love-sick student with the comment that his illness was induced by love, for studying seldom has such an effect.[44] Luther even wrote to students' parents when appropriate to urge their consent to a son's marriage. To Anton Rudolf, wine-master in Weimar, he wrote that his son Niclaus was in love with a pious girl and wished to marry her according to God's ordinance. The son complained that Herr Rudolf was proving to be hard and resistant, but the father should now give his consent to an honorable marriage.[45] In another case he even ventured to urge a mother to agree to the marriage of her son Johann to a maiden of honorable family, for he was in ashes and longed for his mother's blessing.[46]

Perhaps the most important aspect of Luther's social concern for students had to do with their call to serve society, in church, state, or a private vocation, and his placement efforts in their behalf. Luther's doctrine of vocation is so central to his entire social ethic and marked such a radical change from the medieval conception that many scholars have examined it in depth.[47] It is astonishing, however, to discover how nearly all approach the problem almost exclusively in terms of abstract theology or of Luther's statements on the subject in general treatises or sermons, rather than in the context of real situations in which concrete recommendations and actual decisions on occupations and positions had to be made. It will be valuable after a brief discussion of vocation, in order to make explicit certain implicit assumptions, to see how Luther applied his understanding of vocation in expressing his social concern for his students.

Luther believed that all Christians are called by the gospel to be children of God. As children of God, all are given the command to serve their fellow man. All men have external offices, jobs to do, as members of society. For Christians the tasks involved in their stations in life give them an opportunity to work creatively with God, to serve as His masks and as channels for His creative work. "What is all our labor in the field, in the garden, in the city, in the house, in controversy, in governing," he asked, "than a kind of child's play through which God wishes to bestow His gifts on field, house and everything? They are our Lord God's masks behind which He wishes to be hidden and do everything."[48] Christians are not coerced by God to service, but a life of service is an act of love toward neighbor giving expression to their faith in God. This call is not a call to serve God, as though good works were an offering toward salvation, but a call to serve a neighbor. "Since God does not need our work," Luther wrote, "and also did not command us to do anything for Him other than to praise and thank Him, so the man sallies forth and gives himself entirely to his neighbor, serves him, helps and comforts him entirely freely."[49] The *vocatio* or *Beruf* is, therefore, in its first sense a call to faith in Christ, in its second sense a call to service to neighbor.[50] Only in a tertiary or related sense does vocation include a call to a specific position, trade, or job.

The use of the word *calling* for a man's occupation must be properly understood. For Luther the vocation is general, a call to work *coram deo*, devoting oneself to the good and service of other men. Vocation extends to all aspects of a Christian's life,

to the biological orders such as marriage and family relationships as well as to his occupation or position in civil society. He
is called to serve and before him are a number of stations in life
through and in which he can respond to the call. The call to witness and work as a Christ to one's neighbors is not *to* an occupation, but *in* one.[51] Luther's radical innovation was in applying
the concept of vocation to secular tasks, making no spiritual distinctions and drawing upon no value scale as long as each task
was in accord with God's command.[52] There is work to be done
of a special nature in the church. All baptized Christians are
called by a *vocatio generalis* to preach and administer the sacraments, for, Luther asserted, the example of Stephen still holds.
But the call to the public preaching office requires a *vocatio spe-
cialis*, for other Christians in a congregation and in authority
must choose and call one for this office.[53] The office of the ministry holds a unique position at the summit among all callings, for
through it the gospel is preached. Even among occupations in
worldly society there are variations in importance and levels of
responsibility for service. There are, however, among callings no
spiritual distinctions, for none contribute to a man's justification
before God, and all are willing acts of service and love for the
faithful's fellow man.

A misconception of Luther's view of the social order and of
the individual's place in it, very common in the older literature
and still appearing occasionally in the newer, is that Luther simply took over the medieval notion of the three major estates in
society and that each man was obliged to remain in the estate
to which he was born and the occupation he had inherited. A
Scripture passage to which Luther often referred was 1 Corinthians 7:20: "Every one should remain in the state in which he
was called." In a sermon of 1515 Luther still used *vocatio* for
the estate of the monk, married people, and parents. In a sermon of 1520 Luther used *vocatio* for the estate in which a man
has his work to do for his support. In the *Churchpostil* of 1522
Luther listed several different kinds of estates. Gradually he
came to see the linking of *vocatio spiritualis* and *vocatio externa*
as a useful association, and from then on developed his mature
view of vocation.[54] One must, as Saint Paul says, always remain

in the state to which he was called, to faith in God and loving service to his neighbor; but does that mean that he is forever frozen in an occupation? Is there to be no social mobility? Luther argued strongly only against selfish or irresponsible change of positions or vocations, not against well-considered changes required by love of neighbor.

Questions remain as to whether a man's individual abilities and talents (*ingenium*) are to be considered in his own choice of an occupation; how and to what extent changes in occupation are acceptable; and how the call to a different position takes place, can be recognized, assessed, and decided upon. Vocation is situational and varies from person to person. For that reason the mere imitation of another person, even literal mimicry of Christ's life, is not only inadequate but wrong insofar as it seeks to increase one's own holiness on the pattern of another's. Other criteria for determining the specific nature of a vocation and ground rules more complex than mere role-acting or model emulation came into play. An examination of the real-life situations in which Luther was involved in the calls, placement, and vocational changes of the students and university alumni will add concreteness to his theoretical statements and shed light upon such scholarly confusion as may still exist.

Luther himself had used the university, however briefly, to take up the profession of law thereby and rise above his father's station in life, for law was a ladder for social mobility. Countless sons of peasants, craftsmen, or nobles, many former priests and monks, young men from all walks of life came to Wittenberg for the kind of liberal arts and professional education that would help them get ahead in life. The largest numbers came streaming in to study evangelical theology, but Luther encountered some who were more interested in law or medicine; and he, like Melanchthon, even counseled some to switch to other fields more suitable to their gifts and talents. Johann Krafft is a case in point. Breslau had given him a stipend of twenty gulden for six years and he had taken an A.B. and an M.A. in theology. Now he decided for medicine, and Luther wrote the captain and council in Breslau asking that his stipend be enlarged so that he could continue in the higher faculty of medicine and that he be relieved of the obligation to return to teach school for a time. Luther said he was a good man for theology, sensible, moral, conscientious, and gifted with a good understanding of Scriptures, and if his constitution were not too weak for preaching, he would want him to do that. But under the circumstances he advised him to go into medicine.[56] On another occasion Luther recommended a doctor of medicine from Wittenberg, Erasmus Flock, to Veit Dietrich in Nürnberg as being "most worthy of the favor and honor of all for his integrity and piety."[57]

The faculty diploma for Heinrich Schmedstedt spelled out all the virtues of a model candidate in theology.[58] Although few of the regular graduates were model candidates, they all had something to commend them, and Luther considered their personal qualifications in recommending them. He recommended Franz Günther for the parish in Lochau because he was eloquent and could speak the Word powerfully before a large auditorium of people.[59] He spoke highly of Michael Stifel as a preacher because "he is a pious, learned, ethical, and diligent person" who would be of good use. Later he recommended Stifel for the parish in Lochau, telling Elector John that he could marry the widow of the former preacher, Franz Günther, and care for the two children.[60] Luther in the name of Wittenberg University authorized the ordination of Joachim Pfuhl, a former monk of the monastery of Lehnin who had been reeducated in evangelical theology, as minister in Schönewald.[61] Another interesting case is that of Hieronymus Nopos. Luther wrote the council of Regensburg that he and Melanchthon had told Nopos to take their call, but that he would practice preaching in Wittenberg until Lent, and would then come to be heard and tried out. Since he was a good teacher, Luther added, he could not be a bad preacher.[62] A conflict of calls required Luther's intervention in the case of Michael Besler, who had just taken a master's degree at Wittenberg and a call to a small parish of Saint George in Sprottau. Now Luther wrote Veit Dietrich that the council and city of Sprottau had asked him to intervene so that the more prestigeous Nürnberg would not call Besler away.[63]

He did not, however, promote all of his own as parish preachers. He recommended Georg Norman to King Gustav of Sweden as tutor for his son, characterizing him as "a man of holy life, modest, sincere and learned, suitable and altogether worthy of being a pedagogue of the king's son."[64] Luther and Bugenhagen urged Anton Lauterbach in Pirna to recommend Magister Johann Götz to the council as schoolteacher.[65] Luther agreed with Elector John Frederick that Veit Örtel of Windsheim should give the Greek lectures, for he was a good man, had given lectures, was older, and had worked well with Melanchthon.[66]

Luther's concern for his students and their contribution to the evangelical cause continued long after their graduation. Years later he continued to advise the alumni on accepting calls, about leaving positions, or deciding in the case of conflicting calls; and he even actively intervened to gain a better income for them or to support them against critics. He encouraged them to help each other, as when he wrote to Andreas Kauigsdorf that he would help the woman he had recommended find a job and that he, in turn, should help his colleague Nicolaus Foraneus find a different parish as soon as possible.[67] Wolfgang Brauer wrote Luther that he was undecided about his call to Zeitz, saying he first must know precisely about the salary, the cost of living there, and the education of his sons, which cause alone moved him, and that he would appreciate Luther's counsel and wish. In the end he did not go to Zeitz.[68] Luther recommended Magister Engelbert Scheteken to the council in Riga for the position of superintendent, but in this case the council acted against Luther's advice.[69] In 1541 Luther wrote to that old stalwart Wenzeslaus Linck in Nürnberg that in view of the Nürnbergers' despising of the Word he was ready to help Linck find another position. The Lord would provide one, and Luther stood ready to help.[70] He and several colleagues recommended Martin Gilbert, who had spent eight years at Wittenberg, to Elector John Frederick for the position of pastor at Liebenwerda.[71] With this brief beautiful note he congratulated Joachim Mörlin in Arnstadt on his call to Göttingen:

> Grace and peace in the Lord! We congratulate you on your call, my Lord Doctor, and we pray a mighty benediction of the Holy Spirit

upon you and the people of Göttingen, so that you may produce very much fruit to the glory of God. Go in peace and the Lord be with you. Amen.[72]

Luther was for standing firm in the face of local opposition or annoyances, observing that changing a position is easy, improving on it difficult, and in the end those who move around a great deal find that their circumstances have deteriorated rather than improved. Certainly mere ambition or personal whimsy should never be considered decisive, for only loving service to the neighbor must be the basic criterion. Thus he warned Jakob Propst in Bremen not to leave his post, just as he told Conrad Cordatus in Zwickau not to lose his courage because of the hardheartedness and thanklessness of the people.[73] He advised Johann Lonicer not to give up his professorship of Greek at Marburg until he had received a call elsewhere.[74] In a "damn the torpedos" letter he advised Andreas Kauigsdorf in Eilenburg not to give up the ministry of the Word unless driven out by force or called elsewhere, for Satan and impious people are everywhere.[75] He repeated this same "stand fast" counsel to Clemens Ursinus in Bruck (who evidently had complained about the parishioners' slowness to believe), saying that Christ, too, bore the slowness of the Jews a long time and that being driven out was truly to be ground to dust.[76] Luther and Melanchthon intervened with a letter to Elector John Frederick in the case of Magister Cunradus Klaus, who had been their student for several years. They spoke of him as a "very learned and deeply pious man" and expressed their displeasure with the hypercritical and assertive peasants.[77]

Luther was also concerned with the financial welfare of the alumni, asking a raise for a pastor with six children; urging a higher salary for another; telling the congregation in Zwickau that if they did not cancel the debts of a preacher they had let go, he would see to it that they would never get another; and urging all along the way to help a poor preacher get from Saxony to Württemberg.[78]

These examples from real life decision-making situations shed much light on the matter of vocation. Clearly no mysterious or mystical voice is involved in a call to any specific occupation or position. The call comes through real people, God's masks. The education and learning of the candidate are essential qualifications, coupled with his piety and willingness to serve. A man's personal characteristics are important in determining his professional choice, medicine or theology, for example. In the case of a conflict of calls the need and opportunity for service should be decisive. But not infrequently, other things being equal, the personal preference of the candidate, his health, the income, living conditions, or other factors that might affect his effectiveness are to be considered. A candidate may even go and inspect a parish to see if he likes a place better. It is not even wrong, given proper motivation, to seek a call. There is absolutely no divine coercion for, as Luther declared, the Lord does not wish to compel or drive anyone with commandments. No one should change positions simply because of levity or instability, but only if forced out or if a greater opportunity for service presents itself.

Luther's concern was not merely for the cause as such but for the students and alumni as persons who were moving the cause forward. He was concerned with their social welfare as well as with their education, for he was a student-oriented professor. "Let them call us doctors and masters if they please," he said, "but youth is the seed and the fount of the church."[79] But for all that, a student, after hearing Luther preach for the first time, is reported to have said that he would strike Luther on the head with a stone in church if he preached like that again.

1. *WA Br*, No. 102, 1:218–19; Luther to Spalatin, [Augsburg, shortly after October 14, 1518].

2. See Harold J. Grimm, "Luther and Education," *Luther and Culture* (Decorah, Iowa, 1960), pp. 73–142; Theodore Tappert, "Luther in His Academic Role," *The Mature Luther* (Decorah, Iowa, 1959), pp. 3–55; Lewis W. Spitz, "Luther as Teacher," *Lutheran Education* 103, No. 2 (October, 1967):50–60.

3. Oskar Thulin, *A Life of Luther* (Philadelphia, 1966), pp. 99–100.

4. *WA, Tischreden*, No. 3599, 3:433.

5. *WA Br*, No. 614, 3:70–71; Luther to Spalatin, Wittenberg, [*ca.* May 20, 1523]. Looking after Major was a lifelong occupation, it seems, for Luther years later asked Elector John Frederick for a prebend for him; ibid., No. 3384, 8:548–49; Luther to Elector John Frederick, [Wittenberg], September 7, 1539. A sec-

ond letter of this nature to Spalatin asked aid for two plebs (ibid., No. 699, 3:222; Luther to Spalatin [Wittenberg, 1523?]).

6. Ibid., No. 1284, 4:485–86; Luther to Elector John, Wittenberg, June 20, 1528.

7. Ibid., No. 1411, 5:57. Luther to Duke John Frederick of Saxony, [Wittenberg], April 19, 1529.

8. Ibid., No. 1959, 6:361–63; Luther, Jonas, and Melanchthon to Elector John Frederick [Wittenberg], prior to September 18, 1532.

9. Ibid., No. 1968, 6:378–80; Luther to Elector John Frederick [Wittenberg], October 18, 1532.

10. Ibid., No. 2180, 7:162; Luther and Melanchthon to Elector John Frederick of Saxony, Wittenberg, March 2, 1535. A collective effort at persuasion was the request for a stipend for Kilian Windisch, ibid., No. 3577, 9:332–33; Luther, Jonas, Bugenhagen, and Veit Amerbach to Elector John Frederick and Duke John Ernest, Wittenberg, February 20, 1541. Windisch was later deposed from a parish as a Flacianer. See also ibid., No. 3631, 9:449–51, Kilian Windisch to Luther, [Wittenberg], June 12, [1541].

11. Ibid., No. 2217, 7:221; Elector John Frederick to Luther, Torgau, August 3, 1535.

12. Ibid., No. 3976, 10:544–45; Luther to Elector John Frederick, [Wittenberg], March 26 (or July 8?), [1544].

13. Ibid., No. 4057, 10:720–21; Elector John Frederick to Luther, Torgau, December 29, 1544.

14. Ibid., No. 3107, 7:593; Luther to Duke Henry V of Mecklenburg, [Wittenberg], November 18, 1536.

15. Ibid., No. 3443, 9:48–50; Luther and Melanchthon to Margrave Georg of Brandenburg, Wittenberg, February 12, 1540.

16. Ibid., No. 3989, 10:563–64; Duke John Ernest of Saxony to Luther, Coburg, May 8, 1544.

17. Ibid., No. 3998, 10:586; Luther to Prince George of Anhalt, [Wittenberg], May 28, 1544.

18. Ibid., No. 3627, 9:428–33; King Gustav of Sweden to Luther.

19. Ibid., No. 3712, 9:616–17; King Christian of Denmark to the University of Wittenberg, Gottorp, February 12, 1542; in behalf of Master Peter of Gjenner. Ibid., No. 4112, 10:101–2; King Christian III of Denmark to Luther, Kolding, May 16, 1545; promising aid for a lad from Flensburg. Ibid., No. 4170, 10:218–19; Luther to King Christian III of Denmark, [Wittenberg], November 26, 1545; in behalf of Magister Georg Stur.

20. Ibid., No. 813, 3:413–14; Luther to [the Nürnberg Council?], [Wittenberg, before 1524?]. On Gluenspiesz see also ibid., No. 1061, 4:144–45; Luther to Philipp Gluenspiesz in Mansfeld, [Wittenberg, end of 1526].

21. Ibid., No. 1839, 6:144; Luther to the council at Memmingen Wittenberg, July 2, [1531].

22. Ibid., No. 1896, 6:247–48; Luther to the council of Torgau, [Wittenberg], January 12, 1532.

23. Ibid., No. 2016, 6:462–63; Luther to the council of Torgau, Wittenberg, May 6, 1533.

24. Ibid., No. 1993, 6:416–17; Luther to Nicholas von Amsdorf in Magdeburg, Wittenberg, January 14, 1533.

25. Ibid., No. 1996, 6:423–25; Luther to the burgomaster and council at Rothenburg o.d.T., [Wittenberg], January 26, 1533.

26. Ibid., No. 4151, 10:176; Luther to the magistrate and council of Bayreuth [Wittenberg], September 15, 1545.

27. Ibid., No. 3316, 8:399; Luther to the council of Wittenberg [Wittenberg, March or April, 1539?]. On the shortage of bread in 1539, see ibid., No. 3314, 8:397; Luther to Melanchthon in Frankfurt a.M., [Wittenberg], March 26, 1539.

28. *Works of Martin Luther* (Philadelphia, 1931), 4:178; *WA*, 30:Pt. 2, 587.

29. *WA Br*, No. 1988, 6:407–10; Luther to Dorothea Jörger in Keppach, [Wittenberg], January 1, 1533. Ibid., No. 2015, 6:461–62; Luther to Dorothea Jörger in Keppach, Wittenberg, May 6, 1533. Ibid., No. 2063, 6:546–47; Luther to Dorothea Jörger [Wittenberg], October 24, 1533. Ibid., No. 2109, 8:60–61; Luther to Dorothea Jörger, Wittenberg, April 27, 1534. Ibid., 2187, 7:172; Luther to Frau Dorothea Jörger, [Wittenberg], April 8, 1535. Ibid., No. 3054, 7:481; Luther to Dorothea Jörger in Keppach, Wittenberg, July 31, 1536.

30. Ibid., No. 1125, 6:225–26; Luther to the Rector of the University, Heinrich Stockmann, [Wittenberg, Summer, 1527], the case of the medical student. Ibid., No. 3090, 7:564–65; Luther to the burgomaster and council at Saalfeld, [Wittenberg], October 9, 1536. Ibid., No. 3091, 7:565–66; The council of Saalfeld to Luther, [Saalfeld], October 20, 1536. Ibid., No. 3106, 7:592; Luther to the burgomaster and council at Saalfeld, [Wittenberg], November 15, 1536.

31. Ibid., No. 105, 1:224–25; Luther to Spalatin, Wittenberg, October 31, 1518. Ibid., No. 107, 1:227–29; Luther to Spalatin, Wittenberg, November 12, 1518. Ibid., No. 108, 1:229–30; Luther to Spalatin, Wittenberg, November 13, 1518.

32. *LW*, 34:107–8.

33. Ibid., p. 149.

34. *WA Br*, No. 2188, 7:173–74; Luther to Johann Cario, [Wittenberg], April 13, 1535.

35. Ibid., No. 1868, 10:199–200; Burgrave Friedrich II of Dohna to Luther, Benatek in Bohemia, September 20, 1531.

36. Ibid., No. 1876, 6:212–13; Luther to Matthias Kuntzsen and his wife Magdalena in Husum (?), [Wittenberg], October 21, 1531 (?); Luther tells them their son died a Christian, is resting with Christ, and will be with them again in eternal joy. Ibid., No. 1930, 6:300–302; Luther to Thomas Zink, [Wittenberg], April 22, 1532.

37. Ibid., No. 1670, 5:518–20; Luther to Hieronymus Weller in Wittenberg [July (?) 1530]; ibid., No. 2139, 7:104–06; Luther to Matthias Weller, Wittenberg, October 7, 1534.

38. Ibid., No. 3153, 8:79–80; Luther to Konrad Cordatus in Niemegk [Wittenberg], May 21, 1537; tr. in Theodore G. Tappert, ed., *Luther: Letters of Spiritual Counsel*, Library of Christian Classics, vol. 18 (Philadelphia, 1955), pp. 98–100. Chapter 3, pp. 82–108, includes the letters to the Weller brothers and a translation of the *Table Talks* on this subject.

39. Ibid., No. 2209, 7:206–08; Luther to Elector John Frederick, [Wittenberg], July 9, 1535.

40. Ibid., No. 3030, 7:422–23; Luther to Margrave George of Brandenburg [Wittenberg], May 29, 1536.

41. Ibid., No. 3426, 8:654; Luther to Justus Jonas [Wittenberg, 1539?].

42. Ibid., No. 3958, 10:498–504, especially 500–501. In the next letter as well, Luther opposed clandestine betrothals, ibid., No. 3959, 10:504–09; Luther to Bugenhagen, Asmus Spiegel, and Kilian Goldstein, [Wittenberg, after January 22, 1544].

43. *LW*, 45:379–93.

44. *WA Tischreden*, No. 2894b, 3:58.

45. *WA Br*, No. 3020, 7:408–09; Luther to Anton Rudolf, *Weinmeister* in Weimar, [Wittenberg], May 12, 1536.

46. Ibid., No. 3344, 8:453–55; Luther to Ursula Schneiderwein, [Wittenberg], June 4, 1539. A fine treatment of Luther's attitude toward marriage is William H. Lazareth, *Luther on the Christian Home. An Application of the Social Ethics of the Reformation* (Philadelphia, 1960).

47. The most excellent study is that of Gustaf Wingren, *Luthers Lehre vom Beruf* (Munich, 1952), with bibliography; translated as *Luther on Vocation* (Philadelphia, 1957), in which the author sets vocation in the larger theological setting of earth and heaven, God and the devil, man in his temporal and spiritual situations.

48. *WA*, 31:Pt. 1, 436; *Der 147. Psalm, Lauda Jerusalem, ausgelegt*, 1532.

49. Ibid., 17:Pt. 2, 276, *Festpostille*, 1527, on Luke 12:35–40. "By faith he [the Christian] is caught up beyond himself into God, by love he sinks down beneath himself into his neighbor," Luther wrote in "An Open Letter to the Christian Nobility," *Works of Martin Luther* (Philadelphia 1943), 2:342–43.

50. Some of the older works on the subject were in error in arguing that there was no impelling connection between faith and love, e.g., Karl Eger, *Die Anschauungen Luthers vom Beruf. Ein Beitrag zur Ethik Luthers* (Giessen, 1900), p. 160, thus ascribing the development of a non-religious ethic to the heritage of the reformation theology. Far better are George Forell, *Faith Active in Love. An Investigation of the Principles Underlying Luther's Social Ethics* (New York, 1954) and Donald C. Ziemke, *Love for the Neighbor in Luther's Theology. The Development of His Thought 1512–1529* (Minneapolis, 1963).

51. Lazareth, *Luther on the Christian Home*, p. 158.

52. Karl Holl already observed, *Luther*, vol. 1: *Gesammelte Aufsätze zur Kirchengeschichte*, 6th ed. (Tübingen, 1932), p. 475, that the new element in Luther on vocation is that he changed not only the content of the word "calling" but recast the word itself. The new element is that in his maturity he saw the "call of God" exclusively in the secular tasks, and thus tied together precisely the two things that for Catholic thought were opposites, difficult to fit together. See also Hans Preuss, *Martin Luther. Seele und Sendung* (Gütersloh, 1947), pp. 168–70. A fair summary of recent research is Ruth Hinz, "Der Berufsgedanke bei Luther nach dem heutigen Stande der Forschung," *Luther, Mitteilungen der Luthergesellschaft*, No. 2 (1961):84–94.

53. See Hellmut Lieberg, *Amt und Ordination bei Luther und Melanchthon* (Göttingen, 1962), pp. 132–67.

54. Helmut Gatzen, *Beruf bei Martin Luther und in der Industriellen Gesellschaft* (Münster, ca. 1964), pp. 31, 82–89. Friedrich Risch, "Der Berufsgedanke bei Luther, *Luther. Zeitschrift der Luther-Gesellschaft*, 34: No. 3 (1963):112–21. Risch discusses Alfons Auer, *Zum Christlichen Verständnis der Berufsarbeit* (1959), which compares Luther and Thomas, arguing that both relate calling and reason to God's order of creation. This comparison holds on one level, but is inadequate precisely at the faith and love juncture in their respective theologies. Richard M. Douglas, "Ideas of Work and Vocation in Humanist and Protestant Usage," *Comité International des Sciences Historiques*, 12 (Vienna, 1965), is mistaken when he argues: "To Luther and Calvin 'particular' vocation to work in the temporal kingdom was God's institution, not a matter of man's decision. 'To be called' to a temporal vocation is to be acted upon, just as grace calls a man to a 'spiritual vocation' toward faith and the Word of God," p. 75; "Luther warned

that Satan in turn will use every trick or talent of his own (*omne ingenium*) to lure people from their proper calling and to seduce them into work for which they were never intended, as if God could be ignorant of his own commands," p. 81. Douglas's confusion in assuming that Luther held that each man must remain in one special external office (calling) seems to derive from a failure to appreciate the fact that for the most part Luther distinguishes between vocation and occupation and his antecedent failure to recognize the inseparable connection in Luther between the Christian's inner call to be a child of God and the outer call to serve in the temporal kingdom. A Christian is called to a life of service in general, not to one specific temporal vocation. I owe this acute criticism to Mr. Robert N. Cox in his history senior honors essay, "Luther's View of Man's Vocation," Stanford University. Douglas is excellent on the humanists, however, and otherwise sound on the reformers.

55. G. Wingren, *Luther on Vocation*, pp. 172–81.

56. *WA Br*, No. 3867, 10:294–96; Luther to the captain and council of Breslau, [Wittenberg, April 16, 1543].

57. Ibid., No. 4152, 11:177–78; Luther to Viet Dietrich in Nürnberg, [Wittenberg], September 23, 1545.

58. Ibid., No. 3765, 10:92–95; Zeugnis [Wittenberg, July 10, 1542].

59. Ibid., No. 326, 2:165–66; Luther to Spalatin, Wittenberg, August 14, 1520.

60. Ibid., No. 884, 3:523–24; Luther to Christoph Jörger at Tolleth, Wittenberg, September 3, 1528.

61. Ibid., No. 1314, 4:544–45; Luther to Bernhard von Mila, Captain at Schweinitz, [Wittenberg], September 2, 1528.

62. Ibid., No. 3818, 10:208–9; Luther to the council at Regensburg, [Wittenberg], November 27, 1542.

63. Ibid., No. 3878, 10:319–20; Luther to Viet Dietrich in Nürnberg, [Wittenberg], May 11, 1543.

64. Ibid., No. 3323, 8:411–13; Luther to King Gustav of Sweden, [Wittenberg], April 18, 1539.

65. Ibid., No. 3551, 9:267–68; Luther and Bugenhagen to Anton Lauterbach in Pirna, Wittenberg, November 11, 1540.

66. Ibid., No. 3649, 9:482–84; Luther to Elector John Frederick, [Wittenberg], August 3, 1541.

67. Ibid., No. 1413, 5:59–60; Luther to Andreas Kauigsdorf in Eilenburg, [Wittenberg], May 1, 1529.

68. Ibid., No. 3370, 8:518–19; [Wolfgang Brauer] to Luther, [Issen, August 1?, 1539].

69. Ibid., No. 3527, 9:220–21; Luther to the council at Riga, [Wittenberg], August 26, 1540.

70. Ibid., No. 3665, 9:510–12; Luther to Wenzeslaus Linck in Nürnberg, [Wittenberg], September 8, 1541.

71. Ibid., No. 4067, 9:13–15; Luther, Bugenhagen, Cruciger, Major and Melanchthon (author) to Elector John Frederick, Wittenberg, January 14, 1545.

72. Ibid., No. 3966, 10:524–25; Luther to Joachim Mörlin in Arnstadt, [Wittenberg], February 6, 1544.

73. Ibid., No. 1444, 5:110–11; Luther to Jakob Propst in Bremen, [Wittenberg], July 10, 1529.

74. Ibid., No. 2176, 7:158–59; Luther to Johann Lonicer in Marburg, [Wittenberg], February 8, 1535.

75. Ibid., No. 1023, 4:95; Luther to Andreas Kauigsdorf in Eilenburg, [Wittenberg], June 29, 1526.

76. Ibid., No. 1089, 4:177–78; Luther to Clemens Ursinus, Wittenberg, March 21, 1527.

77. Ibid., No. 4125, 9:119–10; Luther and Melanchthon to Elector John Frederick, [Wittenberg], June 13, 1545.

78. Ibid., No. 1968, 6:378–80; Luther to Elector John Frederick, [Wittenberg], October 18, 1532. Ibid., No. 3915, 10:398–400; Nikolaus Baserinus, Pastor at Mügeln, to Luther; and Luther's response, ibid., No. 3918, 10:402–3; Luther and the Commissioners of the Consistory to Elector John Frederick, [Wittenberg], September 30, 1543. Ibid., No. 1855, 10:163–65; Luther to Matthias Kratsch in Zwickau, [Wittenberg], August 18, 1531. Ibid., No. 2195, 7:185–86; To all Brothers in Christ, especially to Clerics, Wittenberg, May 15, 1535.

79. *WA Tischreden*, No. 5557, 5:239.

ALBRECHT DÜRER'S "FOUR APOSTLES": A MEMORIAL PICTURE FROM THE REFORMATION ERA

Gerhard Pfeiffer

The interpretation of the "Four Apostles" has been an object of controversy to the present moment.[1] A contemporary of Dürer, the calligrapher Johann Neudörfer,[2] is the source of the interpretation that in the four likenesses are represented "properly speaking, a sanguine, choleric, phlegmatic, and melancholic temperament." This interpretation subsequently became the prevailing one. In 1627, during the negotiations between Elector Maximilian I of Bavaria and the city of Nürnberg over the transfer of these pictures, they were referred to as two panels "upon which the four complexions (i.e., temperaments) of man are painted in the guise of four apostles."[3] In Joachim von Sandrart's *Akademie der Künste*,[4] the panels are characterized as "four Evangelists in the form of the four complexions," and they confront the devotee of Dürer's art in the nineteenth century exclusively as the "four temperaments." This view still has adherents today. Erwin Panofsky fit it into the context of contemporary history with Dürer's interest in psychosomatic problems.[5] It was repeatedly the authority of Neudörfer, "who surely must have known," which led art historians to this interpretation. Indeed, Karl Neumann even stated that Neudörfer must "have heard this statement from Dürer's own mouth."[6] However, if one takes a close look at Neudörfer's statement, no direct conclusion can be drawn from it in regard to the artistic intention of Dürer. For that reason, some individuals have rejected this interpretation.[7] It included the necessity of viewing a phlegmatic in the apostle Peter.[8] Wölfflin rejected it;[9] Theodor Hampe and Heidrich declared, in view of their work with the inscriptions that Dürer had affixed to each of the two panels, that the depiction of the four temperaments could not have been Dürer's point of departure.[10] Thausing, therefore, tried to modify the original theory of the temperaments by the observation that on the one panel more contemplative natures, and on the other, more active characters are depicted.[11] This juxtaposition of *vita contemplativa* and *vita activa* is more an evaluation of Dürer's art of characterization than an interpretation of the representation *in toto* or an elaboration of what Dürer "actually" intended to say.

One would surely think that Dürer himself had pointed out to us the way to an interpretation since he supplied inscriptions for the panels; and no one can protest that they can "not be used as evidence, since they do not derive from Dürer."[12] For when Neudörfer reports a statement that Dürer made "in his workshop" as "I inscribed these four pictures at his feet and recorded some sayings of holy Scripture,"[13] he does not of course lay claim for himself to the intellectual authorship for the selection of the texts. The young, and also, vain calligraphist was only an agent of execution; Dürer called upon him because of his recognized calligraphic ability.

Assuming, therefore, that Dürer chose these annotations, we still face the question of their meaning, which is a subject of much debate. The inscriptions[14] begin with the statement that in these dangerous times all secular powers must justifiably heed the purity of the Word of God, as it is heard in the warnings in 2 Peter, 2; 1 John, 4; 2 Timothy, 3; and Mark, 12. An attempt to explain the pictures from these inscriptions easily resulted in viewing the "Four Apostles" as an expression of religious conviction. Dürer was supposed to have removed himself from the path of religious error by the rejection of false prophets, to have warned the viewer, above all the city council of Nürnberg, of them, and in a positive vein, to have given recognition to the "true doctrine." Krodel[15] even believes that Dürer created the pictures in order to escape all the accusations that could be raised against him because of his connection with the Zwinglians, who were viewed as "enthusiasts." Thausing formulates such ideas in the sense that the two panels represent Dürer's decision over the direction to be followed in the ecclesiastical troubles.[16] In the final analysis, then, the panels were viewed not only as Dürer's artistic legacy but also as his religious legacy.

Dürer's artistic "legacy" can, however, be deduced better from his theoretical writings than from his paintings. In the many drafts for his planned pedagogical writing on painting (*Speiss der Malerknaben*), he expressed his views on the function of painting in constantly recurring formulation. He wrote that the art of painting is used in the service of the church and in that way the Passion of Christ and many other good subjects are depicted; it also preserves the form of man after death. The survey of the earth, the waters, and stars has become intelligible by means of paintings, and is made known to many through paintings.[17] Dürer thus names three tasks of painting: first, the picture painted in the service of the church, with christological and exemplary representations; the memorial picture; and the didactic picture, thus scientific illustration.

Dürer did not intend the Apostle panels for an altarpiece. For, according to the background story of the panels, the hypothesis is excluded that they originated as wings of an altarpiece that was not executed and that they "were converted from panels that had become purposeless . . . into the document of a personal conviction."[18] There is no sort of circumstantial evidence for an ordering of an altarpiece and for a cancelling of the order. The hypothesis of Ephrussi and Thausing that the two panels were planned as the wings of a triptych, a medieval winged altarpiece whose middle section was not executed, that Dürer was not able to complete the entire work, and that it had remained an "apparent whole completed in makeshift fashion,"[19] is an unproven supposition. This assumption is not saved by Karl Voll's suggestion[20] that the triptych of Giovanni Bellini in the Frari Church in Venice was Dürer's model, one suddenly awakened in Dürer's memory when he composed the figures of the two panels. Since Ephrussi the central panel has even been conceived as five male nude studies that could be composed into a "Last Judgment."[21] Anton Springer thought of a crucifixion,[22] Wustmann of "the word of God, the New Testament, the teach-

ing of Christ," which he imagined symbolized by a "countenance of Christ,"[23] and Panofsky conceived of a "sacra conver-
sazione."[24]

The variety of hypotheses alone points out the lack of a real
foundation for the thesis that the tables are the uncompleted
remnants of an altarpiece. Wölfflin expressed it succinctly: "No
one ordered the pictures, no one bought them, neither were they
intended for a church."[25] Panofsky concludes from this that the
"Four Apostles" are a "first testimony to an autonomous artistic
need for expression."[26]

Such a need for expression becomés evident if one considers
another possibility among the tasks of painting set forth by
Dürer. In the letter accompanying the presentation of the "Four
Apostles" to the Nürnberg City Council,[27] Dürer himself explained that he had been wishing for a long time to demonstrate
to the council his admiration by means of a memorial picture,
but that he had not wanted to present the council with paintings
of a lesser quality. He also believed, he said, that no one was
more worthy to keep this latest painted panel "for a memorial"
than the city council.

One interpretation of these passages from the letter maintains
that Dürer presented the "Four Apostles" to the council in memory of himself. I consider this wrong, even though the secretary
of the chancellery made an entry in the council records (*Ratsbuch*) that Dürer had made the four portraits "as a memorial to
himself."[28] Rather, the statements of Dürer about the meaning
of painting suggest that he wanted to preserve the memory of
persons or events that the subjects represent, just as he had once
planned to paint Luther "as a lasting memorial,"[29] or, as he allows in the *Unterweisung der Messung,* as a victor, to preserve
by means of a memorial column the memory of a battle that has
been won.

As early as the 1870s a connection to historical contexts was
sought, and it was believed that the inscriptions expressed a
warning against false prophets, Anabaptists, and so-called enthusiasts such as Carlstadt, Müntzer, and Hans Denck, the rector
of the Sebald school in Nürnberg.[30] Ernst Heidrich sought in a
detailed study to explicate the references to contemporary his-

tory in the inscription texts. Based on his results, one cannot "see simply a monument to the Reformation" in the pictures.[31] According to his explanation, they are rather Dürer's testimonial to the council in the struggle against religious revolution, against the spoilers of the attempts at ecclesiastical renewal, against Anabaptists, against unauthorized lay preachers, who sneak into widows' houses; they are directed primarily against Hans Denck. In other words, Dürer professed his faith in the bases of civil and religious order, which the city council held firm in its hand.

Heidrich saw the occasion for the conception of the pictures in the trial that the council conducted against the so-called godless painters Sebald and Barthel Behaim and Jörg Pencz and against Hans Denck. "The desire for a public justification in the face of secret accusations may have been Dürer's point of departure."[32] Friedrich Winkler takes up this thesis: "The views of his pupils and co-workers were remote from Dürer, but he felt that he had to bear witness in the midst of the disorders which were bringing civil rule in Nürnberg into serious danger."[33] Helmuth Rössler even pushed this view to the point of maintaining that Dürer "painted his four Apostle pictures as atonement for his own share of spiritual guilt for the disorders of the times."[34] Such views are based in the final analysis on the supposition of rather close connections between Dürer and the individuals accused in 1525.[35] It was first maintained in 1609 that the brothers Behaim were pupils of Dürer.[36] Did there really exist a confidential relationship with the Behaims, who were reproached after Dürer's death for plagiarism of the master's works? The opinion that Georg Pencz was a very close coworker of Dürer is based only on the identification of Pencz with a servant (Jörg) in Dürer's house who was mentioned in 1523.[37] Denck had come as a stranger to Nürnberg upon the recommendation of Oecolampadius. Pirckheimer invited the new rector of the Sebald school to his house, which was known for its hospitality[38] and where Dürer may have met him. Nothing is known about a closer relationship of Dürer to Denck. Dürer's relations with Carlstadt are recorded for the period of time in which Luther and his Wittenberg colleagues took no offense at his doctrinal concepts.[39] Is it not necessary to raise against Heidrich's view

the objection that he himself presented against an antipapal interpretation of the inscriptions: "What would be the purpose of
. . . this warning about the past?"[40] Hence one may not seek
the explanation for Dürer's painting in one episode, such as is
presented by the trial against the "godless painters." Instead, the
intellectual-religious climate of the years 1525-26, to which
Dürer was exposed when he created the "Four Apostles" as a
memorial picture, should be researched. Four outstanding events
should be examined: the Nürnberg religious colloquy, the Peasants' Revolt, the founding of a *Gelehrtenschule* in Nürnberg,
and the dispute over the sacrament of the Eucharist.

As a *Genannter* of the great council, Dürer was surely invited to participate in the religious colloquy of 1525.[41] He had
the opportunity to follow the theological discussions that led to
the decisions of the council on ecclesiastical policy. There is no
direct written evidence about Dürer's reaction to this discussion.

Dürer's attitude toward the Peasants' Revolt has not become
an object of discussion until recent years. In these discussions
there has been, in my opinion, no attention paid to the shock effect of the war upon Dürer. This effect was expressed in a dream
that Dürer had on the night of June 7, 1525; he awoke from it
full of terror, his whole body trembling. He preserved it in a
sketch: water fell from the skies and inundated the whole land,
"four miles from here." Deeply troubled, he adds to the report:
"May God direct all things for the best!"[42] The association interpreted into the dream, "four miles from here," refers to the
Kirchehrenbach peasant band that had participated in the destruction of castles during May and was now approaching the
city of Nürnberg.[43] In the first days of June anxiety rose to its
highest point in Nürnberg. On June 2 the provost of Saint Sebald
lost his nerve and wanted to resign his office.[44] On the same day
the council issued a mandate[45] in which it made extensive concessions to the common man in its declaration regarding liberal-
izing currency regulations and the redemption of house rents,
the abolition of paramount rights (*Obereigentum*), the reduction of direct and indirect taxes, and the suspension of the market tax. On June 3, the council rejected the demand of the
Kirchehrenbach band for the delivery of weapons.[46] Soon there-

after, the situation of the Würzburg group became critical as a result of the approach of the army of the Swabian League.[47] Through its measures the council sought at the last moment to prevent the outbreak of revolts in the vicinity of Nürnberg, since that would certainly have caused a vendetta by Georg Truchsess of Waldburg, the leader of the army of the Swabian League. The council viewed the complaints of the peasantry as partially justified, deplored the excessive tyranny of the nobles and their persecution of the Word of God, and condemned the indiscriminate slaughtering of peasants by the army of the League, just as it had expressed its disapproval of Thomas Müntzer and the violence of the peasant rebellion. The council saw in the battle between peasants and nobles punishment from God, in which both sides were instruments of God's wrath over the sins of men.[48] Starting from the same conception, Dürer feared a new flood. The Würzburg *Magister* Lorenz Fries also interpreted the events in this way:[49] there arose from the vapors of our sinful guilt-ridden lives mists that fell from heaven as a pitiful flood, not of water but of blood.

Dürer rejected the murdering of peasants by the Swabian League and Margrave Casimir, which had been imminent since the beginning of June. In his *Unterweisung der Messung,* which appeared in 1525, he published sketches for memorial columns:[50] for the victor over powerful enemies, a column formed from captured military equipment; for him who "would want to erect a victory figure for having overcome the rebellious peasants," a column formed from captured farm equipment, such as oat bins, a butter churn, cheese mugs, pitch forks, a milk jug, the whole thing crowned by a peasant figure stabbed from behind; finally, a monument for a drunkard with a beer barrel, playing board with figures, and feed-bags. The bitter irony of Dürer in his judgment of the fashion in which the victorious princes went about their work is clear; one surely cannot observe in it a "manifestation passionée de solidarité"[51] with the peasants, but rather, probably, a stand against the reaction of the princes, which also had an effect on ecclesiastical affairs. The few bits of evidence indicate that Dürer shared the view of the council in checking this reaction by attempts at mediation, in protecting

the justified interests of the peasantry, and in preventing an ecclesiastical restoration. How great the concern of the council was
in the peasant question can be recognized from the fact that the
eruption of a peasant rebellion in the Salzburg area in April,
1526, once again led the council to pronounce a prohibition of
the right of assembly and to issue a warning to the Nürnberg
peasants.[52]

This happened in the days when the new school was opened
in Nürnberg. The founding of this school was, in my opinion,
the actual occasion for Dürer to make a gift—precisely, of the
"Four Apostles"—to the council as a memorial picture. Previous
Dürer research has offered a valuable starting point in this direction. In his general impression that the figure of John represents
the type of a German thinker, Rettberg as early as 1854 believed
that he found a similarity to Schiller and to Melanchthon.[53] This
vague reference to Melanchthon was later repeated; Heidrich[54]
explained in 1909 "that the shape of John is reminiscent of the
Melanchthon portrait." Wölfflin[55] confirmed Melanchthon's
"undeniable similarity to John." Other researchers followed this
thesis. According to Wilhelm Waetzold,[56] Dürer "let Melanchthon's features pass into the head of John," and Friedrich Winkler[57] termed this similarity no chance occurence and declared that
Melanchthon served as the model.

Since Dürer engraved Melanchthon's portrait in copper in
1526 (see Fig. 1), a comparison of the two representations is
quite possible. If one disregards the fact that Dürer omitted the
rather unkempt beard and slightly straightened the ridge of the
nose, then the remaining essential physiognomical elements are
in agreement. It may even be said of the coloration that Melanchthon had reddish hair, according to the testimony of Lucas Cranach's Melanchthon portrait. That Dürer made the acquaintance
of Melanchthon on the occasion of the latter's first stay in Nürnberg in mid-August, 1518, is doubtful. But two extended visits
of Melanchthon in Nürnberg in November, 1525, and in May,
1526, gave the artist the opportunity to come into contact with
Melanchthon.

Melanchthon's Nürnberg sojourns were the result of the council's plan for the establishment of a secondary school.[58] On Oc-

tober 18, 1524, the council decided to invite Melanchthon to move to Nürnberg and assume the instruction of the citizens' children in exchange for appropriate remunerations.[59] Hieronymus Ebner and Bernhard Paumgartner, both of whom stood in personal contact with Melanchthon, were charged with execution of the decision. Ebner had had his son of the same name study under Melanchthon, and Paumgartner's younger brother Hieronymus belonged to Melanchthon's intimate circle of pupils in Wittenberg.[60] Instead of drafting an official letter from the council, Ebner and Paumgartner had Hieronymus Paumgartner communicate in private to his teacher the ideas of the council concerning the founding of a philosophers' school.[61]

The plan for establishing the school met to a great extent Melanchthon's wishes, even if he himself could not follow the summons because of the duties that held him in Wittenberg. Only after the ecclesiastical problem had finally been settled in Nürnberg and the Peasants' Revolt was over could the council take up the plan again. On September 16, 1525, it decided to summon Melanchthon to Nürnberg. It now wrote officially that its conscience and the burden of its office and its authority impelled it to the sovereign duty imposed by God of establishing a respectable Christian school and equipping it with respectable, wise, and learned people in accordance with the needs of the pupils and the opportunity for language study. It asked him to come to Nürnberg to bring this laudable Christian work to completion.[62] Melanchthon agreed and brought along Joachim Camerarius.[63]

The decisive discussions were prepared in November, 1525, by the three friends Melanchthon, Camerarius, and Paumgartner. Based on the recommendation of Melanchthon, the council decided on November 17 to offer the position of rector to Camerarius. He was to be assisted by Michael Roting as a second teacher. Roting was another of Melanchthon's prize pupils who had been a confidant of Luther's and had been received by Melanchthon into his house.

The founding of the school, which was supposed to be opened at Easter, 1526, was therefore due to a circle of intimate collaborators. But it was not until May 6 that Melanchthon arrived in

Nürnberg with Michael Roting. Camerarius and Eobanus Hessus, who was being considered as another teacher, came later. The consultations were concluded on May 21, 1526. Eobanus was chosen as the third teacher, and on May 22 the council published a notice[64] in which the parents were invited to send their children to the new school without paying any tuition. On May 23 the school was opened with an official speech by Melanchthon.[65] In it the Wittenberg scholar praised the decision of the council to create a home for learning. He praised the usefulness of a scholarly education. Law, justice, and religion guarantee the continuation of the human community; "nam nisi literis conservatis durare religio et bonae leges non possunt; praeterea exigit Deus, ut liberos vestros ad virtutem ac religionem instituatis." He was able to vouch fully for the teachers he had recommended: their erudition, he said, enabled them to discharge the task they had assumed, and their character assured that they would keep the highest faith in the execution of their duties.

Similar ideas recur in the school ordinance Melanchthon drafted.[66] The idea also appears here that "sine literis religionis et aliarum virtutum praecepta satis percipi nequeunt." God charged the rulers and the authorities with the duty of the education of the youth, for it is their concern, "doctrinam religionis conservare, quae quidem sine cognitione literarum ac linguarum doceri recte non potest." Camerarius also completely embraced this line of thought. When the council visited the school four weeks after the opening day, it requested Camerarius to make suggestions for the removal of deficiencies. He thereupon stressed that "good art must be exercised for the preservation of righteousness." Whoever took instruction in school, he said, was fit for spiritual and worldly tasks. He asked that God might bless the continuation of the work of promulgating His holy Word. Injury to the proper preaching of the Word of God could, however, in his opinion, be met only by the cultivation of art and teaching.[67]

Thus, a small circle of Christian humanists of similar persuasion inspired and arranged the Nürnberg secondary school. If one attempts to get a visual impression of these men, he will become aware, in my opinion, that their facial features recur in

Fig. 1. Philip Melanchthon. Copper engraving by Albrecht Dürer. German-isches National-Museum, Nürnberg.

Fig. 2 (*above*). Joachim Camerarius the elder. 1559.

Fig. 3 (*below*). Ieronymus Paumgartner. Medal by Joachim Deschler in 1553. Reproduced in Paul Grotemeyer, *Da ich het die Gestalt* (Munich, 1957), plate 59.

ÆTATIS SVÆ.LVII.
Exprelsa imago.
Michaëlis Rotingi
senioris.

Fig. 4. Michael Roting. Copper engraving in the Stadtbibliothek, Nürnberg. Reproduced in G. W. Panzer, *Verzeichnis von Nürnbergischen Portraiten* (Nürnberg, 1970).

Fig. 5. "The Four Apostles," by Albrecht Dürer. Bayer. Staatsgemäldesammlungen, Munich.

Dürer's "Four Apostles." The features of Joachim Camerarius the elder are preserved for us in a medal (Fig. 2) produced when he was 59 years old, thus, in 1559.[68] As far as this small piece allows a judgment of his facial features, the similarity of Paul's portrait to him is assured. The portrait of Hieronymus Paumgartner (Fig. 3) is familiar to us from a medal by Joachim Deschler in 1553.[69] When comparing Paumgartner with Dürer's Mark, we must take into account that the artist of the medal was not able to render so characteristically the liveliness of the glance, which the painter was capable of depicting, nor, given the small size of the medal, the eyebrows, which Dürer sketched with particular affection. Otherwise, the similarity of the features is clear. For Peter, a comparison with the copper-engraved portrait of Michael Roting in the city library of Nürnberg (Fig. 4) is inevitable.[70]

The supposition that historical personalities were models for Dürer in the fashioning of the "Four Apostles" can, of course, be challenged by the argument that portrait similarities alone cannot suffice for the interpretation of the picture and can easily lead to mistakes. Thus it was claimed that the features of Hieronymus Holzschuher could be recognized in the figure of Paul, but this is surely wrong.[71] Stuhlfauth claimed that he could discern a "striking similarity" between Mark and Cranach's "Luther als Junker Jörg."[72] That is certainly misleading. Dürer would scarcely have fulfilled his wish, announced in a letter to Spalatin, of making a portrait of Luther by shoving him into the background in a group picture. Thus my interpretation of the pictures, presented for the first time in 1960, was greeted not only with agreement but also with skepticism and rejection.[73] Even if the attempt at discerning portrait similarities is constantly endangered by a subjective component, it is methodologically legitimate. For Anton Springer had already confirmed[74] that these four figures "breathe . . . such a forceful life and bear to such an extent so very much the stamp of a personality which has developed from the inside to the outside, that we instinctively transform their historical names into psychological ones"; or, as I would formulate it, that we seek to transform their biblical names into historical ones. Karl Neumann[75] saw in the panels "a combination of unique individuality and comprehensive characterization." Wilhelm Waetzold[76] expressed the opinion that "Dürer trained himself to create those powerful figures from study of the portraits of living, famous people" and considered it impossible that the master of individual portraiture would have "produced arbitrarily four character heads from his study folders." Friedrich Winkler[77] finally declared flatly that Peter was "no more and no less than a study after a model." Dürer's own statements support the opinion that the artist adhered to portraits. Dürer confided, in a personal conversation with Melanchthon, that he had learned with age and endeavored to imitate nature; in the course of the discussion he is supposed to have remarked how difficult it is not to deviate from the natural image.[78]

A small observation may strengthen the conviction that we are really dealing with paintings after models: the position of the pupil in the corner of the eye of the Apostle Paul.[79] It is found now and then in Dürer's half-profile portraits, in the portraits of Oswald Krell and Hieronymus Holzschuher, and in the self-portrait on the All Saints picture. It can easily be explained psychologically by the sideways glance that the person being painted made at the work of art being created.

It is apparent from various statements that Melanchthon not only met Dürer but even included him in his conversation. Their common interests are reflected in a report by Melanchthon's son-in-law Caspar Peucer[80] that he had heard from Melanchthon on more than one occasion about the lively participation of Dürer in a discussion on the question of the Eucharist in Pirckheimer's house.

Camerarius, Melanchthon's alter ego in Nürnberg as it were, became friends with Dürer after he moved to Nürnberg. He composed a laudatory literary monument to him in the preface to his Latin translation of Dürer's theory of proportion. The Paumgartner family had been connected with Dürer for a long time. He had already depicted two members of the family, Stefan and Lucas, cousins of Hieronymus, in portrait form as Saint George and Saint Eustachius in a winged altarpiece.[81] Relations between Dürer and Michael Roting can be assumed, since Melanchthon asked Camerarius in a letter to convey his greetings to Eobanus Hessus, who had been painted by Dürer, to Roting and to Dürer.[82]

In addition, it seems to me that there is a reference to the pictures in progress in a letter Philip Melanchthon wrote to Joachim Camerarius on September 7, 1526, about four weeks before the presentation of the painting to the council.[83] The letter dealt with the concept of "dodrans" (i.e., $3/4$ of a foot), and the stature of the Emperor Augustus. Melanchthon had by this time measured out the foot as Leonhard Porcius (in his recently printed work about measures and weights) indicated it for Rome, and had noticed that the statement of Suetonius that the emperor was five feet and a "dodrans" tall, did not at all infer an uncommonly small physical height. Melanchthon added: "Nam me aliquantum excedit ea magnitudo et opinor a tui corporis modo non multum abesse." ("For this size exceeds mine somewhat and I believe that it is not far from your stature.")

So that Camerarius could gain a safe judgment about their mutual relationship in height, he drew on the edge of the letter what was a half foot according to Porcius' data and stated that the passage in Suetonius was now clear. Then Melanchthon continued: "Therefore, it is not necessary to trouble Dürer, and if he has served us in this matter, you should offer him many thanks and tell him that I have recanted and corrected an opinion which I wrote imprudently and before examination of the facts."

Thus data concerning the size of Melanchthon and Camerarius have been added to our previous argument. In the case of the text referring to Dürer we must ask: How could the two correspondents trouble Dürer? Can this question refer exclusively to the interpretation of a passage in Suetonius' works? Camerarius was not supposed to trouble the painter, who was competent in questions of measurement, for such collaboration; indeed, he was to thank him and communicate to him that Melanchthon had taken back an imprudent statement? Or must we not think that this statement refers to the panels that were about to be completed and to the physical stature of Melanchthon and Camerarius mentioned in the letter. Dürer had employed his earlier apostle studies for the physical form of the figures, had placed his portrait heads, as it were, on draped pedestals and achieved that super-elevation of the depicted personalities that removed them from the sphere of everyday life. In the process he had not only neglected the absolute size of the small, slender, or, as Luther said, poor scrawny little fellow[84] Melanchthon, but had even slightly reversed the relationship in size of Melanchthon to Camerarius. When compared with the Apostle Paul, John gives the impression of being physically larger or at least equally large. Cannot the inconvenience, the service that Dürer rendered the two, the silly, hasty judgment that Melanchthon retracted,[85] refer to this relationship in size and its eventual correction? The fact that the smallest of the four apostles is Peter also speaks in favor of Dürer's efforts to hold to the relationship of the physical sizes of the persons depicted and thus also in favor of my identification of the "models" of the "Four Apostles." In the letters of Melanchthon, Roting's first name Michael is distorted to "Mica" (tiny crumb) in good-natured joking, yet certainly in reference to his physical size. Roting was also the oldest of the four; he felt old before his time and unfit, but he reached an advanced age.

The observation of art historians that John is the least carefully executed figure[86] also finds a natural explanation in the thesis that the four figures were painted after the contemporaries of Dürer whom I have indicated. For Dürer had the opportunity to observe Camerarius, Paumgartner, and Roting into early October, but Melanchthon's two sojourns lasted only a short time, November 12–25, 1525, and May 6–29, 1526. In addition Melanchthon's two visits were completely filled with deliberations and preparations for the founding of the school, with the writing of a brief on the liturgy and the endowment laws, and with presentations of personal opinions.[87]

The identification of the "models" of the "Four Apostles" also gives insight into the genesis of the pictures. November, 1525, is an important time period for this work.[88] The sketch of John dated 1525 already records Melanchthon's features. On the other hand, the sketch seems to have been completed before the last third of May, 1526, since Eobanus Hessus, who was summoned on May 21, is no longer included.[89]

Even though, in my opinion, the establishment of the new school supplied the essential impetus for the memorial picture of the "Four Apostles," Dürer was certainly also influenced in 1526 by the dispute over the Eucharist. Based on the attribution of the title-page border of the anonymous work, *Anzaygung etlicher irriger mengel, so Caspar Schatzgeyer barfüsser in seinem büchleyn wider Andream Osiander gesetzt hat*, to Dürer by art historians, one can conclude that Dürer stood in somewhat close contact to a "third party."[90] The question of the Eucharist, which is the chief subject of this pamphlet, led to discussions in inns and secret assemblies. The council reacted on June 16, 1526, with a proclamation on "enthusiasts."[91] It gave a warning to those who speak of the sacrament with disrespect, reject the pure words of Christ and drag them into these human quarrels, or even commit the blasphemy of making disrespectful gestures during the celebration of the Eucharist and so give rise to sects, mistaken notions, and disturbance of peace in the city. The enemy of eternal truth, it stated, wants to lead men to rely on their own devices and their blindness. The battle against this craftiness of the devil, through which sects are formed and the unity of the citizens is destroyed, remained the task of the council, which admittedly could not and would not force anyone to believe. It threatened to punish those who spread erroneous notions and hold conventicles. It warned against such assemblies and disputations and recommended to those seeking instruction and advice to seek out the two preachers to whom the proclamation of the Word of God was entrusted. The council also acted against this movement by banning as "the work of the devil" and "ensnarement" the tracts of Carlstadt, Oecolampadius, Zwingli, and their followers as well as the publications about the religious colloquy in Baden.[92]

Dürer was also under the influence of this spiritual altercation when he chose the inscription texts for the "Four Apostles."

The New Testament texts are introduced by the statement that all secular powers should, in the present dangerous times, justifiably adhere to the divine Word instead of human "ensnarement," because God (according to Apoc. 22, 18f.) does not want anything added to or taken away from His Word.

The words that follow this explanation admit of two possible interpretations: "Darauf horent dise trefflich vier menner Petrum, Johannem, Paulum und Marcum ire warnung." "Horent" was earlier considered unhesitatingly as second person plural imperative; the entire passage was thus interpreted as an exhortation to the person observing the pictures, particularly the council. Dürer, however, uses the ending -*ent* also as third person plural indicative as well as present participle.[93] Thus the interpretation: "Accordingly these four excellent men heed the warning of Peter, John, Paul and Mark" is completely possible. Such a syntactic separation of the "excellent four men" as subject of the sentence from the New Testament authors as object of the sentence would remove a striking feature of the inscriptions, the designation of the New Testament authors as "excellent men," which would mean their secularization, an equation of them with the famous authors of antiquity, a divesting from them of their function as bearers of divine revelation. The opposing argument, that the epithet "excellent four men" corresponds to the saint ideal of the humanists and can be expected from Dürer, I do not find justified after an examination of Dürer's writings for his usage of epithets for saints. According to my interpretation, the inscriptions would prove that the memory of the men who deserve esteem for the founding of the school is held in honor. The council summoned them as Christian teachers and they knew how to teach and live as such. So much are they permeated by the admonitions and teachings of the four authors of the New Testament that they confront the viewer as the living representatives of these men of God; therefore, they also can justly claim their attributes: book, sword, and keys, and the tasks symbolized by these attributes, teaching, punishment, and the absolution from punishment. This motif of combining portrait and saint's figure, which had also been utilized by Dürer in the Paumgartner altarpiece, found in the "Four Apostles" a new, deepened realization.[94]

The conjoined participial construction, which Seebass also prefers,[95] would, however, more strongly emphasize the admonition to the council to heed the words of the New Testament witnesses; that these witnesses have taken on the shape of living personalities who are known to the council would be accidental. Independent of this alternative, however, one must keep in mind the fact that Dürer viewed the attitude of the circle of people upon whom the gift was bestowed, i.e., the council, as memorable; namely, its striving to determine the pure Word of God by means of a religious colloquy, to preserve it from misinterpretations in the Peasants' Revolt and among the sacramentarians, and to insure its proclamation in the future as well by means of the founding of the school. He adopted the "Protestant principle."[96]

The selection of texts must be viewed as a personal achievement of Dürer. Dürer thus turns out to be an excellent biblicist. This he had already proved in the shaping of the pictorial series of the Apocalypse, the Passions, and the Life of Mary. My attempts to trace the use of all four Bible passages to a literary model were unsuccessful. 2 Peter 2:1 f. is found as an argument among traditionalists and reformers in Dürer's time. This passage is cited in the brief of the preachers of Saint Sebald, Saint Lorenz, and the Spitalkirche in Nürnberg, printed with the title "Ein gut Unterricht und getrewer Ratschlag." It also occurs in Hans Sachs and Luther,[97] as well as among the opponents of the Reformation in the "truthful declaration" (*Wahrhafte Erklärung*) of Kaspar Schatzgeyer and with Linhard Ebner in the Nürnberg religious colloquy.[98] 1 John 4:1 ff. was first used in the *Confutatio* of the counsel of the Ansbach monastic prelates, which was not published until the twentieth century.[99] The *Confutatio* was used to contradict the reproach that the Reformation faction interpreted Holy Scripture according to the letter and not according to the spirit. I found the words of the Apostle Paul, 2 Timothy 3: 1 ff. in Erasmus' *Ratio verae theologiae*,[100] turned against the monks: "Obsecro te, lector, an tibi non videtur digito demonstrare quosdam ex istorum ordinibus, qui . . . monachos se vocant." Mark 12, 38, I found in Hans Sachs's *Ein neuer Spruch, wie die geystlicheit und etlich hantwerker uber den Luther clagen*, as an allusion in the judgment of Christ concerning those who sell vigils, anniversaries, and masses for the souls of the dead.[101]

An interpretation of the inscriptions will thus have to illuminate without literary help the conduct of the council that is worthy of the memory of ensuing generations. If the text of the Epistle of Peter about the false prophets who introduce ruinous sects, deny the Lord, and blaspheme the path of truth, points directly to the council's proclamation of July, 1526, then the passage from the Epistle of John leads to the subject of the Eucharistic dispute itself, to Christology as a criterion for the judging of true and false prophets. The quote from the Letter of the Apostle to Timothy points to the contemporary situation, to the "last" times in which the sovereigns must be consoled by Holy Scripture. For there will continue to be greedy, haughty, wicked people who feign a pious way of life. They constantly are given the opportunity to "learn" the gospel, but the recognition of the truth remains closed to them. Even the scribes fall short: long prayers are a pretext for them to exploit widows, and in spite of the influence and the respect that they know how to procure for themselves, damnation awaits them. Whoever is convinced that Dürer would not and could not step before the council with his finger raised in exhortation, and is therefore convinced that he created the "Four Apostles" as a memorial picture, might read in the last two texts that the council did not allow itself to be shaken by its disappointment over the way of life of fellow men and especially of theologians and adhered to its ecclesiastical policy. In respect to the founding of the school it would be necessary to explain that the inaugurators of the new school hear and preach the admonitions of Holy Scripture, that the council has no new disillusionments to fear here.

An analysis of the "Four Apostles" cannot avoid a judgment about Dürer's position on the religious conflicts of his times. As soon as the factional dispute over Dürer's adherence to Protestantism or Catholicism, forced upon us by the nineteenth century *Kulturkampf* question, has been overcome, there remains the less crude question[102] as to what position Dürer took in regard to the actions of the council and the manifestations produced by them in the life of his fellow citizens. It is possible to conclude from the choice of the inscriptions to the "Four Apostles" that Dürer shared with the council its rejection of ruinous sects and false prophets, wherever these stood. If the word *sects* was a subject of dispute in the Nürnberg religious colloquy—applied first to monasticism, then to the new heresy,[103] then by Pirckheimer to the "godless painters"[104]—nevertheless, the term applied in 1526 above all to men like Carlstadt, Oecolampadius, and Zwingli.[105] Like Hans Sachs,[106] Dürer knew how to distingush between true and lip-service Christians. With Willibald Pirckheimer and the nuns from his family, he saw how the sensual, sinful life was glossed over with the Word of God, how the preachers of the city influenced the council and looked out for their own interests,[107] how, according to a letter from Pirckheimer to Melanchthon, the preachers preached *contumeliose et arroganter* and how *concionatorum illorum facta haudquaquam dictis quadrent.*[108]

In order to determine Dürer's position in these years, one must also consider, while not forgetting his marked intellectual independence, the circle of those people with whom he was personally connected. The common denominator of these personalities, who differed religiously, is a similar interest in scholarly questions. From the standpoint of humanism Dürer could maintain relations with the antipodes Lazarus Spengler and Willibald Pirckheimer[109] whereby the judgment about Pirckheimer that he returned to the lap of the old church[110] is reached only anachronistically and with disregard of his wavering statements. Humanistic interests connected Pirckheimer and Dürer with Thomas Venatorius, at that time preacher at the Spitalkirche in Nürnberg. Pirckheimer maintained, with regard to Phrygio, that Venatorius would have been relieved of his office as preacher, since he openly expressed much that displeased him, if friends had not intervened.[111] Executor of the writings left behind by Pirckheimer, to whom he dedicated his pamphlet against the Anabaptists, Venatorius was connected to Dürer by his interest in art theory. He is supposed to have edited a second edition of Dürer's *Unterweisung der Messung*.[112] As one of Dürer's conversation partners, he composed after the master's death a humanistic "monody" to the deceased.[113] In regard to church affairs he proved to be pugnacious in questions of the regulation of feast days, church organization, and the rejection of mendicant orders.[114] As one of those who harassed the nuns of Saint Catherine's,[115] he found himself confronted with the problem of normalizing his relationship to a nun through marriage, and asked Pirckheimer for advice in this situation.[116]

Mathematical interest surely connected Dürer also with the councilman Christoph Koler, to whom he dedicated his *Befestigungslehre*, as is proven by an extant colored title page,[117] and who prevailed upon Joachim Camerarius to translate Dürer's *Proportionslehre* into Latin.[118] The Koler family chronicle[119] characterizes Christoph as a shrewd man who was trained in the arts and particularly in mathematics and music, who had mastered perspective and possessed good discernment in questions of architecture and painting, and who had also studied Roman law. The fear of the Lord and fervent love of the gospel, which are ascribed to him, can be verified by the official sources for the years 1524–26:[120] his services were requested by the council as early as the first peasant uprisings in 1524; he was given the task of negotiating with the provosts over the changes in the regulation of the liturgy in June, 1524; he participated in the censorship of books; he was charged with carrying out the orders of the council in the arrangement of the alms box and the reforming of the endowment laws; he was engaged in the regulation of the monasteries; he took a decisive part in the preparation and execution of the Nürnberg religious colloquy; he was active in the commission set up for the establishment of the school, for which he appointed the mathematician;[121] and finally, he was busy as an official adviser on theological questions.[122] The mutual esteem between Koler and Dürer, which can be inferred from the written sources, points likewise to a position of Dürer in regard to the council that allows recognition of the painter as a representative of Christian humanism in a time of turmoil. Should not the "Four Apostles" also be a witness to this humanistic spirit as well as a witness to Dürer's respect for the council's decisions?

1. In 1960, the year commemorating the 400th anniversary of the death of Melanchthon, I turned my attention to the subjects of Dürer's "Four Apostles." This lecture was published in an annual bulletin of the Melanchthongymnasium

in Nürnberg, where it was not easily accessible, and is consequently presented here in substantially revised form, especially for an American audience. I thus have the opportunity to utilize works that have appeared since 1960 and some archival sources (translated by David Armborst, revised by Jackson Spielvogel). Gerhard Pfeiffer, "Die Vorbilder zu Albrecht Dürers 'Vier Aposteln': Melanchthon und sein Nürnberger Freundeskreis," *Wissenschaftliche Beilage zum Jahresbericht des Melanchthon-Gymnasiums* (Nürnberg, 1960).

2.   Johann Neudorfer, *Nachrichten von Künstlern und Werkleuten*, ed. Georg Wolfgang Karl Lochner (Vienna, 1875), pp. 132–3.

3.   StAN. Verlässe der Herren Älteren of August 8, 1627, printed in Joseph Baader, *Beiträge zur Kunstgeschichte Nürnbergs*, I (Nördlingen, 1860), pp. 94 f. BB 246 (for the year 1627), fol. 707 ff., in Baader, 1, 72 ff. RV 2073, fol. 38; 2074, fol. 18, Akt S I L 148, No. 26. For a summary, see Anton Ernstberger, "Kurfürst Maximilian I und Albrecht Dürer, in Anton Ernstberger, *Franken-Böhmen-Europa*, I (1959):187 ff.

4.   Edited by Peltzer (Munich, 1925), p. 67.

5.   Erwin Panofsky, "Zwei Dürerprobleme," *Münchner Jahrbuch der bildenden Kunst*, New Series, 8 (1931): 42 ff. Kurt Martin has once again taken up the question as it is formulated here (Kurt Martin, *Albrecht Dürer, Die Vier Apostel* [Stuttgart, 1963]).

6.   Carl Neumann, "Die Vier Apostel von Albrecht Dürer," *Zeitschrift für deutsche Bildung* 6 (1930):452.

7.   Anton Springer, *Albrecht Dürer* (Berlin, 1892), p. 155.

8.   Engelhard, "Albrecht Dürer," *Christliches Kunstblatt* (1877), p. 189; H. Merz, "Die Bedeutung der 'Vier Apostel' Albrecht Dürers," *Christliches Kunstblatt* (1897), p. 13; A. von Eye, *Albrecht Dürers Leben* (Wandsbek, 1892), p. 79, speaks of the "opinion of the forward *Schreibmeister*." Also Karl Voll, "Entstehungsgeschichte von Dürers Vier Aposteln," *Süddeutsche Monatshefte* 3 (1906): 79 rejects this interpretation.

9.   Heinrich Wölfflin, *Die Kunst Albrecht Dürers*, 5th ed. (Munich, 1926), p. 348.

10.   Theodor Hampe, "Albrecht Dürer als Künstler und als Mensch," *MVGN*, 28 (1928):56; Ernst Heidrich, *Dürer und die Reformation* (Leipzig, 1909), p. 57.

11.   Moritz Thausing, *Dürer, Geschichte seines Lebens* (Leipzig, 1884), 2:279.

12.   A. Weber, *Albrecht Dürer* (Regensburg, 1894), p. 70.

13.   Also Markus Zucker, *Dürers Stellung zur Reformation* (Erlangen, 1886), p. 47, says that Neudörfer made the suggestions for the choice of the pictorial passages. According to Grimm, *Deutsches Wörterbuch*, 1, 1796, the only questionable thing is the meaning "aufma!en," "aufzeichnen," for the word "bezeichnen" used by Neudörfer, not "aufmerksam machen auf."

14.   Hans Rupprich, *Dürers schriftlicher Nachlass*, (Berlin, 1956), 1:210 f.

15.   Gottfried Krodel, "Nürnberger Humanisten am Anfang des Abendmahlstreits," *Zeitschrift für bayerische Kirchengeschichte* 25 (1956):46.

16.   Thausing, *Dürer*, 2:286; a variation is represented by the formulation of Arno Max Vogt, "Albrecht Dürer, Die Vier Apostel," *Festschrift Kurt Badt* (Berlin, 1961), that the "four Apostles" are, as it were, custodians for the continuation of the Word of the Bible.

17.   Rupprich, *Nachlass*, 2:133; previous sketch versions, pp. 112, 113, 131.

18.   Panofsky, "Zwei Dürerprobleme," p. 39; that the Nürnberg council was, by the way, at the time of the Reformation in principle not hostile to art is shown still by the inventory of the Nürnberg churches today; another trait is

characteristic: in a circular to the pastors on the occasion of the Turkish threat (October 4, 1526; RB, No. 13, fol. 154), primary reference is made to the fact that the Turk destroys churches and also scorns, defiles, and treads upon pictures of our God and Savior Jesus Christ.

19. Charles Ephrussi, *Albrecht Dürer* (Paris, 1832), p. 343; Thausing, *Dürer,* 2:288 f.

20. Karl Voll, "Dürers Vier Aposteln," p. 74; then Klaus Lankheit, "Dürers 'Vier Apostel,'" *Zeitschrift für Theologie und Kirche* 49 (1952):238 ff.: "The inscriptions have moved in the imagination into the spot of the middle piece." Also Klaus Lankheit, *Das Triptychon als Pathosformel* ("Abhandlungen der Heidelberger Akademie der Wissenschaften, philologischhistorischer Klasse;" Heidelberg, 1959), particularly pp. 20 f.; Kurt Martin, *Albrecht Dürer,* p. 25.

21. Friedrich Winkler, *Die Zeichnungen Albrecht Dürers* (Berlin, 1939), 4:No. 890.

22. Springer, *Albrecht Dürer,* p. 153.

23. Rudolf Wustmann, *Albrecht Dürer,* 2d ed. (Leipzig, 1929), p. 91.

24. Erwin Panofsky, *Albrecht Dürer* (Princeton, N.J., 1948), I:225 ff.; Panofsky's interpretation has also influenced Kurt Martin, *Albrecht Dürer,* pp. 21 ff.; and Herbert von Einem, "Dürers 'Vier Apostel,'" *Anzeiger des Germanischen Nationalmuseums* (1969), p. 89.

25. Wölfflin, *Die Kunst Albrecht Dürers,* p. 346.

26. Panofsky, "Zwei Dürerprobleme," p. 40.

27. Rupprich, *Nachlass,* 1:117.

28. In the RB, No. 13, fol. 158, there is recorded for Saturday, October 6, that Dürer had "painted" (and delivered) "a panel with four pictures to his memory" ("ein tafel mit vier Bilden zue seyner gedechtnus gemalt"). The marginal gloss was later added: "Gedechtnus Albrecht Dürers kunst" (memory of Albrecht Dürers art). Also in the negotiations of the year 1627, in which the council sought to prevent the surrender of the panels to Maximilian I of Bavaria, it refers to Dürer's endowment that will serve his memory in his Bavarian hometown. StAN, S.I L. 148, No. 26.

29. Rupprich, *Nachlass,* p. 86.

30. H. Merz, *Kunstblatt,* pp. 29 ff.; Engelhard, "Albrecht Dürer," p. 189.

31. Heidrich, *Dürer und die Reformation,* p. 1.

32. Ibid., p. 39.

33. Friedrich Winkler, *Albrecht Dürer, Leben und Werk* (Berlin, 1957), p. 335, writes in a similar vein as von Einem that Dürer viewed the foundation of the civic social order as threatened by the forces that the Reformation had unleashed.

34. "Geschichtliche Entwicklung (Frankens) vom 15. Jahrhundert bis 1815," *Franken, Land, Volk, Geschichte und Wirtschaft,* 2 (Nürnberg, 1959):79.

35. This was challenged already by Theodor Kolde, "Hans Denck und die gottlosen Maler von Nürnberg," *Beiträge zur bayerischen Kirchengeschichte* 8 (1902):21 f.

36. Adolf Rosenberg, *Sebald und Barthel Beham* (Leipzig, 1875), p. 5. Concerning the Behaims' plagiarism at Dürer's expense, see Rupprich, *Nachlass,* pp. 311 f.; in the proceedings of the trial the painters name Hans Denck as their teacher.

37. Joseph Baader, *Beiträge zur Kunstgeschichte Nürnbergs,* 1:9.

38. Georg Baring, "Hans Denck und Thomas Müntzer in Nürnberg," *ARG,* 50 (1959):147.

39. The dedication by Carlstadt now in Rupprich, *Nachlass*, pp. 92 f.; in addition pp. 264 f. Concerning Carlstadt, see Hermann Barge, *Realencyclopädie für prot. Theologie*, 13 (Leipzig, 1903), especially p. 75, and the same in *Religion in Geschichte und Gegenwart* 2d ed. (Tübingen, 1929), 3:634.

40. Heidrich, *Dürer und die Reformation*, p. 9.

41. Gerhard Pfeiffer, *Quellen zur Nürnberger Reformationsgeschichte* (Nürnberg, 1968), RV 363; Dürer had been a *Genannter* since 1509, and therefore a member of the large council.

42. Rupprich, *Nachlass*, 1:214 f.

43. Wilhelm Stolze, *Der deutsche Bauernkrieg* (Halle, 1907), pp. 137 ff. Martin Gückel, *Beiträge zur Geschichte der Stadt Forchheim im 16. Jahrhundert* (Schulprogramm, Bamberg, 1898), p. 31. Rudolf Endres, "Probleme des Bauernkrieges in Franken," *Jahrbuch für fränkische Landesforschung* 31 (1971).

44. Pfeiffer, *Quellen*, RV 736.

45. Ibid., Brief 231.

46. Ibid., Brief 232.

47. On June 4, the battle of Ingolstadt and Giebelstadt; see Günther Franz, *Der deutsche Bauernkrieg* (Darmstadt, 1956), pp. 206 f.

48. City of Nürnberg to Mühlhausen, Pfeiffer, Brief 225; see also Brief 209, 227, 288; Walter P. Fuchs, *Akten zur Geschichte des Bauernkrieges in Mitteldeutschland*, 2 (1942); No. 1597; Günther Franz, *Quellen zur Geschichte des Bauernkrieges*, No. 99; Dürer was familiar with the position of the council not only from its proclamations but also because the *Genannten* were informed by the city council (StAN RB, No. 13, fol. 1).

49. Scheffler-Henner, *Die Geschichte des Bauernkrieges in Ostfranken vom Magister Lorenz Fries* (Würzburg, 1883), pp. 2 f.; Renate Maria Radbruch, *Der deutsche Bauernstand zwischen Mittelalter und Neuzeit* (Munich, 1941), cites on pp. 19 f. the verse: Whoever does not die in the year 1523, does not perish in the water in the year 1524, and is not slain in 1525, can surely speak of wonders.

50. In the third booklet: *Von den körperlichen Dingen*; see an abridged edition by Alfred Peltzer (Munich, 1908).

51. Thus, Pianzola, *Peintres et vilains* (Paris, 1962), pp. 89 f.; Wilhelm Fraenger, "Düres Gedächtnissäule für den Bauernkrieg," *Albrecht Dürer: die künstlerische Entwicklung eines grossen Meisters* (Berlin, 1954), pp. 86 ff. The same in *Beiträger zur sprachlichen Volksüberlieferung* (Berlin, 1953).

52. StAN, RB, No. 13, fol. 80, 86.

53. R. von Rettberg, *Nürnbergs Kunstleben* (Stuttgart, 1854), p. 117.

54. Ibid., p. 76.

55. Ibid., p. 350.

56. Wilhelm Waetzold, *Dürer und seine Zeit* (London, 1938), p. 250.

57. Winkler, *Albrecht Dürer*, p. 333.

58. Georg Theodor Strobel, *Nachricht von Melanchthons öfterm Aufenthalt und Verrichtungen in Nürnberg* (Altdorf, 1774); Georg Wolfgang Karl Lochner, *Philipp Melanchthon und das Gymnasium zu Nürnberg* (Nürnberg, 1853); Heinrich Wilhelm Heerwagen, *Zur Geschichte der Nürnberger Gelehrtenschulen* (Nürnberg, 1860); Karl Hartfelder, *Philipp Melanchthon als Praeceptor Germaniae* (Berlin, 1889).

59. Pfeiffer, *Quellen*, RV 183.

60. Cf., e.g., *CR*, 1:664, No. 282; concerning Hieronymus Paumgartner, see Otto Puchner, *Neue Deutsche Biographie*, 1:664.

61. *Corpus Reformatorum*, 1:678, No. 291.

62. Otto Clemen, *Supplementa Melanchthoniana*, 1 (Leipzig, 1926):301, No. 335b.

63. *CR*, 1:759, No. 758.

64. Reprint of the mandate also in Strobel, *Nachricht*, p. 23.

65. Speech printed in *CR*, 11:column 106 ff.; discussed in Paul Tschackert, *Melanchthons Bildungsideale* (Göttingen, 1897), p. 12.

66. The school ordinance is in Karl Hartfelder, *Melanchthoniana Paedagogica* (Leipzig, 1892), pp. 7 ff.

67. StAN Y 102 (Copy). Eobanus Hessus also stresses in his *Consolatio paraenetica in afflictam bellis intestinis Germaniam* and in a section of the *Norimberga illustrata* about the *schola nuper instituta* the idea that the internal confusion would be overcome by true education.

68. An obviously reworked later cast is in the Germanisches Nationalmuseum, Nürnberg; cf. Georg Habich, *Die deutschen Schaumünzen des XVI. Jahrhunderts* (Munich, 1934), vol. 2, Pt. 2, No. 3262, size 29 mm.; the piece that was earlier located in the Rosenheim collection could not be traced for me by the British Museum.

69. Modern reproduction in Paul Grotemeyer, *Da ich het die Gestalt* (Munich, 1957), plate 59.

70. G. W. Panzer, *Verzeichnis von Nürnbergischen Portraiten* (Nürnberg, 1970), p. 204; Karlheinz Goldmann, *Melanchthon und Nürnberg. Ausstellung aus Anlass der 400. Wiederkehr seines Todestages* (1960), No. 65c.

71. Cf. Leopold Kaufmann, *Albrecht Dürer* (Cologne, 1881).

72. Stuhlfauth, p. 844; meant is the wood-cut, e.g. in Johann Jahn, *Lucas Cranach als Graphiker* (Leipzig, 1955), p. 104.

73. von Einem; Martin; Michel Hofmann, "Joachim Camerarius in der Maske des Apostels Paulus," *Fränkische Blätter* 13 (1961):35 f.; Carl C. Christensen, "Dürer's '4 Apostles' and the Dedication as a Form of Renaissance Art Patronage," *Renaissance Quarterly* 20 (1967):325–34.

74. Springer, *Albrecht Dürer*, p. 155.

75. Neumann, "Die Vier Aposteln," p. 452.

76. Waetzold, *Dürer und seine Zeit*, pp. 248, 249.

77. Winkler, *Albrecht Dürer*, p. 335. Springer had already stated (p. 155) that for the figure of Peter, Dürer had "borrowed the essential features by spying on nature." Elfried Bock, "Dürers Zeichnungen zu den Münchner Aposteln," *Kunstchronik* 58 (1923):284, asked: "The figure of Mark is surely no model-study?" Markus Zucker, *Albrecht Dürer*, p. 140, sees in the Four Apostles "entirely free imaginative creations of his artist's phantasy."

78. Rupprich, *Nachlass*, p. 289, following *CR*, 6:No. 3666 (Report of December 17, 1547, to Georg von Anhalt). Rupprich, *Nachlass*, following *CR*, 8:855 (Report to Hardenberg). Also, Thausing, *Dürer*, p. 285; Hans W. Singer, *Albrecht Dürer* (Munich, 1918), p. 41, circumscribes Dürer's conception in his old age to the effect that "the final art lines in facsimilization."

79. Concerning the position of the pupil in the corner of the eye, cf. Elfried Bock, "Dürers Zeichnungen," p. 280; C. Neumann, "Die Vier Aposteln," p. 451.

80. Caspar Peucer, *Tractatus historicus de clarissimi viri Ph. Melanchthonis sententia de controversia coenae Domini* (Amberg, 1596), p. 11.

81. Wilhelm Krag, *Die Paumgartner von Nürnberg und Augsburg* (Munich, 1919), p. 26.

82. Rupprich, *Nachlass*, p. 275, No. 98 and p. 276, No. 100; *CR*, 1:803, No. 389; and 805, No. 391 (Report of July 2 and 12, 1526).

83. Rupprich, *Nachlass*, p. 276; *CR*, 1:815, No. 404.

84. *WA, Tischreden*, 2:No. 1245.

85. Perhaps even ill-feeling lasted for a time between Dürer and Melanchthon: the name Dürer disappears in the period that followed from Melanchthon's correspondence (exception: undated letter, Rupprich, *Nachlass*, p. 279, No. 118), and Melanchthon received the news of Dürer's death very coolly (ibid., p. 281, No. 127). In 1527 he conveys his greetings, in distinction to his earlier habit, only to Eobanus Hessus and Michael Roting, not to Dürer, *CR*, 1:855, No. 431.

86. Voll, "Dürers Vier Aposteln," p. 75; concerning recent investigations based on art technology and x-rays, cf. Martin, *Albrecht Dürer*, pp. 21, 23.

87. Here belongs also the much noted exchange of opinions between Melanchthon and the abbess of the Nürnberg convent of Saint Clara, Charitas Pirckheimer. Cf. now the new edition of the *Denkwürdigkeiten* of Charitas done by Josef Pfanner (Landshut, 1962), pp. 131–2.

88. Winkler, *Zeichnungen*, p. 873.

89. The hypothesis of Voll and Panofsky of a later addition of Mark and Peter seems to be untenable according to Martin's statements.

90. G. Pfeiffer, "Albrecht Dürer und Lazarus Spengler," *Festschrift Max Spindler* (Munich, 1969), pp. 396 ff.

91. StAN. RB, No. 13, fol. 115, 117.

92. Ibid., No. 13, fol. 114.

93. E. Hartmann, *Beiträge zur Sprache Albrecht Dürers*. Ph.D. diss. (Halle, 1922, p. 26. The ending "ent" (-end) used by Dürer as second person plural imperative, Rupprich, *Nachlass*, 1:49, 86: *wissent*! pp. 44, 49, 53; *sagent*! Alongside these forms are found imperative forms without "n"; *wisset* (ibid., 1:64, 67; ibid., *nembet* for High German *nehmt*!) *gedenkt* (ibid., 1:37). But third person plural present tense, p. 172: *ligent; tund (tunt)* pp. 102, 103, 135; *ferstend* (=*verstehen*) p. 46; *hand* pp. 52 and 58; *gand, geend*, pp. 126, 205, and 209, *stend* (ibid., 2:60). As a present participle in Dürer's letter to the council of early October, 1526, on the occasion of the presentation of the paintings: *derhalb ich auch die selben . . . pittent*. As a present participle also *dienent* (ibid., 2:91). Perhaps the final word can be said after Dürer's language is fed into the Erlangen computer, which gives hope certainly for a judgment about the validity of the "Lutherklage" in Dürer's diary of his trip to Holland; likewise about the use of epithets for saints in Dürer's writings.

94. Cf. Gerhard Pfeiffer, "Judas Iskarioth auf Lucas Cranachs Altar der Schlosskirche zu Dessau," *Festschrift Karl Oettinger* (Erlangen, 1967):389 ff.

95. Cf. Gottfried Seebass, "Dürers Stellung in der reformatorischen Bewegung," *Albrecht Dürers Umwelt* (Nürnberg, 1971), pp. 119 f.

96. Concerning this concept: Stephan Skalweit, *Reich und Reformation* (Berlin, 1967), pp. 200 ff. My opinion about the recognition expressed in Dürer's words for the actions for the council is shared also by Seebass, "Dürers Stellung," p .120.

97. *Die fränkischen Bekenntnisse*, ed. Wilhelm F. Schmidt and Karl Schornbaum (Munich, 1930), p. 433; Hans Sachs, *Werke*, ed. H. Keller ("Bibliothek des literarischen Vereins Stuttgart," vol. 201; Stuttgart, 1843), p. 7; *WA*, 17:Pt. 1, No. 35.

98. Pfeiffer, *Quellen*, p. 140.

99. *Die fränkischen Bekenntnisse*, p. 351.

100. Erasmus, *Opera*, (Hildesheim, 1962), 5:112.

101. Hans Sachs, *Werke*, p. 507.

102. Seebass's work might well, in my opinion, warn for the future away from factional, broad, sweeping judgments as being anachronistic. Judgments like that of Georg Weise, *Dürer und die Ideale der Humanisten* (Tübingen, 1953), pp. 46 ff. are, one might suppose, surely antiquated. He stated that it was well known "that Dürer, in spite of his initial enthusiasm for the appearance of Luther, did not adhere to the Reformation." Also Heinrich Lutz, "Albrecht Dürer und die Reformation," *Miscellanea Bibliothecae Hertzianae* (Munich, 1961), pp. 175 ff.

103. Pfeiffer, *Quellen*, pp. 131 f., 140 f., 452 f., still in the entry in the Ratsbuch for June 6, 1525 (Pfeiffer, p. 98) the notation that nuns' habits produce "sects which lead the faithful astray."

104. Pfeiffer, *Quellen*, Brief 115.

105. Also *WA, Briefwechsel*, 4:98 (of March 27, 1526), 1032 (of August 11, 1526); Seebass, "Dürers Stellung," p. 121, simplifies too much.

106. Waldemar Kawerau, *Hans Sachs und die Reformation* (Halle, 1889), pp. 46 ff.: Hans Sachs' "gesprech eynes euangelischen Christen mit einem Lutherischen." Cf. also the letter from Heinrich Stromer to Pirckheimer of October 2, 1525 (Pfeiffer, *Quellen*, Brief 259): Mihi tamen persuadeo nunnullos vestros non modo verbis, sed et opere esse Christianismi professores.

107. Letter of February 4, 1525, from Pirckheimer to Phrygio (Pfeiffer, *Quellen*, Brief 115): quibus vero cauponacionem verbi tam obscenam displicere sensere, in eos egregie declamarunt.

108. Pfeiffer, *Quellen*, Brief 252.

109. Pfeiffer, "Albrecht Dürer und Lazarus Spengler."

110. Krodel, "Nürnberger Humanisten," p. 46.

111. Pfeiffer, *Quellen*, Brief 115.

112. Rupprich, *Nachlass*, 3:311.

113. Ibid., 1:302, 318.

114. Pfeiffer, *Quellen*, passim.

115. Ibid., RV 751.

116. Theodore Kolde, "Thomas Venatorius," *Beiträge zur bayerischen Kirchengeschichte* 13 (1907):193.

117. Rupprich, *Nachlass*, 3:453; Joseph Meder, *Dürer-Katalog* (Vienna, 1932), No. 284.

118. Rupprich, *Nachlass*, 1:312.

119. In the Nürnberg city archive (Stadtarchiv).

120. Cf. Pfeiffer, *Quellen*; and StAN, RB, No. 13.

121. RB, No. 13, fol. 107.

122. An example also in Gottfried Seebass, "Zwei Briefe von Andreas Osiander," *MVGN* 57 (1970):206.

THE SIGNIFICANCE OF THE EPITAPH MONUMENT IN EARLY LUTHERAN ECCLESIASTICAL ART (CA. 1540–1600): SOME SOCIAL AND ICONOGRAPHICAL CONSIDERATIONS

Carl C. Christensen

Although historians generally have noted that Luther and his followers took a less critical view of religious imagery than either the Anabaptists or the founders of the Reformed tradition, very little has been written in English concerning early Lutheran ecclesiastical art. Several types of religious art prevalent in medieval life found continued favor among German Protestants. Building upon the patronage customs of the preceding era, private benefactors continued to provide churches with new altars and altar paintings, ornately carved pulpits, richly decorated rood lofts, stained glass, and wall paintings.[1] But the epitaph constituted by far the largest single group of art monuments installed in Protestant churches in sixteenth-century Germany.[2] As Hans Preuss noted years ago, these works deserve closer study.[3]

The term *epitaph*, as used in German art history, does not refer merely to a written funerary text.[4] An epitaph, rather, is an artistically conceived memorial or monument, honoring the deceased, and normally containing a portrait, the representation of a religious theme, and a commemorative inscription. The epitaph need not stand in close proximity to the place of interment; thus, it serves a different purpose than the burial marker or tomb monument. Frequently one finds both a tombstone and an epitaph in honor of the same individual.

Even today many ancient churches in Protestant areas of Germany still contain large numbers of these epitaphs, a significant number of them deriving from the sixteenth century. The monuments from this early period vary greatly in size, format, placement, and artistic merit. Some consist of little more than plaques adorning a pillar or side wall. Others are ostentatiously elaborate structures, rising as much as twenty-five feet or more in height. Memorials to princely or aristocratic personages typically are of stone, whereas middle-class Lutherans usually preferred the less costly wood construction.[5]

The epitaph was no new invention of the Reformation period; it arose in the later Middle Ages and continued to enjoy widespread popularity in both Protestant and Catholic lands up to the end of the eighteenth century. It was the special conditions resulting from the introduction of the Reformation, however, combined with the growing Renaissance spirit of self-advertisement, which served to make the epitaph the most common type of art endowment in sixteenth-century Lutheran churches.

One reason for the new importance of the epitaph, relative to other forms of ecclesiastical art, can be found in the demise of many of the cultic practices associated with medieval Roman Catholicism. The pious Christian of an earlier period who wished to make a gift to his church could choose from a wide range of possibilities. The custom of endowing commemorative masses for the souls of the dead had created a large need for supplementary or side altars—not to mention the complete furnishings of those chantry chapels that lined the walls of many of the great medieval cathedrals.[6] From an elaborate and dramatic eucharistic ritual there had resulted an almost endless demand for vestments and vessels. Lutheran worship required less in the way of liturgical art.[7] Private masses having been abolished, only one altar—the high altar—normally was needed. Indeed, considering the fact that the first Lutherans usually took over existing church structures, along with their furnishings, they frequently found the problem to be a superabundance rather than a scarcity of ecclesiastical art.

Possibilities for further art endowments, it is true, did not entirely vanish with the coming of the Reformation. There occurred some new church construction, with a resulting need for ecclesiastical furnishings.[8] Then, existing works could be replaced for a variety of reasons. The change in theology brought with it a somewhat altered conception of the importance of certain of the traditional art forms. For example: private donors sometimes responded to the greater emphasis now placed upon preaching by contributing large and impressive pulpits, elaborately carved with sculptural relief in the Renaissance manner.[9] Works, such as altar panels, that in their contents did not conform to Lutheran doctrinal standards might be supplanted with new ones.[10] Aesthetic factors also no doubt played a part. It can be assumed that some sixteenth-century Lutherans, in their desire to adorn God's house with objects of beauty, preferred art works harmonizing with the stylistic tastes of their own time to the inherited monuments. With respect to most of the usual types of eccesiastical art, however, the nature of Lutheran worship placed definite restrictions upon the opportunities for new benefactions. The use of the epitaph monument offered the greatest potential for growth. The number of these memorials that might be installed in a given church was limited only by the physical space available.[11] Indeed, from an aesthetic standpoint, these works perhaps compensated for the earlier side altars and private chapels (at least in the instances where these had been removed).[12]

It was not difficult to find theological justification for the use of epitaph monuments in the churches. Luther, especially in his later career, had warmly endorsed the legitimacy of Christian art.[13] He valued particularly its potential contribution to religious pedagogy. Along with altar paintings and other art forms, the epitaphs helped to propagate the Lutheran conception of the gospel message.[14] In addition to providing religious instruction and edification to the onlooker, moreover, these funeral memorials also served as a witness to the faith of the donor and gave expression to the eschatological hope of the Christian community.

A survey of the evidence suggests, however, that the intentions of those who provided for the epitaph monuments were not always exclusively pious in nature. The sixteenth century in Germany witnessed not only the religious revival of the Reformation but also the spread and popularization of secular Renaissance ideals. Panofsky has shown that funerary art reflects as clearly as any other the heightened sense of individual worth and the increased concern for personal glory that the classical revival brought with it.[15] The tomb sculpture of the primitive Christian church had avoided eulogistic elements; it was "prospective," rather than "retrospective," to use Panofsky's suggestive terms. It "emphasized not what the deceased had been or done but what would happen to him on account of his faith."[16] The more extreme examples of Renaissance sepulchral art, on the other hand, seem to suggest that some individuals now were as much concerned to achieve worldly immortality (in the form of enduring fame) as Christian salvation. The mundane spirit was not entirely lacking in sixteenth-century German Lutheranism, as later examples will suffice to show.

We begin our analysis with a survey of the religious subject matter of the paintings and relief sculpture forming the main composition or central panel of the epitaphs.[17] The first point to be noted is that the religious themes usually are scriptural in inspiration.[18] In the context of the Reformation, with its strong emphasis upon *sola scriptura*, religious art meant essentially biblical art.

Among the various themes depicted, the most numerous appear to be those of the Crucifixion of Christ, or a Crucifix (the two are not always easy to distinguish, due to the practice of including contemporary portraits, sixteenth-century clothing, and German landscape backgrounds in both types). The Crucifixion was a traditional theme, of course, in Christian funerary art. For early Lutherans, the event took its greatest significance from the fact that the atoning death of Christ stood as the necessary prerequisite for personal salvation.[19] As the Wittenberg Reformer expressed it in his widely used[20] *Small Catechism*: "I believed that Jesus Christ, . . . has redeemed me, a lost and condemned creature, delivered me and freed me from all sins, from death, and from the power of the devil, not with silver and gold but with his holy and precious blood and with his innocent sufferings and death."[21]

The Resurrection of Christ and Christ as the triumphantly Resurrected One are also very common themes on early Lutheran epitaphs. In Luther's theology the expectation of a life beyond death had always been based on the fact of the resurrection of Christ.[22]

He liked to remark that the Christian's own resurrection is more than half accomplished already, through that of Christ, the Head.[23] The motif, to be sure, could claim no novelty; it had been commonly employed on epitaphs in the later Middle Ages.

A number of compositions, on the other hand, draw their inspiration from Luther's own distinctive emphasis upon the contrast between the judgment of the Law and the blessings of the gospel.[24] This theme has been given various names by art historians: The Law and the Gospel; the Allegory of Law and Grace; The Fall and Salvation. The motif was a very popular one in early Lutheran circles, and can be found on everything from altar panels to carved bridal chests. It had its origin in a collaboration between Luther and Lucas Cranach the Elder (1472–1553) and can, with some justification, be called a uniquely Lutheran contribution to the iconographical tradition of Christian art.[25] The treatment of the theme varies somewhat from work to work, but all derive their basic inspiration ultimately from a panel now in a museum in Gotha, painted in 1529. This prototype shows the picture space divided down the middle by a tree, barren on the left and fruitful on the right. The left side of the panel contains scenes of the Fall of Man; the Hebrew Encampment in the Wilderness and the Brazen Serpent; Moses with the Tablets of the Law; Old Testament Prophets; Christ as Judge of the World; and the Pursuit of Fallen Man by Death and Satan—all reminders of man's lost condition and alienation from God. The right side portrays the Annunciation to the Shepherds; the Resurrected Christ; and the Triumph of the Lamb of God over the prostrate figures of Death and Satan—all symbols of man's salvation. Near the center there appears the figure of Saint John the Baptist directing the attention of naked "representative man" to the saving gospel events at the right. As a virtual summary, in pictorial form, of the Lutheran understanding of the message of the Christian faith, the Law and Gospel theme found appropriate use also on epitaphs, where it consoled the bereaved and warned the indifferent of the fate of those who died under the Law and without coming to an acceptance of the Gospel.

Christ Blessing the Children, another typically Lutheran theme, adorns a group of epitaphs commemorating children who had expired in their infancy or early childhood. Lucas Cranach the Elder (drawing upon the passage from Saint Matthew 19: 13–15: "Let the children come to me, and do not hinder them."[26]) originated the archetypal representation of this subject also, with his panels characteristically depicting Jesus holding an infant in his arms, while indicating his sympathy and favor toward the circle of mothers and children who press in about him. The author of an important study on early Protestant iconography argues that the sudden prominence of this theme in Reformation art derives primarily from the concern of the Lutherans to buttress and give visual expression to their arguments in favor of retaining infant baptism.[27] Quite apart from any such polemical purpose, however, it should be noted that this biblical episode, with its emphasis upon the especial receptivity of Jesus to little children, must have seemed particularly appropriate for this type of funerary monument.

One subject used in early Lutheran epitaph art presents slightly more difficulty in interpretation: the portrayal of the Baptism of Christ. The relevance of this event to death perhaps is not immediately apparent. As an artistic motif it was employed in the early and medieval church as a standard symbol of the trinitarian doctrine ("It had the advantage of being supported by a phrase of the Gospels which affirms that at the moment of the baptism of Jesus there was a simultaneous theophany of the three Persons: the voice of God the Father was heard descending from heaven; God the Son stood in the waters of the Jordan; and God the Holy Ghost appeared as a dove hovering over the Son.")[28] It is not impossible that the intention here too may have been to affirm Lutheran orthodoxy with respect to another doctrine that was being challenged by a few of the more radical spirits in the Left Wing of the Reformation.[29]

But the Baptism of Christ scene also can be more directly related to the eschatological hope associated with death in Christian theology. From the very beginning of Christian art this event had been understood as the prototype for all later baptisms.[30] And the sacrament of baptism itself, of course, signified for the Christian the ultimate promise of eternal salvation; in his *Small Catechism* Luther includes in the section on baptism the verse from the Gospel of Saint Mark (16:16): "He who believes and is baptized will be saved."[31]

In that same section of the *Small Catechism*, however, the Reformer provides what well may be another reason for the use of the Baptism of Christ motif on several epitaphs. He quotes directly from Saint Paul's letter to the Romans (6:4): "We were buried therefore with him by baptism into death, so that as Christ was raised from the dead by the glory of the Father, we too might walk in newness of life."[32] Thus, the themes of baptism and death are linked together in a much more than purely formal manner. Luther's meaning is made even clearer by his discussion of the matter in his 1520 tract *The Babylonian Captivity of the Church*: "Baptism, then, signifies two things—death and resurrection, that is, full and complete justification. When the minister immerses the child in the water it signifies death, and when he draws it forth again it signifies life."[33] Further, the Reformer strongly emphasizes that baptism is not merely a once-in-a-lifetime event which loses its significance as the believer progresses in the faith. The Christian lives his entire life in his baptism and then dies in its promise: "The sooner we depart this life, the more speedily we fulfill our baptism."[34] Death also is the fulfillment of God's promise made to the Christian in his baptism, in that his sin is finally and completely put to death.[35] It seems reasonable, therefore, to view the epitaph representations of the Baptism of Christ as an interesting manifestation of the influence of Luther's Pauline theology even upon the iconography of funerary monuments.[36]

The theme of the Raising of Lazarus is not uncommon on early Lutheran epitaphs. This story of Jesus restoring a deceased man to life constituted for the church an important New Testament prefiguration of the resurrection of the dead;[37] the motif had appeared in Christian burial art from a very early date.[38] The biblical passage describing this event, quite appropriately, was one of those most commonly read at Lutheran funeral services in sixteenth-century Germany.[39]

The ultimate significance of death for the individual's eternal destiny is suggested in some works by the depicting of the Last Judgment. The Augsburg Confession (1530), major creedal

statement of the Lutheran church, had devoted a separate article to this doctrine (Article 17):

> Our churches also teach that at the consummation of the world Christ
> will appear for judgment and will raise up all the dead. To the godly
> and elect he will give eternal life and endless joy, but ungodly men
> and devils he will condemn to be tormented without end.[40]

The motif itself, to be sure, was another of those inherited from
earlier funerary art.[41]

Various other biblical themes also appear as the major composition on early Lutheran epitaphs. Among them there might
be mentioned several portraying events associated with the Incarnation, or Birth of Christ: the Annunciation; the Nativity;
the Adoration of the Shepherds; and the Presentation in the
Temple. Other episodes in the Passion of Christ (besides the
Crucifixion) are depicted: the Agony in the Garden of Gethse-
mane; Christ Carrying the Cross; the Entombment of Christ.

An occasional Old Testament motif also can be found (the
Fall; the Expulsion from the Garden of Eden; the Flood; etc.),
but these are more frequently used on the secondary panels of
large epitaphs, a practice that perhaps might be thought of as
maintaining the medieval tradition of the concordance of the
Old and New Testaments:[42] scenes from the Creation; the Tree
of Life; Jacob's Dream; the Brazen Serpent; Ezekiel's Vision of
the Valley of Dry Bones; Jonah and the Whale; and others.[43]

Monuments with more than one tier frequently display as the
subject matter of their upper panel the scene of the Ascension
of Christ—an unusually apt selection from both a stylistic and
theological point of view.

On a number of early Lutheran epitaphs one also finds auxil-
iary figures representing or personifying the theological virtues:
Faith; Hope; and Charity or Love. Only slightly less popular
were the moral virtues, such as: Justice; Wisdom or Prudence;
Fortitude; and others. Renaissance usage tended to impart to
the latter group a rather secular function, employing them as
"character witnesses" to "enhance the merits" of worldly men
—instead of as testimony to the piety of the godly deceased.[44]

Early Lutherans perhaps intended them to suggest God-given graces rather than purely personal attributes.[45]

The religious subject matter of the paintings or relief sculpture frequently is elaborated upon in the inscriptions provided for these epitaphs. Scriptural passages are directly quoted in some instances and often serve to explicate the theme represented in the art composition. Many of the German texts, in particular, contain explicit reference to the hope of personal resurrection. A very common feature also is the petition, offered by the family or donors of the epitaph, that God might be gracious unto the soul of the departed. The onlooker, on the other hand, may be cautioned to reflect on the fact that one day he too will have to confront death ("Hodie mihi, cras tibi").

The content of the inscriptions is not always exclusively religious in character, however. Often the texts reflect in a rather obvious way important sociological factors underlying the donation of these works. A concrete example helps to make the point clear. In 1558 the widow of Michael Meyenburg, syndic and burgomaster of the free imperial city of Nordhausen, commissioned Lucas Cranach the Younger (1515–86) to paint an epitaph in honor of her deceased spouse. The monument consisted of two panels: the painting, and a separate inscription plaque.[46] Both are very revealing historical documents. The painting has as its major theme a representation of the Raising of Lazarus. In addition to the central participants and a circle of spectators, there stands off to the left a group made up of Luther, Melanchthon, Erasmus, and several of the lesser-known leaders of the German reform movement.[47] The deceased, his two wives, and their children, all portrayed in a kneeling position, appear in a row in the foreground. Finally, there is displayed rather prominently at the very base of the panel the coats of arms of Meyenburg and his two spouses.

The portraits of the Reformers in this composition probably were intended, in part at least, as a testimonial of the close personal relationship between several of them and the deceased. Although his friendship with Luther had cooled considerably in later years, Meyenburg knew the German prophet and even had hosted him in his home once in the 1520s.[48] Justus Jonas, another of the Lutheran Reformers portrayed here, originated from Nordhausen and also was a friend.[49] But, it was with Philip Melanchthon, above all, that the humanistically inclined municipal official had close personal contacts. The latter relied heavily upon Melanchthon over the decades for advice upon how to steer his city safely through the religious controversies and political crises of the period. When the famous professor was forced to abandon Wittenberg for a time during the Schmalkaldic War, he found asylum in Meyenburg's home. Melanchthon provided counsel concerning the education of his friend's sons. This long friendship finally resulted in a 1558 marriage between Meyenburg's son and the granddaughter of Melanchthon—an event that the Nordhausen syndic did not live to see.[50]

The painting's suggestion of his close personal relationships with the great men of his time reflects considerable honor upon Meyenburg. This note of individual importance is further accentuated by the prominence of his own portrait in the center foreground and the easy visibility of his family's armorial bearings in the composition. The rather secular attitudes or values manifested by these features of the painting are rendered most explicit, however, by the attached Latin inscription.[51] Even when allowance is made for the customary humanistic rhetorical flourish, this eulogy must be viewed as a remarkable example of the glorification of the deceased. The only references to religion are those that laud Meyenburg as a God-fearing man and defender of the true faith. On the other hand, we are reminded, in a rather pointed fashion, of his close friendship with Melanchthon; of his numerous and inimitable services to his city; of the high regard in which he was held by the emperor and the imperial government; and of his sterling character and unimpeachable integrity. The writer finally concludes with the bombastic assertion that if such a man's fame and reputation were to be interred, all the world would demand to be buried with him.

The apparent incongruity between worldly pride and Christian piety is suggested in a particularly sharp fashion by this monument—and thus it should not be considered as entirely typical. But the basic contrast appears in many of the early Lutheran epitaphs. Among the inscriptions, those with a Latin text manifest a secular or Renaissance spirit much more noticeably than their more sober German counterparts. The Latin memorials, in fact, often derived from the pen of a prominent local humanist;[52] in some cases they are even signed.[53] The revived classical tongue provided a rich store of laudatory adjectives with which to describe the deceased: *clarissimus, eximius, spectabilis, ornatissimus, praestantissimus, illustrissimus, venerabilis*, and so on. The German texts, though usually less flamboyant, frequently contain more or less equivalent expressions: *wohlweise, tugentsam, ehrbar*, and the like. Aside from official titles there also can be found occasional direct references to social class.

The writers of the inscriptions in some instances make specific mention of the meritorious deeds or generosity of the person honored. The epitaph for Duchess Dorothy Susanna of Saxony (d. 1592) proclaims that she had been a patroness of the church and refuge of the poor.[54] That of Duke John Frederick III of Saxony (d. 1565) extols his zeal for the preservation of orthodox (Protestant) religion in his lands.[55] A panel honoring the pastor Peter von Friemersheim of Lübeck (d. 1574) praises him as the first to preach the restored gospel in his church.[56] Gifts or bequests made by the decedent sometimes are recorded. Thus, the epitaph for the Flensburg merchant, Gerdt van Merfeldt (d. 1597), carefully notes that he had bequeathed a "well-earned and honorable" sum of 25,000 marks for the support of students and the needy.[57]

Aside from the inscriptions, the element of personal or family pride is reflected in other ways.[58] First of all, the works generally contain portraits, foremost of the departed, but often also of his family. In primitive Christian funerary art the use of the portrait apparently arose from the rather naïve wish to provide an aid in the identifying of the deceased upon the day of resurrection.[59] Since the sixteenth-century epitaph, more often than not, stood physically removed from the burial site, this no longer could be the motive. The funerary effigy, in fact, had come to assume something of the nature of an ordinary donor portrait.[60] Although it is true that the rather worldly effect resulting from

the use of personal likenesses on these epitaphs could be,[61] and
in many cases was, mitigated by portraying the decedent in an
attitude of prayer—often kneeling before a crucifix—one cannot overlook the well-known significance of the portrait as an
indicator of the heightened Renaissance sense of individual
worth.

The widespread use of armorial bearings—even on memorials
to middle-class individuals—provides further tangible evidence
of the frequent intrusion of a somewhat mundane spirit.[62] The
coat of arms, often fairly conspicuous in its size and placement
on the monument, served publicly to identify the deceased and
his family.[63] The application of these heraldic devices no doubt
should be interpreted, in part, as a reflection of the prevalent
view of ecclesiastical endowments as remaining, in some sense,
private or family property.[64] But by the time of the Reformation, the provision of all types of ecclesiastical art—suitably em-
blazoned with the familial insignia—had long since become established as a more or less socially acceptable way in which to
advertise wealth and social standing.[65]

Yet even though the displaying of armorial bearings upon
gifts of art works to the church had become a traditional practice, it is significant that already in the later Middle Ages a few
of the more spiritually sensitive observers had begun to com-
plain of the vanity and ostentation inevitably suggested by these
ornaments.[66] Indeed, the practice does seem to have been carried to excessive lengths: there are Lutheran examples from the
sixteenth century of a conspicuous placing of the donor's coat of
arms even upon the very pulpit from which the Word of God
was proclaimed.[67] Luther himself once expressed some reservations concerning the adorning of burial sites with armorial
bearings.[68]

Having surveyed both the religious subject matter and the
more secular features of these epitaphs, it might be well to ask,
finally, if there is any possible harmonizing of the two. Within
the context of sixteenth-century thought and practice, the answer is, to some degree at least, yes. For example, with respect
to the eulogistic inscriptions, it should be pointed out that in

some early Lutheran circles the practice of celebrating the merits of the deceased was considered to be theologically justifiable. The instructions for burial services provided in sixteenth-century church ordinances (*Kirchenordnungen*) in some instances allowed for the commemoration of an individual's virtues, as long as the remarks were kept within a properly Christian framework. The good works of the departed were not to be extolled for their own sake, but as a sign of the presence and working of God's grace—as the fruits of a justifying faith.[69] Thus, the Lutheran of that era apparently could accept as tolerable within the church that which is likely to strike the modern viewer as a somewhat incongruous mixture of the spiritual and the mundane. One is reminded of the statement contained in the otherwise highly laudatory inscription for an imposing epitaph monument in the City Church of Wittenberg—the site of much of Luther's most effective preaching in an earlier day: "Every virtue, every wisdom of the world, without God, however great, is inimical to God."[70]

1. This observation is based upon personal inspection of a large number of German churches, plus examination of relevant volumes of those great multivolume sets of inventories of surviving art and historical monuments compiled for most regions of that country (for specific examples, see the following footnote).

2. The following study of the early Lutheran epitaph derives from careful analysis of approximately seventy examples of this particular art genre, dating from ca. 1540–1600 and drawn from churches and museums in about a dozen towns and cities widely distributed over the Protestant portions of Reformation Germany. For supplementary documentation, I relied upon the following: Gustav Schönermark, *Beschreibende Darstellung der älteren Bau- und Kunstdenkmäler der Provinz Sachsen*, New Series, Vol. 1: *Die Stadt Halle und der Saalkreis* (Halle a. d. S., 1886); Hermann Grössler and Adolf Brinkmann, *Beschreibende Darstellung der älteren Bau- und Kunstdenkmäler der Provinz Sachsen*, vol. 19: *Der Mansfelder Seekreis* (Halle a. d. S., 1895); Cornelius Gurlitt, *Beschreibende Darstellung der älteren Bau- und Kunstdenkmäler des Königreichs Sachsen*, vol. 17: *Stadt Leipzig* (Dresden, 1895); Karl Becker *et al.*, *Die Kunstdenkmale der Provinz Sachsen*, vol. 1: *Die Stadt Erfurt* (Burg, 1929); Paul Lehfeldt, *Bau- und Kunst-Denkmäler Thüringens, Grossherzogthum Sachsen-Weimar-Eisenach*, vol. 1: *Verwaltungsbezirk Weimar* (Jena, 1893); Theodor Goecke, *Die Kunstdenkmäler der Provinz Brandenburg*, vol. 2, part 3: *Stadt und Dom Brandenburg* (Berlin, 1912); Theodor Goecke, *Die Kunstdenkmäler der Provinz Brandenburg*, vol. 6, part 2: *Stadt Frankfurt a. O.* (Berlin, 1912); Ludwig Rohling, *Die Kunstdenkmäler des Landes Schleswig-Holstein*, vol. 7: *Die Kunstdenkmäler der Stadt Flensburg* (Munich, 1955); Dietrich Ellger, *Die Kunstdenkmäler des Landes*

Schleswig-Holstein, vol. 10: *Die Kunstdenkmäler der Stadt Schleswig* (Munich, 1966); F. Hirsch, G. Schaumann, and F. Bruns, *Die Bau- und Kunstdenkmäler der Freien und Hansestadt Lübeck*, vol. 2: *Petrikirche, Marienkirche, Heil.-Geist-Hospital* (Lübeck, 1906); J. Baltzer and F. Bruns, *Die Bau- und Kunstdenkmäler der Freien und Hansestadt Lübeck*, vol. 3: *Kirche zu Alt-Lübeck, Dom, Jakobikirche, Ägidienkirche* (Lübeck, 1920); P. J. Meier and K. Steinacker, *Die Bau- und Kunstdenkmäler der Stadt Braunschweig* (Braunschweig, 1926). These works also were useful: Ingrid Schulze, *Die Stadtkirche zu Wittenberg* (Berlin, 1966); Eva Schmidt, *Die Stadtkirche zu St. Peter und Paul in Weimar* (Berlin, 1955); Alfred Overmann, *Die Predigerkirche* (Erfurt, 1928).

3. Hans Preuss, *Die deutsche Frömmigkeit im Spiegel der bildenden Kunst* (Berlin, 1926), p. 228.

4. For an excellent general article on the epitaph monument, see Paul Schoenen, "Epitaph," *Reallexikon zur deutschen Kunstgeschichte*, ed. Ludwig Heinrich Heydenreich and Karl-August Wirth, 5 (1967): cols. 872–921. There are also some useful comments in Erwin Panofsky, *Tomb Sculpture* (New York, n.d.), p. 55 and passim.

5. For the purposes of this paper it has not seemed necessary to elaborate upon the distinctions usually made between the various social groups under consideration here. The German Protestant princes, lesser nobility, and urban patrician class—however different they may have been in other ways—all shared a common concern for honor, prestige, and ostentatious public display. Both the landed and urban aristocracies (or at least the more successful elements thereof) seem to have enjoyed an even more exalted social position, if anything, during the second half of the sixteenth century than was true in the later Middle Ages and early Reformation years. For the tendency toward increasingly rigid social stratification in Germany, see Bernd Moeller, *Reichsstadt und Reformation* (Gütersloh, 1962), pp. 71–75; Harold J. Grimm, "The Reformation and the Urban Social Classes in Germany," *Luther, Erasmus and the Reformation*, ed. John C. Olin, James D. Smart, and Robert E. McNally, S.J. (New York, 1969), p. 78; Hajo Holborn, *A History of Modern Germany: 1648–1840* (New York, 1964), pp. 36–39.

6. For late medieval endowments of altars and chapels by the urban patrician and merchant classes in Germany, see Fritz Rörig, *The Medieval Town* (Berkeley, Calif., 1967), p. 131.

7. See Vilmos Vajta, *Luther on Worship: An Interpretation*, trans. U. S. Leupold (Philadelphia, 1958).

8. Friedrich Buchholz, *Protestantismus und Kunst im sechzehnten Jahrhundert* (Halle a. d. S., 1928), pp. 23 ff.

9. Rohling, *Die Kunstdenkmäler*, pp. 98–102, 162–66.

10. For examples of early Lutheran altars, see Oskar Thulin, *Cranach-Altäre der Reformation* (Berlin, n.d.); also Rohling, *Die Kunstdenkmäler*, pp. 90–96.

11. One church (St. Gotthardt's), in the city of Brandenburg, contains yet today nine epitaphs dating from the second half of the sixteenth century.

12. This is suggested by Hans Carl von Haebler, *Das Bild in der evangelischen Kirche* (Berlin, 1957), p. 23. Von Haebler's book contains some useful material on early Lutheran funerary art.

13. See Paul Lehfeldt, *Luthers Verhältnis zu Kunst und Künstlern* (Berlin, 1892); Christian Rogge, *Luther und die Kirchenbilder seiner Zeit* (Leipzig, 1912); Hans Preuss, *Martin Luther: Der Künstler* (Gütersloh, 1931); Hans Frhr. v. Campenhausen, "Die Bilderfrage in der Reformation," *Zeitschrift für Kirchengeschichte* 68 (1957):96–128 and "Zwingli und Luther zur Bilderfrage," *Das*

Gottesbild im Abendland, ed. Günter Howe (Witten and Berlin, 1957), pp. 139–72; Carl C. Christensen, "Luther's Theology and the Uses of Religious Art," *Lutheran Quarterly* 22 (1970):147–65.

14. Ulrich Gertz, *Die Bedeutung der Malerei für die Evangeliumsverkündigung in der evangelischen Kirche des XVI. Jahrhunderts* (Berlin, 1936), passim.

15. Panofsky, *Tomb Sculpture,* p. 67.

16. Ibid., p. 39.

17. For information on the iconography of pre-Reformation epitaphs in Germany, see Schoenen, "Epitaph," cols. 890–903.

18. A content analysis of the subject matter of the compositions found on the central or main panel of the epitaphs here under consideration reveals the following frequency of themes: Crucifixion, or Crucifix—13; Resurrection of Christ, or Christ as the Resurrected One—11; the Law and the Gospel theme—4; Christ Blessing the Children—3; the Baptism of Christ—3; the Raising of Lazarus—3; the Last Judgment—3; various events associated with the Incarnation, or Birth of Christ—5; the Passion of Christ (scenes other than the Crucifixion)—4; assorted Old Testament scenes—4; other religious themes—8; non-religious subject matter (portraits, coats of arms, or inscriptions only)—13. In the small number of instances where an epitaph had more than one major composition of equal size and prominence, rather than a single central panel, the additional compositions were all included separately in this list. It should be remembered that, given the extent and variety of the scriptural writings, the number of possible iconographical themes was very large indeed.

19. For a helpful explanation of Luther's doctrine of the Atonement, see Paul Althaus, *The Theology of Martin Luther,* trans. Robert C. Schultz (Philadelphia, 1966), chap. 17. But note the interesting statement made by Panofsky (p. 43) that where the cross was used on early Christian funerary art it was intended as a symbol not of Christ's death but of his resurrection.

20. Bernd Moeller, "Das religiöse Leben im deutschen Sprachgebiet am Ende des 15. und am Ende des 16. Jahrhunderts," *Comité International des Sciences Historiques, XIIe Congrès International des Sciences Historiques Vienne, 29 août–5 septembre 1965. Rapports III, Commissions* (Vienna, 1965), p. 137; Franz Lau, "La vie religieuse dans les pays protestants de langue allemande à la fin du XVIe siècle," *Colloque d'histoire religieuse Lyon, octobre 1963* (Grenoble, 1963), p. 110.

21. *The Book of Concord: The Confessions of the Evangelical Lutheran Church,* trans. and ed. Theodore G. Tappert (Philadelphia, 1959), p. 345; for the original text, see *Die Bekenntnisschriften der evangelischlutherischen Kirche,* 6th ed. rev. (Göttingen, 1967), p. 511.

22. Althaus, *Martin Luther,* p. 411.

23. Ulrich Asendorf, *Eschatologie bei Luther* (Göttingen, 1967), p. 289.

24. For this aspect of Luther's theology, see Althaus, *Martin Luther,* pp. 251–66.

25. This theme has been given more careful and detailed study than any other in early Lutheran iconography. See Richard Foerster, "Die Bildnisse von Johann Hess und Cranachs 'Gesetz und Gnade'," *Schlesiens Vorzeit: Jahrbuch des schlesischen Museums für Kunstgewerbe und Altertümer,* N.F., 5 (1909): 117–43, 205–6; Karl Ernst Meier, "Fortleben der religiös-dogmatischen Kompositionen Cranachs in der Kunst des Protestantismus," *Repertorium für Kunstwissenschaft,* 32 (1909):415–35; Thulin, *Cranach-Altäre,* pp. 128–48; Donald L. Ehresmann, "The Brazen Serpent: A Reformation Motif in the Works of Lucas Cranach the Elder and His Workshop," *Marsyas* 13 (1966–67):32–47.

26. Revised Standard Version.

27. Christine O. Kibish, "Lucas Cranach's 'Christ Blessing the Children': A Problem of Lutheran Iconography," *Art Bulletin* 37 (1955): 196–203. For this theme, see also Gertrud Schiller, *Ikonographie der christlichen Kunst*, 2d ed. (Gütersloh, 1969), 1:166. On Luther's doctrine of infant baptism, see Jaroslav Pelikan, *Spirit versus Structure: Luther and the Institutions of the Church* (New York, 1968), chap. 4.

28. Andre Grabar, *Christian Iconography: A Study of Its Origins* (Princeton, N.J., 1968), p. 115.

29. It has been pointed out that the Counter-Reformation fully appreciated the Trinitarian implications of this theme. Schiller, *Ikonographie*, 1:152.

30. Ibid., 1, 138.

31. *The Book of Concord*, p. 349; *Die Bekenntnisschriften*, p. 516.

32. Die *Bekenntnisschriften*, p. 517.

33. *LW*, 36:67–68; for the original text, see *WA*, 6:534.

34. *LW*, 36:69; *WA*, 6:535.

35. Althaus, *Martin Luther*, p. 407.

36. Apparently, Luther's view of baptism as the death and resurrection of the believer differed somewhat in emphasis from that of Saint Paul. This point, however, does not seem to me to invalidate the conclusion that I am attempting to draw here. Nor does the fact that the theme can be found also on pre-Reformation epitaphs. For a comparison of Luther and Saint Paul on this question, see Althaus, *Martin Luther*, pp. 356–59.

37. Schiller, *Ikonographie*, 1:190.

38. Grabar, *Christian Iconography*, p. 10.

39. See Aemilius Ludwig Richter, ed., *Die evangelischen Kirchenordnungen des sechzehnten Jahrhunderts* (Nieuwkoop, 1967), 1:366; 2:21, 141, 274.

40. *Book of Concord*, p. 38; *Die Bekenntnisschriften*, p. 72. For the details of Luther's views on the Last Judgment, see Althaus, *Martin Luther*, pp. 414–17.

41. Schoenen, "Epitaph," col. 892.

42. For the concordance of the Old and New Testaments in medieval art, see Émile Mâle, *Religious Art in France: XIII Century. A Study in Mediaeval Iconography and Its Sources of Inspiration*, trans. Dorra Nussey (London, 1913), pp. 140 ff.

43. For the traditional allegorical interpretation of the Jonah episode as a sign or symbol of the resurrection, see George Ferguson, *Signs and Symbols in Christian Art* (New York, 1966), pp. 26, 31.

44. Panofsky, *Tomb Sculpture*, pp. 73–74.

45. See von Haebler, *Das Bild*, p. 29.

46. This epitaph is no longer in existence, having been destroyed in World War II. For an impressive set of detailed photographs of the original, see Thulin, *Cranach-Altäre*, pp. 75–95.

47. It has been suggested that the portraying of the Reformers together with the Raising of Lazarus motif might have been intended, in part at least, as a reference to the revival of the true faith in the Reformation. See Hans Patze and Walter Schlesinger, eds., *Geschichte Thüringens*. Vol. 3: *Das Zeitalter des Humanismus und der Reformation* (Cologne, 1967), p. 342.

48. Ibid., pp. 60, 105; also G. Kawerau, "Meienburg: Michael M.," *Allgemeine Deutsche Biographie*, 52 (Leipzig, 1906):286–87.

49. Kawerau, "Meienburg," p. 286; also Martin Lehmann, *Justus Jonas: Loyal Reformer* (Minneapolis, Minn., 1963), pp. 46, 116.

50. For Meyenburg's relations with Melanchthon, see Kawerau, "Meienburg," pp. 286–87; also Patze and Schlesinger, "Das Zeitalter," pp. 105, 107, 308.

51. I have been unable to secure a copy of the original Latin text; for a modern German translation, see Thulin, "Cranach-Altäre," p. 164.

52. Eva Spitta, "Haltung und Geschichtskreis niederdeutscher Bürger in 15. und 16. Jahrhundert," *Niedersächsisches Jahrbuch für Landesgeschichte*, 16 (1939): 139.

53. Schmidt, *Die Stadtkirche*, p. 110.

54. Ibid., p. 111.

55. Ibid., p. 109.

56. Baltzer and Bruns, *Kirche*, 3:408–9.

57. Rohling, *Die Kunstdenkmäler*, pp. 107–8.

58. This, in spite of the common characterization of early Lutheran art as simple, sober, and unostentatious. See Preuss, *Die deutsche Frömmigkeit*, p. 187; also, Buchholz, *Protestantismus*, pp. 17–18.

59. Panofsky, *Tomb Sculpture*, p. 39.

60. Ibid., p. 55.

61. von Haebler, *Das Bild*, p. 25.

62. For some very suggestive remarks on the social and political significance of titles of honor, and the armorial bearings by which these are symbolized (albeit in a different national setting), see especially the opening pages of the article by Lawrence Stone, "The Inflation of Honours 1558–1641," *Past & Present*, 14 (November, 1958):45–70.

63. Klemens Stadler, "Entwicklung und Recht der Familienwappen," *Schwäbische Blätter für Volksbildung und Heimatpflege*, 5 (1954):2. In Germany, the family continued to be an extremely important social unit in the sixteenth century. See Ermentrude von Ranke, "Der Interessenkreis des deutschen Bürgers im 16. Jahrhundert," *Vierteljahrschrift für Sozial- und Wirtschaftsgeschichte*, 20 (1928):476.

64. Gustav A. Seyler, *Geschichte der Heraldik* (Nürnberg, 1885), pp. 333–37. The donors of ecclesiastical art commonly were considered to retain some sort of property rights to these artifacts: see Charles Garside, Jr., *Zwingli and the Arts* (New Haven, Conn., 1966), pp. 102, 105, 151, 156; also Carl C. Christensen, "Iconoclasm and the Preservation of Ecclesiastical Art in Reformation Nuernberg," *Archiv für Reformationsgeschichte*, 61 (1970): 212, 219.

65. Christensen, "Iconoclasm and the Preservation," pp. 213–14.

66. G. G. Coulton, *Art and the Reformation* (Oxford, 1928), pp. 334–35; also Seyler, *Geschichte der Heraldik*, p. 509.

67. Rohling, *Die Kunstdenkmäler*, pp. 99–100, 163–65. For an imposing Lutheran high altar (1598) bearing prominent bust portraits of the donors, see the same work, pp. 91, 96.

68. Preuss, *Martin Luther*, p. 75.

69. "Und wo der Herr an den verscheiden leuthen etwas besonder genaden in jrem leben vnd sterben bewisen, vnd vns exemple des glaubens fürgestelt, die sollen zum preisz des Herren vnd besserung der gemeinden Gottes, mit mesziger Gotsförchtiger erzelung, gemeldet vnd geprisen, Doch in dem durch die Prediger veissig vffgesehen werdenn, das die den menschen nichts zugefalln redenn, sonder allein aus lauterem hertzen die besserung der kirchenn, mit dem

preisz der gaben Gottes fürderen. . . ." (Richter, *Die evangelischen Kirchenord-nungen*, 2:158).

70. "Omnis enim virtus, omnis sapientia mundi absque deo, quamvis magna, inimica deo est." The epitaph is that of Matthias von der Schulenburg (1571). For the inscription, see Ernst Adolf Zitzlaff, *Die Begräbnisstätten Wittenbergs und ihre Denkmäler* (Wittenberg, 1896), pp. 110–11.

PART THREE: THE ORGANIZATION OF THE REFORMATION

THE LUTHERAN CHURCH OF THE REFORMATION: PROBLEMS OF ITS FORMATION AND ORGANIZATION IN THE MIDDLE AND NORTH GERMAN TERRITORIES

Irmgard Höss

The organizational form of the Lutheran church in Germany from its establishment in the sixteenth century until the fall of the monarchy in 1918 was the so-called territorial church government (*landesherrliches Kirchenregiment*). To be sure, the structure of church government varied from territory to territory; the tendency toward state churches, however, was typical. The close ties of the German Lutheran church to the state, which it preserved beyond the collapse of monarchical power, now appears questionable to the church as a result of the painful experiences of the 1930s. The modern critique echoes in part concerns that Luther expressed toward the end of his life. It overshoots the mark, however, insofar as it sometimes overlooks the fact that the territorial states were the decisive political force in Germany of the sixteenth century. The development of the new church organization was accomplished within the framework of these states even though the delineating of jurisdictions may have remained open in detail. We want to concern ourselves here with the problems of the formation and organization of the Lutheran state church in a few specific cases, and address ourselves to the question of the extent to which the direction of development was inevitable.[1]

In the years after the outbreak of the Reformation, the Augustinian monk and professor of theology at Wittenberg began by denouncing the improper preaching of indulgences and other abuses within the church, and even questioning the teachings of the Roman Church on the sacraments. His aim, however, was not to create a new church but to revitalize the existing one.

317

His theological opponent, the Ingolstadt professor Johann von Eck, as well as Erasmus and Luther's humanist friend at the court of Electoral Saxony, Georg Spalatin, saw more clearly and recognized sooner the implications of Luther's powerful rhetoric. The doctrinal system that Luther attacked at the same time held together the entire external order of the church; its destruction therefore threatened the entire institution. The church was deeply anchored in the economic and social life of the period. It was possessor of land and wealth. The episcopal jurisdiction had absorbed wide areas of civil law, above all the entire scope of marriage law.

In the early 1520s and especially as the Peasants' Revolt disturbed the German territories, including Thuringia, where the Ernestines had substantial holdings, the traditional order was everywhere shaken. This was especially true for the lands of the Ernestine line of the House of Wettin, because Frederick the Wise, elector of Saxony, to an unusual extent for a prince of this time, pursued an intentional policy of moderation. Thus the following situation was created: since the bishop's jurisdiction no longer functioned—or more precisely, since the bishop no longer could depend on the support of the secular authority —the most serious confusion prevailed in the administration of marriage law. The priests, vicars, chaplains, and other spiritual leaders were left generally in dire straights by the refusal of the populace to pay tithes. The willingness of congregations and of individual church members to give offerings declined visibly, for people interpreted Luther's teaching on "good works," to which the giving of offerings had been reckoned, as being of no use in achieving salvation. Man, by God's grace, was justified "through faith alone" in Christ's redeeming death. The order of service was no longer uniform from place to place as it previously had been. In most cities the congregations had adopted new forms when they gave up the Roman mass without having prescribed a standard form. Luther's German mass, it must be remembered, first appeared in 1526. It came to the point that even in individual cities a unified liturgy could not be guaranteed, for the monastic and collegiate churches usually persisted in the use of the Roman mass, thereby providing grounds for endless strife.

After the Peasants' Revolt, when the countryside was outwardly again at peace, it became increasingly important to end
this confusion. Because of the close relationship between spiritual matters and secular order in early sixteenth century society,
religious confusion without doubt carried with it a latent danger for order in the state. Who then could set about to bring
help and establish order? Within the circle close to Frederick the
Wise, the issue was first articulated and put into writing at the
end of September 1523.[2] At that time Spalatin advised the elector
to find a temporary solution to the question of church order in
concert with the estates until the time when a general council
could undertake reforms. As is clear from the passages he cites
from the Old and New Testaments[3] in his memorandum, Spalatin believed that the intervention of the prince in the affairs of
the church was a direct princely obligation. Frederick the Wise
avoided such requests and did not himself seize the initiative to
carry out the Reformation.

And what possibilities did Luther see? In hindsight one may
say that for a surprisingly long time he hesitated in executing
the reforms he had put forth, and he was overtaken by some of
his original supporters and later opponents, like Carlstadt and
Müntzer. Sooner or later the question of the reorganization of
worship services had to lead to the larger problem of the organizational structure of the new reformed church. Scholars have
continually put forth the question: How did Luther originally
conceive of the outward form of the new church? This question has been answered in very different ways, for Luther himself expressed different opinions about this problem. Moreover,
his statements often lacked the necessary precision; Luther was
not especially gifted in dealing with organizational questions.
Though at the beginning Luther may have desired more freedom for the congregations than they later in fact acquired and
than he then regarded as desirable, nevertheless, there can be
no question that Karl Holl, who argued that Luther's original
intention was to found a definite congregational church organization, overemphasized these tendencies in Luther.[4] It remains
unmistakable that Luther, from the beginning, suggested a certain tie to the secular authority in the question of the outward
ordering of the church. Finally, as early as 1520 he turned with

his desired reforms, which still aimed at the renewal of the traditional church, to the Christian nobility of the German nation, that is, to secular authority. This is not difficult to understand, for Luther grew up in a late medieval German territory; like the west European kings the German territorial princes had long since achieved a certain guardianship over the churches in their respective territories. The privileges the princes had received from the pope had already contributed to a loosening of diocesan structure. The house of Wettin had been especially successful in these efforts, and exerted de facto if not de jure governmental authority over the bishoprics of Merseburg, Naumburg-Zeitz, and Meissen in its territory.[5]

Frederick the Wise's secret protection of Luther early established a certain tie between Luther and the will of the court, although Luther certainly opposed this relationship on different occasions. The break with those who departed from the direction of Luther's conception of reform, whom Luther liked to call "enthusiasts" (*Schwärmer*) and "radical sectarians" (*Rottengeister*), pushed him even more to the side of the governing authority. One thing became clear in Luther's dispute with Carlstadt and Müntzer: under no circumstances did Luther wish to construct the elect community on the model of the original apostolic congregation.

The impressions that Luther gathered during his travels throughout the countryside, especially in the area of the Thuringian Peasants' Revolt, convinced him of the necessity of princely intervention. At first Luther made use of the intercession of Spalatin. On October 1, 1525, the latter informed Elector John in a letter that Luther considered it essential that the elector take possession of all the glebe lands in his realm. Out of the revenues from these properties the elector should pay the salaries of the pastors, preachers, curates, and other persons active in the church's service. Without these measures, they could not expect to find a lasting solution either to the question of liturgy or to other problems that might arise. Luther expressed his willingness to help conduct a visitation, but expected that the elector, on his part, would not permit anyone to continue with or try to reintroduce the old church ceremonies.[6]

On October 31 Luther himself wrote to the elector; without

again mentioning the question of ceremonies, he now stated his desire that the secular authority intervene only to settle the question of church property, regulation of the parishes, and the endowment of the pastors, church personnel, and schoolmasters, whose situation was serious.[7] These were questions that Luther had for a long time considered to be within the competence of the secular power. In more detailed discussion relative to the visitations, he found himself ready to support a qualified right of the prince to intervene in internal issues in the church. He recognized that having two kinds of worship services within a single congregation created a serious situation that might well produce revolt and tumult. Since the intervention of the bishops, who were actually responsible for stopping such developments, was no longer possible, Luther acknowledged the emergency powers of the territorial prince to resolve these questions.

The first attempt to carry out an inspection of the churches had been ordered by Elector John the previous year in Western Thuringia. Shortly thereafter the area was swept by the Peasants' Revolt.[8] Even at that time, however, the procedures of later visitations were already discernible: electoral authorization, cooperation between theologians and advisors to the elector or his officials, a report by the visitation committee to the elector, and instructions to the civil servants, chief magistrates and mayors of the cities, priests, village magistrates, and congregations in the villages. Now the elector took up Luther's requests. After giving orders on Christmas Day, 1525, that the mass henceforth should be said in the German language, he commissioned two partial visitations at the beginning of 1526, one in a Saxon, the other in a Thuringian district. Apparently, in view of the forthcoming diet, the prince purposely avoided taking measures that would include the entire territory. The recess of the Diet of Speyer of 1526, which postponed enforcement of the Edict of Worms, left it to each state to act in a manner answerable to God and the emperor in matters concerning religion and the Edict of Worms until a council could meet. Because of this recess, the elector of Saxony felt sufficiently secure to undertake a new ordering of the church in his lands after his return from Speyer.

After Luther again formally proposed on November 22, 1526,

that visitations be conducted in the churches and schools,[9] it was decided in a conversation between him and the representatives of the elector (Brück and Grefendorf or vom Ende) to create a four-member commission. Two members of the commission were to be qualified to evaluate doctrine and personnel, and two were to have a good understanding of interest and properties. According to the wish of the elector, the University of Wittenberg selected the jurist Dr. Hieronymus Schurff and Melanchthon as experts in doctrine and personnel for the commission. On the electoral side the official from Grimma, Hans von der Planitz, and Asmus Haubitz were named to the commission.[10]

On June 16, 1527, after months of preparation the electoral Instruction was finished and the announcement was ready to be sent to the nobility. The formulation of the electoral Instruction gave the visitation, which was suggested by Luther, a different character in one essential point. Luther had accorded only an emergency right to the secular lord to intervene in internal church affairs—that is with reference to doctrine. In the Instruction, however, Elector John came to the fore as the instrument of the princely power who authorized and executed the visitation. He saw the visitors as his agents, to whom the congregational representatives and the noble patrons had to report, indicating what their obligation was with regard to external order and matters of faith. With this Instruction—and this I wish to maintain in opposition to the recent work of H. W. Krumwiede, who denies it—the Lutheran territorial church government came into being, although, to be sure, it would have to go through some developments.[11]

The work, which the visitation committee had to accomplish, was unpleasant, troublesome, and apparently also rather unsuccessful. Since many questions that arose had not been sufficiently clarified in the preparatory work of the chancellery, the committee was forced to improvise. Jurist Schurff seemed to be especially unhappy; by September 15, 1527, he had already had himself relieved of his duties on the committee, although the work of the visitation was not yet complete. There was a serious reason underlying his action; we know from evidence, in a law dissertation from Tübingen that appeared in 1967, that Schurff throughout his life held fast to canon law with respect to church property.[12] Schurff's position on the visitation committee was filled by another jurist, Georg Spalatin, who in the meantime had become the pastor in Altenburg.

As it had proved necessary to work out a written direction for the pastors, who up to this point had no guidelines at hand for their work within the context of the new doctrine, Melanchthon, on the basis of the notes he had made during the questioning of the pastors, drew up the first draft for the Instruction of the Visitation Committee to the Churchmen in the Electorate of Saxony. The elector requested Luther and Bugenhagen to submit their opinions of this document to him. In two conferences held in Torgau during September and November, 1527, the instructions for the visitation were edited. By the end of March of the following year, the Instruction was printed and, by the beginning of the visitation of 1528–29, which encompassed the entire territory, it was possible to have it in the hands of the pastors.

This direction, which was actually written by Melanchthon and for which Luther prepared a preface,[13] dealt only briefly with the old church's doctrines, institutions, and ceremonies that were rejected by the Reformers. Withholding of the cup in Communion was treated in detail. Apparently, in Wittenberg it was felt that the traditional church no longer posed a serious danger. Indeed, the directive warned churchmen against unnecessary and overzealous opposition to the pope and bishops, and urged them to allow those who were weak in the faith the opportunity for a time to receive Communion in one kind. The main point of the Instruction concerned an appeal to the pastors to concentrate on ethical and religious edification. In the sermon the emphasis should be on the chief points of doctrine—repentence, faith, and the problem of good works. Other issues, which the simple people could not understand, should be left alone. At the same time the pastors should give judgment against mistaken opinions about matters of faith and Christian freedom, and educate the congregation to be obedient to the secular authority. Infant baptism was made the norm, and was defended against dissenting opinions. The tone of the Instruction made one thing clear: the main concern was no longer to overcome the old church doctrine and form, but rather it was the solving of problems in ethical and religious life, the disturbing of peace and quiet in the state, and the doctrines, which had gone beyond the direction indicated by Luther. The propaganda of the Anabaptists, the youngest branch of the radical reform movement, had, since the beginning of 1527, reached the borders of the Ernestine territories. As a guide for the correctness of doctrine, the Instruction, as had the directive before it, appealed simply to the Word of God, that is, to the Holy Scriptures. It was only after the 1530s, after the wide possibilities for interpretation of the Holy Scriptures became apparent, that such doctrinal statements as the Augsburg Confession and Apology displaced the Holy Scriptures as the doctrinal standard.

After the publication of the visitation Instruction, it was almost half a year before the subjects of the elector were informed of the forthcoming general visitation. The work was entrusted to six different commissions, made up of theologians and representatives of the nobility and officials. Most of the officials named to the commissions were lawyers; among the theologians were some, like Jonas and Spalatin, who also had completed a course of legal study. The work of the visitation, whose goals were to create a new church organization and to achieve a uniformity of doctrine and order of service, lasted altogether more than a decade. The visitation had to work in two directions. On the one hand, it examined the qualifications and teachings of the pastors, preachers, and schoolteachers. In the interest of preserving peace in the land it had to bring about a general acceptance of the doctrines of the Wittenberg theologians that Elector John had declared obligatory. Those who deviated doctrinally were urged to resign, and at the same time—as far as it was a matter of deviating in the direction of the old church—preparations were to be made for their material welfare. On the other hand, the visitation had to establish the extent of municipal and rural church property before it had been confiscated and initiate its recovery, for the ruler wanted to take it into his care. The confiscation had taken place because, in the face of criticism of the old church, all members of society believed they were entitled to take church property in one form or another.

In connection with the first great state visitation of 1528–29 the church's supervisory structure was outlined. At the head of the structure stood an approved clergyman as "superattendent." This term is a translation from the Greek *episkopus* into Latin. The "superattendents" were to inspect the priests and school personnel in their districts and examine their qualifications for appointment. In addition, they were responsible for administrative expenditures and assisted provisionally in cases dealing with marriage law. Thus they assumed the judicial functions of the former archdeacons.

The visitation was carried out within the framework of the territorial state; the territory determined the geographic boundaries of the new church, which was drawn up as a territorial church. The boundaries of the "superattendent's" jurisdiction could no longer be attached to the old archdiaconates and deaneries for the traditional administrative districts of the church were older than the territorial states, and thus cut across their boundaries. So the structuring of the administrative districts of the new Lutheran church corresponded to the official secular divisions. To be sure, not every secular division received a "superattendent." Only in especially large districts, for example, in Altenberg, was this the case. As a general rule, several areas were united into one "superattendency."[14]

The comprehensive reorganization of the church properties in 1528–29 included only the cities. In the countryside the pre-Reformation financial arrangements continued in force. The elector, taking into consideration his relations with the emperor and the empire, still refrained from sweeping changes in the cloister and foundation properties. Privately, however, he had begun to bring the monasteries under close princely supervision. When the Diet at Augsburg was again unable to solve this complex of questions, the provincial diet at Zwickau decided in January, 1531, to deal with this problem on the provincial level. The estates insisted that the cloister and foundation properties should not be taken under the immediate administration of the prince, but rather should be placed under sequestration and secured a right to participate in administration.[15] To carry out the resolution, several sequestration commissions were created and attached to the newly created large administrative districts

(*Hauptkreise*). For each district a four-member commission was appointed. Visitation and sequestration were supposed to supplement each other, but in the beginning they often worked at cross-purposes. The sequestrators tried to prevent the monastic goods for which they were responsible from being reduced in size, and the visitation committee wished to draw upon these resources to improve the endowment of the pastorates. Only in the course of time was it possible to harmonize the work of the two commissions, so that they fitted together into the total scheme of the reorganization of church relationships. Because of the extraordinarily high administrative costs, Elector John Frederick would have gladly done away with the administrative involvement of the estates even during the 1530s. This he did not accomplish, however, until 1543, when his request to a committee of the provincial diet resulted in placing the administration of monastic property in the hands of electoral officials.

The revenues from the former cloister and foundation properties, which could be increased through improved administration, were used—aside from administrative expenses, which these funds covered—for the indemnification of the orders' personnel. Indemnification payments decreased in the course of time, and the endowment income was increasingly used to supplement the salaries of pastors and schoolmasters. In addition some of the funds helped to subsidize the refunding of Wittenberg University in 1536. The revenues were used sparingly for purposes of the common good, but they were used liberally for purposes of the state, especially for the liquidation of debt. The use of such funds for secular purposes was not entirely unknown to men of that time, for spiritual and temporal problems were closely related. In 1538, for example, Martin Bucer frankly declared in a brief dealing with the question of church property that spiritual wealth, as well as being used for purposes of religious instruction, ministerial work, education, and caring for the poor, could also be used in time of governmental emergency for the protection of the land and its people, for war against the Turks, and for maintainence of the worthy patrician families.[16] Likewise, Luther, as early as 1531, addressed himself to the question of whether the prince ought to withhold a portion of the church property for himself or for others. Certainly without grasping the significance of his answer, he announced that the revenue, which is left over after the fulfillment of responsibilities for the care of souls and for schools, could be taken without danger for use by the secular government, "which is also service to God."[17]

All of the directions for the establishment of the Lutheran reformation church in Electoral Saxony at first came personally from the elector, and were worked out in the chancellery. The first special authorities, which were not constituted with the intention of being a permanent institution, were the visitation commissions. The next organ developed in the territorial church was the "superattendent," who at that time was given the difficult responsibility of directing marriage courts. They gladly sought Luther's advice or requested briefs from the university, but they placed particularly difficult cases before the elector for his decision. He in turn requested, when necessary, briefs either from university theologians or from jurists of the court council. Not until 1539 did another fixed office of the territorial church arise: the consistory in Wittenberg, which at first was given jurisdiction in marital cases. (This was left over from the more comprehensive plan of a committee of the estates, which had recommended the creation of a number of consistories.) Half of the members of the consistory were lawyers, half theologians. In a later phase its powers were broadened; in cooperation with the university it was responsible for guarding the unity of doctrine, which became necessary during the doctrinal strife of Luther's followers. Thus the fully developed government of the state church of Electoral Saxony (held from 1548 on by the Albertine branch) was based on four pillars: consistory, university, "superattendents," and parish clergy.

The organization, first gradually erected and tested in the Ernestine territory, was then extended to other areas. Upon the death in April, 1539, of Duke George of Saxony, the eager defender of the old faith, his brother and successor, Duke Henry, immediately wanted to introduce the Reformation into the Albertine lands. Up to that time the Reformation had secured a footing there only in Henry's own domains of Freiburg and

Wolkenstein. Here the organization of the church was already based on the model of the Ernestine visitation order, and in the drafting of a visitation order for Henry's new lands, the electoral order of 1527 served as the pattern for the work of the Wittenberg theological faculty, which had to advise on its adaptation. The duke also drew upon experienced helpers from the Ernestine lands in carrying out the first hurried visitation, which encompassed only the cities. The task of the visitation committee in Albertine Saxony was in part more difficult and in part easier than that of their colleagues in the Ernestine lands had been: more difficult, in that it was extremely hard to find qualified pastors for the construction of a new church in an area that had been held to the old church with such determination and prudence. However, since the administrative machinery, including that for church real estate, was intact, it was easier to ascertain the church's wealth in this area than in a territory that had been involved in the Peasants' Revolt, although here, too, ecclesiastical institutions attempted to get rid of documents, as has been shown for Pforte.[18] The task was also easier, because the fundamental disagreement with the emperor and the imperial estates over the confiscation of ecclesiastical holdings had already been settled by the members of the Schmadkaldic League.[19]

The first Albertine order remained in effect only a few years, only during the rule of Duke Henry, who at first formulated his Reformation law without securing the support of the estates upon whom he was financially dependent because of their right to approve taxes. Thus the first provincial diet at Chemnitz in November, 1539, produced heated discussions. As a result, the duke was not allowed to call upon anyone in Ernestine Saxony to aid in the second visitation of 1539–40. For a number of concessions, including the recognition of the privileges of the estates, the duke extracted approval from the estates for the confiscation of ecclesiastical properties. By so doing, the estates assumed joint responsibility with the duke over against the empire for the measures introduced.

On the advice of his father-in-law, Landgrave Philip of Hesse, the young Duke Maurice, who succeeded Henry in the summer of 1541, managed to avoid his father's mistakes. He understood how to work with the estates and at the same time limit their influence. In January, 1543, Maurice presented his great project for the improvement of the educational structure to a committee of the provincial diet at Dresden. He was able to convince the estates that the establishment and financing of three ducal schools and the raising of stipends at the university would only be possible through the sale of unremunerative monastic properties. Through the sale of the properties to the nobility, the prince gained not only financial freedom of movement but also the allegiance of the nobles in the defense of the new church order against opposition from the emperor or the empire. In Albertine Saxony the wealth formerly held by the church was largely spent on education after the expenses for church administration were covered; a number of well-known city schools also received subsidies.[20]

The industrious prince even surpassed his Ernestine cousins in the establishment of a fully developed consistorial organization. In 1545 he founded consistories in the former bishoprics of Merseburg (for Leipzig), and Meissen (for Dresden). Two theologians, two jurists, one prothonotary, a secretary, and a courier were appointed to each consistory. These collegiate organs were secular authorities subordinate to the prince, who from now on held the highest jurisdiction in ecclesiastical questions. The visitation committee and the "superattendents" were in this manner pushed into the background. It was just such a development as this that Spalatin formerly had feared would occur in Ernestine Saxony, when the question of consistories was reviewed. In a letter to Dresden "Superattendent" Daniel Greiser, on October 22, 1543, Luther polemicized against an innovation in Duke Maurice's church ordinance of 1543, which placed final jurisdictional power in matters of excommunication in the hands of the prince. In this he saw a mixing of the secular and spiritual duties and argued: "When it comes to the point that the court wishes to rule the churches according to its own will, then God will not give his blessing and the future will be worse than the past."[21] Here Luther was frightened by a development he himself had introduced, albeit by necessity, when he had called upon the help of secular authority in establishing the new church. The involvement of the secular authority precluded a free development of the external organization of the Reformation church.

In the new Electoral Saxony (Albertine), the principle of the territorial church found its strongest advocates among the humanist cryptocalvinist forces. With their second defeat at the end of the sixteenth century, another form of territorial church prevailed, which was shaped by a dualism between the prince and the estates.[22]

The visitation Instruction of Electoral Saxony in the form of a revision for Albertine Saxony also became the basis for the Reformation in the territory of Duke Henry the Younger, of Brunswick-Wolfenbüttel, when the troops of the Schmalkaldic League occupied his land and forcibly introduced the Reformation.[23] The three-part visitation instruction of 1542 underwent only certain modifications, which resulted from the special conditions of an occupied territory. The issuers of the credentials and general Instruction for the visitation committee were the governor and councils of the occupied territory who were appointed in the name of the two leaders of the Schmalkaldic League. Only the special Instruction that designated Bugenhagen (for Ernestine Saxony) and Corvin (for Hesse) for the visitation of the foundations and cloisters was issued directly by John Frederick and Landgrave Philip. The church order for Wolfenbüttel published in the following year, 1543, likewise followed the Saxon model. In the chapter "Concerning Doctrine," under the literature recommended to the pastors appeared the Apology to the Augsburg Confession—as one might well expect after the 1530s. The confession was not expressly mentioned, but knowledge of it was assumed. As in Saxony "superattendents," now more often called superintendents, were appointed, whose duty it was to watch over the doctrinal teachings of the pastors in their districts. They were empowered to take disciplinary measures against the pastors when necessary. Difficulties that emerged were to be referred to the governor in Wolfenbüttel, until the supervision was taken over by a consistory established for the territory and a general superintendency. The organization of the new superintendencies was detached from the old divisions of the archdiaconates and attached to the political jurisdictions, here called courts (*Gerichte*) and half-courts (*Halbgerichte*).

During the political development of the following years, this arrangement in Brunswick-Wolfenbüttel was not developed further. After returning to his territory, Duke Henry the Younger carried out his harsh, Catholic policy. Thus only after Henry's death in 1568, when his Lutheran son, Julius, succeeded him, did Brunswick-Wolfenbüttel gain a Lutheran church order established by its own prince. Quite understandably the duke avoided making the organization of the church like that which the Schmalkaldic occupation had introduced. Thus in the formulation of the Wolfenbüttel church ordinance of 1569, he looked for help to Brunswick's current city superintendent, Martin Chemnitz, and to Tübingen's university chancellor, Jakob Andreä. The church ordinance of 1569, with reference to Old Testament passages, emphasized the point that the government was directly responsible for the organization of the church and its services.[24] This emphasis was much stronger than it had been in the new church ordinance that Electoral Saxony had influenced and that the leaders of the Schmalkaldic League or their representatives had decreed. This church ordinance had referred to the governor's Christian duty in addition to the responsibilities deriving from his office. Inasmuch as the duke also directly claimed the right to instruct his subjects (to complete their doctrinal learning), the supreme episcopate of the prince was already evident here. Here, too, the duke immediately created, as an instrument of his church government, a consistory, the first nominees to which were all jurists. The immediate establishment of a consistory was due on the one hand to the influence of Andreä, who was familiar with the consistory from Württemburg, and on the other hand to the special needs of a territory that had been held so long by the Catholic faith that considerable difficulties were expected from the introduction of the new ordinance. But the establishment of the consistory may be explained above all by chronology: at this time a consistorial organization already existed in Albertine Electoral Saxony and in Ernestine

Ducal Saxony. The duties of the consistory were outlined in the foreword to the church ordinance: the removal of deficiencies that the visitation discovered, the naming of general and special superintendents as well as pastors and curates, the leadership of the biannual visitation carried out by the superintendents, and the preservation of doctrinal unity and supervision of discipline and morals.

Finally let us take a look at a Protestant territorial church, which not only varied from the above organizations but also preceded the formation of the Reformation church in Electoral Saxony. The rise of the Prussian church is connected with the bankruptcy of the state of the Teutonic Knights.[25] It is particularly interesting because it had at first an episcopal constitution, and one might assume that a Lutheran church headed by bishops could maintain more freedom of movement and more independence from princely directives than was possible in a church such as in Electoral Saxony. This question was investigated by one of my students in his *Staatsexamen* project, the results of which I rely on here.[26]

The situation in the lands of the Teutonic Order after the loss of the economically productive portion of its territory at the second Peace of Thorn in 1466 was hopeless. It became even worse as a result of the Knights' War of 1520–21. Polish mercenaries occupied the bishopric of Pomesania, while the Teutonic Knights were stationed in the northern part of the bishopric of Ermland, which had been ceded to Poland. Administration in the knights' territory was completely outdated in comparison with the type of administration used in most territorial states of the sixteenth century. Margrave Albert of Brandenburg-Ansbach saw only one possibility for the modernization of his state: the transformation of the territory into a secular hereditary dukedom. The achievement of such a goal had to lead to conflict with the emperor and the pope, and was for all practical purposes impossible to attain within the framework of the old church.

The grand master of the order inclined toward the new evangelical doctrine from early on, but had to work carefully in every respect because of the politically explosive nature of his plans. It was also necessary to prevent the weakening of the Teutonic Order through withdrawals, as was happening to other religious orders, for without the Teutonic Knights the grand master would not be able to maintain his position in the territory. The acquisition of the first Lutheran preacher for the Teutonic lands in Prussia documents the first close connection with Wittenberg. In September, 1523, the former Franciscan, Johann Briessmann, arrived in the North. Briessmann came originally from Kottbus, was of the same generation as Luther and the grand master, and had the year before taken a degree of doctor of theology at Wittenberg. While the way was being prepared for the introduction of the Reformation to the Teutonic lands, the grand master was away. He had left as early as 1522 to prepare the way for negotiations with the empire and Poland for his proposed political solution. During his absence he had appointed as regent Georg von Polentz, bishop of Samland. Polentz, who came from a noble family in Meissen, had studied law and had accompanied Maximilian I on the campaign against Venice in 1509. It was during this campaign that Albert had met Polentz. The latter joined the Order of Teutonic Knights after Albert became grand master, and was given far-reaching authority. Albert sent him to Prussia and nominated him for bishop of Samland when Günther von Bünau, the former bishop, died in 1518. It is important to know something about the background of Polentz in order to evaluate properly events in the Teutonic lands in the decisive years 1523–25.

While the grand master had to hold himself in check, the Prussian bishops placed themselves at the head of the movement. One might think at first that this distinguished the Reformation in the Prussian lands of the Teutonic Order from all other areas of Germany. But Georg von Polentz was not only bishop of Samland but also regent, and, during a year and a half vacancy (from May, 1522, to October, 1523), he also administered the bishopric of Pomesania. The bishop of Samland caused a great stir on Christmas Day, 1523, by delivering three major evangelical sermons; Briessmann advised Polentz on the theological content of the sermons. In January, 1524, the bishop issued his first reform mandate for the bishopric of Samland.

By Easter it was already possible to introduce a Lutheran reform of public worship in the churches under his jurisdiction.
Several weeks later all of the altars other than the main altar
were removed from the churches. No reaction was expected
from the populace, which had been christianized in the not-too-
distant past. In addition, no resistance from the priests material-
ized. From October, 1523, on, the bishop's prudent measures received support from Erhard von Queiss, bishop of Pomesania,
residing in Riesenburg. Queiss, who like Polentz was born in
Lausitz and was trained in law, had been elected by his cathedral chapter according to correct procedure, but he no longer
held the church's consecration and papal approbation. On January 1, 1525, Queiss issued a very cautious, carefully thought
out reform mandate.

The grand master, who had asked many people for their
opinions about the state of the Teutonic Order's territory, had
also requested Luther's advice. This the latter gave in a conversation late in November, 1523, at which Melanchthon was
present. Luther favored putting aside the rule of the order and
changing the Teutonic lands in Prussia into a secular duchy.
To carry out this plan it was necessary to come to an agreement
with Poland. On April 8, 1525, shortly before the expiration
of the truce, a treaty was drawn up in Cracow. On the basis of
this agreement Albert was to rule the Prussian lands of the Teutonic Order as a secular hereditary "Duke in Prussia," and to
hold his duchy as a fief of the king of Poland in conjunction
with his brothers.

Returning to Prussia as its hereditary duke, Albert stepped
clearly to the head of the Lutheran territorial church. He har-
vested the fruits of the prudent preparatory work that the bish-
op-regent had achieved—acting less in his capacity of bishop
than as the administrator for the grand master. The bishops remained in office, but were placed under the authority of the territorial prince. Indeed, two days after the prelates and the remaining members of the estates had taken the oath of fealty,
Polentz relinquished his secular authority over the third of the
bishopric that had been granted to him to the prince, and con-
tented himself with the revenue from two offices that had been

assigned to him. In justifying his step, he argued first of all that it was appropriate for him, as prelate and bishop, to preach the Word of God, but not to govern land and people. This position accorded with the ideas of Luther, who had no objection to the office of bishop insofar as it was returned to its spiritual function. Secondly, Polentz argued that the duke, as a result of the recent war and the debts of his predecessors, was burdened with such heavy debts that he was in desperate need of financial help.[27] Thus the reorganization of the ducal finances was one of the openly avowed purposes of secularization.[28] The economy of the bishopric of Pomesania was in desperate straits in the wake of the departure of the occupation troops; therefore, Queiss did not follow Polentz's example until two years later, when the economic conditions in his bishopric were somewhat stabilized.

Thus for the time being the bishoprics remained in force within the framework of the Lutheran church in the duchy of Prussia. This was possible because the bishops themselves voluntarily agreed to the limitation of their function to purely spiritual responsibilities. That this course of action could be carried out —indeed, done so without conflict— can be explained on the one hand by the historical development of the position of the Prussian episcopal office during the time of the rule of the Teutonic Order.[29] On the other hand, it occurred because the men who were bishops in Prussia were not members of dynastic families, but rather members of the nobility, who were used to serving the prince.

We have only to ask now whether the Lutheran bishops in Prussia were successful in fulfilling their spiritual functions in relative independence. With regard to the appointment of pastors, the territorial ordinance of 1525 assigned to the bishops the right of examining the candidates presented by the feudal lord. Since in the great majority of parishes the right of patronage lay in the lands of the territorial lord, the bishops played a subordinate role. The territorial lord had inherited the parishes incorporated into the Teutonic Order, which included also the former churches of episcopal patronage. There is no known instance of the rejection of a candidate nominated by the duke.[30] With respect to the preservation of doctrinal purity the bishops were successful in achieving a certain predominance, especially in comparison with the court theologians. Polentz, however, wanted nothing at all to do with dogmatic disputes. The final decision on matters of correct doctrine rested with the dilatory duke, from whom too much was demanded. However, only by means of the rulers' authority was the suppression of dissenting opinions possible. One of the most important duties of episcopal administration, in the view of the Reformers, was the visitation, in which the Lutheran bishops in Prussia always diligently involved themselves. For the first Prussian church visitation in 1526, Duke Albert and the bishops Polentz and Queiss issued the authorization to the visitors, Paul Speratus and the court adviser Adrian von Waiblingen. Two years later the two bishops were only recipients of the ducal visitation edict. After that the bishops, for all practical purposes, exercised their authority in the visitation only by the ordinance of the territorial lord. They took care of the spiritual jurisdiction through an official. However, the prince exercised appellate jurisdiction for the marriage courts, which operated under the supervision of the bishops. When adultery cases were pending, a secular adviser was even sent to the proceedings in the bishop's court.

It must be concluded therefore, that the Lutheran bishops in Prussia were unable to establish their office as an independent ecclesiastical institution; rather, it was understood as a kind of territorial church office. One cannot say that they were frustrated in their attempt to develop an independent Lutheran episcopal office, for they did not even try to do this. Polentz achieved a very real contribution to the creation of a Prussian Reformation church, and himself shared in the development that led to the establishment of a territorial church government. As a result of the secularization, the bishops had also become financially dependent upon the territorial lord.[31]

It was thus consistent that Duke Albert later tried to dissolve the episcopal organization and organize his state church according to the model of Electoral Saxony. In 1542 he presented the estates with his plan for a church order headed by superintendents. In spite of the financial benefits of the plan, the estates rejected the proposal. Indeed, he now even had to accept the fact that the episcopal organization would be established firmly in the territorial constitution, in the so-called *Regimentsnotel* of 1542, although the bishops were to be selected by the elector alone. Nevertheless, Duke Albert did not give up his plan. After the death of Polentz, he appointed in 1554 only a president to the bishopric of Samland (Johann Aurifaber). He followed the same course when he appointed Paul Speratus to succeed Queiss in the bishopric of Pomesania.

The estates, which feared that their influence could be reduced, resisted all of the duke's attempts to allow the office of bishop to fall into disuse and to replace it with consistories after the examples of Electoral Saxony and Brandenburg. They found support for their endeavor in Poland, and were able to force the reintroduction of the office of bishop in 1566. At the same time they were able to establish new regulations for the election of bishops, which assured the predominance of the estates in the electoral procedure. In these later quarrels over the bishop's office, it was not a question of how the church could win a greater freedom from the intervention of secular power (whether of the prince or of the estates). Rather, the bishop's office had become a bone of contention in the struggle between the prince and the estates.[32] In the end, however, the Prussian reformation church did not retain the bishop's office. Ignoring the objections of the estates, the territorial regent, Margrave Frederick of Brandenburg-Ansbach, abolished the office of bishop in 1584 and introduced the consistorial organization in accord with the models of Brandenburg and Saxony. He established a consistory for each of the two previous bishoprics. Thus, also for the Prussian reformation church the territorial church organization became the pattern, with an unequivocal supreme episcopate for the prince.

1. This essay grew out of a presentation given to a meeting of Erlangen historians on October 22, 1969. I have profited from the discussion that followed that meeting. (Translated by Jann Whitehead Gates.)

2. See Irmgard Höss, *Georg Spalatin 1484–1545: ein Leben in der Zeit des Humanismus und der Reformation* (Weimar, 1956), pp. 238–39.

3. 2 Kings 23, Paralipomena, and Acts 15.

4. Karl Holl, *Gesammelte Aufsätze zur Kirchengeschichte*, 5th ed., vol. 1 (Tübingen, 1927). From the extensive literature on this problem the especially penetrating studies of Franz Lau should be noted: *"Äusserliche Ordnung" und "weltlich Ding" in Luthers Theologie* (Göttingen, 1933); and Franz Lau, *Luthers Lehre von den beiden Reichen* (Berlin, 1953). See also Edgar M. Carlson, "Luther's Conception of Government," *Church History* 15 (1946):257–70.

5. Justus Hashagen, *Staat und Kirche vor der Reformation* (Essen, 1931). Hashagen approaches the problem in its broad western context. For a study dealing with the Wettin lands and incorporating especially the older specialized studies see Irmgard Höss, "Die Problematik des spätmittelalterlichen Landeskirchentums am Beispiel Sachsens," *Geschichte in Wissenschaft und Unterricht* 10 (1959): 352–62; and Karl Bosl, "Der Wettinische Ständestaat im Rahmen der mittelalterlichen Verfassungsgeschichte," *Historische Zeitschrift* 191 (1960):349–56.

6. See Höss, *Spalatin*, pp. 321 ff.; here also and passim for the different interpretations of Luther and Spalatin on the rights of the territorial prince as opposed to those of the church.

7. *WA Br*, 3:No. 937.

8. On the visitations that took place before the Peasants' Revolt, see Irmgard Höss, "Humanismus und Reformation," *Das Zeitalter des Humanismus und der Reformation*, vol. 3, *Geschichte Thüringens*, ed. Hans Patze and Walter Schlesinger (Cologne, 1967), pp. 74 ff., and note, p. 306.

9. *WA Br*, 4:No. 1052.

10. Hans-Walter Krumwiede, *Zur Entstehung des landesherrlichen Kirchenregiments in Kursachsen und Braunschweig-Wolfenbüttel* Studien zur Kirchengeschichte Niedersachsens, vol. 16 (Göttingen, 1967), pp. 69 ff. has recently made the assertion that the university also exerted an influence on the selection of the representatives by the elector. In my opinion this is incorrect; Krumwiede clearly misunderstood the pertinent passage in the letter of the elector to Luther on November 26, 1526, *WA Br*, 4:No. 1054. See my critique in *Archiv für Reformationsgeschichte* 61 (1970):144–47, especially pp. 145–46.

11. Krumwiede, *Kirchenregiment*, pp. 88 and 261, argues that the development of the territorial church government first took place after 1527–28. He must admit, however, that the conclusion of the instruction emphasizes the narrow aristocratic character more strongly than its beginning. Helga-Maria Kühn's interpretation of the instruction in *Die Einziehung des geistlichen Gutes im albertinischen Sachsen 1539–1553* ("Mitteldeutsche Forschungen," vol. 43; Cologne, 1966), p. 45, follows my own.

12. See Wiebke Schaich-Klose, "D. Hieronymus Schürpf; Leben und Werk des Wittenberger Reformationsjuristen, 1481–1554" (dissertation, Tübingen, 1966). Later published as *D. Hieronymus Schürpf. Der Wittenberger Reformationsjurist aus St. Gallen, 1481–1554* (St. Gallen, 1967), pp. 49 ff.

13. An analysis of the "Instruction of the Vistation Committee" is the focus of the study by Krumwiede, *Kirchenregiment*, pp. 91–119.

14. On the superintendencies see Höss, "Humanismus und Reformation," pp. 84 ff. On the late medieval church organization see Karlheinz Blaschke, Walther Haupt, and Heinz Wiessner, *Die Kirchenorganisation in den Bistümern Meissen, Merseburg und Naumburg um 1500* (Weimar, 1969).

15. See Höss, "Humanismus und Reformation," pp. 90 ff. There is only one detailed study for the eastern portion of the Ernestine territory: A. Hilpert, "Die Sequestrationen der geistlichen Güter in den kursächsischen Landkreisen Meissen, Vogtland und Sachsen 1531 bis 1543," *Mitteilungen des Altertumsvereins zu Plauen* 22 (1912).

16. See Kühn, *Einziehung des geistlichen Gutes*, p. 41.

17. Ibid., p. 42; *WA Br*, 6 (1935):No. 1766.

18. See Robert Pahncke, *Schulpforte; Geschichte des Zisterzienserklosters Pforte* (Leipzig, 1956).

19. See Kühn, *Einziehung des geistlichen Gutes*, p. 113.

20. Ibid., pp. 103 ff.

21. *WA Br*, 10 (1947):No. 3930; Kühn, *Einziehung des geistlichen Gutes*, p. 78. I have used Kühn's translation.

22. See Franz Lau in his bibliographical essay "Luther und die Welt der Reformation," *Luther-Jahrbuch* (1969), pp. 112–13, for his comments on Krumwiede's study.

23. See Krumwiede, *Kirchenregiment*, pp. 146–240.

24. Ibid., p. 201.

25. Walther Hubatsch, "Die inneren Voraussetzungen der Säkularisation des Deutschordensstaates in Preussen," *Archiv für Reformationsgeschichte* 43 (1952): 145–72. See also Walther Hubatsch, *Geschichte der evangelischen Kirche Ostpreussens*, 3 vols. (Göttingen, 1968).

26. Dieter Diehnelt, "Georg von Polentz: erster evangelischer Bischof im Bereich der deutschen Reformation. Ein Beitrag zum evangelischen Bischofsamt der Reformationszeit unter besonderer Berücksichtigung des Verhältnisses von geistlicher und weltlicher Gewalt in Preussen" (unpublished *Staatsexamenarbeit*, 1969). This study is based on printed material; with an examination of the pertinent archival materials, it could form the basis of a doctoral dissertation.

27. Ibid., p. 47.

28. Walter Hubatsch, *Albrecht von Brandenburg-Ansbach Deutschordens-Hochmeister und Herzog in Preussen 1490–1568*, Studien zur Geschichte Preussens, 8 (Heidelberg, 1960):141–42.

29. The Prussian bishops' freedom of movement was limited early through the incorporation of the cathedral chapter into the Teutonic Order and also through legislation that thwarted the expansion of the secular authority of the bishops (*Amortisationsgesetz*). The previous grand master, Frederick of Saxony, had effectively put an end to the independence of the bishops with the establishment of a high court of justice as the highest court of appeal for all courts in the territory. This move was also aimed at the ecclesiastical courts. The Defensive Order of 1507 also reduced episcopal independence, for it redivided the entire territory, including the area under the bishop's sovereignty, according to a strategic plan, into four or five regions—recruiting districts. From this time on the bishops were appointed directly by the grand master; the election by the cathedral chapter was only a formality.

30. To support this statement, which is based upon only a few examples, a thorough sifting of primary sources is still required.

31. How difficult it was for a Lutheran bishop to secure enough room for movement is demonstrated by the frustrated attempt in Naumburg. See Peter Brunner, *Nikolaus von Amsdorf als Bischof von Naumburg*, Schriften des Vereins für Reformationsgeschichte, vol. 179 (Gütersloh, 1961).

32. Jürgen Petersohn, "Bischofsamt und Konsistorialverfassung in Preussen im Ringen zwischen Herzog und Landschaft im letzten Viertel des 16. Jahrhunderts," *ARG* 52 (1961):188–205.

PROTESTANT ENDOWMENT LAW IN THE FRANCONIAN CHURCH ORDINANCES OF THE SIXTEENTH CENTURY

Hans Liermann

Revolutionary change in eccesiastical-religious thought was not the only development of the century of the Reformation. Important forces emanated from the changes in theological thought that deeply influenced society and that also brought about decisive alterations in the legal ordinances. Legal institutions, which for centuries had been an integral part of medieval society, having been imprinted by medieval religious thought, were now altered through the dynamics of Reformation thought. This transformation was decisive for their further development. Called upon to perform different functions, the legal ordinances had to adapt. Jurisprudence was led into new paths by theology. Consequences resulted from the spiritual wrestlings of the great *homo religiosus*, Martin Luther, that must be pursued to their most intricate ramifications in legislative and juristical thought.[1]

A legal institution exemplifying these theologically inspired changes in legal form and judicial position is the ecclesiastical endowment, which had grown out of the medieval church's emphasis on good works. The Reformation doctrine of justification by faith abolished this emphasis, and this deeply affected the practice of establishing endowments. The spread of the Reformation manifested itself in the newly formulated sixteenth-century church ordinances of the evangelical territories. When one examines the numerous volumes of the comprehensive collection *Die evangelischen Kirchenordnungen des XVI. Jahrhunderts*, which was begun by Emil Sehling and has recently been continued at Göttingen by the Institut für evangelisches

Kirchenrecht of the Lutheran Church in Germany, one finds everywhere legal regulations concerning endowments. This phenomenon has already been referred to several times in the literature on the subject.[2]

Despite over-all conformity, local peculiarities can be found. It is, therefore, exciting and at the same time instructive to examine the evangelical endowment laws of a particular territory. Through such an examination it can be demonstrated how the enduring, universally similar legal opinions were adopted by the authorities, and how they took shape in reference to the local situation. The volume in the Sehling collection that deals with the church ordinances of Bavarian Franconia is an excellent, fertile, and, in view of its completeness, unsurpassable source for such an examination.[3] It contains material on a center of the Reformation that differs essentially from Saxony and Thuringia, with which Sehling dealt in the first volume of his collection. The difference lies in the fact that Franconia consists not of large, expansive territorial states but rather of an aggregation of regions of diverse sizes. In addition to more important territories such as Brandenburg-Ansbach-Kulmbach of the Franconian Hohenzollern margraves and the powerful imperial city of Nürnberg, one finds smaller imperial cities, earldoms, territories belonging to imperial knights, and imperial villages.

Furthermore, there are few codified endowment laws, except for some alms regulations and regulations for the common chest (the compilation of all endowments under a common administration). More often, the individual regulations concerning endowments appear at random. For example, the law concerning benefice endowments is treated with the law concerning the priesthood; the law concerning endowments for the benefit of the soul, in connection with the establishment of a common chest. In spite of all this, however, it is possible to glean a theologically based system of evangelical endowment law from the Franconian church ordinances.

The theological dogmatics out of which the new thinking concerning this legal position of endowments could proceed can be found particularly in the Nürnberg legal code. The great

imperial city was at the time of the Reformation a focal point
for spiritual argumentation. This fact expressed itself directly
in early ecclesiastical legislation which set forth fundamental
beliefs of the Reformation. The *23 Nürnberger Lehrartikel* of
1528 include a comprehensive section entitled "Concerning
Proper Good Works."

The theological passages of this section contain opinions that,
when transferred into the legal world, signify the removal of
certain categories of endowments that had been customary until that time. Thus number 10 of the section states: "That good
works are only such works with which one serves God according to His Word and the neighbor in brotherly love."[4] This
passage recognizes as conforming to the gospel those church endowments that make it possible to serve God according to His
Word, and also all charitable endowments that serve a neighbor in brotherly love. At the same time it rejects endowments
for masses for the benefit of the soul and the votive masses
(masses read for the benefit of a particular concern of the person who paid for the mass), which were widely practiced in the
medieval church. Their purpose was not directly concerned with
service to God but more concerned with the good of the donor's
soul—in the case of votive masses, even his temporal well-being.

A still sharper rejection of such endowments is contained in
article 12 in the section dealing with good works: "That all
those works are wicked and vain which God has not commanded and which are not demanded by brotherly love."[5] Finally, the *23 Nürnberger Lehrartikel* of 1528 even designate as
simony those endowments based on the notion of work righteousness. In the section "Concerning Simony" it states:

7.   That bishops, clerics, monks, and nuns practice simony when
they sell their good works, their meritorious deeds, confraternity benefits, fast days, masses for the souls, even though these may be proper
in themselves, for money, interest or endowments.

8.   That all who endow or buy such deeds also practice simony.[6]

Traditional endowments are divided into two groups by Reformation theology. There are those that are commendable and

worthy of encouragement. These include ecclesiastical endowments, insofar as they are dedicated to the pure service of God, as defined by the Reformation. In addition, charitable endowments dedicated to the service of the neighbor are also acknowledged as having a right to exist. To the second group belong those endowments that owe their origin to a false teaching of good works, and that must, therefore, be rejected as contradictory to the gospel. Endowments for the benefit of the soul and endowed votive masses are particularly rejected as unevangelical. With regard to these two practices the evangelical legislators envisioned for themselves a double assignment. They first of all had to prevent such endowments in the future. That was comparatively easy to accomplish. Second, they had to determine what to do with those already existing. This task caused great difficulties.

The Reformation era was a time of slow transition in Franconia. This was so particularly because the larger evangelical territories, especially the imperial city of Nürnberg, proceeded very carefully. Margrave Casimir of Brandenburg-Ansbach remained a Roman Catholic until his death in 1527, even though the Reformation succeeded in his territory. Thus, instead of strict prohibitions of unwanted endowments in the early church ordinances, one finds only careful formulations that aim at the elimination of endowments. The decree of the Ansbach provincial diet of 1526 provides an example. It states, "Furthermore, no mass shall be celebrated for money in the future, but only for the sake of the honor and love of God, when the celebrant has the proper devotion and the proper attitude for such a celebration."[7]

This ordinance did not serve to abolish endowments for masses, but rather to extricate them from materialistic entanglement. Two years later, the fifteenth question of the *Ansbacher 30 Fragen* of 1528 quite obviously points in the same direction. The visitors should ask the pastor: "Whether it is proper to read votive masses for private concerns, also in the German language, as a response to endowments, gifts, or other favors."[8] These thirty questions were the basis for the first church visitation in the Ansbach territory.

The actual condemnation of such masses came only when the Reformation had been carried out in its entirety both in Nürnberg and in the Franconian principalities of Brandenburg-Ansbach and Brandenburg-Kulmbach. The Brandenburg-Nürnberg Church Ordinance of 1533 announced unequivocally that the Eucharist had been made into a business and a "business has been made of the Eucharist and it has been adulterated with all kinds of unchristian songs and prayers which are contrary to the Word of God, and countless similar abuses, so that it has finally come to this, that that Lord's Supper has had to serve all sorts of transactions and businesses. For the mass has not only been read for fever and all kinds of sickness, but also for poverty, etc. Yes, magic has even been practiced with it."[9]

The question of what should be done with the existing endowments for masses caused some perplexity. For this reason, the city council of Nürnberg requested an opinion from Melanchthon in 1525. Some of the donors were still living, and they requested the return of their endowments. At the same time, there were heirs of donors who wanted to increase their inheritance by also reclaiming such endowments. Melanchthon decided that the money should be returned to the living donors at their request. On the other hand, the demand of the heirs should be rejected.[10]

Moreover, in Nürnberg as in Ansbach, the existing endowments were dealt with very carefully at first. Basically they were preserved, though with the condition that they should in time become a part of the common chest, called the *Grosse Almosen* in Nürnberg, a large, communal foundation that united all of the charitable endowments.[11] The Order of the Nürnberg City Council for the *Grosse Almosen* of the year 1522 states, "For good reasons the honorable city council, nevertheless, wishes to preserve in their customary fashion the old, previously endowed donations and soul baths [at the death of a donor the poor received a bath and were entertained in connection with the mass that was read for the donor; this was done so that they would pray for the well-being of his soul], of course, with the intention that they should also eventually be incorporated into the *Grosse Almosen*."[12]

The decree of the Ansbach provincial diet of the year 1526 takes a similar, conservative stand. Existing endowments should be dealt with "according to prevailing practice and according to ancient tradition." Nothing should be changed "until this matter has been discussed at a general Christian council or a national assembly and a decision has been published, or until a further decree is published." When pastors have religious scruples, "and, on account of their conscience, cannot or do not wish to fulfill what the endowments demand of them, the donors or their heirs must decide whether they wish to use the annual proceeds of the endowment capital in such a manner that they call upon another person to fulfill the obligations which the endowment requires." If there are several donors who cannot agree, "then that group should be followed which wishes to preserve the endowment." Finally, when none of the donors or their heirs are any longer available, and no one wishes to observe the anniversaries, the endowment should be deposited by the authorities.[13]

It becomes apparent from this that at that time people still wished to preserve the endowment practice, if this was at all possible. Finally, the deposition by the officials of the margraves is, of course, a preliminary step to the accession of the endowments to the treasury when its purpose could no longer be fulfilled.

The proceedings in Kitzingen were similar to those in Nürnberg. The citizens of Kitzingen established a common chest in their Beggars Ordinance of 1523, but they preserved the anniversaries and similar endowments. The city council, nevertheless, addressed the request to the authorities that they might give such endowments willingly into the common chest "so that the alms could be divided in a more efficient manner than had been done up until then."[14] In this last sentence secular and rational considerations come to the surface. Poverty must be combatted more efficiently through the centralization of the individual alms endowments.

Endowments for masses in the evangelical territories had to cease in the course of the sixteenth century; they had lost their meaning and reason for existence. Statute laws regulating their

fate are not to be found in the Franconian church ordinances.
In time they were probably incorporated into the *Grosse Almosen* or elsewhere into the common chest, as the Nürnberg alms
regulation of 1522 indicates. Otherwise, the state treasury incorporated them when there was no longer an interested party.

The common chest, which could incorporate such endowments, was established everywhere in the cities, and its existence
was soon taken for granted. This fact is illustrated in the Church
Visitation in the margravate of Brandenburg *unter dem Gebirg*
of the year 1536. In this document the common chest is simply
considered to be the responsibility of the curates and assistants
in the parishes: "They should carefully promote the poor-
box."[15]

The centralization of the endowments was so complete in certain areas that they became a legal part of the common fund.
In other areas their individuality was preserved, and they were
merely subordinated to the central administration of the common chest.[16] This administration differed from place to place.
Windsheim proceeded moderately, though even there the endowments for masses and their proceeds were eventually incorporated into the common chest. The Windsheim Ordinance
for the Common Chest states: "In time the previously endowed
donations and soul baths will also be transferred into this
'[Grosse] Almosen.' "[17]

But this transfer of the endowments into the common chest
meant merely that their administration was removed from the
priests and transferred to city officials.[18] The purpose of the endowment was also carried on, if this was at all possible. This
can be established from the fate of a Windsheim endowment,
the so-called *Jungferngeld*. This endowment for the dowry of
poor brides was, of course, subject to the common chest, like all
endowments. But it is stated specifically in the ordinance of
1524 that "certain pious daughters of burghers who have
reached the age suitable for marriage and cannot marry because
of their poverty [they lacked the means for a dowry]" should
also be supported from the common chest.[19]

The endowments for masses, then, were either transformed
or wholly incorporated into the common chest, since they were

irreconcilable with the basic doctrinal position of the Reformation. On the other hand, the ecclesiastical endowments, which were considered to be the property of the clerics in medieval thought and which were to serve the cult and the maintenance of the church building, were generally taken over from canonical law in their old form. As a matter of fact, the canonical law concerning ecclesiastical endowments already had a feature in the medieval church common with the Reformation. The administration of ecclesiastical endowments was in the hands of laymen. In Franconia these men were called *Heiligenpfleger* (administrator of the property of the saint to whom the church was dedicated, which was considered to be his personal property) or *Gotteshausmeister* (master of the church that was designated as the house of God). The laymen were, therefore, already allowed to participate in these matters before the time of the Reformation. The *Heiligenpfleger* were supervised by the visitors in their administrative activity. Thus the Chapter Ordinance of 1565 states that the visitors, when they come to a congregation, should invite the mayor and other secular officials "together with the administrators of the property of the ecclesiastical endowment or also several people from the congregation to a discussion early the following morning."[20]

The Consistorial Ordinance for Brandenburg-Ansbach-Kulmbach of 1594 provides detailed instructions concerning the supervision of the administrators of the property derived from ecclesiastical endowments. This is done in section 9, which is entitled "Concerning Churches, Common Chests, Administrators of Church Property, and their Functions." The administrators were required to give precise accounts of their activities before a magistrate of the margrave and the pastor.[21]

It is interesting that in the earldom of Castell, according to the Village Ordinance for Obereisenheim of 1579, the fines for blasphemy, cursing, and swearing, as well as for parents who did not send their children to school went wholly or in part into the ecclesiastical endowment where the procurator (*Gotteshausmeister*) should receive them and charge them to an account.[22] This ordinance is evidence of the beginning of the bureaucratic state that handled ecclesiastical discipline and thereby it helped support the church financially. The benefice endowments experienced much greater change than the ecclesiastical endowments. There was some opposition on the part of the people to the fact that the clergy were the beneficiaries of the benefices. This disposition, of course, influenced benefice rights in certain places. An especially revolutionary anticlerical disposition is expressed in the admonition with which the mayor and the congregation of Wendelstein received their new pastor in 1524, shortly before the outbreak of the great Peasants' War:

> Since in past times we have been burdened frequently by clerics with offerings, with the pastor's interest in the inheritance, with the special payments, and other fees, we have accumulated great expenses. And since we have now been taught by the gospel that the Lord gives freely, and that His gifts should not be sold for money, we are of the opinion and have resolved that neither you nor anyone else should have a claim to such payments.[23]

On the basis of the *ius divinum* (Matt. 10:8) various payments are denied to the holder of the benefice. Nevertheless, the residents of Wendelstein preserved the benefice, which they claimed to have been endowed by their ancestors, although they cited no exact evidence for this assertion. The admonition to the pastor states further:

> Because the servants of the Word should have their livelihood, we are aware that this incumbency has been provided with property out of which the pastor should receive his sustenance. We do not wish to take anything from whatever belongs to it, taxes, woodland, meadows, and fields, nor do we wish to interfere with the extent of its borders. Whatever else has been used previously by others without authorization and has been taken from the lambs of Christ in a hardhearted manner, that you may not request, and you must be satisfied with the aforementioned possessions.[24]

The benefices were interfered with not only from below but also from above, on the part of the sovereign. This interference was justified by the assertion that there had been some abuse of the benefice. If nothing else, strict supervision of the benefice and its administration was initiated. An Ansbach Mandate of March 16, 1528, concerning the filling of the benefices demands: Since "much misuse has been practiced with regard to the investiture of benefices on persons of the Roman Church and in other ways," no one should from now on be invested with a benefice "without our knowledge and our volition."[25]

The supervision of the benefice was extended during the course of the sixteenth century. The Consistorial Ordinance for Brandenburg-Ansbach-Kulmbach of 1594 delineates precise instructions in its seventh section. Glebe lands were to be neither exchanged nor leased against the wishes of the pastor who at the time was using the benefice. The pastors should not hew wood at will in the forests owned by the church, and they should not allow the parishioners to graze their cattle in those woods.[26]

The Consistorial Ordinance also placed particularly great value on the physical condition of the buildings belonging to the benefice. In section 8 it treats the topic "concerning the construction of churches, parsonages, and homes for the teachers in the principality." It requests the shifting of building responsibility to the patrons, especially the monasteries and bishoprics where they have the right of patronage. In this section there also emerges a rather charming concern that the pastor have an opportunity and place for quiet study: "A study should be built for every pastor so that he can study undisturbed."[27]

Through the visitations it also became apparent that frequently proceeds from endowments did not suffice for the support of the pastors. It is a well-known fact that even before the Reformation pastors left their congregations because they could no longer live on their incomes.[28] In order to reestablish normal conditions, it was necessary to seek some assistance in such situations. The Wassertrüding Chapter Ordinance of 1545 states concerning this condition: "When someone does not have the income due to him as a pastor, he should report this. Thereupon his superiors should turn to his lord concerning this lack, so that his salary may be given to him."[29]

It is possible to affirm a great deal of variation in the handling of the benefices. In the rural areas they were preserved for the most part. In the cities, on the other hand, they were in many cases combined in special treasuries out of which the pastors received a salary.[30] This centralization of benefices can be found in numerous cities, as, for example, in Schweinfurt[31] and Rothenburg o. d. T. The latter had a dual system: some of the benefices were preserved, and there were also pastors who received a salary. The imperial city confiscated the benefices and paid the pastor a salary particularly when a dispute arose between the pastor and the congregation over the proceeds of the benefices. This is illustrated in the Rothenburg Instruction How the Church Ordinance Should Be Handled and Carried Out of 1558, which states:

> 3. When the new pastors are installed, the congregations are commanded that where a salary is not alloted to the pastors, nothing should be removed from their possessions and rights which belong to the benefice.
>
> 4. Since quarrels often arise between the pastors and their congregations, it is established that a definite salary be alloted to the pastors.[32]

The justification for this measure according to the Instruction is that the pastors could use the time for study that they would otherwise spend in argumentation with the peasants.

Not infrequently the benefices were also added to the monastic funds that were taken over by the state; this was the case in Rothenburg o. d. T.[33] and in Brandenburg-Kulmbach.[34] Rothenburg o. d. T. also collected the income from vacant benefices.[35]

In general, it is possible to assert that the benefices were much more exposed to government interference than the ecclesiastical endowments. The reason for this may be related to the fear of robbing God when tampering with ecclesiastical endowments, whereas tampering with benefices involved only the taking from a man, the pastor. Claiming of benefices for the state is connected with the confiscation of monastic property, as seems to be the case in Brandenburg-Kulmbach and Rothenburg o. d. T. The monasteries controlled the benefices of the parishes incorporated in them, so that the benefice endowments that belonged to the monastery became part of the state treasury with the confiscation of monastic property. Unoccupied benefices were also at times converted into academic scholarships. One of the questions of the church visitation in the margravate of Brandenburg *unter dem Gebirg* of the year 1536 was, therefore, "how should the benefices that had been given to the schools be used."[36]

A very peculiar medieval endowment remained untouched by the Reformation in its legal position, namely, the hospital. It was an institutional endowment to which one neither could nor wanted to give another purpose; its incorporation into public funds would have been senseless. It served its purpose as an eleemosynary endowment after the Reformation as it had before. In its administration and financial organization it was, of course, subordinate to the visitation. Otherwise it was simply taken for granted by various visitation ordinances. Thus the question was also asked in the Ansbach Ordinance of Church Visitation of 1536, "What to do with the hospitals?"[37] The Ansbach Retaxierte Chapter Ordinance of 1578 suggests that the visitors ask "how the hospital administrators conduct themselves in their position?"[38]

In summarizing the results of this examination of the endowment law of the Franconian church ordinances, it is possible to confirm that in general an attempt was made in these ordinances to preserve the pre-Reformation endowments and, after changing their purpose, to incorporate them into the new ecclesiastical life. Some exceptions did, of course, occur. Within this context, then, the Reformation was not a revolution. On the contrary, one finds an attempt to preserve and to promote the essential character of endowments. The visitations served this goal. In addition to the spiritual *superiores*, secular officials were appointed to be visitors for the particular purpose of protecting the endowment fortunes. The decree of the Ansbach provincial diet of 1526 demanded that "[state] officials should be brought in for the supervision of the endowments."[39]

Furthermore, the Consistorial Ordinance of 1594 specifies at the end of the century:

The members of the highest ecclesiastical administrative authority (the consistories), especially the president and the secular councilors, should see to it that that be correctly administered which has been donated previously for the support of the churches and schools and which has been designated for it by us [the sovereign] after the accomplishment of the Reformation, or which shall be designated for it in the future out of generosity. All such endowments together with the rights due them should be correctly used, defended, and preserved, so that nothing be taken from them and so that they not be employed falsely against the evangelical regulations.[40]

This statement demonstrates the beginnings of the supervision and protection of endowments by the state, as is still the case today, and gives evidence to one of the many long-range effects of Luther's Reformation that reaches to our present day.

1. This essay appeared in the original German in *Vierhundertundfünfzig Jahre lutherischer Reformation 1517–1967 Festschrift für Franz Lau* (Göttingen, 1967) under the title "Reformatorisches Stiftungsrecht in den fränkischen Kirchenordnungen des 16. Jahrhunderts." It has been revised for its inclusion in this volume. (Translation by Kurt Hendel.)

2. *KO. Cf.* H. Lehnert, *Kirchengut und Reformation* (Erlangen, 1935), p. 148, with Hans Liermann, *Handbuch des Stiftungsrechts: Geschichte des Stiftungsrechts* (Tübingen, 1963), pp. 124 ff., and the literature cited there.

3. *KO*, p. 768.

4. Ibid., p. 131 a. "Das das allein gute werk sein, damit man Got nach seinem wort und dem negsten nach bruderlicher liebe dienet."

5. Ibid., p. 131 b. "Das alle werk, die Got nicht bevolhen und des nechsten lieb nichterfordert, bos und unnustz seim."

6. Ibid., p. 134 a. "7. Das bischoff, pfaffen, monchen, nunnen, simonei treiben, wann sie ir gebet, gute werk, verdienst, bruderschaft, vigilien, seelmessen, wann die schon sunst recht weren, umb gelt, gult, stiftung verkauen." "8. Das alle, die solichs stiften und kaufen, auch simonei treiben."

7. Ibid., p. 91 a. "Es soll auch hinfüro kein mess umb gelt, sunder allein umb der ere und lieb Gotts willen, so der celebrierer rechte andacht und begird darzu hat, gehalten werden."

8. Ibid., p. 126 b. "Ob sich auch gezime, umb gestiften oder andere presenz oder nutzung verdinglich mess auch in deutscher sprach ze halten."

9. Ibid., p. 182 a. "allerlei unchristliche gesang und gebet, dem wort Gottes ungemess und entgengen, darein gemischt, und solicher missbreuch so unzelich vil, bis es zuletzt dahin ist kummen, das des Herrn abentmal . . . hat zu allerlei handeln und gescheften müssen dine. Dann man hat nicht allein mess gelesen für fieber und allerlei krankheit, sundern auch für armut, für gefar leibs und guts etc. Ja, man hat auch zauberei damit getrieben."

10. Cf. Liermann, *Handbuch*, p. 143 f.

11. The centralization of endowments for the purpose of charity and for social welfare, which was referred to as the "common chest" in the law code of the

evangelical territories, was a phenomenon of the time which could also be found in the Roman Catholic territories. Cf. Lierman, *Handbuch*, p. 146 ff.

12. *KO*, 11:29 a. "Gleichwoh wil ein erber rat aus guten ursachen die alten hievor gestiften spend und seelpad in irem wesen wie bisher beruen lassen des versehens, das die mit der zeit auch in dises almusen gezogen werden sollen."

13. Ibid., p. 94 b. "wie die beschehen und mit alter herkummen sein . . . bis auf ferner handlung und beschluss eins gemeinen christlichen concilien oder nationalversamlung oder unsern weitern bescheid . . . solch stiftungen irs gewissens halben nit halten könten oder wolten, . . . so soll in der fundatores oder irer erben willen steen, die stiftung von der jerlichen abnutzung durch ander person halten zu lassen . . . so soll hierinen dem teil gevolgt werden, der die Stiftung gehalten haben will."

14. Ibid., p. 72 b. "damit solich almusen, bass dann bisher geschehen, ausgetailt wurden."

15. Ibid., p. 319 a. "Item den casten der arenm leut sollen sie getreulich furdern."

16. Cf. in general Liermann, *Handbuch*, p. 148.

17. *KO*, 11:675 b. "Sich werden auch die alten, gestiften schpent und seelbad mit der zeit auch in dies almosen begeben."

18. Ibid., p. 672.

19. Ibid., p. 675 b. "etliche fromme burgerstöchter, die ihre mannbar jahr erreicht und doch armut halber sich könten verheiraten."

20. Ibid., p. 352 a.

21. Ibid., p. 395 a.

22. Ibid., p. 687, 689.

23. Ibid., p. 78 a, b. "Item diewel wir verschiner zeit von der pfaffhait manifeltig sein bemuet und angefochten worden, als mit opfern, seelgerect, belonungen und andern erdichten dingen, dadurch wir in unkosten sein gefürt worden. Und so wir nun durch das evangelion bericht worden, das unser mainung und endlicher beschluss das man weder dir noch einem andern solcher ding aus gerechtigkait kains geben sol."

24. Ibid., p. 78 b. "Seind aber die diener des worts enthaltung und leibs nottdurft gewarten und haben sollen, ist uns gut zu wissen, das ditz ampt oder pfarr von unsern voreltern sein begabung hat, davon gemainer diener und pastor sein enthaltung have kan und sol, davon wir (als vom lehen) nicht willens sein, etwas zu nemen solcher zugehöre, nemlich etlich zins, holzmark, wisen und ecker, wie die dann verraint und verstaint sein. Magstu dich zur leibs notturft, als ein getreuer diener, wie oben begriffen ist, gebrauchen. Was aber uber das vorhere durch ander unbillich begert und von den scheflein Christi geschunden ist, das soltu kain ferner anfordrung haben, sunder dich an solchem (wie billich) genügen lassen."

25. Ibid., p. 106 a.

26. Ibid., p. 393 a, b.

27. Ibid., pp. 393 b–394 b. "Und nachdem die notturft erfordert, das die pfarrer zue irem studiren ein besonder ort haben, da sie von weib, kindern und hausgesind ungehindert und ungeirret demselben mit vleis abwarten können, soll jedem pfarrherr . . . nach gelegenheit jedes orts ein studirstueblein gebaut werden."

28. In a register of the diocese of Mainz one finds the following entry of the year 1506: "propter paupertatem aufugit" ("He left because of poverty"). Cf.

C. A. H. Burkhardt, *Geschichte der sächsischen Kirchen-und Schulvisitationen von 1524 bis 1545* (Leipzig, 1879), p. 325.

29. *KO*, 11:332 b. "Auch wen einer sein priesterliche, zimliche leibnarung nit genugsam hette, soll er das anzaigen. Alsdann sollen und wöllen die superiores gegen seinen lehenherren des mangels halben sich bewerben, auf das ime sein taglon und lidlon gegenben werde."

30. Ibid., p. 293.

31. Ibid., p. 621.

32. Ibid., p. 610 b. "3. Desgleichen auch jeder zeit, wo neue pfarrer angenomen und uf die pfarren confirmiert, inen ernstlich uferlegt und bevolhen, wo inen kein genandte competenz verordnet, das der pfarr an iren güter und gerechtigkeiten nichts entzogen werde."
"4. Nachdem auch je und allwegen sich zwüschen den pfarren und iren zuhören allerlai zenk und beder . . . zugetragen . . . solte nicht ungeraten sein, wa es auderst füeglich gesein möchte, das den pfarern ein genannte competenz verordent. . . ."

33. Ibid., pp. 564 ff.

34. Ibid., p. 362 a, b.

35. Ibid., p. 563.

36. Ibid., p. 323 a.

37. Ibid.

38. Ibid., p. 94 b.

39. Ibid.

40. Ibid., p. 382 b. "Zum neunten, die consistorialn besonders der president und ime zugeordnete politische räte, sollen insonderheit, was zue unterhaltung der kirchen und schulen von alters gestift und nach beschehener christlicher reformation von uns darzu verordnet, auch künftig aus mildraichen herzen sampt deselben anhangend jura gehandhabet, vertaidigt und erhalten werde, damit nichts entzogen oder anderstwohin und obangezogener reformation und ordnung zuewider gewendet werdet."

THE SECOND NÜRNBERG CHURCH VISITATION

Gerhard Hirschmann

The great importance of documents concerning church visitations to historical research has been recognized for a long time.[1] The last decades have seen great progress in the concern for these documents and their publication.[2] In Germany, certainly the pre-Reformation visitations of the fifteenth century have been recognized as equal in importance to the post-Reformation visitations of the sixteenth century. In many instances the results of the visitations have been used polemically by both Catholic and Protestant church historians. This is justifiable if the judgments of both parties give due consideration to the fact that what was objectionable is especially emphasized in the visitation reports. This fact is realized today in a time when the ecclesiastical situation in Germany in the fifteenth and sixteenth centuries is more clearly understood by researchers.

In Franconia, as far as the history of the areas that became Lutheran is concerned, the main interest has been in the first post-Reformation church visitation in 1528, conducted in the principalities of Brandenburg-Ansbach, Brandenburg-Kulmbach, and the territory of the imperial city of Nürnberg. After the work of Hermann Westermeyer in 1894, the documentary fragments preserved from the principality of Ansbach were published by Karl Schornbaum in 1928 in honor of the four-hundredth anniversary of the visitation.[3]

Unfortunately, the notes concerning the visitation in the territory of the imperial city of Nürnberg were destroyed near the end of the eighteenth century. Only fragmentary copies of the parishes of Kornburg and Ottensoos[4] as well as the curates' visitation in the Nürnberg city parishes of Saint Sebald, Saint Lorenz, and the New Hospital Church[5] have been preserved for us. On the basis of this evidence and a manuscript in the German National Museum in Nürnberg entitled "Reports of the Church Visitation of 1528,"[6] Adolf Engelhardt, in 1937, published a detailed account of the visitation in the Nürnberg territory.[7]

But there has remained a lack of any thorough description of the second Nürnberg visitation of 1560–61. The importance and extent of the second visitation, which, unlike the first, was conducted in the individual parishes themselves, combined with the fact that excerpts of the records and, in part, even the original protocol is extant, justify the writing of a coherent narrative of the planning and implementing of the second visitation.

A glance at the sources and the previously published accounts of the visitation indicates that it was carried out in two phases over a period of two years. The first phase lasted from May 26 to July 1, 1560, and included visitations to the administrative districts (*Ämter*) of Hersbruck, Velden, Lauf, Heideck, Hilpolstein, Allersberg, and some other selected Nürnberg parishes. The second phase extended from September 1 to October 23, 1561. It included the administrative districts of Gräfenberg, Hiltpoltstein, Betzenstein, Altdorf, Lichtenau, and individual parishes north and south of the imperial city.[8]

Excerpts of the protocols of both phases of the visitation are extant.[9] They were read to the Nürnberg City Council upon the completion of the visitation. Furthermore, there exists a very concise record, published in 1913 by Karl Schornbaum, entitled "Wie die priester auf dem lande in examine seind graduirt worden 1560."[10] This contains evaluations written in both German and Latin. Although occasionally somewhat lengthier, they usually are no longer than four or five words. Johann Christian Siebenkees published a similar brief account in 1792.[11]

The most important source, at least for the second phase of the visitation in 1561, is the extant original record that Schornbaum hoped to discover fifty years ago.[12] Part of these protocols is deposited in the Staatsarchiv, Nürnberg.[13] Heinz Dannenbauer used this for the first time, along with the previously mentioned excerpts, in his work "Die Nürnberger Landgeistlichen bis zur 2. Kirchenvisitation."[14] He did this, however, without a thorough collation of this important document with other sources. From the voluminous manuscripts, he printed only short digests of selected statements that were related to the pastors. I have located the other previously unknown part of the original records of the visitation in the Nürnberg city archives.[15]

Furthermore, there exist exact accounts of the expenses of the visitation,[16] the decisions of the Nürnberg government concerning the conduct of the investigation,[17] and the "Considerations Concerning the Visitation of Pastors and Sacristans in Rural Areas," prepared by order of the council by the two preachers Besold and Heling.[18] Also extant is a copy of the visitation articles insofar as they relate to the pastors,[19] and, finally, the conclusions compiled by the city council upon the completion of the visitation, on the basis of the protocol abstract.[20]

The plan to conduct another visitation in Nürnberg originated in 1558, thirty years after the first visitation. On February 15, 1558, the council resolved, "As it appears beneficial to correct and abolish the spreading confusion in rural areas through an orderly visitation of pastors, it is ordered that it be considered and suggested how such a visitation could be established and implemented."[21] Councilmen Hans Stark and Joachim Haller were entrusted with this assignment.

The confusion the council's order referred to was the consequence of the Second Margrave's War. The territory of Nürnberg was at that time, in 1552–53, severely afflicted. A large number of villages were burned and destroyed or at least pillaged. Acts of violence against the people were very common and this must have had an effect upon them. In addition one must consider that a second generation now filled the pastorates, the members of which had not directly and actively experienced the profound movement of the Reformation.

Apart from this particular situation, there was a general awareness that repeated visitations were an important means of reestablishing order and leadership in the life of the church. Hence, visitations were repeated at the same time in the principalities of Ansbach and Bayreuth, in Electoral Saxony in 1555,

Electoral Upper Palatinate in 1557, and in the Neuburg Palatinate in 1553, 1558, and 1561.[22]

On the basis of the council's decision, the previously mentioned "Considerations" were drawn up by the preachers Besold and Heling. These comprised eight pages, and were signed by the two preachers and dated March 12, 1558. The authors explained at the beginning that they wanted to avoid the impression "that we wish to establish anything new." Therefore, as they wrote later, they took the "ordinance of the visitation as it was established and approved by Philip Melanchthon and other God-fearing men and as it was implemented by the elector, Duke August, in his territory" as their model, and following it, prepared an abstract "according to the situation of this land." In mentioning the ordinance of the visitation of Elector August of Saxony, the authors of the "Considerations" were making reference to the visitation in Electoral Saxony in 1555. The instructions of March 3, 1555,[23] which Melanchthon helped to draw up, were printed by Hans Lufft in Wittenberg.[24] Two years later the "General Articles and Public Report" of May 8, 1557, was published in Dresden.[25] This presented a church order written on the basis of the results of the visitation of 1555. Both publications could have been available to the Nürnberg theologians in their work and could have served as a model for their ideas, even though the "Considerations" appears, externally, to have been compiled independently with many variations.

They suggested "two preachers and two or more God-fearing and understanding men" should be selected as visitors. A notary should also accompany them in order that everything would be duly recorded. The document was divided into two main parts. The first contained a lengthy list of questions that the [secular] administrators, community representatives, church administrators, pastors, schoolmasters, citizens, and peasants would be required to answer. The second part contained the "Admonitions" to the individual groups visited. In the conclusion of the document, the authors suggested that this kind of visitation be conducted annually, and in an appendage they recommended that the people be urged diligently to receive private absolution.

After the council's decision of 1558 and the request for advice from the two theologians, the visitation was temporarily postponed. Only after two years (early in 1560) were the plans for the church visitation taken up again. On April 8, 1560,[26] the council, "as a Christian government," concluded that a visitation to all church personnel, school children, and parishioners in the imperial city's territory should be undertaken. The preparations were made by Joachim Haller and Hieronymus Schürstab (1512–73) who replaced Hans Stark. Schürstab had served on the city council since 1545.[27] Haller, somewhat younger (1524–70), joined the council in 1550 and advanced in the official hierarchy to the position of junior *Losunger*.[28]

Schürstab and Haller were to examine and possibly revise the advice of Heling and Besold concerning the establishment of the visitation. They then were to study the evidence from the first visitation of 1528 and prepare recommendations concerning the participants of the visitation, the time limits, and the itinerary of villages to be visited.

On Friday, May 17, 1560, the whole affair was taken up by the council.[29] The recommendations of Schürstab and Haller were read to the council, and new resolutions were drawn up. The governing authorities agreed to the establishment of a visitation into the individual parishes to be conducted by the two preachers, Hieronymus Besold of the Heilig-Geist-Spital and Moritz Heling of Saint Sebald. Because of his familiarity with the area, territorial administrator Christoph Fürer (1517–61)[30] was to participate as was Matthias Schiller, a man connected with the Calvinists.[31] Schiller was to serve as secretary and amanuensis.

Besold and Heling, two of the most reputable theologians of the imperial city, were entrusted with the spiritual leadership of the visitation. Besold was the son of a Nürnberg citizen. After his studies at Wittenberg, he became the noonday preacher at Saint Jacob and, from 1547 on, was preacher at the Heilig-Geist-Spital. In 1548 he had married Osiander's daughter; in 1562 he was named preacher at Saint Lorenz. He died of the plague on September 4, 1562.[32] Heling, born in 1522 in Friedland in Prussia, also studied at Wittenberg. He came to Nürnberg with Melanchthon in 1555. At Melanchthon's suggestion he was appointed to the position of preacher at Saint Sebald, which was open because Leonhard Culmann had been removed from office after being convicted of adhering to Osiandrian errors. Heling was a follower of Melanchthon and stood on the side of the Philippists in the violent and drawn-out controversy in Nürnberg. As such, he was relieved of his preaching obligations in 1575. Heling died on October 2, 1595.[33]

Besold, unlike Heling, was a practical man who avoided theological controversy and who remained a loyal follower of Luther. The two clergymen (to whom the council gave the title of superintendent), though of different leanings, had worked well together in the past. In 1558 Besold, supported by Heling, assumed the position of overseer of the children and the recitation of the catechism at Sunday church services. In the same year with other Nürnberg clergy, they repudiated the Consensus Formula of the Frankfurt Recess and in 1561 rejected the proposal to send observers to the Council of Trent. One may assume that they were able to work well together on the visitation.

Let us now return to the council meeting of May 17, 1560, and the resolutions concerning the establishment of the visitation. The investigation was not to limit itself to ecclesiastical affairs but, as in 1528, persons "in the villages visited who live scandalous lives should be summoned to be called into question and to be exhorted to repentance." At that time it was simply a matter of course for territorial lords to be concurrently lords of the church. The council, therefore, claimed the right of supervision over the moral condition of its subjects.

The draft of the Visitation Articles was thoroughly discussed at the council meeting. Unlike the Articles of 1528, at least a copy of that part of the final draft of the Articles of 1560–61 dealing with the pastors has been preserved.[34] The council was satisfied with the draft and accepted it with only minor alterations. For example, in the eighth question, a sentence was added stipulating that the pastors should report those persons to the city council who, after verbal admonitions, refused to give up their vices. In this way the supervisory duty of the governing authority over the Christian life style of its subjects was strongly emphasized. The fourth question was supplemented with an admonition to the pastors not to be severe with elderly people who were no longer able to learn the catechism verbatim. Also administrators (*Pfleger*)—that is, the leading officials of the imperial city's administrative districts—were warned that subjects were not allowed to miss the church service or sermons in the execution of any official duties. Furthermore, pastors should be permitted to threaten disrespectful and unrepentant parishioners with excommunication and suspension, after prior instruction and arrangement with the council.

Finally, the council included a resolution concerning a visitation to several parishes "which belong to Nürnberg but are located over the water." They here referred to parishes west of the river Rednitz over which Nürnberg exercised church patronage rights even though they were in the territory of the margrave of Ansbach. In the visitation of 1528, conducted together with Ansbach, officials of the margrave were entrusted with the responsibility of visiting these parishes "out of good will but with no justification." Times had changed; now the city council resolved to include these parishes in the Nürnberg church visitation and await "whether and in what way the margrave would wish to amend the decision."

After all of the provisions for the visitation were fulfilled, there was nothing further to hinder its initiation. On Sunday, May 26, 1560, the visitation commission left Nürnberg and went first to Hersbruck.[35] Altogether there were fourteen or fifteen men and eleven or twelve horses. Joachim Haller, the leader of the visitation, had, on the previous day, received an advance of 100 gulden from the treasury (*Losungsstube*) to cover expenses. At the end of the visitation he presented a detailed account of individual expenses. This gives us a most welcome record of the outcome and cost of the project. The first money spent went to the children of the German and Latin school in Hersbruck "because of their prayer habits." Each child received three pfennigs. From Hersbruck the commission went to Engelthal where the three pastors from Engelthal, Entenberg, and Offenhausen were visited. Next on the schedule was the parish of Alfeld.

On the return trip from Alfeld, the visitors had their noon meal
with Herr von der Grün at Thalheim castle. Since he refused
to take any money from his guests, they "honored" his wife,
three daughters, grandchildren, and servants with six and one-
half talers. The pastor of Förrenbach received one taler "in
consideration of his advanced age and poverty." From Hersbruck, the parishes of Vorra, Eschenbach, Pommelsbrunn, Reichenschwand, and Henfenfeld were visited. (The combined
parish of Alfalter-Artelshofen was, at that time, unoccupied.)
In each place the school children, and occasionally the pastor,
received gifts. The commission stayed ten days and eight nights
in Hersbruck and paid a total of eighty-two gulden, one pound,
and sixteen pfennigs for their room and board.[36] The administrator's wife and children received ten talers "for the household's inconvenience and general disturbance of the household
order, also, for the kindling wood, salt, and lard for which there
was no bill." The servants received two talers.

Having finished their work in Hersbruck, the commission
traveled to the administrative district (*Pflegamt*) of Velden.
On the way it had to pay two pounds twelve pfennigs for "an
extra team of horses to cross the mountain" between Eschenbach and Velden. It also needed a carriage guide, whom it paid.
The visitors stayed in Velden two days and two nights. The
wife of the constable, Hans Ott, was confined at that time. At
his request the commission gave him one-half taler for childbed
supplies. On the return journey to Hersbruck it stopped in the
parish of Kirchensittenbach. The pastor there could not be
questioned because he had suffered a stroke that left him barely
able to speak and very hard of hearing.

The commission then turned back toward Nürnberg, stopping three days and three nights in Lauf, during which time it
visited the parishes of Behringersdorf, Rückersdorf and Leinburg. The office of the territorial administrator (*Landpflegamt*) in Nürnberg had sent Veit Sauermann, the morning
preacher (*Frühmesser*) of Ottensoos to Lauf to be examined.
This was done to ascertain if he would be suitable for an appointment as morning preacher at Artelshofen. Sauermann did
not pass his examination but at least received one-fourth of a

taler for his journey. The wife and eight children of the administrator at Lauf received monetary gifts. Likewise, the city watchman and the host of the inn, where the horses were quartered, received payment. The schoolchildren everywhere received small gifts of money. On the journey home the parish of Mögeldorf was also visited. Here the travelers dined in the castle of Sebastian Imhoff.

The commission arrived in Nürnberg on June 15. However, after its reception it immediately took another advancement of 300 gulden for the journey to the districts of Allersberg, Hilpolstein, and Heideck. Nürnberg had held these districts in pledge since 1542; consequently, they fell under the ecclesiastical authority of the city. The commission first went to Heideck, where it remained for six days and nights. From Heideck it conducted visitations in the parishes of Jahrsdorf, Zell, Rednitzhembach, Aberzhausen, Liabstadt, Walting, Kalbensteinberg, and Liebenstadt. The wife of the pastor of Liebenstadt received a taler as a gift because of great poverty and a long illness. The pastor of Bechthal came to Heideck for his interview. After visiting Schwimbach, the commission traveled to Hilpolstein, where it remained for eight days and nights. From here it visited the parishes of Meckenhausen, Mörsdorf, and Heuberg. Monetary gifts were again presented. After remaining one day and one night in Allersberg, the commission again returned to Nürnberg on July 1.

During this last visit costs of four gulden, four pounds, and twelve pfennigs were incurred for barber and laundry services as well as for services from a saddler, smith, and wheelwright. Mentioned also was the expenditure of nine gulden, two pounds, twelve pfennigs "for 103 catechisms, some of which have been distributed, others of which still remain to be distributed in various schools in the countryside." These catechisms were probably editions of Luther's *Small Catechism* of 1529. The six coaches and the drivers who "waited for the gentlemen" received thirteen gulden, one pound, six pfennigs. Altogether the thirty-four-day visitation of 1560 cost 49 gulden. Hieronymus Schürstab and Joachim Haller received travel pay for thirty-four days. Christoph Fürer, who apparently participated for only a short time, received travel compensation for five days.

At the conclusion of the visitation, reports on each parish were compiled from the records made during the actual visit. These reports are the so-called Church Visitation Book.[37] A summary of this was made and read at the council meetings of August 20, 22, 23, 27, and 30, 1560. The government's conclusions, which were then made public, are contained in the volumes of the council's official protocol, the *Ratsverlässe*. A closer study will be made of these after a discussion of the second half of the investigation.

A year later the second phase of the visitation began. The commission once again consisted of fourteen to fifteen persons; Joachim Haller again was in charge. Councilman Paul Koler, a brother-in-law of Christoph Fürer, took the place of Hieronymus Schürstab. There is no evidence to indicate whether or not Schürstab participated. The spiritual responsibilities fell, as before, to Heling and Besold. The latter was given two students from the Hospital school who were to "attend him at different times." Instead of Matthias Schiller, chancery secretary Johann Ketzmann was responsible for keeping records of the proceedings. It is noteworthy that four young boys accompanied the visitors for a few days "for the sake of preserving the memory." They were the eleven-year-old son of Haller, Willibald, the eight-year-old Paul Koler, the visitor's son, and the sons of Johann Ketzmann and council secretary Christoph Lindner. Each of the four boys was presented with one-half gulden "as a prayer pfennig." Here one can see the preservation of the old German legal custom of involving children in legal matters to secure witnesses for later times. It is reminiscent of the famous "Ohrenziehen."[38]

In order to depict the second phase of the visitation we can refer to the original protocol and appendages, such as the drafts of invitations to the pastors and the pastors' responses, and other similar documents.[39] Also, unlike the year before, the accounts record specific dates. This makes it possible to follow exactly the itinerary and performance of the visitation.

On the day before departure Haller again received an advance of 200 gulden from the treasury. Before the visitation began, the commission paid "ten pfennigs for fifty good writing quills, twenty pfennigs for two writing rulers, twenty-five pfennigs for paper shears." On August 31, 1561, the commission left Nürnberg and rode, on twelve horses, to Gräfenberg, stopping for a drink on the way in Heroldsberg. In Eschenau, alms were distributed to the poor and disabled. The mason and the whitewasher working on the administration building in Gräfenberg were also given gratuities.

The commission lodged in Gräfenberg for a week, and from there carried on its business. On Monday morning, September 1, 1561, the pastor, schoolmaster, administrator, mayor, and councilmen of Gräfenberg were examined. The same afternoon the pastor and administrator of Hiltpoltstein were interviewed. On September 2, the pastor of Grebern (Walkersbrunn) was visited. The pastor of Stöckach appeared in Gräfenberg on the same day. He asked to be excused from the examination as he had been installed by the bishop of Bamberg and feared difficulties would arise if he were to submit to the Nürnberg investigation. The commission referred the problem to the council for instructions. The response came quickly, on September 3, advising the representatives, "with regard to the examination . . . do not pressure the pastor. Merely indicate to him that he should adhere to the religion which he has been advocating in his church." However, the pastor of Stöckach would not return to Gräfenberg a second time, even though the administrator of Hiltpoltstein, Sebald Lang, went personally to Stöckach to persuade him.[40]

On September 2 the commission examined the pastors of Igensdorf and Kirchrüsselbach. September 3 it rode to Hiltpoltstein, where it spent one night. While there, it questioned the jurors and legal personnel. The administrator there received six talers for the expenses incurred. On the next day, September 4, it traveled to Betzenstein, where it examined the pastor in the morning. At noon it held two public examinations, for the city of Betzenstein itself and for the surrounding villages. At that time the pastor presented a detailed memorandum[41] concerning practices in the church at Hüll, which appeared to him to be blasphemous. In the afternoon a public examination took place in Hüll. The proceedings dealt with a popular cultic pilgrimage to a picture of the Madonna in the church at Hüll. The pastor portrayed the cult very vividly:

> A matter has come to my attention in the neighboring succursal chapel of Hüll where I must assist several times in the course of a year. I have found there a distasteful and wicked idolatrous abuse. There are pilgrimages, processions around the altar with crosses, banners, lamps, and idolatrous pictures. The pictures are offered money, votive candles, and human hair. Children genuflect before the picture and offer petitions. The picture of the Madonna has two poles attached to it and is covered with rags and old and new church veils.

The pastor had, in vain, attempted to abolish this cult. Two "idolatrous men," Sebald Walther and Winterer, appear to have been the principle instigators of the cult.

The commission remained over night in Betzenstein. On the next morning, September 5, it interrogated the church administrator of Hüll in Betzenstein. It then issued to him and to the pastor "a final decree regarding the offering at Hüll." In this it stipulated, "Therefore the administrator must order that the altar with the Madonna's picture be removed and a crucifix like one which can be found in Nürnberg is to be installed in place of the picture. The picture of Saint Martin in the other altar can be removed since the altar itself remains sufficiently decorated with its painting." The following year a crucifix was brought to Hüll.[42]

On Saturday, September 6, the examination of the congregation in Kirchrüsselbach took place. The pastor there, who was characterized as an "excellent little elderly man," received four gulden, two pounds, twelve pfennigs because of his meager income. On Sunday, September 7, the commission concluded examination of the community of Walkersbrunn with the questioning of the church administrator, captains, and the community representatives. On September 8, "after breakfast," the examination of the parish community of Igensdorf took place. Finally, on the morning of September 9, the examiners questioned the two pastors of Beerbach and Eschenau in Gräfenberg. (Their parishes were not visited until later, on September 25 and 26.) On the same day the commission began its journey home. The seven-day stay in Gräfenberg cost more than sixty-three gulden. Added to this expense were remunerations for the wife and children of the administrator. The visitors stayed overnight with Hans Stark in Röckenhof on September 9 before arriving in Nürnberg.

On Monday, September 15, the commission resumed its itinerary. Passing through Saint Peter, they arrived in Fischbach, where the pastor, village captains, and community representatives were examined. There then followed a public examination of the entire community. The noonday meal was taken in the castle of Georg Scheurl, who, like other hosts, refused to accept payment. The visitors, however, did present his wife with four gulden. Toward evening, after having been refreshed with an "afternoon drink" at the home of Wolf Pessler's widow, they proceeded to Feucht where they sought lodging in a local inn. A peasant who served as a guide from Fischbach to Feucht received one pound, twelve pfennigs.

On Tuesday, September 16, the visitation was carried out in Feucht. The following day the commission visited Röthenbach in Saint Wolfgang, where it spent the night in an inn. The pastor of Kornburg was summoned to Röthenbach for the following day and was then examined. The pastor from Büchenbach in Schwabach, who had also been summoned, failed to appear, basing his refusal on the fact that he fell under the jurisdiction of the margrave. On Thursday, September 18, the commission rode to Altdorf. It stayed there for a week with the administrator, Balthasar Baumgartner. The city council gave the visitors some jugs of wine as a gift. Three boys played music in the administrator's hourse, presumedly during meals. A student from Neustadt in Coburg, Hieronymus Cunrad, received money for provisions from the commission in Altdorf "because of the conditions about which he had petitioned."[43] The visitors planned their stay so that they could hear the sermon preached Friday morning in the church, after which they examined the pastor and two curates. On Saturday they interrogated the administrator and the schoolmaster, and visited the school. They concluded by questioning the council secretary, the councilmen, and the community representatives (called in Altdorf *Achter* instead of the *Vierer*). On Sunday and Monday, September 21 and 22, the investigators held three public examinations in the church for the parishoners. The people incorporated into the Altdorf parish from outside the city proved to be more poorly prepared than those in the city itself.

On September 23 a public examination took place in the parish of Rasch, which was served by the two curates of Altdorf. The departure document concerning the results of the visitation is dated September 24, the same day on which the commission left Altdorf. Before leaving, it presented a gift to the administrator's wife "in remembrance of her good victuals and the great pains she had taken." Her seven children also received gifts, as did the curates, keeper of the watchtower, the fieldguard, the disabled, the constable, and the watchman.

The visitors traveled to Lauf via Letten, where they presented a gift to the local fishermen. On September 25 they arrived from Lauf at the parish of Beerbach to begin the visitation. They remained two days and nights in the castle of Eschenau as guests of Gabriel Muffel; the master of the house received sixteen gulden. On Friday, September 26, the visitation of the community of Eschenau took place; the same day the visitors summoned the parish leaders of Kalchreuth and Heroldsberg to Eschenau for examination. The parishes themselves underwent public examination on Sunday morning in the Kalchreuth church and on Sunday afternoon, September 28, in the church at Heroldsberg. The visitors conducted the examination in Heroldsberg after having attended church services there. When this was finished, they returned to Nürnberg.

On October 1 the commission resumed its journey, this time heading west to the parishes in the administrative district of Lichtenau. On the way it distributed alms to the poor at the Frauentor, to the disabled at Saint Leonhard, and to a poor man in Lichtenau. On Thursday, October 2, it questioned the pastor of Immeldorf, who managed the Lichtenau parish, and the pastor of Sachsen in Lichtenau. In the afternoon it held a public examination in Sachsen; it examined parishoners of Lichtenau and Immeldorf the following day. The visitation in the district (*Pflegamt*) of Lichtenau ended on Saturday with the interrogation of the Lichtenau administrator, Georg Hass, the jurors, the captain, and the church administrators of Immeldorf and Sachsen.

The visitation turned toward the northern parishes of Nürnberg on October 8. The examiners took lodging in Grossgründlach, staying there for nine days as guests of the Nürnberg administrator, Franz Gruner.[44] From there they traveled, on October 9 and 10, to examine the pastor of Tennenlohe, who also served Eltersdorf, and the pastors of Kraftshof and Poppenreuth. On October 10 they were dinner guests of Frau Kress in Kraftshof. Sunday, October 12, a public examination took place in Eltersdorf. As usual, the sacristan and children who pray in the church (*Betkinder*) received gifts. On October 13 the examiners summoned the pastors of Bruck and Puschendorf to Grossgründlach and questioned them. The next day they interviewed the pastors of Lonnerstadt, Möhrendorf, Saint John in Nürnberg, and Sambach. All of these men received gifts of two gulden each. The commission questioned the pastor of Hausen bei Forchheim on October 15. A high fever prevented the pastor of Burgfarrnbach from coming to Grossgründlach; he was questioned later in Nürnberg on November 14.

By special order, the Nürnberg City Council waived the execution of a public examination in Fürth because of a quarrel over jurisdiction in capital offenses with the Bamberg Cathedral provost. Only the pastor was subsequently examined, on October 17, in Grossgründlach. Likewise the commission did not examine the communities of Puschendorf, Burgfarrnbach, Möhrendorf, Lonnerstadt, Sambach, and Hausen, since they fell under foreign jurisdiction. It questioned the parishioners of Poppenreuth in the church on two successive days, October 15 and 16; this was necessary because of the large size of the parish. The visitors spent the night in Vach as "guests of Lindner." On October 16 the village captains and the community representatives of Thon, Grossreuth, and Kleinreuth underwent examination in Grossgründlach; they were reimbursed for their travel expenses. The total expenditure for the stay with the administrator in Grossgründlach was eighty-one gulden, one pound, sixteen pfennigs. The accounts of total expenditures for lodging is still extant.[45] The administrator's wife received six gulden "as a parting gift."

The last visitation journey began in Nürnberg on Monday, October 20, 1561. The work began in the morning with the examination of the pastor from Eibach. Next, the visitors questioned the church administrator, village leaders, and representatives of the parish of Eibach in Reichelsdorf, where the commission took lodging in an inn. Monday afternoon it also examined the pastors from Regelsbach and Saint Leonhard in Nürnberg. The pastor of Gustenfelden excused himself in order to visit his father, who was seriously ill.

The public examination for the community at Eibach took place in the Eibach church on Tuesday afternoon, October 21. The commission held a public examination for the communities of Sünderbühl, Gibitzenhof, Sandreuth, and Steinbühl at noon on Wednesday, October 22, in Saint Leonhard's Church. On Thursday, October 23, the communities of Lichtenhof, Hummelstein, Obergalgenhof, Untergalgenhof, the two Ziegelhüttens, Weiherhaus, Tafelhof, Hümplesshof (Himpfelshof), and Bleich auf der Deutschherrnwiese were also examined in the church of Saint Leonhard. In Eibach and Saint Leonhard, the sacristan, pastor, and children received gifts of money. Early on Thursday, October 23, in Saint Leonhard's parsonage, the captains of Steinbühl, Gibitzenhof, and Sündersbühl were questioned; the pastor then received his written departure document. The commission had their noonday meal with Joachim Tetzel in Saint Leonhard and gave his wife and four daughters five talers. It then returned to Nürnberg, having concluded the visitation. The cost of the 1561 visitation was 645 gulden, five pounds, ten pfennigs. In addition, there was travel pay for forty-five days. The two councilmen, Haller and Koler, received forty-two gulden, seven pounds, six pfennigs; the secretary, Johann Ketzmann, received six gulden, three pounds, eighteen pfennigs.

As was the case in 1560, the notes taken during the visitation were recopied in the "Church Visitation Book," and simultaneously a summary was prepared to be read to the city council. This summary, however, was not read to the council until the summer of 1562 on June 11, 26, and 29, July 1, and October 16, 17, and 19.[46]

How were the diverse grievances that the visitation discovered dealt with? Trivial matters and questions directly concerning public worship were disposed of by the visitors. Thus they forbade the practice at Altdorf of placing a small reed in the chalice at communion services because it was not done in the Nürnberg area and because "it was frought with many dangers." The church veils on the picture of the Madonna on the altar at Altdorf were to be removed early in the morning while the congregation was not present.[47]

The commission referred more serious situations, especially those which involved finances, to the city council for decisions. The council relieved very poorly qualified pastors, like those at Laibstadt, Jahrsdorf, and Heuberg, of their offices.[48] The pastor of Regelsbach was also dismissed. The commission censured and threatened to punish some clergy and many parishioners for their improper life styles. It also chastised persons for failure to attend church services and infrequent attendance at Communion. Censures were enacted against superstitious and idolatrous practices such as bell-ringing to chase away thunderstorms, the blessing of cattle,[49] and the using of medicinal herbs;[50] such practices were especially widespread in the parishes of Grossgründlach and Eltersdorf. The pastor of Kirchrüsselbach was forbidden to distribute wine in the parsonage. The canons regular of Hilpoltstein were forbidden to sing the office. The Velden parish had to sing all hymns in German in the future, for the village lacked a Latin school.

Several pastors, such as those of Entenberg, Gräfenberg, Beerbach, Eibach, Walkersbrunn, and Liebenstadt, as well as the curates of Förrenbach and Hersbruck, received salary increases. In order to increase the pastors' interest in studying, and to improve public worship, the authorities sent books to various parishes, including Alfeld (*Book of Family Devotions*), Entenberg, Heroldsberg (*Service Book*), Offenhausen, and Vorra. The authorities ordered the parish of Altdorf to obtain the

Tomos Lutheri and to use the revenue of "church lands" to do so. The same means, which the city council had administered since the time of the Reformation, were used to supply Allersberg with a new chalice. For the payment of incidental fees, the council suggested to the other parishes (namely Eltersdorf and Saint John in Nürnberg) to follow the example of the tariff that had been introduced in Mögeldorf. The authorities censured intemperance at baptisms and weddings.

The visitation resulted in building improvements for the parsonage in Schwimbach, for the stables of the Gräfenberg and Kraftshof parsonages, for the churches in Heuberg and Mörlach, and for the cemetery wall in Allersberg. The government considered the possibility of building a house for the pastor in Lichtenau so that he could stay there rather than commute from Immeldorf. Finally, the city council concerned itself with the schools; various schoolmasters, such as those in Altdorf and Gräfenberg, received salary increases. The council ordered new schools constructed in Engelthal, Happurg, and Meckenhausen.

Within the scope of this essay, it is not possible to investigate individual cases further. That must await publication of the complete visitation protocol. However, one may at least present the results of the visitations to the pastors of Sachsen, Saint John in Nürnberg, and Saint Leonhard in Nürnberg, for a discussion of these three parishes is not included in Dannenbauer's work.[51]

Sachsen.[52] Johann Kissling of Windsheim has been pastor of Sachsen since the feast of the Chair of Peter. The Ansbach chapter conferred the benefice on him; the administrator of Lichtenau installed him. He does not know his annual income as he has not yet been there for a full year. He has no money; his only income is the small tithe. He answered moderately well in his questioning and passed the examination fairly well. He has a Bible, the *Loci* of Melanchthon, the Augsburg Confession, the Homilies of Brenz, Philip Melanchthon, and Luther. He uses ceremonies in the church. When he has communicants, he uses vestments; when there are no communicants, he does not use them. He found the situation thus when he arrived: There was a *Service Book* (*Agendbüchlein*) at the parish, which he diligently follows. Heretofore he has held instruction in the catechism of Luther and Karg on Sunday afternoon, but so far has not accomplished much. The reason for this is that the parishioners do not attend church very often. Except on Sundays and holidays, the only church ceremony is private absolution. There are only "about twenty children" and about three women who live in Sachsen who attend afternoon catechism. They are coarse people who understand very little. The neighbors are anxious for him to hold school. He is willing to receive children and hold classes, but the government should give him special wood for the project.

Nürnberg, Saint John. Pastor Johann Mittenhuber has been pastor there for six years. He did moderately well in the examination and requested a better salary. As he has no regular parishioners, he was not given a written departure document but was told that he should study hard, and recite the six parts of the catechism in the church early every Sunday and holiday. Likewise, he was told to read slowly from the *Service Book*. When communicants from the city or other places come to him, he should examine each of them carefully before administering private absolution. The commission gave him a *Service Book*.

Nürnberg: Saint Leonhard. Pastor Frörer, born in Bernau in the Upper Palatinate, has been pastor of Saint Leonhard for more than five years. He did moderately well on the examinations and was listed among the moderate achievers. He has a Latin and a German Bible, the homilies of Luther and Master Veit (Dietrich) as well as those of Brenz and Melanchthon, Brenz's commentary on John, the homilies of Spangenberg, the *Service Book* and the Church Order. He holds services as prescribed in the *Service Book*. He does not hold catechism lessons, for the villages are too far away for the parishioners to come to vespers. He does have "about twenty children" near him and goes over the catechism with them. At night he goes out if he is called for.

After describing the development of the visitation an assessment of its results is necessary. This evaluation, however, can only emphasize the most important elements.

The individual parishes received a thorough investigation.

The visitation always began with the examination of the pastor, which especially emphasized an assessment of his knowledge, his execution of official responsibilities, and finally his library. Next came the "public examination" of the parishioners held in connection with a public worship service at which the pastor was required to preach a sample sermon.[53] A special attempt was made to discover the adults' knowledge of the catechism as well as what kind of drilling the schoolchildren received in the catechism. The examiners also checked church and Communion attendance as closely as they did general morality. The jurors, village captains, and representatives of the communities had to testify concerning morals. They also had to give an evaluation of the pastor. The visitation extended to the schoolmasters and their schools, financial questions, and building assessment. The clergy used this opportunity to put forth their salary petitions and construction needs.

At the conclusion of the visitation, the commission composed a "recess" in which it itemized all objectionable findings and included recommendations for corrections. Sometimes the commission gave direct orders. More important situations, as we have already noted, it referred to the city council for decisions at the conclusion of the entire project.

What kind of general conclusion can one draw from the results of the visitation? How did the pastors and congregations fare? First, something must be said about the scope of the visitation. There were eighty parishes[54] that were to be included in the visitation. The wide scope of the project is remarkable. On the one hand were the parishes under foreign jurisdiction such as Bamberg's Sambach, where the Ebner family had patronage rights, and the margrave's Möhrendorf, where the Schürstab family had patronage rights. On the other hand was Sachsen, where Nürnberg was the territorial lord but where the religious establishment of Saint Gumbertus in Ansbach possessed the right of church patronage. Nürnberg derived its right of ecclesiastical jurisdiction (and thus also its right of conducting visitations) from the possession of territorial as well as patronage rights. However, the council did make the concession of examining only the pastor and not the parishioners in parishes that lay under foreign jurisdiction.

The visitation excluded the twelve parishes that lay in the districts of the New Palatinate (Allersberg, Hilpolstein, and Heideck), had been pledged to Nürnberg in 1542. These parishes were not reformed until 1542–43; as Dannenbauer noted, their pastors clearly differed from the standard of the pastors of the older Nürnberg territories. Sixty-eight parishes remain. Of these, four (Bergen, Büchenbach, Hausen, Stöckach) could not be visited because they lay under foreign jurisdiction, and the pastors, therefore, did not appear before the visitors. Four other parishes (Alfalter, Gustenfelden, Kirchensittenbach, and Ottensoos) were excluded from the visitation either because the pastors were unable to appear or because the parish was vacant at the time of the visitation. Six more parishes were excluded because they did not have their own pastors but were combined with neighboring parishes (Artelshofen, Altenthann, Eltersdorf, Lichtenau, Rasch, and Veitsbrunn).

There remained fifty-four parishes, which were actually visited.[55] Of these, seventeen of the pastors received a good classification. They were marked as "good," "very good," or "excellent." Twenty-five pastors were classified as having done moderately well. These were designated as "moderately good," "somewhat good," or "having received a moderate classification." Twelve of the pastors received a poor evaluation. They were classified as "passed, but not among the best," "passed, having done poorly," "passed, having done very poorly," or "unfit." Five curates were included with the pastors. Two of them received "good," two "moderately good," and one a "poor" classification. Altogether, forty-six of the fifty-nine clergymen received classifications of either good or satisfactory. This was more than three-fourths of those visited.

In contrast to these good results, the three districts held in pledge fared poorly; of twelve pastors and one curate only two were classified as "good," five as "moderately good," and six as "very poor."

In contrast, how did the parish communities fare? We only have information for the visitation of 1561; the original protocol for the 1560 investigation is no longer extant, and the summaries do not include the evaluations of the communities.[56] In addition, as already mentioned, the commission examined only the pastors in village parishes that lay within a foreign jurisdiction. Consequently, there are evaluations for only twenty-four parish congregations for 1561. This number is increased by one because of the situation in Altdorf, where there were two examinations, one for the city itself and one for those people outside the city who, nevertheless, belonged to the city parish. Fifteen of these parishes received classifications of "passed fairly well" or "passed rather well." Eight of the parishes received poor classifications, having done "not very well" or "very poorly" in the exam. In two cases (Eltersdorf and the city of Altdorf) the classification was "passed, some poorly, some well." No congregation earned a "passed very well" rating. Thus, the parishioners fared significantly worse than their pastors.

These relatively unfavorable results were, most certainly, related to the Second Margrave's War and its effect on the people of the area. As is always the case, war no doubt destroyed many good and moral patterns of life. The new beginnings of the Reformation did not develop as thoroughly as they would have done in peacetime. The particular specialty of the Reformation —instruction in the articles of Christian faith and especially in the catechism—was not yet able to attain everywhere the desired result. The primary aim of the visitation, that for which "the whole event was devised,"[57] was to obtain some idea of the peoples' knowledge of the catechism and to intensify and revive catechetical instruction, especially for the young. The distribution of numerous copies of the catechism served this end.

In conclusion, one may say that the second church visitation represents an important step in the attempt to establish a new regulation of the church's life in the territory of the imperial city of Nürnberg. It is therefore fortunate that at least half of the protocol of the investigation is extant. It gives us, four hundred years later, a vivid record of the Christian spirit that filled the examiners and pastors. It also shows us how that spirit was fostered in the communities where it was lacking.

1. This essay originally appeared in *Zeitschrift für bayerische Kirchengeschichte* 32 (1963), 111–32. It has been revised for inclusion into this volume

(translation by Frank P. Lane). A general assessment of the visitation documents and recommendations for an edition is contained in Gg. Müller, "Visitation als Geschichtsquelle," *Deutsche Geschichtsblätter* 8 (1907):287–316; 16 (1915):1–32; and 17 (1916):279–309.

2. Müller, "Visitation," pp. 305–16 includes a survey of the literature dealing with visitations organized by territories. Additional literature can be found in Karl Schottenloher, *Bibliographie zur Deutschen Geschichte im Zeitalter der Glaubensspaltung 1517–1585* 6 vols. (Leipzig, 1933–39), 4:Nos. 38944–39134. The most recent publication on the topic is Hellmuth Heyden, ed., *Protokolle der pommerschen Kirchenvisitationen 1535–1539*, Quellen zur pommerschen Geschichte, Fourth Series, vol. 1 (Cologne, 1961).

3. Hermann Westermayer, *Die Brandenburgisch-Nürnbergische Kirchenvisitation und Kirchenordnung 1528–1533* (Erlangen, 1894); Karl Schornbaum, *Die erste Brandenburgische Kirchenvisitation 1528*, Einzelarbeiten aus der Kirchengeschichte Bayerns, vol. 10 (Nürnberg, 1928).

4. StAN S. I L. 296 No. 7. Printed in Karl Schornbaum, *Beiträge zur bayerischen Kirchengeschichte*, 2 (1905): 218–22.

5. *Hist.-diplomat. Magazin für das Vaterland und angrenzende Gegenden*, 2 (1783):375–86.

6. Germanische Nationalmuseum, Nürnberg, Merkelsche Sammlung, Hs. Nos. 508 and 978.

7. Adolf Engelhardt, "Die Reformation in Nürnberg," *MVGN* 34(1937): 69–107.

8. StAN, Stadtrechnungsbelege, No. 228.

9. StAN, Kirchen auf dem Lande, No. 453, fol. 1^r–22^r, and No. 454, fol. 1^r–36^r.

10. Karl Schornbaum, "Zur zweiten Nürnbergischen Kirchenvisitation 1560/61," *Beiträge zur bayerischen Kirchengeschichte*, 19(1913):22–27.

11. Johann Christian Siebenkees, "Von der 1560 and 1561 in der Nürnbergischen Landschaft angestellten Kirchenvisitation," *Materialien zur Nürnbergischen Geschichte*, 4 vols. (Nürnberg, 1792–95), 1:236–247.

12. Schornbaum, "Nürnbergischen Kirchenvisitation," p. 22.

13. StAN, Kirchen auf dem Lande, No. 454, fol. 51^r–247^r.

14. Heinz Dannenbauer, "Die Nürnberger Landgeistlichen bis zur zweiten Nürnberger Kirchenvisitation 1560/61," *Zeitschrift für bayerische Kirchengeschichte*, 2–4 (1927–29), 6–9 (1931–34), 25 (1956). A short treatment of the second church visitation can be found in Gunther Petsch, "Das Nürnberger protestantische Kirchenrecht der reichsstädt. Zeit," (dissertation, Erlangen University, 1933), pp. 16 ff.

15. StAN, Amb. 658, fol. 1^r–95^r.

16. See note 8.

17. See notes 21 and 26.

18. Germanisches Nationalmuseum, Nürnberg, Archiv, Reichstadt Nürnberg ex. 15. Thanks to Dr. Ludwig Veit for this reference.

19. StAN, Akten der E-Laden, No. 93. Printed as an appendix to this essay.

20. StAN, Kirchen auf dem Lande, No. 453, fol: 23^r–36^r, and No. 454, fol. 37^r–42^r. The original entries are contained in the Ratsverlässe volumes.

21. StAN, RB, No. 30, fol. 78^r, RV No. 1152, fol. 23^r. The intention of holding a church visitation is inferred in the Ratsverlässe for the years 1535, 1536, 1540, and 1548. Thanks for helpful references from Dr. Gottfried Seebass of Erlangen University.

22. Matthias Simon, *Evang. Kirchengeschichte Bayerns*, 2d ed. (Nürnberg, 1952), p. 292.

23. Emil Sehling, *Die evangelischen Kirchenordnungen des XVI. Jahrhunderts*, sec. 1, part 1 (Leipzig, 1902), pp. 305–11. A detailed description is in Wilhelm Schmidt, *Die Kirchen- und Schulvisitation im sächs. Kurkreise von 1555*, Schriften des Vereins für Reformationsgeschichte, vol. 90 (Halle, 1904) and vol. 92 (Halle, 1906).

24. *KO*, sec. 1, part 1, p. 105.

25. Printed in ibid., pp. 316–35.

26. StAN, RB 31, fol. 63ᵛ; RV 1181, fol 19ʳ.

27. StAN, Rep. 52a, No. 249, fol. 378ᵛ.

28. Johann Gottfried Biedermann, *Geschlechtsregister des Patriciats zu Nürnberg* (Bayreuth, 1748), Table 139.

29. StAN, RB No. 31, fol. 77ᵛ–79ʳ; RV No. 1183, fol. 4ʳ–5ᵛ.

30. Biedermann, *Geschlechtsregister*, Table 372.

31. *MVGN*, 40 (1949):1, and note 5a. He became council secretary in 1578; from 1577 until his death in 1602 he was one of the *Genannten* of the large council. Johann Ferdinand Roth, *Verzeichnis aller Genannten des grössern Raths*, (Nürnberg, 1802), p. 93.

32. Andreas Würfel, *Diptycha Ecclesiae Laurentianae* (Nürnberg, 1756), pp. 7 f.; Georg Andreas Will, *Nürnbergisches Gelehrtenlexicon* 2 vols. (Nürnberg, 1755), 1:108.

33. Andreas Würfel, *Diptycha Ecclesiae Sebaldinae* (Nürnberg, 1756), pp. 9–12; Will, *Gelehrtenlexicon*, 2:80 ff.

34. See note 19.

35. The following presentation of the progress of the visitation of 1560 and 1561 is based on the account records (StAN, Rep. 54b II, No. 228), the protocol summaries (see note 9), and on the original protocol extant for the year 1561 (see notes 13 and 15).

36. The cost accounting of the visitation is based on the system of coinage equivalencies in Paul Sander, *Die reichsstädische Haushaltung Nürnbergs* 2 vols. (Leipzig, 1902), 2:742 f. I was not able to ascertain clearly the method of reckoning. It appears that the ratio taken as the basis is: 1 gulden = 8 old pounds = 60 pfennigs. See Ernst Scholler, *Der Reichsstadt Nürnberg Geld-und Münzwesen in älterer und neuer Zeit* (Nürnberg, 1916), pp. 242 f.

37. Cited in StAN, Kirchen auf dem Lande No. 454, fol. 48ʳ. This book was extant in the eighteenth century. A manuscript in the Germanisches Nationalmuseum (Merkelsche Sammlung, Hs. No. 978) states that "the documents concerning the visitation and the examination are entered in a book bound in folio in red leather."

38. Editors' note: In the case of lengthy legal procedings, the children who were present as witnesses would have their ears pulled. The idea was that they would remember the pain and at the same time also the legal proceedings, which they would then be able to bear witness to for the rest of their lives.

39. See notes 13 and 15.

40 StAN, Kirchen auf dem Lande No. 454, fol. 38ʳ. The entire proceeding can be reconstructed well through the correspondence of the commission with the council contained in the visitation protocol. This should be used to correct the presentation of Joseph Baader, "Zur Geschichte der Pfarrei Stöckach während der Reformationsperiode," *Berichte des Historische Vereins Bamberg*, 31 (1869).

41. Stadtarchiv, Nürnberg, Amb. 658, fol. 56ʳ–63ʳ.

42. Alfred Schädler (ed.), *Kunstdenkmäler von Bayern, Landkreis Pegnitz* (Munch, 1961), p. 295.

43. His written petition is contained in the protocol, see note 13, fol. 76ʳ, f.

44. Grossgründlach was directly under the office of Territorial Administration (*Landpflegamt*) from 1542 to 1547. C. *MVGN* 5 (1884):112–14.

45. StAN, Kirchen auf dem Lande No. 454, fol. 239ʳ–246ʳ.

46. A copy of the council's decision is in StAN, Kirchen auf dem Lande, No. 454, fol. 37ʳ–41ʳ.

47. StAN, Kirchen auf dem Lande, No. 454, fol. 95ʳ.

48. See the special protocol for these three parishes: StAN, D-Akt., No. 1127.

49. See note 46, fol. 143ᵛ. Printed in Dannenbauer, "Nürnberger Kirchen-visitation," 4 (1929):237. See note 14.

50. See note 46, fol. 145ʳ. An herb for healing the symptoms of illness indicated by "Geschoss." Hanns Bächtold-Stäubli, ed., *Handwörterbuch des deutschen Aberglaubens*, 3:755.

51. Furthermore, Dannenbauer omits a discussion of the visitation to the Entenberg, Offenhausen, and Mögeldorf parishes. These parishes were also visited; however, no general summary of the visitation protocol was prepared for the council, with the reason given that "the protocol should be heard for it is not long," or, in the case of Mögeldorf, "it is necessary to hear the protocol, for no special summary could be prepared."

52. Gg. Rusam, *Geschichte der Pfarrei Sachsen bei Ansbach* (Ansbach, 1940), p. 107, cites three very short sentences concerning the visitation protocol of 1561. For the following discussion, see note 35.

53. Germanisches Nationalmuseum, Merkelsche Sammlung, No. 978, fol 9ʳ.

54. The total number of parishes was ascertained on the basis of Dannenbauer's survey. See note 50.

55. The survey printed in Schornbaum (see note 10) supplies the qualifications of the pastors of Entenberg, Offenhausen, and Mögeldorf (see note 50) missing from Dannenbauer.

56. Ascertained from the original visitation protocol of 1561.

57. So wrote an unknown writer in the eighteenth century who had the *Kirschenvisitationbuch*. See note 52, fol. 8ʳ.

58. StAN, Akten der E-Laden, No. 93.

Appendix

The Visitation Articles of the Nürnberg

Church Visitation of 1560[58]

Questions and admonitions for the pastors.

1. What books they should read.

2. They should not read the catechism to the people only once; rather, they should regularly repeat it and examine the people over it.

3. They should allow no one, be they young or old, to receive Com-

munion unless they are able to recite their prayers and the articles of faith and know and understand how these benefit them.

4.   The pastor is ordered not to be too severe or harsh with the old or the young who are not able to learn the catechism by heart or are unable to read or write. Rather he is to act in accordance with the ability of each person and exercise Christian discretion.

5.   They are to maintain unity and harmony among the people and not create dissension. They themselves are to live and associate harmoniously with the people.

6.   They are to abstain from all revelry, avoid going to the taverns, not play games at parties or participate in any other unseemly pastimes.

7.   They are to admonish parents faithfully to bring their children to church and to have regular prayer in their homes.

8.   The pastors should report to the council all parents and heads of households who are found to be remiss in the above-mentioned things and who have been sufficiently threatened with punishment through sermons and the Word of God and who yet persist in their public sins and vices.

9.   In their sermons the pastors should encourage the congregations to attend Communion frequently and to hear the Word of God diligently.

10.   Pastors should threaten unrepentant parishioners with excommunication and exclusion from the sacraments.

11.   They should not, however, undertake excommunication without the special knowledge and order of the council as the sovereign authority.

12.   The pastors should indicate the names of those who have not received Communion for a long time so that if they do not improve, the government may constrain them to do so.

13.   The pastors who live near cities and larger country towns where, once a week, a sermon is to be delivered in addition to the Sunday sermon, must go into the city or country town on that day and listen. Furthermore, they must confer with the learned pastor about the teaching, and, at that time, take instruction.

14.   The city council has told the imprudent pastors, who neither improve nor abstain from their annoying way of life, that they will be removed.

NOTES ON THE CONTRIBUTORS

Roland H. Bainton, formerly Titus Street Professor of Ecclesiastical History at Yale University, is the author of *Here I Stand: A Life of Martin Luther* (1950); *Erasmus of Christendom* (1969); and *Women of the Reformation* (1971).

Phillip N. Bebb, a former student of Harold J. Grimm, is assistant professor of history at Ohio University.

Lawrence P. Buck, assistant professor of history at Widener College and a former student of Harold J. Grimm, is the author of "Die Haltung der Nürnberger Bauernschaft im Bauernkrieg," *Altnürnberger Landschaft Mitteilungen* (1970).

Carl C. Christensen, a former student of Harold J. Grimm, is associate professor of history at the University of Colorado and the author of "Municipal Patronage and the Crisis of the Arts in Reformation Nuernberg," *Church History* (1967); "Dürer's Four Apostles and the Dedication as a Form of Renaissance Art Patronage," *Renaissance Quarterly* (1967); and "Iconoclasm and the Preservation of Ecclesiastical Art in Reformation Nuernberg," *ARG* (1970).

Richard G. Cole, associate professor of history at Luther College, studied under Harold J. Grimm and is the author of "The Pamphlet and Social Forces in the Reformation," *Lutheran Quarterly* (1965); "Propaganda as a Source of Reformation History," *Lutheran Quarterly* (1970); and "French and German Pamphlets and the Formation of Cultural Attitudes in the Sixteenth Century," *Yearbook of the American Philosophical Society* (1970).

Charles E. Daniel, Jr., a former student of Harold J. Grimm, is assistant professor of history at the University of Rhode Island.

Karl H. Dannenfeldt, academic vice-president of Arizona State University, is the author of *Leonhard Rauwolf: Sixteenth Century Physician, Botanist, and Traveler* (1968), and *The Church of the Renaissance and Reformation* (1970). He is the editor of *The Renaissance: Medieval or Modern?* (1959).

Hans J. Hillerbrand, professor of history at the City University of New York, is the author of *The Reformation: A Narrative History* (1964); *A Fellowship of Discontent* (1967); and *Christendom Divided* (1971).

Gerhard Hirschmann, the director of the Nürnberg City Archive, is the author of *Das Landgebiet der ehemaligen Reichsstadt Nürnberg* (1951); *Die Annalen der Reichsstadt Nürnberg des Ratsschreibers Johannes Müllner von 1623* (1971); and *Das Nürnberger Patriziat im Königreich Bayern 1806-1918* (1971).

Irmgard Höss, professor of history at Erlangen University, is the author of *Georg Spalatin: Ein Leben in der Zeit des Humanismus und Reformation* (1956); "Das religiös-geistige Leben in Nürnberg am Ende des 15. und am Ausgang des 16. Jahrhunderts," *Bibliothèque de la Revue d'Histoire Ecclesiastique* (1967); and "Duldung, Glaubenszwang, und Widerstand: Eine Stellungnahme Johann Spangenbergs aus dem Jahre 1541," *ARG* (1970).

Robert M. Kingdon, professor of history at the University of Wisconsin, is the author of *Geneva and the Coming of the Wars of Religion in France, 1555-1563* (1956), and *Geneva and the Consolidation of the French Protestant Movement, 1564-1572* (1967). He is the co-editor of *Registres de la Compagnie dex Pasteurs de Genève au Temps de Calvin* (1964).

Hans Liermann, professor of legal history at Erlangen University, is the author of *Richter, Schreiber, Advokaten* (1957), and *Handbuch des Stiftungrechts* (1963). He is the editor of *Kirchen und Staat* (1954).

Gerhard Pfeiffer, professor of history at Erlangen University, is the author of *Fränkische Bibliographie* (1965), and *Nürnberg: Geschichte einer europäischen Stadt* (1971). He is the editor of *Quellen zur Nürnberger Reformationsgeschichte* (1968).

Gottfried Seebass, assistant at the Institute for Reformation Research of Erlangen University, is the author of *Das reformatorische Werk des Andreas Osiander* (1967); "Dürers Stellung in der reformatorischen Bewegung," in *Albrecht Dürers Umwelt: Festschrift zum 500. Geburtstag* (1971); and *Bibliographia Osiandrica: Bibliographie der gedruckten Schriften von Andreas Osiander* (1971).

Kyle C. Sessions, associate professor of history at Illinois State University and a former student of Harold J. Grimm, is the editor of *Reformation and Authority: The Meaning of the Peasants' Revolt* (1968). He is the author of "The Sources of Luther's Hymns and the Spread of the Reformation," *Lutheran Quarterly* (1965), and "Music and the Schools in the Reformation of German Towns," *Illinois State University Journal* (1968).

Jackson Spielvogel, assistant professor of history at the Pennsylvania State University and a former student of Harold J. Grimm, is the author of "Willibald Pirckheimer's Domestic Activity for Nürnberg," *Moreana* (1970).

Lewis W. Spitz, professor of history at Stanford University, is the author of *Conrad Celtis: The German Arch-Humanist* (1957); *The Religious Renaissance of the German Humanists* (1963); and *The Renaissance and Reformation Movements* (1971).

George H. Williams, Hollis Professor of Divinity at Harvard University, is the author of *Anselm: Communion and Atonement* (1960); *Wilderness and Paradise in Christian Thought* (1962); and *The Radical Reformation* (1962).

Jonathan W. Zophy, associate professor of history at Lane College, Jackson, Tennessee, has completed a study of Christoph Kress under the direction of Harold J. Grimm.

INDEX

Aberzhausen, 363
Acosta, Christoval, 239
A Dialogue or Conversation Between a Father and His Son About Luther's Doctrine, 98-99
Adige River, 168-69, 187
Adige Valley, 169
Aemylius, Georg, 233-34, 243
Aesticampianus, 227
Aetius of Amida, 227, 237
Agricola, George, 236
Aicholtz, Johann, 239, 243
Albert, margrave of Brandenburg-Ansbach, 332, 334, 336-37
Albertine (Electoral) Saxony, 328-331, 336-37, 357-58. *See also* Saxony
Aleppo, 241
Alexandria, 164, 184
Alfalter-Artelshofen, 362, 375
Alfeld, 361-62, 371
Allersburg, 350, 363, 375
Allgäuer Alps, 137
Allin, Rose, 215
Alsace, 124
Altdorf, 356, 367-68, 371, 376
Altenburg, 41, 45, 47, 252, 323, 325
Altenthann, 375
Althaus, Paul, 106
Amerbach, Johann, 139
Amsdorf, Nicholas von, 254
Anabaptists, 28, 35-36, 156-98, 274, 289, 292
Andreä, Jakob, 331
Ansbach, 287, 343-45, 348, 355, 357, 372, 374; "Ordinance of Church Visitation," 351; Retaxierte Chapter Ordinance, 351

Antitrinitarianism, 161, 188
Antwerp, 239
Apuleius Barbarus, 227, 238
Aretius, Benedict, 235
Aristotle, 227
Arnstadt, 263
Arras, 239
Artelshofen, 362, 375
Askew, Anne, 209-11
Asolo, 174, 179-84
Atherton, Ralph, 220
Auerbach, 231
Augsburg, 21, 36, 60-61, 101, 231, 238, 241, 243; Confession of, 303-4, 324, 330, 372; diet of, 117, 325
August, duke of Saxony, 236, 358
Augustinians, 20-21, 23, 41, 57, 307, 317; canons, 251; monastery of, 20, 25, 47
Augustus, Emperor, 283
Aurifaber, Johann, 230, 337
Auspitz, 189
Austin Canons, 179
Austria, 64, 239
Avicenna, 226-27, 230, 241

Baghdad, 240
Bainton, John, 209
Baltringen, 123
Bamberg, 24-25, 66, 82, 255, 369, 374; bishop of, 24-27, 54, 61, 66-67, 83, 365
Bartholomew of Padua, 192
Basel, 139, 223, 228, 231, 237; university of, 139
Bauhin, Casper, 242
Baumgartner, Balthasar, 367

Bavaria, 48, 271
Bayreuth, 254, 357
Bechthal, 363
Beerbach, 366, 368, 371
Behaim, Barthel, 275-76
Behaim, Sebald, 275-76
Beheim, Georg, 60
Behringersdorf, 362
Bellini, Giovanni, 273
Belon, Pierre du Mans, 235-36, 242
Benden, Alice, 214
Benedictines, 251
Benet, Mother, 220
Bergamo, 185
Bergen, 375
Bern, 235
Bernau, 375
Besler, Michael, 20
Besold, Hieronymus, 357-61, 364
Bessler, Georg, 22
Betzenstein, 356, 365-66
Biel, Gabriel, 94
Bildhausen, 122
Black Forest, 124, 166
Blaurock, George, 169
Bleich auf der Deutschherrnwiese, 370
Bobart, Jacob, 243
Bock, Jerome (Hieronymus Tragus),
    223, 231; *New Kreütter Buch*, 223,
    231
Bødker, Claus, 96
Bohemia, 231, 235, 256
Bologna, 59, 81, 157, 171, 183, 187,
    232, 240; university of, 55
Bolsec, Jerome, 10
Bolzano, 169
Bonaduz, 169
Bonger, Agnes, 218-19
Bostrup, Jens, 99
Bragora, 190
Brandenburg-Ansbach, 337, 341, 344,
    357; -Kulmbach, 344, 350, 357;
    Consistorial Ordinance of, 347, 349,
    351
Brant, Sebastian, 139
Brassavola, Antonius Musa, 232
Bratislava, 238
Brauer, Wolfgang, 263
Bremen, 264
Brenner Pass, 169
Brenta, 168

Brenz, Johann, 48, 372-73
Brescia, 168
Breseña, Isabella, 175, 179
Breslau, 261
Breyn, Jacob, 242
Briessmann, Johann, 333
Brixen, bishop of, 166-68
Bruck, 264, 369
Brück, Georg, 322
Bruneck (Brunico), 169, 182
Brunfels, 231
Brunswick-Wolfenbüttel, 330-31
Bucella, Nicholas, 191, 195
Bucer, Martin, 115, 326; *Gesprech-
    Buechlin Neuw Karsthans*, 115
Büchenbach, 367, 375
Bugenhagen, Johann, 103, 143-44,
    253, 263, 323, 330
Bullinger, Henry, 171, 176, 185-86
Bünau, Gunther, 333
Burgau, 137-38, 140, 144, 148
Burgfarnbach, 369
Burgos, Edict of, 68
Busale, Bruno, 174, 176, 178, 184
Busale, Jerome, 161-65, 175-81, 183-
    84
Busale, Matthew, 176-78
Busalu, Julius, 179
Busman, Johann, 254

Cadolzburger, Niklas, 22
Cajetan, Cardinal, 62
Callezaro, Julius, 180
Calvin, John, 4-14, 111, 176, 186, 188,
    198, 250
Camerarius, Joachim the elder, 228-29,
    233, 240, 279-84, 290
Camerarius, Joachim the younger, 228,
    240, 242-43
Campeggio, Giovanni, 61
Campeggio, Cardinal Lorenzo, 61-65,
    67
Canitz, Hans von, 252
Canitz, Ulrich von, 252
Canitz, Wolf von, 252
Cantimori, Delio, 158-59
Capistrano, Giovanni di, 163
Capuchins, 174-75
Careless, John, 219-21
Carlsbad, 231

Carlstadt, Andreas, 27-28, 35, 97, 274-75, 285, 289, 319-20
Carmelites, 255
Carnesecchi, Peter, 175
Carraciolo, Marquis Galeaszzo, 8
Carthusian monastery, 29
Casimir, margrave of Brandenburg-Ansbach, 277, 343
Caspano, 171
Cassel, 241
Castell, 347
Castelnuovo (Podgrad), 182
Celtis, Conrad, 20, 59
Chalcedonian, 157, 197
Charles V, Emperor, 63, 68, 93, 179
Chemnitz, 235-36, 328
Chemnitz, Martin, 331
Chiavenna, 171, 181, 187, 196
Chon (Cohon, Kune), 152
Christian III, king of Denmark, 253
Chur, 185-86
Cistercians, 177
Cittadella, 175, 182, 191
Clusius, Carolus, 239, 242-43
Coburg, 367
Cochläus, Johann, 106
Colditz, 41
Cologne, 78, 227, 232, 251
Constantine, Emperor, 215
Constantinople, 184
Constance, 17
Cooper, Elizabeth, 219
Cordatus, Conrad, 257-64
Cordus, Euricus, 229
Cordus, Philippus, 231
Cordus, Valerius, 229-36, 238, 242; *Dispensatorium pharmacorum omnium*, 230
Cornarius, Janus, 236-37, 242
Corpus Christi College, 217
Corvin, 330
Coverdale, Miles, 218
Cracow, 195, 334
Cramer, A., 13-14
Cranach, Lucas the elder, 278, 281, 301
Cranach, Lucas the younger, 305
Cranmer, Thomas, 218
Cruciger, Casper, 227, 243
Culmann, Leonhard, 360
Cunrad, Hieronymus, 367

Dachau, Johann, 254
d'Alessandria, Nicholas, 179, 182, 184
Damascus, 164, 196
Dannenbauer, Hienz, 356, 372, 375
Danube River, 137, 168-69
Danzig, 230, 233
da Orta, Garcia, 239
d'Asolo, Marc Anthony, 178, 182
da Prato, Marc Anthony, 180
de Apuzzo, Ambrose, 178
del Borgo, Benedict, 175, 179-82
della Sega, Francis, 180, 188, 190-96
del Monte, Cardinal Innocenzo, 185
Denck, Hans, 274-75
Denmark, 96, 253
Deschler, Joachim, 281
d'Este, Cardinal, 62
de Tournefort, J. P., 234
Deutz, 99
de Villafranca, John, 175-77
DeWind, Henry, 159
Dietrich, Veit, 262, 373
Dinstedt, Ulrich, 60
Dioscorides, 226-29, 233, 235-41
Dipperz, 125
Dodonaeus, 239
Dolly (English Protestant), 209
Dominicans, 23, 249
Dorothy Susanna, duchess of Saxony, 307
Doumergue, Emile, 13
Dresden, 329, 358
Dürer, Albrecht, 20, 74, 271-90; *Befestigungslehre*, 290; *Speiss der Malerknaben*, 273; *Unterweisung der Messung*, 274, 277, 289

Ebner, family of, 374
Ebner, Hieronymus, 20
Ebner, Linhard, 287
Ebner, Paul, 227-28, 242
Eck, Johann, 21, 59-60, 318
Edward VI, king of England, 216-17
Egypt, 236
Eibach, 370-71
Eisack (Iscaro), 168
Eisenach, 114-15, 252
Eisenstein, Elizabeth, 93
Eisleben, 60
Elert, Werner, 31
Elizabeth, duchess of Brunswick, 224

Elizabeth I, queen of England, 217
Eltersdorf, 369, 371-72, 375-76
Emser, Hieronymus, 83
Ende, H. vom, 322
Engadine, 191
Engelhardt, Adolf, 356
Engelmann, Nicholas, 152
Engelthal, 361, 372
England, 11, 162, 186, 208, 237
Englender, Johann, 55
Engels, Friedrich, 106
Entenberg, 361, 371
Ephrussi, Charles, 273
Erasmus, 20, 22, 34, 95, 113, 237, 287, 305, 318
Erastus, 11
Erfurt, 148, 151-52; city council of, 124
Erhard, Master, 53
Ermland, 332
Ernestine Saxony, 328, 332. *See also* Saxony
Erzgebirge, 231
Eschenau, 365, 368
Eschenbach, 362
Euphrates River, 241
Evangelical Rationalism, 157-58, 171, 197. *See also* Anabaptists; Socinianism
Eybach, M. Friedrich von, 53

Faber, Petrus, 252-53
Farel, William, 5-6
Ferdinand, Archduke, 61, 63-65, 124, 167
Ferrara, 174, 182, 184, 188, 232, 236
Feucht, 367
Feudalism, 137
Fischbach, 367
Flensburg, 307
Flock, Erasmus, 262
Florence, 12, 81, 174, 232
Florio, John, 186
Florio, Michelangelo, 186; *Apologia di M. Michel Agnolo Fiorentino*, 186
Folkes, Elizabeth, 214
Forchheim, 27, 369
Foreaneus, Nichlaus, 263
Förrenbach, 362, 371
Foxe, John, 208-9, 214-16; *Actes and Monuments*, 208
Fra Andriano, 195

France, 12, 162, 236, 239, 241
Francese, Fra Mattheo, 177
Franck, Sebastian, 187
Francis of Calabria, 181
Franciscans, 23, 93-94, 139, 163, 333; monastery of, 29
Franconia, 27, 53, 340-41, 347, 355
Frankfort a. M., 231, 238-39; Recess of, 360
Frari Church, 273
Frederick the Wise, duke of Saxony, 41, 60, 249, 251, 318-20
Freiburg, 166, 238
Frideswide, Saint, 217.
Friedewald, Nicolaus, 232
Friedland, 359
Friedrich II, baron of Dohna, 256
Friemersheim, Peter von, 307
Fries, Lawrence, 277
Friuli, 182
Frörer, 373
Frosch, Johann, 255
Fuchs, Leonhard, 223, 228-29; *De historia stirpium*, 223
Fugger, Jacob, 124
Funius, Andreas, 252
Fürer, Christoph, 20, 359, 363-64
Fürer, Sigmund, 20
Furth, 369

Gaismair, Michael, 122, 160, 166-68, 198
Galeato, Jerome, 176
Galen, 226-27, 235-37
Gallicius, Philip, 185
Gardiner, Stephan, 210
Gasser, Achilles Pirimius, 239
Gemusaeus, Hieronymus, 228
Geneva, 4, 6, 8-14, 173, 188; Consistory of 4, 6-7, 9, 11, 13-14; government of, 6, 10, 14
Genoa, 177, 185
George, duke of Saxony, 83, 124, 327
George II, duke of Wertheim, 141
George, margrave of Brandenburg-Ansbach, 48, 252, 257-58
George, prince of Anhalt, 253
Gerlach, 99
Germanic National Museum, 356
Germany, 11, 17-18, 52, 95, 101, 112-13, 117, 137, 162, 169, 174, 198,

208, 229, 233, 236-37, 297, 299, 333, 341, 355. *See also* Holy Roman Empire
Gesner, Conrad, 231, 233-39, 243
Gherlandi, Julius, 180, 189-92
Ghini, Lucas, 232
Giacometto (Italian tailor and evangelist), 182
Gibitzenhof, 370
Gilbert, Martin, 263
Glapio, 140
Glascock, Agnes, 219
Gluenspiesz, Philipp, 253
Gonzaga, Julia, 175
Gotha, 241, 252, 301
Göttingen, 263, 340
Götz, Johann, 263
Gräfenberg, 356, 365-67, 372
Graubünden, 174
Grebel, Conrad, 169
Grefendorf, 322
Greiffenberger, Hans, 23
Gregorian Calendar, 241
Greiser, Daniel, 329
Grey, Jane, 186
Greyfriars, 96
Grigioni, 183
Grimma, 252, 322
Groote, Gerard, 94
Grosse Almosen, 344, 346
Grossgründlach, 369-71
Grün, H. von der, 362
Gruner, Hans, 369
Guffidaun (Gudon), 169
Günther, Franz, 262
Günzburg, 137
Günzburg, Johann Eberlin von, 93-94, 98, 102, 113-15, 137-52; *15 Bundgenossen*, 113; *Mich wundert das kein Geld im Land ist*, 98, 114; *True Warning to the Christians in the Margravate of Burgau*, 102, 138-52
Günz River, 137, 140
Gunzenhausen, 22
Gustav, king of Sweden, 253, 262-63
Gustenfelden, 370, 375
Gutenberg, 94
Güttel, Casper, 60

Hadrian VI, Pope, 232
Haetzer, Louis, 197

Haller, Albert, 234
Haller, Anna. *See* Tetzel, Anna
Haller, Joachim, 357, 359, 361, 363-64, 370
Haller, Karl, 78
Haller, Willibald, 364
Hampe, Theodor, 271
Handsch, Georg, 240
Happurg, 372
Hapsburg, house of, 63, 138, 167
Hass, George, 369
Haubitz, Asmus, 322
Hausen, 369, 375
Hawkhurst, 220
Heideck, 356, 363, 375
Heidelberg, 251
Heidrich, Ernst, 271, 274-75
Heilig-Geist-Spital, 359
Heilsbronn, 139
Heinrich, duke of Mecklenburg, 252
Heling, Moritz, 357-60, 364
Henfenfeld, 362
Henry, duke of Freiburg, 255
Henry, duke of Saxony, 327-28
Henry VII, king of England, 215
Henry VIII, king of England, 209-10
Henry the younger, duke of Brunswick-Wolfenbüttel, 330-31
Heracleon (Candia), 184
Herdegen, George, 53
Hereford, 218
Herold, Hieronymus, 234, 243
Heroldsberg, 365, 368
Hersbruck, 356, 361-62, 371
Hesse, 125, 330
Hessus, Eobanus, 280, 283-84
Heuberg, 363, 371-72
Hilpolstein, 356, 363, 365, 371, 375
Hippocrates, 227-28, 238
Hofman, Melchior, 199
Hohenzollern, house of, 341
Holl, Karl, 319
Holland, 211
Holy Roman Empire, 52. *See also* Germany
Holzschuher, Hieronymus, 20, 281-82
Hooper, John, 218
Hornbach, 223
Hügel, Andreas, 255
Hüll, 365-66

Hummelstein, 370
Hümplesshof, 370
Hungary, 189-90, 239
Hus, John, 94
Hut, Hans, 199
Hutten, Ulrich von, 111-13, 117; *Arminius*, 112; *Gesprächbüchlein*, 113; *Monitor I*, 113; *Monitor II*, 113; *Vadiscus*, 112
Hutter, Jacob, 169, 199
Hutterites, 159, 161, 188-95, 198. *See also* Anabaptists
Hüttner, Adularius, 149, 151-52
Hyperius, Andreas, 239

Igensdorf, 365-66
Il Tiziano, 173-75, 180-81, 185
Imhof, Conrad, 85-86
Imhof, Hans, 85
Imhof, Sebastian, 363
Immeldorf, 368-69
Ingolstadt, 223; university of, 59
Inn River, 168
Innsbruck, 80, 167; diet of, 167
Inquisition, 183, 188-89
Institut für evangelisches Kirchenrecht, 340-41
Iscaro, 169
Islam, 199. *See also* Muslims
Istra, 182
Italy, 163, 173-74, 183, 188-89, 197, 199, 229, 238, 241

Jäger, Thomas, 22
Jahrsdorf, 363, 371
Jena, 252
Jews, 162-65, 194. *See also* Judaism
Joachim, elector of Brandenburg, 124
Joachimstal, 235
John, duke of Saxony, 251, 262, 320-22, 324
John Ernest, duke of Saxony, 253
John Frederick, duke of Saxony, 235, 252, 255, 257, 262-63, 326, 330
John Frederick III, duke of Saxony, 307
Jonas, Justus, 252, 255, 258, 306, 324
Jörger, Dorothea, 254-55
Judaism, 161, 165, 177, 197-99
Julius, duke of Brunswick-Wolfenbüttel, 331

Julius III, Pope (Giammaria Ciocchi), 174
Jungandres, Andres, 252

Kaiserberg, Geiler von, 139
Kalbensteinberg, 363
Kalchreuth, 368
Karg, 373
Karthans, 111
Kauigsdorf, Andreas, 262-63
Keppach, 254
Kettenbach, Heinrich von, 111, 115
Ketzmann, Johann, 364, 370
Kirchehrenbach, 276
Kirchensittenbach, 362, 375
Kirchmair, George, 169
Kirchrüsselbach, 365-66, 371
Kissling, Johann, 372
Kitzingen, 102, 252, 345; Beggars Ordinance of, 345
Klaus, Bernhard, 36, 264
Knights' War, 352
Knox, John, 12, 111
Koberger, Anton, 56
Koberger, printing house of, 95
Kock, Hans, 149
Köhler, Walther, 13; *Zürcher Ehegericht und Genfer Konsistorium*, 13
Koler, Christoph, 290
Koler, Paul, 364, 370
Koloszvár, 196
Königsberg, 230-31
Kornburg, 355, 367
Kottbus, 333
Krafft, Johann, 261-62
Krafftheim, Crato von, 230
Kraftshof, 369, 372
Kraus, Josef, 20
Krautheim, Erasmus, 253
Krell, Oswald, 282
Kress, Christoph, 63, 66
Kress, Frau, 369
Krodel, Gottfried, 272
Kronberg, Hartmuth von, 113
Krumwiede, H. W., 322
Kulturkampf, 288

Lactantius, 215; *On the Deaths of the Persecutor*, 215
Laibstadt, 371

Lang, John, 150-51

Lang, Sebald, 365

Lanzenstiel, Leonard, 190, 193

Latimer, Hugh, 211, 218

Lau, Franz, 19

Lauf, 356, 362-63, 368

Laureto, John di Buongiorno della Cava, 175, 177, 184-85

Lauterbach, Anton, 263

Lebanon, Mount, 241, 243

Lehnin, monastery of, 262

Leib, Kilian, 60, 75

Leimbach, Konrad, 252

Leinburg, 362

Leipzig, 230, 237, 329; disputation of, 21; university of, 41, 236, 240

Leisnig, 102

Letten, 368

Leuchtenberg, 83

Leyden, university of, 241

Liabstadt, 363

Lichtenau, 356, 368-69, 372, 375

Lichtenhof, 370

Liebenstadt, 363, 371

Liebenwerda, 263

Linck, Wenzeslaus, 21, 41-49, 263; *A Wholesome Teaching*, 46; *Offene Schuld*, 48-59; *Preparation of Children for Communion*, 47

Lindner, Christoph, 364, 369

Linz, 80, 241

Lithuania, 196

Livorno, 232

Ljubjana, 182

Locke, John, 45

London, 186, 196, 218; bishop of, 210-12

Lonicer, Johann, 236-38, 264

Lonnerstadt, 369

Lübeck, 307

Lucca, 232

Lufft, Hans, 358

Luther, Catherine, 255

Luther, Martin, 17, 19-23, 29, 31, 33-35, 43, 47-49, 139-40, 143, 156, 174, 188, 199, 228, 233, 274-75, 281, 287, 299-303, 305, 308-9, 317-24, 326-29, 333, 335, 340, 352, 360, 363, 372-73; and Peasants' Revolt, 106, 120-21, 124-26; and printing, 108-19; attitude of, toward plants, 223-26; attitude of, toward students, 249-65; on vocation, 259-62; *Address to the German Nobility*, 19, 97, 108; *An die Ratsherren aller Städte deutschen Landes*, 110; *Auslegung des Vaterunsers*, 111; *Babylonian Captivity of the Church*, 97, 303; *Brief an die Fürsten zu Sachsen von dem aufruhrischen Geist*, 111, 116; *Churchpostil*, 260; *Dass eine christliche Versammlung oder Gemeine Recht und Macht habe*, 122; *Ermahnung zum Frieden auf die zwölf Artikel der Bauernschaft in Schwaben*, 106; *Eyne trey vormanung Martini Luther zu allen Christen*, 100; *Grosser Sermon von Wucher*, 109; "Ninety-five Theses Concerning Indulgences," 20, 59, 108, 139, 249; *Sendbrief von dem harten Büchleim wider die Bauern*, 106, 110; *Sermon on Keeping Children in School*, 254; *Sermon von dem Wucher*, 108; *Small Catechism*, 300, 302-3, 363; *Table Talks*, 256; *The Freedom of the Christian*, 97, 110; *Vermahnung zu allen Christen sich zu hüten vor Aufruhr und Empörung*, 111; *Von den guten Werken*, 109; *Von Kaufhandlung und Wucher*, 110; *Von Weltlicher Obrigkeit*, 110; *Wider die räuberischen und mörderischen Rotten der Bauern*, 106

Lyons, 186, 196

Macek, Josef, 160; *Der Tiroler Bauernkrieg und Michael Gaismair*, 160

McLuhan, Marshall, 95

Magdeburg, 45, 254

Magdunensis, Odo, 237

Mahy, M., 150

Main River, 140

Major, Georg, 251

Manelfi, Peter, 157-58, 164, 174-75, 182-83, 188-89, 192-93

Manorialism, 137

Marburg, 229-30, 238-39, 264; university of, 238

Marangone, Anthony, 170

Marpeck, Pilgrim, 169

Marranos, 161, 163, 165, 176, 198

Marstaller, Michael, 55

Martin, Saint, 366

Mary, queen of England, 208, 214, 216, 218

Mattioli, Pier' Andrea, 236, 240, 242

Maurice, duke of Saxony, 328-29

Maximilian I, duke of Bavaria, 271
Maximilian I, Emperor, 333
Meckenhausen, 363, 372
Mediterranean Sea, 242
Medler, Nikolaus, 255
Meissen, 320, 329, 333
Melanchthon, Philip, 47, 49, 139, 143,
    174, 226-28, 232-33, 239-40, 242,
    252, 255, 261-62, 264, 278-80, 282-
    84, 289, 305-6, 322-23, 358, 360,
    372-73
Mellerstadt, Polich von, 226
Memmingen, 17, 137; council of, 253
Merano (Meran), 123, 167; Articles
    of, 167-68
Merfeldt, Gerdt van, 307
Mersburg, 320, 329
Meyenburg, Michael, 305-6
Milan, 182
Miltitz, Carl von, 60
Milwitz, Christoffel, 149
Mittenhuber, Johann, 373
Modiana, 174, 182
Moeller, Bernd, 18-19, 24
Mögeldorf, 362, 372
Möhrendorf, 369, 374
Moibanus, Johann, 238-39
Mönchröden, 252
Montaigne, Michel, 186
Montanus, Giambattista, 231
Montpellier, 239-41
Moravia, 159, 188-89, 191-93, 195-96,
    198
Morison, Robert, 242-43
Morlin, Joachim, 262
Mörsdorf, 363
Muffel, Gabriel, 368
Mühlpfordt, Hermann, 45
Müller, Hans, 151
Mumford, Lewis, 94
Müntzer, Thomas, 27, 35, 116-17, 167,
    187, 274, 277, 319-20, *Ausgedruckte
    Entblössung,* 117; *Hochverursachte
    Schutzrede,* 117
Murner, 119
Muslim, 158, 164, 194
Mussolini, Benito, 162

Naevius, Caspar, 235-36
Naevius, Johann, 236-37
Naples, 161, 164, 175-79, 184-86
Naumburg-Zeitz, 320

Negri, Francis, 181
Neofiti, 165
Neudörfer, Johann, 271-72
Neumann, Karl, 271, 281
Neustadt, 367
Neustift, 166
New Hospital Church, 42, 48, 356
Nicander, 230, 238
Niccoluzzo, Lawrence, 174, 182
Nicene, 157, 197
Nicodemism, 197-98
Niemegk, 257
Noce Valley, 168
Nogaredo, 168
Nopos, Hieronymus, 262
Nordhausen, 305-6
Norman, Georg, 262
Nürnberg, 18, 20-24, 26-38, 41, 44-
    45, 47-49, 52-68, 73-87, 95, 102,
    115, 231, 233-34, 238, 240, 243,
    253, 262-63, 271, 274-82, 287, 289,
    341, 343-44, 355-61, 363, 365-66,
    368-76; -Brandenburg Church Or-
    dinance, 18, 30-31, 37, 344; city
    archives of, 356-57; city council of,
    24-37, 41, 45, 48, 52-68, 73-87,
    253, 272, 274, 280, 286-87, 290,
    344, 356-61, 364, 369; diet of, 64;
    Gelehrtenschule, 34, 276, 278, 288;
    religious colloquy of, 29, 31, 35, 68,
    276, 287, 289-90
23 Nürnberg Lehrartikel, 342
Nützel, Caspar, 20, 66, 80-82

Obereisenheim, 347
Obergalgenhof, 370
Occam, William of, 94
Ochino, Bernardino, 174-75
Oecolampadius, 113, 275, 285, 289
Oertel, Sigmund, 78
Offenhausen, 361, 371
Olevianus, 11
Oliveto, Monte, 177, 179, 184
Oribasisos, 238, 242; *Euporista ad An-
    dramachum,* 238, 242
Örtel, Veit, 263
Osiander, Andreas, 22-23, 25-32, 34-
    38, 48-49, 60, 359
Ott, Hans, 362
Ottensoos, 355, 362, 375
Ottoman Empire, 163-64. *See also*
    Turks, Ottoman
Oxford, 217

Padua, 160-61, 168, 174, 176-80, 182-84, 190-95, 231-32
Palatinate, 83, 358, 373, 375
Pannonius, Christoph, 228
Panofsky, Erwin, 271, 274, 299-300
Papal States, 162
Paris, 235
Paruta, Nicholas, 196
Passau, 231
Pässler, Peter, 166
Pastor, Adam, 197
Paul, Saint, 176, 260
Paul IV, Pope (Caraffa), 163
Paul of Aigina, 237
Paumgartner, Bernhard, 279
Paumgartner, Hieronymus, 279-83
Paumgartner, Lucas, 283
Paumgartner, Stefan, 283
Pausram, 189
Peasants: pamphlets of, 120; revolt of, 41, 116, 137-38, 151, 276-79, 286, 318-21, Twelve Articles of, 121-25, 137, 149; War of, 27, 33, 100, 106-9, 111, 122, 126, 160, 162, 166, 168, 171, 191, 198
Pencz, Jörg, 275-76
Perugia, 182
Pessler, Georg, 55
Pessler, Wolf, 367
Peucer, Caspar, 282
Peuschels, Nikolaus, 252
Peutinger, Conrad, 60
Pforte, 328
Pfuhl, Joachim, 262
Philip, landgrave of Hesse, 328
Phrygio, 289
Piacenza, 179
Pilgrimage of Grace, 107
Pinzgau Valley, 167-68
Pirano (Piran), 182
Pirckheimer, family of, 20
Pirckheimer, Charitas, 35
Pirckheimer, Felicitas, 85
Pirckheimer, Willibald, 21, 23, 74-87, 275, 282, 289-90
Pirna, 263
Pisa, 232
Placotomus, Johann, 230, 233
Planitz, Hans von der, 322
Pliny, 226-28, 230-32, 236, 238
Plunkenet, Leonhard, 243

Poland, 332-35, 337
Pole, Cardinal Reginald, 217
Polentz, Georg von, 333-37
Polesine, conventicle of, 180
Polish Brethren, 158, 164
Pömer, Hector, 22, 60
Pomerania, 235
Pomesania, bishopric of, 332-35
Pommelsbrunn, 362
Pommern, John, 144
Poppenreuth, 369
Porcius, Leonhard, 283
Portugal, 163, 176, 239
Prättigau, 167
Prenner, Georg, 251
Prenninger, Marsilius, 57
Preuss, Hans, 297
Prierias, Sylvester, 100
Propheten, Andres zum, 152
Propst, Jacob, 264
Prussia, 333-37, 359
Puritanism, 3
Puritans, 43
Puschendorf, 369
Puster Valley, 168

Quassow, 252
Queiss, Erhard von, 334-37

Rach, Johann, 227
Ralla, Joachim Johann, 230, 232
Rasch, 368, 375
Rattenberg, 169
Ratzenberger, Caspar, 241-42
Rauwolf, Leonhard, 240-43; *Aigentliche beschreibung der Raiz so er vor diser zeit gengen Auffgang inn die Morgenländer . . . selbts volbracht*, 241
Rebdorf, 60
Rednitzhembach, 363
Rednitz River, 361
Reformation, 55-57
Regelsbach, 370-71
Regensburg, 63-64, 66, 102-3, 231
Regiomontanus, 94
Reichelsdorf, 370
Reichenschwand, 362
Renato, Camillo, 170-71, 181, 185-87
Renato, Francesco, 178

Rettenberg, 168
Reuchlin, Johann, 22, 34, 113
Reviso, 179
Rhaetia, 169, 171, 174-75, 181, 185-87, 196
Rhaetian Confederacy, 160, 166
Rhazes, 230
Rheticus, Georg Joachim, 227, 231
Rienz (Rienza), 168
Rieter, Hans, 76
Rieter, Jörg, 79
Riga, 263
Rindtflaisch, N., 149
Riva di Trento, 187
Rizzeto, Anthony, 188, 191-92, 194-96
Roberts, M., 220
Röckenhof, 367
Roloff, Matthäus, 252
Romagna, 182
Rome, 112, 157, 169-70, 182, 184, 213, 232
Ronciglione, 232
Rondelet, Guillaume, 240-41
Rostock, 230
Rothenburg o. T., 254, 350
Roting, Michael, 279-84
Rotondò, Antonio, 159
Rovigo, 174, 180, 182, 190
Rückersdorf, 362
Rudolf, Anton, 258
Rudolf, Niclaus, 258
Ruel, Jean, 238
Ryff, Walther Hermann, 229, 233, 238

Saalfelden, 241, 255
Sachs, Hans, 23, 28, 33, 114-15, 287, 289; *Dialogue Concerning Greed*, 114-15; "Wächterlied," 23
Sachsen, 368-69, 372-74
Saint Bartholomew, church of, 41
Saint Catherine, convent of, 290
Saint Clara, convent of, 35
Saint Gall, 174, 181
Saint Gumbertus, church of, 374
Saint John, church of, 369, 372-73
Saint Leonhard, church of, 368, 370-73
Saint Lorenz, church of, 22, 48, 54, 60, 287, 356, 359
Saint Petersburg, 151

Saint Sebald: church of, 54, 61, 287, 356, 359-60; school of, 274-75
Salmerón, Alfonso, 192
Salzburg, 123, 231, 278
Sambach, 369, 374
Samland, 333, 337
Samosatenes, 196
Sandrart, Joachim von, 271
Sandreuth, 378
Sangerhausen, 125
San Giovanni, 190
Sanseverino, Catherine, 177
Santa Maria dell' Anima, 232
San Vito, 174
Sarton, George, 223
Sartori, Joseph, 174, 181
Sauermann, Veit, 362
Savonarola, 12
Saxony, 23, 41, 235, 252, 264, 307, 318, 323, 326-30, 337, 341
Schaff, Philip, 100
Scharpff, Hans, 82
Schatzgeyer, Caspar, 287
Schenk, Jacob, 255
Scheteken, Englebert, 263
Scheurl, Christoph, 20-24, 29, 53, 55-68
Scheurl, Georg, 367
Schiemer, Leonard, 169
Schiller, Matthias, 359, 364
Schleupner, Dominikus, 22
Schloffer, John, 169
Schmalkaldic League, 328, 330-31
Schmalkaldic War, 32, 306
Schmedstedt, Heinrich, 262
Schmelz, Johann, 253
Schönewald, 262
Schornbaum, Karl, 355-56
Schott, Cunz, 77
Schreiber, Hieronymus, 231-35
Schreiner, Johann, 252
Schurff, Hieronymus, 322-23
Schürstab, family of, 374
Schürstab, Hieronymus, 359, 363
Schütz, Gregory, 82-84
Schütz, Hans, 79-87
Schütz, Hieronymus, 82
Schwabach, 367
Schwäbisch Hall, 48
Schwaz, 169

Schweinfurt, 350
Schwenckfeld, Caspar, 187
Schwengenfeld, Mattes, 149
Schwimbach, 363, 372
Seamen, Mother, 214
Second Margrave's War, 357, 376
Seebass, Gottfried, 286
Seeberg, 231
Sehling, Emil, 340-41
Serapion, 241
Servetus, Michael, 10, 185-86
Service Book, 371-73
Shaxton, 210-11
Sicily, 164
Sickingen, Franz von, 113, 115
Siculo, George, 187-88
Siebenkees, Johann Christian, 356
Siena, 232, 235
Sittard, Cornelius, 232, 238
Sixtus IV, Pope, 54
Slovakia, 190-91
Smith, Agnes, 220
Snell, Georg, 254
Stella, Aldo, 160-61; *Anabattismo e
    Antitrinitarismo in Italia nel XVI
    Secolo: Nuove ricerche storiche*, 160;
    *Dall' Anabattismo al Socinianismo
    nel Cinquecento: Richere storiche*,
    160
Socinians, 159, 161, 171, 197. *See also*
    Evangelical Rationalism; Anabap-
    tists
Socinus, Faustus, 171, 195, 198
Spain, 162-64, 176, 239
Spalatin, Georg, 60, 98, 249, 251, 255,
    281, 318-19, 323-24, 329
Spangenberg, 373
Spengler, Lazarus, 20-21, 24, 28, 44,
    49, 289
Speratus, Paul, 336
Speziale, Peter, 175
Speyer, 231; diet of, 321
Spiera, Francesco, 187
Spiritualism, 157, 197. *See also* Ana-
    baptists
Spitalkirche, 287, 289
Sponheim, 99
Springer, Anton, 273, 281
Sprottau, 262
Stadler, Ulrich, 169
Stanberger, Balthasar, 115; *Dialogus*

Zwischen Petro und eynem Bawren,
    115
Stark, Hans, 357, 359, 367
Staupitz, Johann von, 20-21, 57, 59
Stein, Heinlin vom, 139
Steinbühl, 370
Stengel, Laurentius, 254
Sterzing (Vipiteno), 169
Stifel, Heinrich, 262
Stöckach, 365, 375
Stöffler, Johann, 228
Stolberg, 231, 242
Strassburg, 17, 102, 223, 233, 235,
    238-39
Strauss, Jakob, 114; *Das Wucher zu
    nemen und geben unserm Christ-
    lichen glauben und bruderlicher lieb
    . . . entgegen ist*, 114; *Haubstück
    und Artikel Christlicher leer wider
    den unchristlichen wucher*, 114
Stringaro, Giacometto, 171-73, 183
Stuhlfauth, 281
Suetonius, 283
Suleiman I, Sultan, 164
Sündersbühl, 370
Swabian League, 28, 79, 277
Swiss Confederation, 166
Swiss War, 77
Switzerland, 11, 163, 165, 181, 239,
    241

Tafelhof, 370
Tauber River, 140
Tennenlohe, 369
Tertullian, 215
Tetzel, Anna, 78-79
Tetzel, Anton, 78-79, 81-82
Tetzel, Joachim, 370
Teutonic Knights, Order of 332-35
Thalheim Castle, 362
Thausing, Moritz, 273
Theophrastus, 226, 235, 241
Thessalonica, 184, 196
Thon, 369
Thorn, Peace of, 332
Thuringia, 148, 234, 318, 321, 341
Tiber River, 232
Tirol, 166
Tizzano, Lawrence, 173, 177-79, 181,
    184-85
Torgau, 253, 323

Touvoie, bishop of, 235
Transylvania, 197
Traona, 186
Trent: bishopric of, 167, 169; Council of, 187
Trentino, 189, 360
Treviso, 178, 180, 182, 188-89
Tripoli, 241
Trieste, 191
Trithemius, 99
Troeltsch, Ernst, 31
Truchsess, George, 227
Tübingen, 228, 231; university of, 223, 331
Tucher, Anton, 20
Tucher, Endres, 20
Tucher, Martin, 20, 66
Turin, university of, 159
Turks, Ottoman, 115, 326
Tuscany, 182, 186
Tyms, William, 218
Tyrell, Master, 215
Tyrol, 160, 162, 165-69, 174, 197-98

Ulm, 137
Unitarianism, 157, 197
Untergalgenhof, 370
Urban, W., 159
Urbino, 174
Ursala (wife of della Sega), 191, 194
Ursinus, Clemens, 264

Vach, 369
Valdés, John de, 175-76
Valdesians, 158, 175-77, 180
Val di Fiemme, 169
Valence, university of, 240
Varrotta, Marcantonio, 196
Veitsbrunn, 375
Velden, 356, 362, 371
Venatorius, Thomas, 289
Veneto, 160, 164, 183
Venice, 157, 160, 168, 170, 175, 178, 182-86, 189, 196, 231, 273, 333; Synod of, 157, 160, 164, 180-83, 188-89, 192-93; Ten Articles of, 188, 190
Vergelius, Marcellus, 238
Vergerio, Peter Paul, 182, 186
Vermigli, Peter Martyr, 175, 217

Verona, 182-83
Vicenza, 171, 174, 177, 180, 182-84, 188-89
Vienna, 239, 243; university of, 239
Viret, Pierre, 8
Viterbo, 232
Volckamer, Clement, 63
Volckamer, Paul, 75-76
Voll, Karl, 273
Volprecht, Wolfgang, 21
Vorra, 362, 374
Voyt, Heinrich, 55

Waetzold, Wilhelm, 278, 282
Waiblingen, Adrian von, 336
Waitzen, 241
Waldburg, 277
Waldensians, 170, 181-82
Waldheim, 41
Waldshut, 124
Walkersbrünn (Grebern), 365-66, 371
Walpot, Peter, 169, 193
Walsingham, 209
Walther, Sebald, 366
Walting, 363
Wardell, Agnes, 216-17
Wartburg Castle, 97
Wassertrüding Chapter Ordinance, 349
Waste, Joan, 214
Weber, Max, 31
Weida, 252
Weiherhaus, 370
Weimer, 258
Weller, Hieronymus, 252, 255-56
Weller, Matthias, 256
Wendelstein, 348
Wertheim, 140-41
Westermeyer, Hermann, 355
Wettin, house of, 318, 320
Whittington, Chancellor, 215
Wilkinson, 218
Wimpfeling, Jacob, 113
Windsheim, 263, 346, 372; and Ordinance for a Common Chest, 346
Winkler, Friedrich, 275, 278, 282
Winshemius, Viet, 230
Winterer, Sebald, 366
Wittenberg, 18, 20, 41, 59-60, 102,

113, 140, 143-44, 223, 226-28, 230-43, 254, 256-57, 262-63, 275, 279-80, 306, 317, 323, 327, 333, 358; city church of, 309; university of, 41, 55, 223, 226-43, 251-57, 261-62, 275, 322, 326, 333, 359
Wölfflin, Heinrich, 271, 274, 278
Wolfgang, Saint, 367
Wolkenstein, 328
Woodman, Richard, 220
Worms: diet of, 117, 139; Edict of, 62-64, 321
Wriosthesley, 210-11
Württemburg, 264, 331

Würzburg, 277
Wustman, Rudolf, 273-74

Young, Elizabeth, 211-14

Zeitelmayer, Johann, 55
Zeitz, 263
Zell, 363
Zerbst, Johann, 252
Ziegelhütten, 370
Zurich, 17, 116, 124, 167, 169, 238
Zwickau, 45, 237, 264, 325
Zwingli, Ulrich, 12, 28, 116, 167-68, 285, 289